GLOBAL SOURCEBOOK OF ADDRESS DATA MANAGEMENT

A Guide to address formats and data in 194 countries

Global Sourcebook of Address Data Management

A guide to address formats and data in 194 countries

Graham Rhind

Gower

Published by
Gower Publishing Limited
Gower House
Croft Road
ALDERSHOT
Hampshire
GU11 3HR
United Kingdom

Gower
Old Post Road
Brookfield VT 05036
USA

British Library Cataloguing in Publication Data
Rhind, Graham R.
Global source book of address data management : a guide to address fomats and data in 193 countries
1.Database marketing – Handbooks, manuals, etc.
I.Title
658.8'4

ISBN 0 566 08109 1

Library of Congress Cataloging-in-Publication Data
Rhind, Graham R.
Global sourcebook of address data management : a guide to address formats and data in 194 countries / Graham Rhind.
p. cm.
Includes index.
ISBN 0-566-08109-1 (hardback)
1. Postal service—Directories. 2. Business—Databases—methodology. 3. database management.
I. Title.
HE6031.R48 1998
383′4—dc21 98–28991
CIP

Typeset in Times New Roman, Greek1 and TransRoman by Graham Rhind and printed in Great Britain by MPG Books Ltd, Bodmin, Cornwall.

Contents

Author's note

No political statement is intended by the placement of any international boundary lines on maps, by the use or mention of specific languages or by any other statements made within this book.

Every effort has been made to ensure that the information provided in this publication is entirely accurate. Should you, however, notice any errors, or have any other comments about the book, I should be very glad to hear of them from you. Please contact the author by e-mail at graham@grcdi.nl, or by mail to:

Postbus 15734
1001 NE AMSTERDAM
The Netherlands

Acknowledgements

A great many people have provided me with the information and skills required to compile this book.

I am indebted especially to the following people for their input: Angelo Comotto, Joan-Carles Ferrer i Pont, John Harris, Marketta Herttua, Bart Lauwereins, Mihály Matura and Ian Morris.

Special thanks to Luistxo Fernandez and Marije Materola, for the work they have put into building and maintaining their Geonative web site containing minority-language place-names, which they have allowed me to reproduce shamelessly in this publication.

Thanks also to the staff of OTS Group and to all those nameless people who so selflessly post useful information on the Internet.

I would also like to thank: Jeannet Aalberts, Rients de Boer, Arnoud Bonemeyer, David J. Dean, Maria-Paolo Eusepi, János Friss, Marion Gunn, Katy Iliopoulou, Robert Jones, Algimantas Kantautas, Tomek Kuzmierz, Christiane Lokcick, Carine Magdelijns, Foltan Miroslav, The NYz Company, Sean O'Fearghail, Marco Orlandi, M.D. Patterson, Martin Reuter, Gabriela Ribiero, Klaus Riedmann, John Ryrie, Jarek Szarejko, Eveline Strudler, Sabine Vandecauter, the Summer Institute of Linguistics and the Unicode® Consortium.

Introduction

Creating a database, especially an address database, is one of those tasks that everybody thinks is so easy that anybody can do it. After all, one only has to create a few fields using any off-the-shelf database package, and then start to type the names. Right?

Wrong. Half-hearted and badly-planned attempts to build international address databases fail. You need to give it more than passing attention to build a database which is to be of optimal use to you, and preventing errors is cheaper in the long run than correcting them after the damage has been done. The database is the core of all your direct marketing work. If it is bad, so will be your direct marketing. It is the single most important factor influencing the effectiveness of any direct marketing activity.

The Global Sourcebook of Address Data Management is not intended to guide you through the best way to build your address database, avoiding expensive pitfalls as you go - I have done this already in my book *Building and Maintaining a European Direct Marketing Database.* This guide is intended to help you to populate your database in the most effective and accurate way; to ensure that you can put your data to its best use and to maintain your advantage, without causing any unnecessary irritation to those people within your database.

Direct marketing has immense advantages over forms of mass-communication because of its directness - your message goes straight to the person for which it was intended. This very directness introduces an increased ability to cause offence or irritation to that person, with its associated detrimental effects on your company. This irritation may be caused by the message itself - your offer or the artwork - but often the greatest irritation is caused by what your contact sees before he or she opens the envelope - the envelope itself and, more specifically, his/her name and address. They will check that you have got your facts right. If you have not, if you have used an incorrect address format, unsightly casing, an inappropriate salutation or the wrong language, you may not only irritate but greatly increase the chance that that person will dispose of your expensive mailing unopened - your artwork wasted.

When you buy a product you will often be highly influenced by the image which you have of the company selling it. You might frequent one shop instead of another because the staff are friendly and helpful, or because the decor gives an image of professionalism, or for some other, intangible, reason. Recipients of your mailings will equally be affected by the image of your company as projected by the mailing, and the first influence of that image is the care which has been taken to ensure that their personal details are correct. Remember that when you send something to somebody, they get the whole package - good and bad. You also know that you have to work hard to remove the bad, because, in the eyes of the recipient one bad will outweigh ten goods in your mailing. A well-printed address, correct in every detail, may not solicit a positive response from potential buyers, but it will not distract them from their progress towards opening the envelope, reading the contents and perhaps buying your product. You can be sure that some degree of negative feeling will occur when something is wrong with the address, and your chances of making the sale or just giving a good impression will be slightly (or greatly) diminished.

But what is a correct address? What do I need to watch out for? How do I prevent causing irritation to my customers in this country? These are some of the questions that this guide seeks to answer for you for 193 of the World's countries. It is intended as a reference work for anybody who maintains or uses a cross-border address database. Foreign addresses need to be treated differently. Not in terms of the data itself - if you build your database properly it will be flexible enough to be used for a mailing in Ulan Bator - but in terms of the way in which the data is output. Addressing German businessmen as Mister instead of Herr, structuring their addresses incorrectly and giving their towns English names will not be appreciated by the recipients, whose confidence in you and your offer will be impaired by your inability to treat them and their personal details correctly. If you are in the direct marketing business, your database is the core of everything that you do and if you are in the direct mailing business, a person's address is central to your success.

The way that you use this guide depends on the purpose for which you hold your database. If you hold, for example, a subscription database, you will be interested in getting your publication as quickly and efficiently as possible to the subscriber - you shall want to follow the norms of the post office concerned, perhaps in order also to profit from postal discounts. You can use this guide to find how the post office of the country concerned prefers that addresses are formatted. If, on the other hand, you are aiming to sell via direct mailing, you will be interested in taking into account cultural aspects of an address, to ensure that it looks good and correct in the eye of the recipient, and does nothing to reduce the efficacy of your message or the quality of your offer. In this case the sections of this guide referring to such aspects as language, salutations, address formats and settlement names will be of more relevance to you.

In any case, if you mail to more than one country, you will constantly be confronted by a series of questions:

- In which format should the address be written?
- In which format should the postal code be written?
- How do I write the word "Postbox" in the local language?
- What language should I use?
- Which diacritical characters shall I need to be able to store and print?
- How can I recognize different parts of the address?
- Should I use upper or lower case?
- Where does the house number belong?
- What salutation do I use?
- In which order do I write the person's name?

and so on. This book is intended as a reference work to allow you to get the answers to these questions (and more) for as many of the World's countries as possible. Years of research have brought together this information into this single source specifically to answer the needs of the database management, database marketing and direct mailing sectors.

I hope that you find this reference work useful, and look forward to hearing from you should you find anything missing.

World Address Formats

Address formats, the order in which different address elements are printed on a label or envelope, differ widely. At the last count, there were 91 different formats. Using the table below, find which format number is used in the country in which you are interested, then refer to that number format in the *Address Formats* section.

NB: In the *Address Formats* section, strings between square brackets ([]) should be typed exactly as written.
Fields or strings between curly brackets ({}) may or may not appear in an address.
The casing of the text indicates the casing of the address. Thus "Thoroughfare" cases, for example, as "Green Lane", "thoroughfare" cases, for example, as "rue" whilst "SETTLEMENT" cases, for example, as "LONDON".

Format Number by Country

Country	*Format number*
Algeria	31
American Samoa	13
Andorra	32
Angola	39
Argentina	33
Armenia	2
Aruba	34
Australia	13
Austria	1
Azerbaijan	2
The Bahamas	35
Bahrain	15
Bangladesh	36
Belarus	37
Belize	14
Belgium	3
Benin	38
Bermuda	16
Bolivia	17
Bosnia-Herzegovina	2
Botswana	40
Brazil	18
British Virgin Islands	14
Brunei	16
Bulgaria	2
Burkina Faso	91
Burundi	42
Cameroon	42

Canada	43
Cape Verde	39
Central African Republic	42
Chad	42
Chile	44
China	8
Colombia	45
Comoros	42
Congo (Democratic Rep. of)	41
Congo (People's Rep. of)	46
Costa Rica	47
Croatia	2
Cuba	48
Cyprus	20
Czech Republic	49
Denmark	3
Djibouti	42
Dominican Republic	50
Ecuador	51
Egypt	52
El Salvador	53
Equatorial Guinea	54
Eritrea	55
Estonia	2
Ethiopia	56
Faeroe Islands	2
Federated States of Micronesia	13
Fiji	14
Finland	3
France	4
French Guiana	4
French Polynesia	4
Gabon	42
Georgia	20
Germany	1
Ghana	56
Greece	2
Greenland	2
Guadeloupe	4
Guam	13
Guatemala	57
Guernsey	5
Guinea	42
Guinea-Bissau	58
Haiti	3
Honduras	59
Hong Kong	21

Hungary	6
Iceland	2
India	16
Indonesia	60
Iran	8
Ireland	7
Isle of Man	5
Israel	8
Italy	61
Ivory Coast	62
Jamaica	22
Japan	23
Jersey	5
Jordan	16
Kazakhstan	63
Kenya	64
Kiribati	65
Kuwait	2
Kyrgyzstan	66
Latvia	67
Laos	20
Lesotho	56
Libya	34
Liechtenstein	1
Lithuania	68
Luxembourg	8
Madagascar	2
Macedonia	3
Malawi	56
Malaysia	8
Maldives	16
Mali	34
Malta	9
Martinique	4
Mauritania	42
Mayotte	4
Marshall Islands	13
Mexico	25
Moldova	2
Monaco	4
Mongolia	24
Morocco	20
Mozambique	69
Myanmar	16
Namibia	56
Nauru	70
Nepal	71

New Caledonia	4
New Zealand	27
The Netherlands	2
Nicaragua	19
Niger	42
Northern Mariana Islands	13
Norway	3
Oman	72
Pakistan	73
Palau	13
Panama	74
Paraguay	17
Peru	28
Philippines	29
Poland	75
Portugal	10
Puerto Rico	76
Qatar	56
Réunion	4
Romania	2
Russia	77
Rwanda	42
St Kitts & Nevis	30
St Lucia	14
St Pierre & Miquelon	4
St Vincent & the Grenadines	14
San Marino	61
São Tomé and Príncipe	34
Saudi Arabia	16
Senegal	46
Seychelles	78
Sierra Leone	14
Singapore	79
Slovakia	3
Slovenia	2
Solomon Islands	80
South Africa	26
South Korea	16
Spain	11
Sri Lanka	26
Sudan	81
Surinam	55
Swaziland	82
Sweden	12
Switzerland (French-speaking)	8
Switzerland (German-speaking)	1

Switzerland (Italian-speaking)	2
Syria	83
Taiwan	16
Tajikistan	2
Tanzania	56
Thailand	84
Togo	42
Trinidad & Tobago	14
Tunisia	2
Turkey	2
Turkmenistan	85
Tuvalu	78
Uganda	56
Ukraine	87
United Arab Emirates	86
United Kingdom	5
United States of America	13
United States Virgin Islands	13
Uruguay	50
Uzbekistan	88
Vatican City	61
Venezuela	89
Vietnam	16
Yemen	90
Yugoslavia	2
Zambia	8
Zimbabwe	14

Address Formats

1) Austria; Germany; Liechtenstein; Switzerland (German-speaking);

To an individual:

Salutation
Contact Name
Thoroughfare[ ]number
postal code[ ]SETTLEMENT

To a company contact:

Company Name
Contact Name
Thoroughfare[ ]number
postal code[ ]SETTLEMENT

2) Armenia; Azerbaijan; Bosnia Hercegovina; Bulgaria; Croatia; Estonia; Faeroe Islands; Greece; Greenland; Iceland; Kuwait; Madagascar; Moldova; The Netherlands; Romania; Slovenia; Switzerland (Italian-speaking); Tajikistan; Tunisia; Turkey; Yugoslavia

Contact Name
Thoroughfare[ ]number
POSTAL CODE[ ]SETTLEMENT

3) Belgium; Denmark; Finland; Haiti; Norway; Macedonia; Slovakia

Contact Name
Thoroughfare[ ]number
postal code[ ]SETTLEMENT{[ ]SORTING CODE}

4) France; French Guiana; French Polynesia; Guadeloupe; Martinique; Mayotte; Monaco; New Caledonia; Réunion; St. Pierre & Miquelon

Contact Name
number[ ]thoroughfare type[ ]Thoroughfare name
postal code[ ]SETTLEMENT{[ ]sorting code}

5) United Kingdom; Guernsey; Isle of Man; Jersey

Contact Name
{internal number[ ]}{Building Name}
{house number[ ]}Thoroughfare
{Thoroughfare}
{Secondary address string}
{Double Dependent Locality}
{Dependent Locality}
SETTLEMENT
POSTAL CODE
{County}

6) Hungary

Last name[ ]First name
postal code[ ]SETTLEMENT
Thoroughfare[ ]number

or

Last name[ ]First name
SETTLEMENT
Thoroughfare[ ]number
postal code

7) Ireland

Contact Name
{internal number}{[ ]Building Name}
{house number[ ]}Thoroughfare name
{Secondary address string}
CITY{[ ]sorting code}
County

8) China, Luxembourg; Switzerland (French-speaking); Iran; Israel; Malaysia; Zambia

Contact Name
number[ ]Thoroughfare
postal code[ ]SETTLEMENT

9) Malta

Contact Name
number[,]Thoroughfare
SETTLEMENT[ ]POSTAL CODE
{Island Name}

10) Portugal

Contact Name
Thoroughfare type[ ]Thoroughfare name[ ]number
{Region}
postal code[ ]SETTLEMENT{[CODEX]}

11) Spain

Contact Name
{thoroughfare type[ ]}Thoroughfare name[,]number{[-]floor/flat/staircase etc.}
postal code[ ]SETTLEMENT[(]Province[)]

12) Sweden

As (2) above, but when addressing a person within a company:

Company Name
Department Name
Contact Name

indicates that the envelope may be opened by others, whilst

Contact Name
Company Name
Department Name

indicates that the mailing is private and to be opened by the addressee only.

In rural areas, some village areas have no street names, so the format is:

Contact Name
Village[,]Farmstead Name
postal code[ ]SETTLEMENT

13) American Samoa; Australia; Federated States of Micronesia; Guam; Marshall Islands; Northern Mariana Islands; Palau; United States of America

CONTACT NAME
number[ ]THOROUGHFARE NAME[ ]THOROUGHFARE TYPE
SETTLEMENT[ ]STATE CODE[ ]POSTAL CODE

14) Belize; British Virgin Islands; Fiji; Sierra Leone; St Lucia; St Vincent & the Grenadines; Trinidad & Tobago; Zimbabwe

Contact Name
number[ ]Thoroughfare
SETTLEMENT

15) Bahrain

Contact Name
number[ ]Thoroughfare
SETTLEMENT{[ ]postal code}

16) Bermuda; Brunei; India; Jordan; Maldives; Myanmar (Burma); Saudi Arabia; South Korea; Taiwan; Vietnam

Contact Name
number[ ]Thoroughfare
SETTLEMENT[ ]postal code

17) Bolivia; Honduras; Paraguay

Contact Name
{thoroughfare type[ ]}Thoroughfare name[ ]number{[ ]staircase etc.}
SETTLEMENT

18) Brazil

Salutation
Contact Name
Thoroughfare type[ ]Thoroughfare name[,]number{[,]apartment etc.}
postal code[ ]SETTLEMENT[-]STATE CODE

19) Nicaragua

Contact name
Thoroughfare[ ]number
SETTLEMENT[ ]postal code

20) Cyprus; Georgia; Laos; Morocco

Contact Name
number[,]thoroughfare
postal code[ ]SETTLEMENT

21) Hong Kong

Street Address:

Contact Name
{Flat/Floor number}
{Building Name}
number[ ]Thoroughfare
CITY/DISTRICT
PART OF TERRITORY

Postbox:

Contact Name
Postbox number
NAME OF POST OFFICE WHERE BOX IS LOCATED
PART OF TERRITORY

22) Jamaica

Contact Name
number[ ]Thoroughfare name[ ]Thoroughfare type
SETTLEMENT{[ ]sorting code}
{PARISH}

23) Japan

Contact Name
number[ ]Thoroughfare{[Chome] Chome name}
{[Ku]Ku name}
CITY
postal code

Since the new postal code has been introduced, the postal code may also be written on the first line as follows:

Contact Name
postal code
number[ ]Thoroughfare{[Chome] Chome name}
{[Ku]Ku name}
CITY

24) Mongolia

Contact name
Address indicators
SETTLEMENT[ ]POSTAL CODE

25) Mexico

Contact Name
{Thoroughfare type[ ]}Thoroughfare name[ ]number{[ ]floor etc. indicators}
{[Col.] Section indicator}
postal code[ ]SETTLEMENT[,]STATE CODE

26) South Africa; Sri Lanka

Contact Name
number[ ]Thoroughfare
SETTLEMENT
postal code

27) New Zealand

CONTACT NAME
NUMBER[ ]THOROUGHFARE NAME[ ]THOROUGHFARE TYPE
{VILLAGE/SUBURB}
SETTLEMENT[ ]postal code

28) Peru

Contact Name
Thoroughfare[ ]number
SETTLEMENT{[ ]sorting code}

29) Philippines

For Manila - Postbox:

Contact Name
postbox number[ ]name of post office
postal code[MANILA]

For Manila - Street Address:

Contact Name
number[ ]street or district
postal code[MANILA]

For Metropolitan Manila - Postbox:

Contact Name
postbox number[ ]name of post office
postal code[ ]City/Municipality[METRO MANILA]

For Metropolitan Manila - Street Address:

Contact Name
number[ ]Street or district{[ ]Village}
District Name[ ]City/Municipality
postal code[METRO MANILA]

For elsewhere - Street Address:

Contact Name
number[ ]Street or district{[ ]village}
District Name[ ]City/Municipality
postal code[ ]PROVINCE

30) St. Kitts and Nevis

Contact name
Address components
SETTLEMENT[,]ISLAND NAME

31) Algeria

Contact Name
number[,]thoroughfare type[ ]Thoroughfare name
postal code[ ]SETTLEMENT

32) Andorra

Contact Name
number[,]thoroughfare type[ ]Thoroughfare name
postal code[ ]SETTLEMENT

33) Argentina

Contact Name
{thoroughfare type[ ]}Thoroughfare name[ ]number{[ ]staircase etc.}
postal code[ ]SETTLEMENT
PROVINCE

34) Aruba; Libya; Mali; São Tomé and Príncipe

Contact name
Thoroughfare type[ ]Thoroughfare name[ ]number
SETTLEMENT

35) Bahamas

Contact Name
[PO Box]ISLAND CODE[-]number
SETTLEMENT[ ]ISLAND ABBREVIATION

or

Contact Name
[General Delivery]
Post office name
ISLAND NAME

36) Bangladesh

Contact Name
Thoroughfare[ ]number
SETTLEMENT[-]postal code

37) Belarus

postal code[ ]SETTLEMENT[-]sorting code
Thoroughfare name[ ]Thoroughfare type[ ]number
Last Name[ ]First Name or Initials

38) Benin

Contact Name
sorting code[BP]number
SETTLEMENT

39) Angola, Cape Verde

Contact Name
Thoroughfare type[ ]Thoroughfare name[ ]number{[ ]staircase etc.}
SETTLEMENT

40) Botswana

Contact Name
[PO Box]number
SETTLEMENT
Postal town

41) Congo (Democratic Republic of)

Contact Name
[BP]number
SETTLEMENT{[ ]sorting code}

42) Burundi, Central African Republic, Cameroon, Chad, Comoros, Djibouti; Gabon; Guinea; Mauritania; Niger; Rwanda; Togo

Contact Name
[BP]number
SETTLEMENT

43) Canada

English-language addresses:

CONTACT NAME
number[ ]THOROUGHFARE NAME[ ]THOROUGHFARE TYPE
SETTLEMENT[ ]PROVINCE CODE[ ]POSTAL CODE

French-language addresses:

CONTACT NAME
number[ ]THOROUGHFARE TYPE[ ]THOROUGHFARE NAME
SETTLEMENT[ ]PROVINCE CODE[ ]POSTAL CODE

44) Chile

Contact Name
{thoroughfare type[ ]}Thoroughfare name[,]number{[,]floor etc.}
SETTLEMENT{[ ]sorting code}

45) Colombia

Salutation
Contact name
{thoroughfare type[ ]}Thoroughfare name[,]house number{[,]floor etc.}
SETTLEMENT{[ ]PROVINCE[ ]sorting code}

46) Congo (People's Republic of); Senegal

Contact name
number[,]thoroughfare type[ ]Thoroughfare name
SETTLEMENT

47) Costa Rica

Contact Name
{thoroughfare type[ ]}Thoroughfare name[,]number{[,]floor etc.}
postal code[ ]SETTLEMENT

48) Cuba

Contact Name
{thoroughfare type[ ]}Thoroughfare name[ ]number
[CP]postal code[ ]SETTLEMENT

49) Czech Republic

Salutation
Contact Name
thoroughfare type[ ]Thoroughfare name[ ]number
postal code[ ]SETTLEMENT{[ ]sorting code}

50) Dominican Republic; Uruguay

Contact Name
{thoroughfare type[ ]}Thoroughfare name[ ]number
postal code[ ]SETTLEMENT

51) Ecuador

Contact Name
{thoroughfare type[ ]}Thoroughfare name[ ]number{[ ]staircase etc.}
POSTAL CODE
SETTLEMENT

52) Egypt

Contact Name
number[ ]Thoroughfare name[ ]District name
Province
postal code

53) El Salvador

Contact Name
{thoroughfare type[ ]}Thoroughfare name[ ]number
SETTLEMENT
PROVINCE[ ]postal code

54) Equatorial Guinea

Contact Name
[Apartado]number
SETTLEMENT

55) Eritrea; Surinam

Contact Name
Thoroughfare[ ]number
SETTLEMENT

56) Ethiopia; Ghana; Lesotho; Malawi; Namibia; Qatar; Tanzania; Uganda

Contact Name
[PO Box]number
SETTLEMENT

57) Guatemala

Contact Name
{thoroughfare type[ ]}Thoroughfare name[ ]number{[ ]staircase etc.}
postal code[-]SETTLEMENT

58) Guinea-Bissau

Contact Name
Thoroughfare type[ ]Thoroughfare name[ ]number
postal code[ ]SETTLEMENT

59) Honduras

Contact Name
{thoroughfare type[ ]}Thoroughfare name[ ]number{[ ]staircase etc.}
postal code[ ]SETTLEMENT[,]PROVINCE

60) Indonesia

Contact Name
number[,]Thoroughfare name
SETTLEMENT[ ]postal code

61) Italy; San Marino; Vatican City

Contact name
thoroughfare type[ ]Thoroughfare name[ ]number
postal code[ ]TOWN[ ]PROVINCE CODE

62) Ivory Coast

Contact Name
sorting code[BP]number
SETTLEMENT[ ]sorting code

63) Kazakhstan

postal code[ ]COUNTRY NAME
SETTLEMENT
street address
Contact name

64) Kenya

Contact Name
[PO Box]number
postal code[-]SETTLEMENT

65) Kiribati

Contact Name
Address elements
Settlement
ISLAND

66) Kyrgyzstan

postal code[ ]SETTLEMENT[-]sorting code
Thoroughfare name[ ]Thoroughfare type[,]number
Contact name

67) Latvia

Contact name
number[ ]Thoroughfare
SETTLEMENT{[-]sorting code}[,]postal code

68) Lithuania

Contact name
Thoroughfare name[ ]number{[-]apartment number}
City[ ]postal code

or

Contact name
Thoroughfare name[ ]number{[-]apartment number}
postal code[ ]City

69) Mozambique

Contact name
Thoroughfare type[ ]Thoroughfare name[,]number
postal code[ ]SETTLEMENT

70) Nauru

Contact Name
District name
[PO Box]number

71) Nepal

Contact Name
Address components
SETTLEMENT[ ]postal code

72) Oman

Contact name
[PO Box]number
GOVERNORATE OR REGION
postal code

73) Pakistan

Contact name
Building information
Street address information
Sector information
SETTLEMENT[-]postal code

74) Panama

Contact Name
Thoroughfare[ ]number
SETTLEMENT{[ ]sorting code}
{PROVINCE}

75) Poland

Salutation
Contact name
thoroughfare type[ ]Thoroughfare name[ ]number
postal code[ ]SETTLEMENT

76) Puerto Rico

CONTACT NAME
{[URB]URBANIZATION DISTRICT}
NUMBER[ ]THOROUGHFARE
SETTLEMENT[PR]POSTAL CODE

77) Russia

postal code[ ]SETTLEMENT[ ]sorting code
thoroughfare type[ ]Thoroughfare name[ ]number{[,]apartment etc. details}
Last Name[ ]First Name or Initials

78) Seychelles; Tuvalu

Contact name
[PO Box]number
Settlement
ISLAND NAME

79) Singapore

Contact name
number[ ]Thoroughfare name[ ]Thoroughfare type
Settlement[ ]postal code

80) Solomon Islands

Contact name
[PO Box]ISLAND CODE number
SETTLEMENT
ISLAND NAME

81) Sudan

postal code[ ]SETTLEMENT
[PO Box]number
Contact name

82) Swaziland

Contact name
[PO Box]number
SETTLEMENT
postal code

83) Syria

Contact Name
Address components
SETTLEMENT

84) Thailand

Contact name
{building/block information}
number[ ]thoroughfare
{village and/or district names}
Settlement
PROVINCE
postal code

85) Turkmenistan

postal code[ ]SETTLEMENT
COUNTRY NAME
Last name[ ]First name or INITIALS
number[,]thoroughfare type[ ]Thoroughfare name

86) United Arab Emirates

Contact name
[PO Box]number
EMIRATE NAME

87) Ukraine

postal code[ ]SETTLEMENT
number[,]thoroughfare
Contact name

88) Uzbekistan

Contact name
{[rayon]district number}
{[dom]building number[, kvartira]apartment number}
postal code[ ]SETTLEMENT
OBLAST NAME

89) Venezuela

Contact Name
{thoroughfare type[ ]}Thoroughfare name[,]number{[ ]floor/flat/staircase etc.}
SETTLEMENT[ ]postal code{[R.C.]route carrier number}

or

Contact Name
{thoroughfare type[ ]}Thoroughfare name[,]number{[ ]floor/flat/staircase etc.}
SETTLEMENT[ ]postal code{[ ]PROVINCE ABBREVIATION}

90) Yemen

Contact name
number[,]thoroughfare
SETTLEMENT

91) Burkina Faso

First name[ ]LAST NAME
[BP]number
SETTLEMENT{[ ]sorting code}

World Postal Code Formats

Knowing the format of a postal code is essential not only to be able to recognize it within an address or database field, but also as using the Postal Code correctly will speed up delivery and reduce returns.

Postal code formats are covered by each country chapter. This data is summarized below for all countries covered:

NB: *9* indicates a numeric digit, *A* a letter.
Strings between square brackets ([]) should be typed exactly as written. Thus for Greenland, *[39]99* indicates that all postal codes begin with 39, are four digits long, and the last two digits are numeric.
Where more than one format is given, each format is possible.

Country	*Format*
Albania	none
Algeria	99999
American Samoa	[96799] [96799-]9999
Andorra	none
Angola	none
Argentina	9999
Armenia	999999
Aruba	none
Australia	9999
Austria	9999
Azerbaijan	999999
Bahamas	none
Bahrain	999 9999
Bangladesh	9999
Belarus	999999
Belgium	9999
Belize	none
Benin	none
Bolivia	none
Bosnia-Hercegovina	99999
Botswana	none
Brazil	99999[-]999
Brunei	9999
Bulgaria	9999
Burkina Faso	none
Burundi	none
Cameroon	none
Canada	A9A[ ]9A9
Cape Verde	none

Central African Republic	none
Chad	none
Chile	none
China	999999
Colombia	none
Comoros	none
Congo (Democratic Republic of)	none
Congo (People's Republic of)	none
Costa Rica	9999
Croatia	99[ ]999
Cuba	99999
Cyprus	9999
Czech Republic	999[ ]99
Denmark	9999
Djibouti	none
Dominica	none
Dominican Republic	9999
Ecuador	A9999A
Egypt	99999
El Salvador	99999
Equatorial Guinea	none
Eritrea	none
Estonia	[EE]9999
Ethiopia	none
Faeroe Islands	999
Federated States of Micronesia	[9694]9 [9694]9[ ]9999
Fiji	none
Finland	99999
France	99999
French Guiana	[973]99
French Polynesia	[987]99
Gabon	none
Georgia	999999
Germany	99999
Ghana	none
Greece	999[ ]99
Greenland	[39]99
Grenada	none
Guadeloupe	[970]99 [971]99
Guam	[969]99 [969]99[-]9999
Guatemala	99999
Guernsey	[GY]9[ ]9AA
Guinea-Bissau	9999
Guinea	none

Guyana	none
Haiti	9999
Honduras	AA9999
Hungary	9999
Iceland	999
India	999999
Indonesia	99999
Iran	99999
Ireland	none
Isle of Man	[IM]9[ ]9AA
Israel	99999
Italy	99999
Jamaica	none
Japan	999[-]9999
Jersey	[JE]9[ ]9AA
Jordan	99999
Kazakhstan	999999
Kenya	99999
Kiribati	none
Kuwait	99999
Kyrgyzstan	999999
Laos	9999
Latvia	9999
Lesotho	none
Libya	none
Liechtenstein	[94]99
Lithuania	9999
Luxembourg	9999
Macedonia	[9]9999
Madagascar	999
Malawi	none
Malaysia	99999
Maldives	99[-]99
Mali	none
Malta	AAA[ ]99 AAA[ ]999 [CMR 0Z]
Marshall Islands	[969]99 [969]99[-]9999
Martinique	[972]99
Mauritania	none
Mayotte	[976]99 [985]99
Mexico	99999
Moldova	9999
Monaco	[980]99
Mongolia	999999
Morocco	99999

Mozambique	99999
Namibia	none
Nauru	none
Nepal	99999
Netherlands	9999[ ]AA
New Caledonia	[988]99
New Zealand	9999
Nicaragua	9999 9999[-]999
Niger	none
Nigeria	none
Northern Mariana Islands	[9695]9 [9695]9[-]9999
Norway	9999
Oman	999
Pakistan	9999
Palau	[96940] [96940-]9999
Panama	none
Paraguay	none
Peru	none
Philippines	9999
Poland	99[-]999
Portugal	9999
Puerto Rico	[00]999 [00]999[-]9999
Qatar	none
Réunion	[974]99
Romania	9999999
Russia	999999
Rwanda	none
St Kitts and Nevis	none
St Lucia	none
St Pierre and Miquelon	[975]99
St Vincent and the Grenadines	none
San Marino	[47031]
São Tomé and Príncipe	none
Saudi Arabia	99999
Senegal	none
Seychelles	none
Sierra Leone	none
Singapore	999999
Slovakia	999[ ]99
Slovenia	9999
Solomon Islands	none
South Africa	9999
South Korea	999[-]999
Spain	99999

Sri Lanka	99999
Sudan	9999
Surinam	none
Swaziland	A999
Sweden	999[ ]99
Switzerland	9999
Syria	none
Tajikistan	999999
Tanzania	none
Thailand	99999
Togo	none
Trinidad & Tobago	none
Tunisia	9999
Turkey	99999
Turkmenistan	999999
Tuvalu	none
United Arab Emirates	none
Uganda	none
Ukraine	999999
United Kingdom	A9[ ]9AA A99[ ]9AA A9A[ ]9AA AA9[ ]9AA AA99[ ]9AA AA9A[ ]9AA [GIR 0AA]
United States of America	99999 99999[-]9999
United States Virgin Islands	[008]99 [008]99[-]9999
Uruguay	99999
Uzbekistan	999999
Vatican City	[00120]
Venezuela	9999
Vietnam	99999
Western Samoa	none
Yemen	none
Yugoslavia	99999
Zambia	99999
Zimbabwe	none

World Postbox Indicators

The following list provides the local-language version of the word *Postbox* by country. Abbreviations and alternative versions are provided in the country chapter concerned:

Country	*Postbox Indicator*
Albania	Kutia Postare Nr.
Algeria	Boite Postale
American Samoa	PO Box
Australia	PO Box
Austria	Postfach
Bahamas	PO Box
Belgium	Postbus / Boite Postale / Postfach
Belize	PO Box
Benin	Boite Postale
Botswana	PO Box
Brazil	Caixo Postal
Burkina Faso	Boite Postale
Burundi	Boite Postale
Cameroon	Boite Postale
Canada	PO Box / Boite Postale
Central African Republic	Boite Postale
Chad	Boite Postale
Chile	Casilla Postal
Colombia	Apoartado Aéro
Comoros	Boite Postale
Congo-Brazzaville	Boite Postale
Congo, Democratic Republic of	Boite Postale
Costa Rica	Case Postale
Denmark	Postboks
Djibouti	Boite Postale
Egypt	PO Box
Equatorial Guinea	Apartado
Ethiopia	PO Box
Fiji	GPO Box
Finland	Posti Loaero / Box
France	Boite Postale
Gabon	Boite Postale
Germany	Postfach
Ghana	PO Box
Grenada	PO Box
Guadeloupe	Boite Postale
Guam	PO Box
Guernsey	PO Box
Guinea	Boite Postale

Guyana	PO Box
Haiti	Boite Postale
Hungary	Postafiók
Iceland	Pósthólf
India	PO Box
Indonesia	Kotak Pos
Ireland	PO Box / Bosca Poist
Isle of Man	PO Box
Italy	Casella Postale
Ivory Coast	Boite Postale
Jamaica	PO Box
Jersey	PO Box
Kenya	PO Box
Lesotho	PO Box
Liechtenstein	Postfach
Malawi	PO Box
Mali	Boite Postale
Marshall Islands	PO Box
Martinique	Boite Postale
Mauritania	Boite Postale
Mayotte	Boite Postale
Micronesia	PO Box
Monaco	Boite Postale
Namibia	PO Box
Nauru	PO Box
Netherlands	Postbus
New Caledonia	Boite Postale
New Zealand	P O Box
Niger	Boite Postale
Nigeria	PO Box
Northern Mariana Islands	PO Box
Norway	Postboks
Oman	PO Box
Palau	PO Box
Philippines	PO Box
Poland	Skrytka Pocztowa
Portugal	Case Postale
Qatar	PO Box
Réunion	Boite Postale
Rwanda	Boite Postale
Saint Kitts and Nevis	PO Box
Saint Lucia	PO Box
Saint Pierre and Miquelon	Boite Postale
Saint Vincent and the Grenadines	PO Box
San Marino	Casella Postale
Senegal	Boite Postale
Sierra Leone	PO Box

Slovakia	Postova Schranka
Slovenia	Postni Predal
Solomon Islands	PO Box
South Africa	PO Box / Posbus
Spain	Apartado / Apartat
Sri Lanka	PO Box
Sudan	PO Box
Surinam	Postbus
Swaziland	PO Box
Sweden	Box
Switzerland	Postfach / Case Postale / Casella Postale
Tanzania	PO Box
Togo	Boite Postale
Trinidad and Tobago	PO Box
Tunisia	Boite Postale
Tuvalu	PO Box
Uganda	PO Box
United Arab Emirates	PO Box
United Kingdom	PO Box
United States of America	PO Box
United States Virgin Islands	PO Box
Vatican City	Casella Postale
Venezuela	Apartado
Wallis and Futuna	Boite Postale
Zambia	PO Box
Zimbabwe	PO Box

Diacritical Marks

Whether you hold your address database information in DOS, Windows™ or on another platform; whether your data is for a single country or for many; you will be certain to be faced with the challenge of storing diacritical marks (accents).

Most of the World's languages (including English) contain one or more diacritical marks. These marks indicate that the letter has a different phonetic value or is stressed differently to the same letter without the mark. Though the marks may appear strange (and possibly irrelevant) to non-speakers of the language concerned, they are required to ensure that the text remains accurate and logical.

The first computer operating systems used a set of character codes called ASCII (American Standard Code for Information Interchange). These are reproduced by holding down the ALT key and typing a 1-, 2- or 3-number code on the key pad. Limited at that time by computer hard- and software to 256 characters, in no way can this system represent each character used in the World's more than 10 000 languages. To overcome this limitation, a number of code pages were created - each of which were supposed to contain sufficient letters with diacritical marks to represent the alphabets of at least one language.

The most common code page used by English-speakers is 437. This contains the following letters with diacritical marks:

á, â, Ä, ä, à, Å, å, Æ, æ, Ç, ç, ê, ë, è, É, é, ï, î, ì, í, ñ, Ñ, ô, Ö, ö, ò, ó, ß, Ü, ü, û, ù, ú, ÿ

This is sufficient for a number of Western-European and Scandinavian languages, but there are serious omissions. A number of languages in the same group, such as Icelandic, are not represented. Certain letters in Scandinavian languages, such as the "Ø" in Danish and Norwegian are missing. Even for French, the letter "Œ" cannot be reproduced. Equally, a number of upper-case equivalents of lower-case letters with diacritical marks cannot be reproduced using this code page.

Code page 850 supplements code page 437 with the following diacritical marks:

Á, Â, À, ã, Ã, ð, Đ, Ê, Ë, È, Í, Ï, Ì, Ó, Ô, Ò, õ, Õ, Þ, þ, Ú, Û, Ù, ý, Ý.

Further code pages are 852 (Slavic languages/Hungarian); 860 (Portuguese); and 865 (Scandinavian).

Whilst this system allows for the most part for the storage of data for a single country or language area, problems arise when trying to store data from more than one country or language area. Whilst using code page 850, for example, will allow the storage of (most) addresses for Western Europe, it cannot allow the correct storage of addresses from Eastern Europe, even for those languages written in the Latin script. In Hungarian, for example, code page 850 misses Á, Í, Ó, ő, Ő, Ú, ű and Ű. For Czech, the following letters with diacritical marks are missing: Á, Č, č, ď, Ě, ě, Í, Ň, ň,

Ó, ř, Ř, Š, ś, ť, Ť, Ú, Ů, ů, ý, Ý, ž, and Ž. Clearly, no accurate representation of the language can succeed without these characters.

On the DOS platform, a character can look different on different code pages but retain the same code value. Of the Icelandic street type HLÍÐ, for example, only the HL will appear correctly when represented using code page 437, though the ASCII codes of its constituent letters remain the same. Changing the code page to 850 will allow this word to be represented correctly.

Changing the code page is done differently under different operating platforms - refer to your documentation. In DOS/Windows™ systems, the code page (for screen output) is set in the *autoexec.bat* file by adding the lines:

MODE CON CODEPAGE PREPARE=((*nnn*) *[drive path filename]*)
MODE CON CODEPAGE SELECT=*nnn*

where *nnn* is the code page number and *drive path filename* is the file containing the code page information (having the extension *.CPI*). For example, for code page 850, the lines might read:

```
MODE CON CODEPAGE PREPARE=((850) C:\WINDOWS\COMMAND\EGA.CPI)
MODE CON CODEPAGE SELECT=850
```

To check which code page is active, type

MODE

at the DOS prompt.

ANSI codes (American National Standard Institute) are used with systems such as Microsoft Windows™. Each ANSI page allows the use of fonts which in turn allow for the reproduction of 224 different characters. This allows the reproduction of most of the characters required for the World's languages in such systems as word-processing programs by changing the font within the document. There are, however, few database programs which allow fonts to be changed within fields or within tables. These programs take as default the ANSI page defined by the underlying Windows™ operating system.

Whilst ANSI allows the output of letters with diacritical marks (assuming a compliant printer and font type), the large problem of data transfer between platforms and software remains. Transferring data between one ASCII page and another; one ANSI page and another; or between ASCII and ANSI pages will necessarily change the appearance (and in the last case the value) of the letter that you are trying to reproduce. This can cause immense damage to the data and make correct storage and output impossible.

An alternative methodology for storing character values is The Unicode™ Standard. This avoids the limitations of hardware, platform and software by not attempting to represent a diacritic using a single character but instead using a four-character code (composed of standard alpha-numeric characters with the same values regardless of code page) to indicate which diacritic mark is to be represented. This code in turn is usually enclosed between other symbols (e.g. <00C1>) to distinguish from the rest of the text. This code system is increasingly being included in new operating systems and software. Here are a number of Unicode™ values:

Á	00C1
á	00E1
Ã	00C3
É	00C9
Ñ	00D1
Ò	00D2
Đ	00F8

Unfortunately, I can only draw your attention to the issue of diacritical marks without providing a solution for reproducing these marks for all languages within a single database system. To the best of my knowledge, an all encompassing solution does not yet exist. Aim, however, to use operating systems and software which have Unicode™ support so that you will in the near future be able to handle diacritical marks better than is currently possible.

Accents

The tables below cover a large number of European languages and some other languages written in Latin script.

The tables show the diacritical marks contained in the language concerned, the alternative 'non-ASCII' equivalent where available (i.e. an alternative without diacritical marks), the ASCII code of the accented letter (if available) in code pages 437 and 850, and the Unicode™ value.

Whilst it is not always possible to type the correctly accented letter using ASCII, accented letters can be output on most printers using alternative ASCII codes. Thus, for example, typing the code to produce a + symbol would, by using an alternative font set, be output as an accented character. To do this, however, means that you have to maintain a consistent platform for your output devices and you will have to use a different printing set for each language to be printed as all accents cannot be covered in a single set.

NB: Alphabetization - in the alphabetization lists, letters between brackets immediately following another letter indicate that this letter is included in the sort for the previous letter. I.e., it is given the same value as the preceding letter for sorting purposes. Those between brackets on their own are letters borrowed from other languages and are sorted, when found, in the position shown. When two "letters" are shown in upper case, these letters form a single letter in the language concerned. The alphabetization tables include only upper case versions of letters - when a lower case form of a letter differs markedly in appearance to its upper case equivalent, the lower case version is printed immediately next to the upper case version.

Albanian

Spoken by about 4 million people, in Albania, in the Serbian province of Kosovo, in Macedonia, Yugoslavia, Bulgaria, Romania and Italy

Letter	*Alternative*	*ASCII code (page 437)*	*ASCII code (page 850)*	*Unicode™*
â		131	131	00E2
Â		na*	182	00C2
ç		135	135	00E7
Ç		128	128	00C7
ë		137	137	00EB
Ë		na	211	00CB

**na = not available as an ASCII code in the specified code page*

Albanian is alphabetized as follows:

A	B	C	Ç	D	E	Ë	F	G	H	I	J	K
L	M	N	O	P	Q	R	S	T	U	V	W	X
Y	Z											

Basque

Basque is spoken by some 700 000 people in the Spanish regions of País-Vasco and Navarra, and in south-eastern France.

Letter	*Alternative*	*ASCII code (page 437)*	*ASCII code (page 850)*	*Unicode™*
ç		135	135	00E7
Ç		128	128	00C7
é		130	130	00E9
É		144	144	00C9
ñ		164	164	00F1
Ñ		165	165	00D1
ü		129	129	00FC
Ü		154	154	00DC

Basque is alphabetized as follows:

A	B	C (Ç)	D	E	F	G	H	I	J	K	L	M
N	Ñ	O	P	Q	R	S	T	U (Ü)	V	W	X	Y
Z												

Breton

Breton, a Celtic language, is spoken in the westernmost parts of Brittany, France, by some 600 000 people.

Apostrophes are used within words in Breton.

Letter	*Alternative*	*ASCII code (page 437)*	*ASCII code (page 850)*	*Unicode™*
â		131	131	00E2
Â		na*	182	00C2
ê		136	136	00EA
Ê		na	210	00CA
ñ		164	164	00F1
Ñ		165	165	00D1
ù		151	151	00F9
Ù		na	235	00D9
ü		129	129	00FC
Ü		154	154	00DC

**na = not available as an ASCII code in the specified code page*

Breton is alphabetized as follows:

A (Â)	B	(C)	Ch	C'h	D	E (Ê)	F	G	H	I	J	K
L	M	N	Ñ	O	P	(Q)	R	S	T	U (Ù, Ü)	V	
W	(X)	Y	Z									

Catalan

There are about 10 540 000 speakers of Catalan - in Spain it is spoken by some 5 980 000 people in Catalonia, 3 350 000 people in Valencia (where it is called Valencian and is considered by some a distinct language), 755 000 people in the Balearic Islands, 48 000 people in the eastern part of Aragon and 2 000 people in Murcia. It is the national language of Andorra and is spoken there by 38 000 people. There are 330 000 speakers in Roussillon in south-eastern France and 37 000 speakers in the town of Alghero (L'Alguer) on Sardinia, Italy.

Letter	*Alternative*	*ASCII code (page 437)*	*ASCII code (page 850)*	*Unicode™*
à		133	133	00E0
À		na*	183	00C0
ç		135	135	00E7
Ç		128	128	00C7

é		130	130	00E9
É		144	144	00C9
è		138	138	00E8
È		na	212	00C8
í		161	161	00ED
Í		na	214	00CD
ï		139	139	00EF
Ï		na	216	00CF
l·		na	na	0140
L·		na	na	013F
ó		162	162	00F3
Ó		na	224	00D3
ò		149	149	00F2
Ò		na	227	00D2
ú		163	163	00FA
Ú		na	233	00DA

**na = not available as an ASCII code in the specified code page*

In Catalan, abbreviations of plurals are doubled. For example, the Spanish abbreviations for the United States is *EE.UU.* The full stops must be added after each double-letter, never between them.

Catalan is alphabetized as follows:

A (À)	B	C (Ç)	D	E (É, È)	F	G	H	I (Í, Ï)	J	K	L
L·l	M	N	O (Ó, Ò)	P	Q	R	S	T	U (Ú, Ü)	V	W
X	Y	Z									

In Catalan a middle dot ("·") may appear within words between ells to indicate differences in pronunciation. "ll" will indicate a single sound as in Castilian Spanish. "l·l" will indicate an ell sound more akin to the English. For example "Paral·lel", "Col·legi". This dot may be found in databases as a "." or a hyphen ("-"). It should not be removed.

Croatian

Although Serbian and Croat are basically the same language, the former is written in Cyrillic script, the latter in Roman. Croatian is spoken by about 6 million people in Croatia, Slovenia, Bosnia-Herzegovina and Serbia.

Letter	*Alternative*	*ASCII code (page 437)*	*ASCII code (page 850)*	*Unicode™*
č	cc	na*	na*	010D
Č	Cc	na	na	010C
ć	ch	na	na	0107
Ć	Ch	na	na	0106
đ	dj	na	na	0111
Đ	Dj	na	na	0110
š	sh	na	na	0161
Š	Sh	na	na	0160
ž	zz	na	na	017E
Ž	Zh	na	na	017D

na = not available as an ASCII code in the specified code page

Croatian is alphabetized as follows:

A	B	C	Ć	Č	D	Đ	E	F	G	H	I	J
K	L	M	N	O	P	Q	R	S	Š	T	U	V
(W)	(X)	(Y)	Z	Ž								

Czech

Czech is spoken by about 10 million people in the Czech Republic.

Letter	*Alternative*	*ASCII code (page 437)*	*ASCII code (page 850)*	*Unicode™*
á		160	160	00E1
Á		na*	181	00C1
č		na	na*	010D
Č		na	na	010C
ď		na	na	010F
Ď		na	na	010E
é		130	130	00E9
É		144	144	00C9
ě		na	na	011B
Ě		na	na	011A
í		161	161	00ED
Í		na	214	00CD
ň		na	na	0148

Ň		na	na	0147
ó		162	162	00F3
Ó		na	224	00D3
ř		na	na	0159
Ř		na	na	0158
š		na	na	0161
Š		na	na	0160
ť		na	na	0165
Ť		na	na	0164
ú		163	163	00FA
Ú		na	233	00DA
ů		na	na	016F
Ů		na	na	016E
ý		na	236	00FD
Ý		na	237	00DD
ž		na	na	017E
Ž		na	na	017D

**na – not available as an ASCII code in the specified code page*

Czech is alphabetized as follows:

A	Á	B	C	Č	D	Ď	E	É	Ě	F	G	H
Ch	I	Í	J	K	L	M	N	Ň	O	Ó	P	Q
R	Ř	S	Š	T	Ť ť	U	Ú	Ů	V	W	X	Y
Ý	Z	Ž										

Danish

Danish is spoken by 5 million people in Denmark, as well as some inhabitants of the Faeroe Islands, Greenland and northern Germany.

Letter	*Alternative*	*ASCII code (page 437)*	*ASCII code (page 850)*	*Unicode™*
á		160	160	00E1
Á		na*	181	00C1
å	ae	134	134	00E5
Å	AE	143	143	00C5
æ	ae	145	145	00E6
Æ	AE	146	146	00C6

é		130	130	00E9
É		144	144	00C9
í		161	161	00ED
Í		na	214	00CD
ó		162	162	00F3
Ó		na	224	00D3
ø	oe	na	155	00F8
Ø	OE	na	157	00D8
ú		163	163	00FA
Ú		na	233	00DA
ý		na	na	00FD
Ý		na	na	00DD

**na = not available as an ASCII code in the specified code page*

Danish is alphabetized as follows:

A (Á)	B	C	D	E (É)	F	G	H	I (Í)	J	K	L	M
N	O (Ó)	P	Q	R	S	T	U (Ú)	V	W	X	Y (Ý)	Z
Æ (Ǽ)	Ø (Ǿ)	Å (AA)										

Dutch

Dutch is spoken by about 14 million people in The Netherlands and about 5 million Belgians. There is a small Dutch-speaking minority in northern France.

Letter	*Alternative*	*ASCII code (page 437)*	*ASCII code (page 850)*	*Unicode™*
æ	ae	145	145	00E6
Æ	AE	146	146	00C6
ä	a	132	132	00E4
Ä	A	142	142	00C4
ë	e	137	137	00EB
Ë	E	na*	211	00CB
é	e	130	130	00E9
É	E	144	144	00C9
è	e	138	138	00E8
È	E	na	212	00C8
ê	e	136	136	00EA
Ê	E	na	210	00CA

ï	i	139	139	00EF
Ï	I	na	216	00CF
ö	o	148	148	00F6
Ö	O	153	153	00D6
ó	o	162	162	00F3
Ó	O	na	224	00D3
ò	o	149	149	00F2
Ò	O	na	227	00D2
ô	o	147	147	00F4
Ô	O	na	226	00D4
ü	u	129	129	00FC
Ü	U	154	154	00DC
ij	ij or y	152	152	0133
IJ	IJ or Y	na	na*	0132

**na = not available as an ASCII code in the specified code page*

NB Only ë and é and their upper case equivalents are *commonly* found in Dutch. Note that the letter ij is a single letter in the Dutch alphabet, coming between y and z, but it is *always,* without exception, typed as two letters - i and j - in normal usage, or it is written as a y. You should also do this. Note, however, that when these occur at the beginning of a real noun, both the I and the J must be in upper case, i.e. Krimpen aan de IJssel.

Dutch is alphabetized as follows:

A (Ä)	B	C	D	E (Ë)	F	G	H	I (Ï)	J	K	L	M
N	O (Ö)	P	Q	R	S	T	U (Ü)	V	W	X	Y	IJ
Z												

English

English is spoken by about 322 000 000 throughout the World, in many countries as a second language. Spoken in the United Kingdom, Ireland, the United States of America, Canada, Australia, New Zealand, South Africa and many former British colonies.

Letter	*Alternative*	*ASCII code (page 437)*	*ASCII code (page 850)*	*Unicode™*
à	a	133	133	00E0
À	A	na*	183	00C0
ç	c	135	135	00E7
Ç	C	128	128	00C7

ë	e	137	137	00EB
Ë	E	na	211	00CB
é	e	130	130	00E9
É	E	144	144	00C9
è	e	138	138	00E8
È	E	na	212	00C8
ê	e	136	136	00EA
Ê	E	na	210	00CA
ï	i	139	139	00EC
Ï	I	na	216	00CF
ñ	n	164	164	00F1
Ñ	N	165	165	00D1
ô	o	147	147	00F4
Ô	O	na	226	00D4
ö	o	148	148	00F6
Ö	O	153	153	00D6

**na = not available as an ASCII code in the specified code page*

English words are often written without diacritical marks because of ignorance, but many words, especially of French origin, such as façade, rôle, éclair, belovèd, naïve and so on, should correctly be written using a diacritic mark.

English is alphabetized as follows:

A	(À)	B	C	(Ç)	D	E	(É	È	Ê	Ë)	F	G
H	I	(Ï)	J	K	L	M	N	(Ñ)	O	(Ö	Ô)	P
Q	R	S	T	U	V	W	X	Y	Z			

Estonian

Estonian is spoken by almost a million people in Estonia, Russia and Latvia.

It is written in the Latin, not the Cyrillic, script.

Letter	*Alternative*	*ASCII code (page 437)*	*ASCII code (page 850)*	*Unicode™*
ä		132	132	00E4
Ä		142	142	00C4
ö		148	148	00F6
Ö		153	153	00D6
õ		na*	228	00F5

Õ		na	229	00D5
š		na	na*	0161
Š		na	na	0160
ü		129	129	00FC
Ü		154	154	00DC
ž		na	na	017E
Ž		na	na	017D

**na = not available as an ASCII code in the specified code page*

Estonian is alphabetized as follows:

A	B	(C)	D	E	F	G	H	I	J	K	L	M
N	O	P	(Q)	R	S	Š	Z	Ž	T	U	V	(W)
(X)	Õ	Ä	Ö	Ü	(Y)							

Faroese

Faroese is spoken by most of the 40 000 inhabitants of the Faeroe Islands. It is related to Icelandic and resembles old Norse.

Letter	*Alternative*	*ASCII code (page 437)*	*ASCII code (page 850)*	*Unicode™*
á		160	160	00E1
Á		na*	181	00C1
æ		145	145	00E6
Æ		146	146	00C6
ð		na	208	00F0
Ð		na	209	00D0
í		161	161	00ED
Í		na	214	00CD
ó		162	162	00F3
Ó		na	224	00D3
ø		na	155	00F8
Ø		na	157	00D8
ú		163	163	00FA
Ú		na	233	00DA
ý		na	236	00FD
Ý		na	237	00DD

**na = not available as an ASCII code in the specified code page*

Faroese is alphabetized as follows:

A	Á	B	C	D	Ð	E	F	G	H	I	Í	J
K	L	M	N	O	Ó	P	Q	R	S	T	U	Ú
V	W	X	Y	Ý	Z	Æ	Ø					

Finnish

Finnish is spoken by about 4.5 million people in Finland, and by about 50,000 people in Russia and 30,000 in northern Sweden.

Letter	*Alternative*	*ASCII code (page 437)*	*ASCII code (page 850)*	*Unicode™*
ä	a	132	132	00E4
Ä	A	142	142	00C4
å	a	134	134	00E5
Å	A	143	143	00C5
ö	o	148	148	00F6
Ö	O	153	153	00D6
š	s	na*	na	0161
Š	S	na	na	0160
ž	z	na	na	017E
Ž	Z	na	na	017D

**na = not available as an ASCII code in the specified code page*

Finnish is alphabetized as follows:

A	B	(C)	D	E	F	G	H	I	J	K	L	M
N	O	P	(Q)	R	S	Š	T	U	V	(W)	(X)	Y
Z	Ž	(Å)	Ä	Ö								

French

French is spoken by about 72 million people throughout the World; 56 million people in France and Monaco, 6 million people in Canada, 4 million people in Belgium, 3 million people in Switzerland, 1 million in the United States and about 300 000 people in Luxembourg. It is also spoken, often as a second language, by inhabitants of France's ex-colonies.

Letter	*Alternative*	*ASCII code (page 437)*	*ASCII code (page 850)*	*Unicode™*
à	a	133	133	00E0

À	A	na*	183	00C0
â	a	131	131	00E2
Â	A	na	182	00C2
æ	ae	145	145	00E6
Æ	AE	146	146	00C6
ç	c	135	135	00E7
Ç	C	128	128	00C7
ë	e	137	137	00EB
Ë	E	na	211	00CB
é	e	130	130	00E9
É	E	144	144	00C9
è	e	138	138	00E8
È	E	na	212	00C8
ê	e	136	136	00EA
Ê	E	na	210	00CA
î	i	140	140	00EE
Î	I	na	215	00CE
ï	i	139	139	00EC
Ï	I	na	216	00CF
ô	o	147	147	00F4
Ô	O	na	226	00D4
œ	oe	na	na*	0153
Œ	OE	na	na	0152
ù	u	151	151	00F9
Ù	U	na	235	00D9
û	u	150	150	00FB
Û	U	na	234	00DB
ü	u	129	129	00FC
Ü	U	154	154	00DC
ÿ	y	na	na	00FF
Ÿ	Y	na	na	0178

**na = not available as an ASCII code in the specified code page*

French-speakers rarely assign accents to capital letters. Some listings will simply omit accents in upper-case letters, others will use the lower-case accented equivalent even where the rest of the word is in upper case.

French is alphabetized as follows:

A (Â, À, Æ)	B	C (Ç)	D	E (É, Ê, È, Ë)	F	G	H	I (Î, Ï)	J	K
L	M	N	O (Ô, Œ)	P	Q	R	S	T	U (Û, Ù)	V
W	X	Y (Ÿ)	Z							

Friesian or Frisian (West)

There are about 300,000 speakers of West Friesian in the province of Friesland in the northern Netherlands.

Letter	*Alternative*	*ASCII code (page 437)*	*ASCII code (page 850)*	*Unicode™*
â		131	131	00E1
Â		na*	182	00C2
ä		132	132	00E4
Ä		142	142	00C4
é		130	130	00E9
É		144	144	00C9
ê		136	136	00EA
Ê		na	210	00CA
ë		137	137	00EB
Ë		na	211	00CB
ï		139	139	00EF
Ï		na	216	00CF
ô		147	147	00F4
Ô		na	226	00DA
ö		148	148	00F6
Ö		153	153	00D6
û		150	150	00FB
Û		na	234	00DB
ú		163	163	00FA
Ú		na	233	00DA
ü		129	129	00FC
Ü		154	154	00DC

**na = not available as an ASCII code in the specified code page*

West Friesian is alphabetized as follows:

A (Â, Ä)	B	C	D	E (É, Ê, Ë)	F	G	H	I (Ï, Y)	J	K
L	M	N	O (Ô, Ö)	P	Q	R	S	T	U (Ú, Û, Ü)	V
W	X	Z								

Friulian

There are some 600 000 speakers of Friulian in Northeast Italy and a small number in Slovenia.

Letter	*Alternative*	*ASCII code (page 437)*	*ASCII code (page 850)*	*Unicode™*
à		133	133	00E0
À		na*	183	00C0
á		160	160	00E1
Á		na	181	00C1
â		131	131	00E2
Â		na	182	00C2
è		138	138	00E8
È		na	212	00C8
ì		141	141	00EC
Ì		na	222	00CC
ò		149	149	00F2
Ò		na	227	00D2
ù		151	151	00F9
Ù		na	235	00D9

**na = not available as an ASCII code in the specified code page*

Friulian is alphabetized as follows:

A	À	Á	Â	B	C	D	E	È	F	G	H	I
Ì	J	K	L	M	N	O	Ò	P	Q	R	S	T
U	(Ù)	V	W	X	Y	Z						

Gaelic

Gaelic is spoken in two distinct varieties in Scotland and Ireland. It has almost 20 000 speakers in the former and some 500 000 in the latter.

Letter	*Alternative*	*ASCII code (page 437)*	*ASCII code (page 850)*	*Unicode™*
à		133	133	00E0
À		na*	183	00C0
á		160	160	00E1
Á		na	181	00C1
é		130	130	00E9
É		144	144	00C9
è		138	138	00E8
È		na	212	00C8
í		161	161	00ED
Í		na	214	00CD
ì		141	141	00EC
Ì		na	222	00CC
ó		162	162	00F3
Ó		na	224	00D3
ò		149	149	00F2
Ò		na	227	00D2
ú		163	163	00FA
Ú		na	233	00DA
ù		151	151	00F9
Ù		na	235	00D9

**na = not available as an ASCII code in the specified code page*

Irish is alphabetized as follows:

A (Á)	B	C	D	E (É)	F	G	H	I (Í)	J	(K)	L	M
N	O (Ó)	P	Q	R	S	T	U (Ú)	V	W	X	Y	Z

The Scottish Gaelic alphabet has 18 letters and is alphabetized as follows:

A (À, Á)	B	C	D	E (È, É)	F	G	H	I (Ì)	(J)	(K)	L
M	N	O (Ò, Ó)	P	(Q)	R	S	T	U (Ù)	(V)	(W)	(X)
(Y)	(Z)										

Galician

Galician is spoken by over 3 million people in Spain.

Letter	*Alternative*	*ASCII code (page 437)*	*ASCII code (page 850)*	*Unicode™*
á		160	160	00E1
Á		na*	181	00C1
é		130	130	00E9
É		144	144	00C9
í		161	161	00ED
Í		na	214	00CD
ñ		164	164	00F1
Ñ		165	165	00D1
ó		162	162	00F3
Ó		na	224	00D3
ú		163	163	00FA
Ú		na	233	00DA
ü		129	129	00FC
Ü		154	154	00DC

**na = not available as an ASCII code in the specified code page*

Galician is alphabetized as follows:

A	Á	B	C	D	E	(É)	F	G	H	I	(Í)	J
K	L	M	N	Ñ	O	(Ó)	P	Q	R	S	T	U
(Ú	Ü)	V	W	X	Y	Z						

German

German is one of the most widely spread languages in Europe, spoken by about 80 million people in Germany, 7.7 million people in Austria, 4.4 million people in Switzerland, 66 000 people in Belgium, 28 500 people in the South Tyrol region of Italy and 29 000 people in Liechtenstein, as well as by smaller minorities in southern Denmark, eastern France and Luxembourg. There are large regional variations in the form of German spoken, especially between Germany, Switzerland and Austria.

Letter	*Alternative*	*ASCII code (page 437)*	*ASCII code (page 850)*	*Unicode™*
ä	ae	132	132	00E4
Ä	AE	142	142	00C4
ö	oe	148	148	00F6
Ö	OE	153	153	00D6
ü	ue	129	129	00FC
Ü	US	154	154	00DC

ß	ss	225	225	00DF

The Scharfes S ("ß") is used only in lower case. The upper case equivalent is SS. This symbol is NOT used in Swiss-German.

Where three esses come together in German, a hyphen needs to be used as follows:

Strauss-strasse

not

Straussstrasse

All nouns in German are written with the first letter as a capital.

German is alphabetized as follows:

A (Ä)	B	C	D	E	F	G	H	I	J	K	L	M
N	O (Ö)	P	Q	R	S (ß=SS)	T	U	Ü	V	W	X	Y
Z												

Greek

Greek is spoken by about 10 million people in Greece and Cyprus. It has its own alphabet which has to be transliterated for use with databases containing Roman script. The table below gives the transliteration symbol of each Greek character. Each character is given in upper case then lower case version:

Letter	*Name*	*Transliteration*	*Unicode™*
Αα	álfa	a	0391, 03B1
Ββ	víta	v	0392, 03B2
Γγ	ghána	gh (y before an e sound)	0393, 03B3
Δδ	thélta	th	0394, 03B4
Εϵ	épsilon	e	0395, 03B5
Ζζ	zíta	z	0396, 03B6
Ηη	íta	i	0397, 03B7
Θθ	thíta	th	0398, 03B8
Ιι	yóta	i	0399, 03B9
Κκ	kápa	k	039A, 03BA
Λλ	lámtha	l	039B, 03BB
Μμ	mi	m	039C, 03BC
Νν	ni	n	039D, 03BD
Ξξ	ksi	ks	039E, 03BE
Οο	ómikron	o	039F, 03BF

Ππ	pi	p	03A0, 03C0
Ρρ	ro	r	03A1, 03C1
Σσς	sigma	s	03A3, 03C3, 03C2
Ττ	taf	t	03A4, 03C4
Υυ	ípsilon	i	03A5, 03C5
Φφ	fi	f	03A6, 03C6
Χχ	hi	h	03A7, 03C7
Ψψ	psi	ps	03A8, 03C8
Ωω	omégha	o	03A9, 03C9

Note that the letter ς is only used at the end of a word.

Greenlandic

Greenlandic is spoken by 40 000 people in Greenland and a further 7 000 people in Denmark.

Letter	*Alternative*	*ASCII code (page 437)*	*ASCII code (page 850)*	*Unicode™*
K‘		na*	na	0138
æ		145	145	00E6
Æ		146	146	00C6
ø		na	155	00F8
Ø		na	157	00D8
å		134	134	00E5
Å		143	143	00C5

**na = not available as an ASCII code in the specified code page*

Greenlandic is alphabetized as follows:

A	B	C	D	E	F	G	H	I	J	K	L	M
N	O	P	Q	(K‘)	R	S	T	U	V	W	X	Y
Z	Æ	Ø	Å									

Hungarian

Hungarian is spoken by about 10 million people in Hungary, 1.5 million people in Romania, and by minorities in Slovakia, Slovenia, Croatia and Serbia.

Letter	*Alternative*	*ASCII code (page 437)*	*ASCII code (page 850)*	*Unicode™*
á		160	160	00E1
Á		na*	181	00C1
é		130	130	00E9
É		144	144	00C9
í		161	161	00ED
Í		na	214	00CD
ó		162	162	00F3
Ó		na	224	00D3
ö		148	148	00F6
Ö		153	153	00D6
ő		na	na*	0151
Ő		na	na	0150
ú		163	163	00FA
Ú		na	233	00DA
ü		129	129	00FC
Ü		154	154	00DC
ű		na	na	0171
Ű		na	na	0170

**na = not available as an ASCII code in the specified code page*

Hungarian is alphabetized as follows:

A	Á	B	C	CS	D	E	É	F	G	GY	H	I
Í	J	K	L	LY	M	N	NY	O	Ó	Ö	Ő	P
Q	R	S	SZ	T	TY	U	Ú	Ü	Ű	V	W	X
Y	Z	ZS										

Icelandic

Icelandic is spoken by 250 000 people in Iceland.

Letter	*Alternative*	*ASCII code (page 437)*	*ASCII code (page 850)*	*Unicode™*
á	a	160	160	00E1
Á	A	na*	181	00C1
æ	ae	145	145	00E6
Æ	AE	146	146	00C6

ð	d	na	208	00F0
Ð	D	na	209	00D0
é	e	130	130	00E9
É	E	144	144	00C9
í	i	161	161	00ED
Í	I	na	214	00CD
ó	o	162	162	00F3
Ó	O	na	224	00D3
ö	o	148	148	00F6
Ö	O	153	153	00D6
œ	oe	na	na*	0153
Œ	OE	na	na	0152
þ	th	na	232	00FE
Þ	TH	na	231	00DE
ú	u	163	163	00FA
Ú	U	na	233	00DA
ý	y	na	236	00FD
Ý	Y	na	237	00DD

**na = not available as an ASCII code in the specified code page*

Icelandic is alphabetized as follows:

A	Á	B	C	D	Ð	E	É	F	G	H	I	Í
J	K	L	M	N	O	Ó	P	Q	R	S	T	U
Ú	V	W	X	Y	Ý	C	Þ	Æ	Ö			

Italian

Italian is spoken by about 57 million people in Italy, San Marino and Vatican City and about 500 000 people in Switzerland.

Letter	*Alternative*	*ASCII code (page 437)*	*ASCII code (page 850)*	*Unicode™*
à		133	133	00E0
À		na*	183	00C0
é	e'	130	130	00E9
É	E'	144	144	00C9
è		138	138	00E8
È		na	212	00C8
í	i'	161	161	00ED

Í	I'	na	214	00CD
ì		141	141	00EC
Ì		na	222	00CC
ï		139	139	00EF
Ï		na	216	00CF
ó	o'	162	162	00F3
Ó	O'	na	224	00D3
ò		149	149	00F2
Ò		na	227	00D2
ú	u'	163	163	00FA
Ú	U'	na	233	00DA
ù		151	151	00F9
Ù		na	235	00D9

**na = not available as an ASCII code in the specified code page*

Italian is alphabetized as follows:

A (À)	B	C	D	E (É, È)	F	G	H	I (Í, Ì, Ï)	J	K
L	M	N	O (Ó,Ò)	P	Q	R	S	T	U (Ú, Ù)	V
W	X	Y	Z							

Ladin

There are about 30 000 speakers of Ladin in Northeast Italy.

Letter	*Alternative*	*ASCII code (page 437)*	*ASCII code (page 850)*	*Unicode™*
â		131	131	00E2
Â		na*	182	00C2
á		160	160	00E1
Á		na	181	00C1
à		133	133	00E0
À		na	183	00C0
ê		136	136	00EA
Ê		na	210	00CA
é		130	130	00E9
É		144	144	00C9
è		138	138	00E8
È		na	212	00C8

î		140	140	00EE
Î		na	215	00CE
í		161	161	00ED
Í		na	214	00CD
ì		141	141	00EC
Ì		na	222	00CC
ô		147	147	00F4
Ô		na	226	00D4
ó		162	162	00F3
Ó		na	224	00D3
ò		149	149	00F2
Ò		na	227	00D2
û		150	150	00FB
Û		na	234	00DB
ú		163	163	00FA
Ú		na	233	00DA
ù		151	151	00F9
Ù		na	235	00D9

**na = not available as an ASCII code in the specified code page*

Ladin is alphabetized as follows:

A	(Â	Á	À)	B	C	D	E	(Ê	É	È)	F
G	H	I	(Î	Í	Ì)	J	K	L	M	N	O
(Ô	Ó	Ò)	P	Q	R	S	T	U	(Û	Ú	Ù)
V	W	X	Y	Z							

Latvian

There are about 1 400 000 speakers of Latvian, mainly in Latvia.

Letter	*Alternative*	*ASCII code (page 437)*	*ASCII code (page 850)*	*Unicode™*
ā		na*	na	0101
Ā		na	na	0100
č		na	na	010D
Č		na	na	010C
ē		na	na	0113
Ē		na	na	0112

ģ		na	na	0121
Ģ		na	na	0122
ī		na	na	012B
Ī		na	na	012A
ķ		na	na	0137
Ķ		na	na	0136
ļ		na	na	013C
Ļ		na	na	013B
ņ		na	na	0146
Ņ		na	na	0145
ō		na	na	014D
Ō		na	na	014C
ŗ		na	na	0157
Ŗ		na	na	0156
š		na	na	0161
Š		na	na	0160
ū		na	na	016B
Ū		na	na	016A
ž		na	na	017E
Ž		na	na	017D

**na = not available as an ASCII code in the specified code page*

Latvian is alphabetized as follows:

A	(Ā)	B	C	Č	D	E	(Ē)	F	G	Ģ ģ	H
I	(Ī)	J	K	Ķ	L	Ļ	M	N	Ņ	O	(Ō)
P	(Q)	R	Ŗ	S	Š	T	U	(Ū)	V	(W)	(X)
(Y)	Z	Ž									

Letzebuergesch

Letzebuergesch, a language related to German, is the official language of Luxembourg and is spoken by some 350 000 people.

Letter	*Alternative*	*ASCII code (page 437)*	*ASCII code (page 850)*	*Unicode™*
â		131	131	00E2
Â		na*	182	00C2
ä		132	132	00E4
Ä		142	142	00C4

é		130	130	00E9
É		144	144	00C9
ë		137	137	00EB
Ë		na	211	00CB
M̂		na	na	004D+0302
m̂		na	na	006D+0302
N̂		na	na	004E+0302
n̂		na	na	006E+0302
ö		148	148	00F6
Ö		153	153	00D6
ô		147	147	00F4
Ô		na	226	00D4
ü		129	129	00FC
Ü		154	154	00DC

**na = not available as an ASCII code in the specified code page*

Letzebuergesch is alphabetized as follows:

A (Ä)	B	C	D	E (Ë, É)	F	G	H	I	J	K	L
M (M̂)	N (N̂)	O (Ö)	P	Q	R	S	T	U (Ü)	V	W	X
Y	Z										

Lithuanian

There are almost 3 million speakers of Lithuanian, mainly in Lithuania.

Letter	*Alternative*	*ASCII code (page 437)*	*ASCII code (page 850)*	*Unicode™*
ą		na*	na	0105
Ą		na	na	0104
č		na	na	010D
Č		na	na	010C
ę		na	na	0119
Ę		na	na	0118
ė		na	na	0117
Ė		na	na	0116
į		na	na	012F
Į		na	na	012E
š		na	na	0161

Š		na	na	0160
ų		na	na	0173
Ų		na	na	0172
ū		na	na	016B
Ū		na	na	016A
ž		na	na	017E
Ž		na	na	017D

**na = not available as an ASCII code in the specified code page*

Lithuanian is alphabetized as follows:

A	(Ą)	B	C	Č	D	E	(Ę	Ė)	F	G
H	(Į	Y)	J	K	L	M	N	O	P	(Q)
R	S	Š	T	U	(Ų	Ū)	V	(W)	(X)	Z
Ž										

Maltese

Maltese, an ancient Arabic language with strong Romance influences, is spoken by about 400 000 people in Malta.

Letter	*Alternative*	*ASCII code (page 437)*	*ASCII code (page 850)*	*Unicode™*
à		133	133	00E0
À		na*	183	00C0
ċ		na	na*	010B
Ċ		na	na	010A
è		138	138	00E8
È		na	212	00C8
ġ		na	na	0121
Ġ		na	na	0120
għ		na	na	g+0127
GĦ		na	na	G+0126
ħ		na	na	0127
Ħ		na	na	0126
ì		141	141	00EC
Ì		na	222	00CC
ĩ		na	na	0129
Ĩ		na	na	0128
ò		149	149	00F2

Ò		na	227	00D2
ù		151	151	00F9
Ù		na	235	00D9
ż		na	na	017C
Ż		na	na	017B

**na = not available as an ASCII code in the specified code page*

Maltese is alphabetized as follows:

A (À)	B	Ċ (C)	D	E (È)	F	Ġ	G	H	Ħ	I (Ì,Î)	J
K	L	M	N	Għ	O (Ò)	P	Q	R	S	T	U (Ù)
V	W	X	(Y)	Ż	Z						

Norwegian

Norwegian is spoken by about 4 million people in Norway.

Letter	*Alternative*	*ASCII code (page 437)*	*ASCII code (page 850)*	*Unicode™*
å	aa	134	134	00E5
Å	AA	143	143	00C5
æ	ae	145	145	00E6
Æ	AE	146	146	00C6
é		130	130	00E9
É		144	144	00C9
ó		162	162	00F3
Ó		na*	224	00D3
ò		149	149	00F2
Ò		na	227	00D2
ø	oe	na	155	00F8
Ø	OE	na	157	00D8

**na = not available as an ASCII code in the specified code page*

Norwegian is alphabetized as follows:

A	B	C	D	E	É	F	G	H	I	J	K	L
M	N	O	Ó	Ò	P	Q	R	S	T	U	V	W
X	Y	Z	Æ	Ø	Å							

Polish

Polish is spoken by about 35 million people, mainly in Poland.

Letter	*Alternative*	*ASCII code (page 437)*	*ASCII code (page 850)*	*Unicode™*
ą		na*	na*	0105
Ą		na	na	0104
ć		na	na	0107
Ć		na	na	0106
ę		na	na	0119
Ę		na	na	0118
ł		na	na	0142
Ł		na	na	0141
ń		na	na	0144
Ń		na	na	0143
ó		162	162	00F3
Ó		na	224	00D3
ś		na	na	015B
Ś		na	na	015A
ź		na	na	017A
Ź		na	na	0179
ż		na	na	017C
Ż		na	na	017B

**na = not available as an ASCII code in the specified code page*

Where an accent cannot be reproduced, it is usually just dropped. However, an apostrophe or a comma may be added immediately following the accented letter to clarify meaning. For example: *was* (=to you), *wa,s* (=moustache).

Opening quotation marks in Polish are usually written on the same level as the text as follows: „Hello''. However most computer systems, even in Poland, do not allow this, and the standard "Western" quotation marks are used.

Polish is alphabetized as follows:

A	Ą	B	C	Ć	D	E	Ę	F	G	H	I	J
K	L	Ł	M	N	Ń	O	Ó	P	R	S	Ś	T
U	W	Y	Z	Ź	Ż							

Portuguese

Portuguese is spoken by about 10 million people in Portugal and 163 million people in Brazil. There are also many second-language speakers in Portugal's ex-colonies. In Portugal, there are Northern dialects and Central-Southern dialects.

Letter	*Alternative*	*ASCII code (page 437)*	*ASCII code (page 850)*	*Unicode™*
á		160	160	00E1
Á		na*	181	00C1
à		133	133	00E0
À		na	183	00C0
â		131	131	00E2
Â		na	182	00C2
ã		na	198	00E3
Ã		na	199	00C3
ç		135	135	00E7
Ç		128	128	00C7
é		130	130	00E9
É		144	144	00C9
è		138	138	00E8
È		na	212	00C8
ê		136	136	00EA
Ê		na	210	00CA
í		161	161	00ED
Í		na	214	00CD
ì		141	141	00EC
Ì		na	222	00CC
ó		162	162	00F3
Ó		na	224	00D3
ò		149	149	00F2
Ò		na	227	00D2
ô		147	147	00F4
Ô		na	226	00D4
õ		na	228	00F5

Õ		na	229	00D5
ú		163	163	00FA
Ú		na	233	00DA
ü		129	129	00FC
Ü		154	154	00DC

**na = not available as an ASCII code in the specified code page*

Portuguese accents should not be replaced by apostrophes as apostrophes may be used in Portuguese to indicate certain contractions, such as *Sant'Ana.*

Portuguese is alphabetized as follows:

A (Á, À, Â, Ã)	B	C (Ç)	D	E (É, Ê)	F	G	H	I (Í)	J	K
L	M	N	O (Ó, Ô, Õ)	P	Q	R	S	T	U (Ú, Ü)	V
W	X	Y	Z							

Provençals

Provençals is a Romance language related to French and Catalan, found in south-eastern France and north-western Italy. It has a number of dialects.

Letter	*Alternative*	*ASCII code (page 437)*	*ASCII code (page 850)*	*Unicode™*
à		133	133	00E0
À		na*	183	00C0
ç		135	135	00E7
Ç		128	128	00C7
é		130	130	00E9
É		144	144	00C9
è		138	138	00E8
È		na	212	00C8
ó		162	162	00F3
Ó		na	224	00D3

**na = not available as an ASCII code in the specified code page*

Rhaeto-Romance

Dialects of Rhaeto-Romance are spoken in Switzerland, western Austria and northern Italy by about 500 000 people.

Letter	*Alternative*	*ASCII code (page 437)*	*ASCII code (page 850)*	*Unicode™*
à		133	133	00E0
À		na*	183	00C0
è		138	138	00E8
È		na	212	00C8
é		130	130	00E9
É		144	144	00C9
ì		141	141	00EC
Ì		na	222	00CC
ò		149	149	00F2
Ò		na	227	00D2
ù		151	151	00F9
Ù		na	235	00D9

**na = not available as an ASCII code in the specified code page*

Rhaeto-Romance is alphabetized as follows:

A (À)	B	C	D	E (È,É)	F	G	H	I (Ì)	J	(K)	L	M
N	O (Ò)	P	Q	R	S	T	U (Ù)	V	(W)	X	(Y)	Z

Romanian

Romanian is spoken by about 20 million people in Romania. A similar language to Romanian, written using the Cyrillic alphabet, is spoken in Moldova.

Letter	*Alternative*	*ASCII code (page 437)*	*ASCII code (page 850)*	*Unicode™*
à		133	133	00E0
À		na*	183	00C0
â		131	131	00E2
Â		na	182	00C2
ă		na	na*	0103
Ă		na	na	0102
è		138	138	00E8
È		na	212	00C8
ì		141	141	00EC
Ì		na	222	00CC
î		140	140	00EE
Î		na	215	00CE

ş		na	na	015F
Ş		na	na	015E
ț		na	na	0163
Ț		na	na	0162
ù		151	151	00F9
Ù		na	235	00D9

**na = not available as an ASCII code in the specified code page*

Romanian is alphabetized as follows:

A	Â	Ă	B	C	D	E	F	G	H	I	Î	J
K	L	M	N	O	P	(Q)	R	S	Ş	T	Ţ	U
V	W	X	(Y)	Z								

Romany

Romany is the language of Europe's Gypsies, and knows many dialects and forms, each strongly influenced by the indigenous languages of the region which its speakers inhabit.

Apostrophes are used in Romany words.

Letter	*Alternative*	*ASCII code (page 437)*	*ASCII code (page 850)*	*Unicode™*
è		na*	na*	010D
š		na	na	0161
ž		na	na	017E

**na = not available as an ASCII code in the specified code page*

Sami

Sami (Lapp) is spoken in the north of Norway, Sweden, Finland and Russia by some 35 000 people.

There are six versions of Sami: Kildin (using the Cyrillic script); Northern, Lule, Inari, Skoly and Southern (using the Latin script). This table encompasses all diacritical characters used for those using the Latin script.

Letter	*Alternative*	*ASCII code (page 437)*	*ASCII code (page 850)*	*Unicode™*
á		160	160	00E1
Á		na*	181	00C1
å		134	134	00E5

Å		143	143	00C5
ä		132	132	00E4
Ä		142	142	00C4
â		131	131	00E2
Â		na	182	00C2
č		na	na*	010D
Č		na	na	010C
Đ		na	209	0110
ð		na	na	0111
ń		na	na	0144
Ń		na	na	0143
ŋ		na	na	014B
Ŋ		na	na	014A
ö		148	148	00F6
Ö		153	153	00D6
õ		na	228	00F5
Õ		na	229	00D5
ø		na	155	00F8
Ø		na	157	00D8
š		na	na	0161
Š		na	na	0160
Ŧ		na	na	0166
ŧ		na	na	0167
ž		na	na	017E
Ž		na	na	017D
ǯ		na	na	01EE

Diacritical characters borrowed from Finnish, Swedish and Norwegian are also used.

**na = not available as an ASCII code in the specified code page*

Slovak

Spoken by about 5 million people, mainly in Slovakia. Slovak is usually written in the Cyrillic script. When transliterated to Latin characters, loss of the diacritical marks should be avoided.

Letter	*Alternative*	*ASCII code (page 437)*	*ASCII code (page 850)*	*Unicode™*
á		160	160	00E1
Á		na*	181	00C1

č		na	na*	010D
Č		na	na	010C
ď or d̆	d'	na	na	010F
Ď		na	na	010E
é		130	130	00E9
É		144	144	00C9
ě		na	na	011B
Ě		na	na	011A
í		161	161	00ED
Í		na	214	00CD
ň		na	na	0148
Ň		na	na	0147
ó		162	162	00F3
Ó		na	224	00D3
ř		na	na	0159
Ř		na	na	0158
š		na	na	0161
Š		na	na	0160
ť or ť	t'	na	na	0165
Ť		na	na	0164
ú		163	163	00FA
Ú		na	233	00DA
ů		na	na	016F
Ů		na	na	016E
ý		na	na	00FD
Ý		na	na	00DD
ž		na	na	017E
Ž		na	na	017D

**na = not available as an ASCII code in the specified code page*

Slovak is alphabetized as follows:

A	Á	B	C	Č	D	Ď	E	É	Ě	F	G	H
CH	I	Í	J	K	L	M	N	Ň	O	Ó	P	Q
R	Ř	S	Š	T	Ť	U	Ú	Ů	V	W	X	Y
Ý	Z	Ž										

Slovenian

Slovenian is spoken by about 1.5 million people in Slovenia and small parts of Hungary and Italy.

Letter	*Alternative*	*ASCII code (page 437)*	*ASCII code (page 850)*	*Unicode™*
č	ch	na*	na*	010D
Č	Ch	na	na	010C
š	sh	na	na	0161
Š	Sh	na	na	0160
ž	zh	na	na	017E
Ž	Zh	na	na	017D

**na = not available as an ASCII code in the specified code page*

Slovenian is alphabetized as follows:

A	B	C	Č	D	E	F	G	H	I	J	K	L
M	N	O	P	(Q)	R	S	Š	T	U	V	(W)	(X)
(Y)	Z	Ž										

Sorbian

Sorbian is a Slavic language spoken by some 50 000 people in two distinct dialects in the south-easternmost part of the former East Germany.

Letter	*Alternative*	*ASCII code (page 437)*	*ASCII code (page 850)*	*Unicode™*
ć		na*	na*	0107
Ć		na	na	0106
č		na	na	010D
Č		na	na	010C
ě		na	na	011B
Ě		na	na	011A
ł		na	na	0142
Ł		na	na	0141
ń		na	na	0144
Ń		na	na	0143
ó		162	162	00F3
Ó		na	224	00D3
ř		na	na	0159

Ř		na	na	0158
ś		na	na	015B
Ś		na	na	015A
š		na	na	0161
Š		na	na	0160
ź		na	na	017A
Ź		na	na	0179
ž		na	na	017E
Ž		na	na	017D

**na = not available as an ASCII code in the specified code page*

Upper Sorbian is alphabetized as follows:

A	B	C	Č	D	DŹ	E	Ě	F	G	H	CH	I
J	K	Ł	L	M	N	Ń	O	Ó	P	R	Ř	S
Š	T	Ć	U	W	X	Y	Z	Ž				

Lower Sorbian is alphabetized as follows:

A	B	Bj	C	Č	Ć	D	DŹ	E	Ě	F	G	H
CH	I	J	K	L	Ł	M	MJ	N	Ń	NJ	O	P
PJ	(Q)	R	Ŕ	RJ	S	Ś	Š	TŚ	TŠ	T	U	(V)
W	WJ	(X)	Y	Z	Ź	Ž						

Spanish (Castilian)

Spanish is spoken by about 27.5 million people in Spain, 81 million people in Central America, 18 million people in the Caribbean, 90 million people in South America, 22 million people in the United States of America and by many others as a second language, especially in Spain's ex-colonies.

Letter	*Alternative*	*ASCII code (page 437)*	*ASCII code (page 850)*	*Unicode™*
á	a	160	160	00E1
Á	A	na*	181	00C1
é	e	130	130	00E9
É	E	144	144	00C9
í	i	161	161	00ED
Í	I	na	214	00CD
ñ	n	164	164	00F1
Ñ	N	165	165	00D1

ó	o	162	162	00F3
Ó	O	na	224	00D3
ú	u	163	163	00DA
Ú	U	na	233	00FA
ü	u	129	129	00FC
Ü	U	154	154	00DC

**na = not available as an ASCII code in the specified code page*

In Spanish, abbreviations of plurals are doubled. For example, the Spanish abbreviations for the United States is *EE.UU.* The full stops must be added after each double-letter, never between them.

Spanish is alphabetized as follows:

A (Á)	B	C	CH	D	E (É)	F	G	H	I (Í)	J	K	L
LL	M	N	Ñ	O (Ó)	P	Q	R	RR	S	T	U (Ú, Ü)	V
W	X	Y	Z									

A recent law passed in Spain has removed "ch" and "ll" as separate letters of the Spanish alphabet, though most Spanish-speakers still use them as such.

Swedish

Swedish is spoken by about 8 million people in Sweden and about 300 000 people in western and southern Finland.

Letter	*Alternative*	*ASCII code (page 437)*	*ASCII code (page 850)*	*Unicode™*
å		134	134	00E5
Å		143	143	00C5
ä		132	132	00C4
Ä		142	142	00E4
é		130	130	00E9
É		144	144	00C9
ö		148	148	00F6
Ö		153	153	00D6
ü		129	129	00FC
Ü		154	154	00DC

**na = not available as an ASCII code in the specified code page*

Swedish is alphabetized as follows:

A	B	C	D	E (É)	F	G	H	I	J	K	L	M
N	O	P	Q	R	S	T	U	V	(W)	X	Y	(Ü)
Z	Å	Ä	Ö									

Turkish

Turkish is spoken by about 57 million people in Turkey, and by minorities in Greece, Bulgaria and Cyprus.

Letter	*Alternative*	*ASCII code (page 437)*	*ASCII code (page 850)*	*Unicode™*
â		131	131	00E2
Â		na*	182	00C2
ç		135	135	00E7
Ç		128	128	00C7
ğ		na	na*	011F
Ğ		na	na	011E
İ		na	na	0130
ı		na	na	0131
î		140	140	00EE
Î		na	215	00CE
ö		148	148	00D6
Ö		153	153	00F6
ş		na	na	015F
Ş		na	na	015E
ü		129	129	00FC
Ü		154	154	00DC
û		150	150	00FB
Û		na	234	00DB

**na = not available as an ASCII code in the specified code page*

Turkish is alphabetized as follows:

A	(Â)	B	C	Ç	D	E	F	G	Ğ	H	Iı
İi	J	K	L	M	N	O	Ö	P	(Q)	R	S
Ş	T	U	Ü	Û	V	(W)	(X)	Y	Z		

Welsh

Welsh is spoken by about 600 000 people in Wales.

There are no accepted alternatives to accented characters in Welsh.

Letter	*Alternative*	*ASCII code (page 437)*	*ASCII code (page 850)*	*Unicode™*
ä		132	132	00E4
Ä		142	142	00C4
â		131	131	00E2
Â		na*	182	00C2
á		160	160	00E1
Á		na	181	00C1
à		133	133	00E0
À		na	183	00C0
ë		137	137	00EB
Ë		na	211	00CB
ê		136	136	00EA
Ê		na	210	00CA
é		130	130	00E9
É		144	144	00C9
è		138	138	00E8
È		na	212	00C8
ï		139	139	00EC
Ï		na	216	00CF
î		140	140	00EE
Î		na	215	00CE
í		161	161	00ED
Í		na	214	00CD
ì		141	141	00EC
Ì		na	222	00CC
ö		148	148	00F6
Ö		153	153	00D6
ô		147	147	00F4
Ô		na	226	00D4
ó		162	162	00F3
Ó		na	224	00D3
ò		149	149	00F2
Ò		na	227	00D2
û		150	150	00FB
Û		na	234	00DB
ü		129	129	00FC

Ü		154	154	00DC
ú		163	163	00FA
Ú		na	233	00DA
ù		151	151	00F9
Ù		na	235	00D9
ŵ		na	na*	0175
Ŵ		na	na	0174
ẅ		na	na	0077+0308
Ẅ		na	na	0057+0308
ẃ		na	na	0077+0301
Ẃ		na	na	0057+0301
ẁ		na	na	0077+0300
Ẁ		na	na	0057+0300
v̈		na	na	0076+0308
V̈		na	na	0056+0308
v̂		na	na	0076+0302
V̂		na	na	0056+0302
ŷ		na	na	0177
Ŷ		na	na	0176
ÿ		na	na	00FF
Ÿ		na	na	0178
ý		na	na	00FD
Ý		na	na	00DD
ỳ		na	na	0079+0300
Ỳ		na	na	0059+0300

**na* = not available as an ASCII code in the specified code page*

The Welsh alphabet has 31 letters and is alphabetized as follows:

A (Â, Á, À, Ä)	B	C	CH	D	DD	E (Ê, É, È, Ë)	F
FF	G	NG	H	I (Î, Í, Ì, Ï)	J	K	L
LL	M	N	O (Ô, Ó, Ò, Ö)	P	PH	(Q)	R
RH	S	T	TH	U (Û, Ú, Ù, Ü)	(V)	W (Ŵ, Ẃ, Ẁ, Ẅ)	(X)
Y (Ŷ, Ý, Ỳ, Ÿ)	Z						

Job Titles

It is very important to code the job titles of contact names within a database because the number of job titles in circulation, with their appropriate contractions and acronyms, is surprisingly high. This means that only a certain proportion of programmatic coding is possible. Coding is required to ensure that you can direct your mail within a company to the appropriate person. If you mail to specialized functions, you may have to look further than this table for correct translations, but this table gives the translations of the most commonly occurring job titles in German, French, Spanish, Italian, Dutch, Portuguese, Norwegian, Finnish, Greek, Danish and Swedish. Note that job titles are often given in a language other than that of the country concerned - for example, German for Eastern Europe and English for Scandinavian countries - so this should be taken into account when creating job-title lookup tables.

In the following table, for the German titles, *-r* indicates a male, *-in* a female. In Dutch, titles ending in *-teur* will usually end in *-trice* for females. The abbreviation (f) indicates that the job title refers to a female, (m) to a male.

English	*German*	*French*	*Spanish*	*Italian*	*Dutch*	*Portuguese*
Accountant	-	(Agent) Compatable	-	Contabile	Accountant	Contabilista
Active Partner	Komplementär(in)	-	-	Socio Gerente	Vennoot (m) / Venote (f)	Sócio Activo
Administration Manager	Verwaltungsdirektor(in)	Directeir Administratif	Director Administrativo	Direttore Amminstrativo	Administratie Manager	Director Administrativo / Chefe de Pessoal Administrativo
Advertising Manager	Leiter(in) Werbung / Werbungsleitung	Directeur Publicité	-	-	Manager Afdeling Advertenties	Gerente de Publicidade
Advisor	Betriebswirt(in)	Conseiller	-	Recercatore	Adviseur	Conselheiro
Area Manager	Gebietsleiter(in) / Gebietsverkaufsleiter(in)	Chef de Secteur	-	-	Regio Manager / Divisie Manager	Area da Gerencia
Art Director	Art Director	Directeur Artistique	-	Direttore Artistico	Art Director	Director Artistico
Assistant Director / Assistant Manager	Assistent(in) der Geschäftsleitung / Assistent(in) der Geschäftsleitung	Directeur Associé / Sous-Directeur / Adjoint Directeur / Associé	Apoderado	Vice Direttore	Adjunct	Assistente do Director / Assistente de Gerencio
Chairman	Vorsitzende(r)	Président	Presidente y Director General	Presidente	Voorzitter (m) / Voorzitster (f)	Presidente
Chairman of the Board	Vorstandsvorsitzende(r)	Président du Conseil	-	Presidente del Consiglio	Voorzitter van de Direktie	Presidente do Conselho
Chairman of the Supervisory Board	Aufsichtsratvorsitzende(r)	Président du Comité de Surveillance	-	Presidente del Consiglio di Controllo / Presidente del Consiglio di Sorveglianza	Voorzitter van de Hoofddirektie	-
Chief Executive	Verleger(in)	Président Directeur Général	Presidente y Director General	Caro Esecutivo	Algemene Directeur	Chefe Executivo

English	*German*	*French*	*Spanish*	*Italian*	*Dutch*	*Portuguese*
Consultant	Fachberater(in)	Conseiller	-	Consigliere	Consultant	Consultor
Commercial Director	Direktor(in)	Directeur Commercial	Director Comercial	Direttore Commerciale / Direttore Vendite	Commercieel Direkteur	Director Comercial
Company Management	Generaldirektor(in)	Administrateur Délégué	Administrador Gerente	Direttore Generale	Afgevaardigd Bestuurder / Hoofddirektie	Gerencia do Empresa
Company Secretary	-	President di Directoire	-	-	Secretaris	-
Creative Director	Kreativ-Direktor(in)	Directeur de la Création / Responsable Création	-	Direttore Creativo	Creative Director	Director Creativo
Deputy Chairman	Stellvertretende(r) Vorsitzende(r)	Vice Président / Sous Directeur	-	Vice Presidente	Plaatsvervangend Voorzitter	-
Director	Direktor(in)	Directeur / Directrice / Direction	Delegado a la Gerencia / Delegado Director	Direttore	Direkteur / Direktrice	Director
Editor	Redakteur(in) / Redaktion	Editeur / Auteur	-	Editore / Redattore	Redacteur	Editor
Editor-in-Chief	Chefredakteur(in)	-	-	Editore Capo / Capo Redattore	Hoofd Redacteur	Editor-Chefe
EDP Director	EDV Direktor(in) / EDV Leitung	-	Director de Informática / Director de Proceso de Datos	Direttore EED (Elaborazione Elettronica dei Dati)	Hoofd Automatisering	Director de EDP
Export Director	-	Directeur d'Exportation	-	-	Uitvoerdirekteur / Export Directeur	Director de Exportacáo
Financial Director	-	Directeur Financier	Director Financiero	Direttore Finanziario	Financieel Direkteur	Director Financeiro

English	*German*	*French*	*Spanish*	*Italian*	*Dutch*	*Portuguese*
Financial Manager	Finanzleiter(in) / Leiter(in) der Abteilung Finanzen	Responsable Financier	-	Direttore Finanziario	Financieel Manager	Gerente Financeiro
General Manager / Managing Director	Betriebsleiter(in) / Handlungsbevollmächtiger / Leitende(r) Mitarbeiter(in) / Bezirksdirektor(in) / Stellvertretende(r) Direktor(in) / Stellvertretende(r) Geschäftsführer(in) / Geschäftsführer(in) / Geschäftsleitung	Directeur Général Gérant / Administrateur	Administrador / Consejero Gerente / Director Generale / Administrador Unico / Administrador Gerente / Administrador General / Gerente	Direttore Generale / Amminstratore Delegate / Amministratore Aggiunto / Direzione Generale	Algemeen Direkteur / Zaakvoerder / Bestuurder / Bedrijfsleider / Vestigingsleider / Chef / Hoofd	Director Geral / Director do Gerencio
General Partner	-	-	-	Socio Accomandatario	-	-
Human Resources Manager / Director	Personalleiter(in)	Directeur du Personnel	Director del Personale	Direttore del Personale	Personeelsdirekteur / Manager Personeelszaken	Gerente Recursos Humanos
Information Systems Director	Systemberater(in)	Directeur Informatique	Director de Informática	Direttore di Informatica / Direzione di Informatica	Direkteur Rekencentrum / Informaticadirekteur	Director Informatinos Sistemas
Joint Managing Director	-	Directuer Générale Adjoint	-	-	Algemeen Adjunct Direkteur	-
Limited Partner	-	-	-	Socio Accomandante	-	-
Manager	Manager(in)	Chef	-	Direttore / Gestore / Gerente	Manager	Gerente
Marketing Manager	Marketingleiter(in) / Marketingberater(in)	Directeur Marketing	Director de Marketing	-	Marketing Manager	Gerente de Marketing

English	*German*	*French*	*Spanish*	*Italian*	*Dutch*	*Portuguese*
Media Manager	Medialeitung	Directeur Communication	-	Direttore Media	Media Manager	-
Member of Co-operative	Genoss(e)(in)	Membre de la Coopérative	-	Membro di Cooperative	Lid van Coöperatie	-
Member of the Board	Vorstandsmitglied / Vorstände	Membre du Conseil	-	Membro del Consiglio	Lid van de Hoofddirektie	Membro do Conselho
Member of the Supervisory Board	Aufsichtsratmitglied	Membre de la Comité de Surveillance	-	Membro del Consiglio di Controllo / Membro del Consiglio di Sorveglianza	Lid van de Hoofddirektie	Membro do Conselha do Super
Nominal Partner	-	-	-	Socio Nominale	-	-
Partner	Gesellschafter(in) / Prokurist(in)	Associé / Partenaire	Socio	Sócio	Partner / Mede-eigenaar	Söcia
President	Präsident(in)	Président / Présidente Directeur Général / Président Direction Général	Presidente / Presidente y Director General	Presidente	President / Direkteur	Presidente
Production Director	Leiter(in) Produktion	Directeur de la Production / Directeur de Fabrication / Chef de Fabrication	Direccion de Produccion / Jefe de Produccion / Cap de Produccion	Direttore di Produzione / Direttore di Stabilimento	Produktie Direkteur	Director de Producós
Project Leader	Projektleiter(in)	Directeur des Projets	-	Direttore dei Progetti	Projektleider	Lider de Projecto
Proprietor	Inhaber(in)	Propriétaire	Proprietario / Titular	Proprietario	Eigenaar	Proprietário
Public Relations Officer	Referent für Öffentlichkeitsarbeit	Sécretaire aux Relations Publique	-	Addetto alle Pubbliche Relazioni	PR-Medewerker	Relações Publicas

English	*German*	*French*	*Spanish*	*Italian*	*Dutch*	*Portuguese*
Publicity Director	Pressesprecher(in)	Directeur de la Publicité	-	-	Publiciteitsdirekteur	Director de Publicidade
Publisher	Herausgeber(in)	-	-	Editore	Uitgever	Publicador / Editor
Purchasing Manager	Einkaufsleiter(in)	Directeur d'Achats	Director de Compras / Director de Approvisionamientas	Procuratore	Inkoopdirecteur	Gerente de Compras
Salesperson	Verkäufer(in)	Commercial / Vendeur	-	Venditore / Commesso [in a shop]	Vertegenwoordiger / Verkoper	Vendedor
Sales Manager	Verkaufsleiter(in)	Chefs des Ventes	Delegado de Ventas / Director de Ventas	Capo Vendite	Hoofd Verkoop / Verkoopsleider	Gerente di Vendas
Secretary	Sekretär(in)	Secrétaire	Secretario	Segretaria (f) / Segretario (m)	Sekretaresse (f) / Sekretaris (m)	Secretária
Secret Partner	-	-	-	Socio Occulto	-	-
Silent Partner	Kommandist(in)	Commenditaire / Bailleur	-	Socio Accomandante	Stille Vennoot	Sócio naó Activo
System Manager	Systemberäter(in)	Responsable Système	Director de Sistemas de información	-	System Manager	Gerente de Sistema
Teacher	Dozent(in) / Fachlehrer(in) / Lehrer(in) / Professor(in)	Professeur / Instituteur (m) / Institutrice (f) / Enseignant (m) / Enseignante (f)	-	Docente / Professore / Insegnante	Docent	Professor
Technical Director	Technicshe(r) Leiter(in) / Technische(r) Direktor(in) / Fertigungsleiter(in)	Directeur Technique / Direction Technique / Responsable Technique	Director Técnico / Direccion Técnico	Direttore Tecnico / Direzione Tecnica / Responsabile Tecnico	Technische Direkteur	Director Técnico
Vice-President	Vizepräsident(in)	Vice President	Vicepresidente	Vice Presidente	Vice-voorzitter	Vice-Presidente

English	*Norwegian*	*Finnish*	*Greek*	*Danish*	*Swedish*
Accountant	Revisor	Tilintarkastaja	Logistis	Revisor	Revisor
Active Partner	Aktiv Kompajong	Vastuullinen yhtiömies	Omorithmos Eteros	-	Aktiv Kompanjon
Administration Manager	Administrasjonssjef	Hallintopäällikkö	Dioikitikos Diefthindis	Administationschef	Administrationschef
Advertising Manager	Annonsesjef	Mainospäällikkö	Diefhindis Diafimisis	Annonce Chef	Annonschef
Advisor	Rådgiver	Neuvonantaja	Simvoulos	Rådgiver	Rådgivare
Area Manager	Distrikssjef	Aluepäällikkö	Diefthindis Periferias	Distrikts Chef	Distriktschef
Art Director	AD	AD	Kallithenikos Diefthindi	Kreativ Chef	Art Director
Assistant Director	Vise Direktør	Apulaisjohtaja	Ipodikitis	Vice-Direktør	Vice Direktör
Assistant Manager	Assisterende Leder	Apulaispäällikkö	Ipodiefthindis	Assisterende Leder	Vice Chef
Chairman	Formann / Ordstyrer	Puheenjohtaja	Proedros	Formand	Ordförande
Chairman of the Board	Styreformann	Johtokunnan puheenjohtaja	Proedros Dikitikou	Bestyrelses Formand	Styrelseordförande
Chairman of the Supervisory Board	Styreformann	Johtokunnan puheenjohtaja	Proedros Epoptikou Simvouliou	-	Styrelseordförande
Chief Executive	Administraterende Direktør	Pääjohtaja	Stelehos	-	Verkstäande Chef
Consultant	Konsulent	Konsultti	Simvoulos	Konsulent	Konsult
Commercial Director	Økonomi Direktør	Kaupallinen johtaja	Emborikos Diefthindis	Økonomi Direktør	Ekonomidirektör
Company Management	Firma Ledelse	Yritysjohto	Diefthinsis Eterias	Firma Ledelse	Ledningsgrupp
Creative Director	Kreativ Leder	Taiteellinen johtaja	Diefthindis Dimiourgikou Tmimatos	Kreativ Leder	Art Director
Deputy Chairman	Vise Formann	Varapuheenjohtaja	Anaplirotis Proedros	Næstformand	Vice Ordförande
Director	Direktør	Johtaja	Dikitis	Direktør	Direktör
Editor	Redaktør	Toimittaja	Sindaktis	Redaktør	Redaktör
Editor-in-Chief	Sjefsredaktør	Päätoimittaja	Arhisindaktis	Chef-redaktør	Chefredaktör

English	*Norwegian*	*Finnish*	*Greek*	*Danish*	*Swedish*
EDP Director	EDB Sjef	ATK-johtaja	Diefthindis Pliroforikis / Mihanografisis	EDB Chef	EDB chef
Export Director	Eksportsjef	Vientijohtaja	Diefthindis Exagogon	Eksportchef	Exportchef
Financial Director	Økonomi Direktør	-	Ikonomikos Dikitis	Økonomi Direktør	Ekonomidirektör
Financial Manager	Økonomisjef	Talouspäällikkö	Ikonomikos Diefthindis	Økonomi Chef	Ekonomichef
General Manager	Daglig Leder	Pääjohtaja	Genikos Diefthindis	Daglig Leder	Direktör
Human Resources Manager / Director	Personalsjef	Henkilöstöpäällikkö	Prosoparhis	Personale Chef	Personalchef
Information Systems Director	Informasjonssjef	Tiedotusjohtaja	Diefthindis Pliroforiakon Sistimaton	-	Informationchef
Joint Managing Director	-	-	Kini Diahirisis Eterias	-	Koncernchef
Manager	Sjef / Leder	Päällikkö / Johtaja	Diefthindis	Chef / Leder	Chef
Managing Director	Direktør	Toimitisjohtaja / TJ	Diefthinon Simvoulos	Direktør	Verkställande Direktor
Marketing Manager	Markedssjef	Markkinointipäällikkö	Diefthindis Marketing	Markeds Chef	Marknadschef
Media Manager	Pressesjef / Markedssjef	Lehdistöpäällikkö	Diefthindis Meson Enimerosis	Presse Chef	Presschef
Member of Co-operative	Medlem av Samvirke	Osuuskunnan jäsen	Melos Sineterismou	Medlem af Samvirke	Medlem av Kooperativ
Member of the Board	Styremedlem	Hallituksen jäsen	Melos Dikitikou Simvouliou	Bestyrelsesmedlem	Styrelseledamot
Member of the Supervisory Board	Styremedlem	Johtokunnan jäsen	Melos Epoptikou Simvouliou	-	Styrelse Medlem
Partner	Kompanjong / Partner	Kumppani (Kni.) / Osakas / Yhtiömies	Eteros	Partner	Kompanjon / Delägare
President	President / Formann	Presidentti / Johtaja	Proedros	-	President
Production Director	Produksjonssjef	Tuotantojohtaja	Diefthindis Paragogis	Produktions Chef	Produktionschef

English	*Norwegian*	*Finnish*	*Greek*	*Danish*	*Swedish*
Project Leader	Projektleder	Projektipäällikkö	Ipefthinos Schediasmou	Projekt Leder	Projektledare
Proprietor	Eier	Omistaja	Idioktitis	Ejer	Ägare
Public Relations Officer	PR-Sjef	PR-päällikkö	Ipefthinos Dimosion Scheseon Diefthindi	PR Chef	PR chef
Publicity Director	-	Mainosjohtaja	Diefthindis Dimosion Scheseon	-	Press chef
Publisher	Forlegger	Kustantaja	Ekdotis	Forlægger	Förläggare
Purchasing Manager	Innkjøpssjef	Ostopäällikkö	Diefthindis Promithion	Indkøbs Chef	Inköpschef
Salesperson	Selger / Salgskonsulent	Myyntimies	Politis	Sælger	Säljare
Sales Manager	Salgssjef	Myyntipäällikkö	Diefthindis Poliseon	Salgs chef	Säljchef
Secretary	Sekretær	Sihteeri	Grammatefs	Sekretær	Sekreterare
Silent Partner	Passiv Kompanjong	Äänetön yhtiömies	Eterorithmos Eteros	Interessent	Passiv Kompanjon
System Manager	Systemansvarlig	Systeemipäällikkö	Ipefthinos Sistimatos	-	System chef
Teacher	Lærer	Opettaja	Daskalos (Kathigitis)	Lærer	Lärare
Technical Director	Teknisk Direktør	Tekninen johtaja	Tehnikos Diefthindis	Teknisk Chef	Teknisk chef
Vice-President	Vise Formann	Varapresidentti / Varajohtaja	Andiproedros	-	Vice President

Salutations

The salutations which are described here are those which are suitable for printing on an address label. Unlike English, some languages use a different salutation in letter headings. This is a translation issue and therefore outside the scope of this book (though it may be referred to below for some languages). For this reason also you should address the recipient in the letter in the language of the letter. E.g., Dhr. van den Broek in The Netherlands should be addressed as Mr. van den Broek in an English letter because 'Dear Dhr. Van den Broek' would be incorrect.

Language	*Male*	*Female (married)*	*Female (unmarried)*	*Female (non-specific)*	*Doctor*	*Professor*
Albanian	Z.			Z.		
Dutch	Mr. / Dhr. (Mijnheer / Deheer)	Mevr. (Mevrouw)	Juff. (Juffrouw)	Mevr. (Mevrouw)	Dr. (Doktor)	
Juffrouw is still used to a limited extent in Belgium. However, for the Netherlands and many Belgian women Juffrouw should not be used - it is not well received. Use instead Mevrouw. A fuller list of salutations used for Dutch-speakers is given in the chapter on The Netherlands. You start a formal letter "Geachte mevrouw/heer".						
English	Mr or M'r (Mister)	Mrs or M'r's (Missus or Missis)	Miss	MS or Ms or m.s.	Dr	Prof.
Ms is best used when the marital status of the (female) recipient is unknown. Equally, there is a large and increasing number of married and unmarried women who prefer to be addressed as Ms in all cases. This preference should be noted in your database.						
Finnish	Hra (Herra)	Rva (Rouva)	Nti (Neiti)	Tri (Tohtori)		
It is very old-fashioned to used titles, especially in the business world. Use only the name of the person, or the job title.						
French	M (Monsieur)	Mme (Madame)	Melle (Mademoiselle)		Dr (Docteur)	
You can start a letter "Messieurs" for both males and females.						
German	Herr	Frau	Fraulein (Frl.)	Frau	Dr.	Prof
It is best not to use the salutation for Fraulein for unmarried women except when specifically asked to do so. Use instead Frau.						
Greek	K.	K.	K.	K.		
Hungarian	Ur	Asszony	Kisasszony		Dr	
Irish					Doctúir	tOllamh
Separate salutations do not exist in Irish. Salutations become part of the name. A form of the title Uasal may be used in official communications. Letters are often started with the name of the person followed by "a chara", meaning "friend". If no name is used, "A chara" is sufficient. Please refer to the chapter on Ireland for more details.						
Italian	Sig. (Signor / Signore)	Sig.^{ra} (Signora)	Sig.^{na} (Signorina)		Dr. (Dottor / Dottore	Prof. (Professore)
Signor is used when followed by the name. Signore simple means 'mister'. You can start a letter "Gentile Signora" for females or "Egregio Signor" for males.						
Norwegian	Hr.	Fr.	Frk.		Dr. (medical only	
The salutation is rarely used if the first name is used. Another preference is to use the job title of the person.						
Polish	Pan	Pani	Panna		Dr (Doktor)	Prof. (Profesor)
The form of "Pan" etc. and the person's name may change according to context. It may be Pan, Pana, Panu, Panie etc. A letter may be commenced "Szanowny Panie (name)" for males or "Szanowna Panie (name)" for females. Pani is often used for both married and unmarried women.						

The academic titles mgr and inz. (inzynicr) may also be used.						
Portuguese	sr. (senhor)	D. (dona), senhora (sra.)	menina		Dr.	Prof.
Senhora is mainly used in rural areas						
Slovenian	Gospod			Gospa		
Spanish	S. (Señor), D. (Don), Señor Don	Sra. (Seññora), Dª (Doña), Señora Doña	Señorita		Dr. (Doctor), Dra. (Doctora)	
Don (male) and Doña (female) are used before first names only. Señor (male) and Señora (female) are used before either surname only or first and surname. Señor Don (male) and Señor Doña (female) are used before first name and surname only. You can start a letter "Apreciado Sr/Sra)						

Mail Return Codes

Envelopes returned to the sender usually give the reason that they were undeliverable on a sticker or stamp on the envelope. A stamp will usually give the reason in the local language only, a sticker will give it in the local language and French, the official language of the Universal Postal Union. The following list provides a translation of these reasons for non-delivery. Note that not all reasons are applicable to all countries.

French	*English*	*German*	*Spanish*	*Italian*	*Dutch*
Absent	Absent	-	-	Assente	-
Adresse Illisible	Addresss unreadable	-	Dirección ilegible	-	Onleesbaar adres
Adresse inexacte	Incomplete address	-	Calle desconocida	Indirizzo inesatto	-
Adresse Insuffisante	Insufficient address	Anschrift ungenügend	Dirección Insuficiente	Indirizzo insufficiente	Ontoereikend adres (B) / Onvolledig adres (NL)
Bureau inexistant	No such post office	-	-	-	-
Décédé	Deceased	Verstorben	Fallecido	Deceduto	Overleden
Déménagé / Parti	Moved / Gone Away	Abgereist	-	-	-
En voyage	Travelling	Verreist	-	-	-
Inconnu	Not known	Unbekannt	Desconocido	Sconosciuto	Onbekend
Introuvable	Unfindable	-	-	Irreperibile	-
Non admis	Non-admissible	-	-	Non ammesso	-
N'habite plus à l'adresse indiquée	Does not live at this address	-	-	-	Woont niet meer op aangeduid adres
Non réclame	Not called for	Nicht abgeholt	No reclamado	Non reclamato	Niet afgehaald
Parti	Gone away	-	-	Partito	-
Parti sans adresse / Parti san laissez d'adresse	Gone away without leaving forwarding address	Unbekannt verzogen	Partió sin delar señas / dirección	-	Vertrokken zonder adres
Raison sociale n'existe plus	Company closed	Firma erloschen	-	-	-
Refusé	Refused	Verweigert	Rehusado	Rifiutato	Geweigerd
Rue inconnue	Unknown street	-	-	-	-
Rue / numéro inexistant(e)	Non-existent street / number	-	-	-	Straatnaam / huisnummer bestaat niet
Transféré	Moved	-	-	Trasferito	-

Using the Country Chapters

When you manage a database for a single country, input, deduplication, merge-purge and output are all relatively simple matters. There are limited issues involving languages spoken, address format, post office required layouts and so on which allow you to build up an expertise to allow the maximum to be extracted from the data.

When you start working with international data, the problems are multiplied many fold. There are over 200 countries and territories in the world where around 100 different address formats are used and 10 000 different languages are spoken. Your approach to managing and outputting this data will make the difference between success and failure in your database marketing activities.

In this edition of *The Global Source-book for Address Data Management*, 194 countries and territories are covered to a greater or lesser extent. Each chapter contains data from a number of different sources brought together to enable you to get the most out of your international address data.

The information provided, the way it is laid out, and the reasons for inclusion, are detailed below.

General formatting information

U This symbol is used in chapters for countries which were covered in the 1994 publication *Building and Maintaining a European Direct Marketing Database* to indicate a section which has been updated. Where a relatively small amount of information has been updated, this symbol has been added to the right of the relevant information. When large amounts of information within a section have been updated, the symbol is used only once, next to the section title.

Because each language has its own alphabetical ordering (refer to the chapter *Diacritical Marks*), all listings have been provided listed according to the English alphabet to create the minimum of confusion. Accented letters are treated as their unaccented equivalents. So, for example, *Ü* is treated as *U* and not as *UE* as it would be in German. The German *ß* is treated as *ss*. Punctuation and casing have been ignored in list ordering.

Where formats are shown, the information between square brackets ([]) should be written exactly as shown, whilst information between braces ({}) occurs in some but not all cases. So, for example,

postal code[ ]Settlement name{[Cédex]}

means that there is an obligatory space between the postal code and the settlement name, and that the settlement name may, in some addresses, be followed by a space and the word *Cédex*.

A *9* is used to indicate a numeric character, an *A* is used to indicate a letter.

If the word in the format is in upper case, the information should be printed in upper case. If the first letter of the first word only is in upper case, the first letter of the text must have an upper case initial letter. Correspondingly, a lower case first letter in a format means a lower case first letter in the text. So, for example,

> number[,]thoroughfare type[ ]Thoroughfare name
> SETTLEMENT

may equate to

> 17, rue de Paris
> LILLE

When common abbreviations are given, they are given only in a single form. Readers should bear in mind that they may appear in a number of formats (with or without punctuation, for example), and remember this when using the abbreviations provided.

Listings, such as of thoroughfare types, are often the same across a number of countries, especially where the same language is spoken. In these cases, the lists are usually not repeated but you are referred to the chapter containing the complete listings. Even where this is not the case, referring to the chapter of a country where the same language is spoken and a great deal of information is provided may often solve any problems that you may have with a country where less information is available.

Country name

The country chapters are sorted and entitled according to their (common) English name. This, of course, is often not how the inhabitants of the country themselves name their country. Where this differs, it is written below the English name. This additionally aids recognition when you come across this name, especially when encoding countries.

Areas of conflict

Below the country name there may be a little extra information about the country. This is often the case when there is a conflict situation in the country. Any conflict will, self-evidently, affect mail deliveries to a greater or lesser extent. The information provided is accurate at the time of going to press, but naturally the situation will change over time. To keep abreast of these situations you must naturally follow current affairs for the country or countries concerned.

Official name

The official name may or may not be the one used when addressing mail to that country. This depends largely on the country from which the mail is being posted and the country concerned. The official name is provided in English and one or more of the country's languages to aid recognition.

Area, Population, Capital, Currency, International telephone access code

For mailing purposes, this data is not required. This book, however, aims to make life easier for the manager of international addresses by providing the maximum amount of information in a single source. The area, population, capital city, currency and international telephone access code are therefore included in these chapters. Note that, unless otherwise stated, the population figures are from censuses or estimates for years later than 1990.

Languages

Mystifyingly, language has always been a poor relation in database marketing. Companies spend enormous amounts of money building, populating and cleaning address databases and then dramatically reduce the effectiveness of their marketing or sales efforts by mailing either in English or in another language which is not the mother language of the recipient. This has the effect not only of reducing the number of effective hits that your mailing has because a number of recipients will not understand, or understand enough of, the mailing, but it can be a great cause of irritation for the recipients. Language has very strong cultural and nationalistic ties for many people, and people will go to great lengths to preserve and use languages. Moves towards political union, such as in Europe, has strengthened rather than weakened this effect as language becomes the most tangible form of cultural identity and national pride as borders fall. Being aware of, and using the languages concerned will not only increase the effectiveness of the mail but will also increase the level of regard the recipients will have for your company.

In each chapter, language use is listed. Listings are limited to indigenous languages except where imported languages have been in use for so long that their usage has become indigenous. Where available, geographical spread of a language is also provided to allow better targetting. More detailed information is provided for industrialized countries where the level of direct mailing is highest. Different language groups have different expectations. The Frisians of The Netherlands, for example, expect to receive mailings only in Dutch. Though mailing to Frisian-speakers in Frisian may increase the response, mailing in Dutch is unlikely to have a detrimental effect. On the other hand, mailing in French to Flemish-speakers in Belgium could, depending on the nature of the mailing, reduce response very dramatically indeed and result in extremely bad feelings towards your company by the recipients. Where available, these expectations are outlined in the text.

Many of the languages have several names. Unless there is a common English name for the language, a local-language version has been used. For further information about the languages, their names and their distributions, you can do no better than to refer to *Ethnologue - Languages of the World* edited by Barbara Grimes. Please refer to the bibliography for further information.

In some cases, the percentage of speakers of languages adds up to more than 100%. This is due to rounding and to the numbers of people who are multilingual.

For the attention of

This section provides the correct form to be used on an envelope in front of the contact name, where "for the attention of" or "Attention:" might be used in English.

Contact names

This section contains information which is of importance when using salutations or for changing upper-case names into the correct mixed-case format. In some cases it also gives naming conventions which can alter in different countries, provinces or language areas for married women and children.

Company names

This section provides, where relevant, the layout of the company name in terms of the company *nature* and the company *name*. The company *nature* is the word or words in the complete name which indicate the activity of the company, for example Baker, Stationer, Printer and so on. The *name*, on the other hand, indicates the unique part of the company name, often the name of a person, an abbreviation and so on.

Company types

Company type refers to a word or abbreviation indicating the legal status of the company, for example Ltd, SA, PLC, etc. It is useful to be able to recognize these so that they can be given a consistent form and put into the correct position within the complete company name or moved into a separate field where desirable.

Addresses / Address format / Example address format

This section is very important for ensuring that address data can be stored consistently and that it can be output in the correct format. An incorrect, ugly or culturally insensitive address format can mean the difference between the envelope being opened or disposed of. Some countries have built strict and extensive rules dictating address format to allow postal discounts and speedy delivery. Others have few rules if any. Where the rules are clear, these are outlined in the section *Address format*. Where the rules are unclear or unknown, an *Example address format* is provided to give at least an indication of formatting.

In these sections, the words *street address* refer to the part of the address which contains the thoroughfare *type*, the thoroughfare *name* and the house number. The term *thoroughfare* is used to indicate the thoroughfare name and type together. So, in the example:

12 Green Street

the *12* is the house number, *Green* is the thoroughfare name, and *Street* is the thoroughfare type. The thoroughfare in this case is *Green Street*.

In the address formats, country names positions are not provided except where they are written in any position other than on the last line of the address. The format of the country name is often dependent on the country from which the mail is being sent.

Building indicators / Thoroughfare types

Lists of building indicators and commonly occurring thoroughfare types and their abbreviations are provided to allow recognition of this address element so that its format can be corrected, the strings within it made consistent, and, if desired, its components moved to different fields.

Other nouns, adjectives and prepositions commonly found in address databases

This section contains lists of nouns, adjectives and prepositions which will be found in company names and addresses. These are provided to aid recognition of these parts of addresses which are common yet often inconsistently written. Recognition of prepositions is also important when changing from upper to mixed case as most prepositions should retain a lower-case first letter.

Postbox

This section provides the word used for postbox in the appropriate local language(s). In some countries recognition of the postbox number is essential as street addresses and mailing addresses (postbox numbers) have different postal codes. Mailings should not be sent with both the mailing address and the street address included as in these cases the post office may attempt to deliver to one of the addresses only, and, should the postal code refer to the other address, the mailing will be returned as undeliverable.

Postal codes

This section is important in that it provides the formatting rules for the postal codes of the country concerned, and gives in some cases the numbers of postal codes which are *not* used, thus allowing basic computer checks for invalid formats and postal codes. Furthermore, the postal codes of the regions where minority indigenous languages are spoken are provided to allow output, if necessary, in these languages for these areas.

Towns

This section gives writing conventions, where necessary, to allow settlement names to be given consistency in your database. Furthermore, corresponding town names are given both in the indigenous languages, where appropriate, and other globally-spoken languages. Response to mailings will improve if the correct local-language version of the settlement name is used (corresponding to the language of the recipient). The inclusion of town names in other major languages is to ensure that data from databases built outside the country concerned (and therefore perhaps containing the non-autochthonal settlement names) can be altered to give the autochthonal name to aid database consistency, and to enable output to be made in the language of the recipient.

Administrative districts

Where these are used in address output, they are listed. In other countries they may also be listed to allow recognition and removal from addresses as required.

Telephone numbers

Where telephone numbers have a given format for the whole of a particular country, this information is provided to allow basic checking of accuracy within a database. Where one area code exists for all numbers within a country, this information is also provided. This information is, however, temporal in nature and subject to change.

Albania
Shqīpëri

Official name: Republic of Albania, Republika e Shqipërisë
Area: 28 748 sq. km (11 097 sq. miles)
Population: 3 303 000
Capital: Tiranë
Currency: 1 Lek (L) = 100 quintars
International telephone access code: 355

Languages

Albanian, the official language, is spoken in two dialects - Gheg, with 300 000 speakers mainly in the North, and Tosk, with 2 900 000 speakers in the rest of the country. There are 60 000 Greek-speakers in the south near to the Greek border; 30 000 Macedonian-speakers along the border with Macedonia; 60 000 Macedo Romani-speakers and 60 000 Vlach Romani-speakers.

Example Address Formats

Erkand Muraku
rruga "Faik Drenova"
Pall Nr. 1, Sh 1, Ap15
TIRANE

Artur Mema
Fshati Zejman
LEZHE

Thoroughfare Types

Below is a list of the most commonly occurring thoroughfare types for Albania:

Albanian	*English*
bulevardi	Boulevard
rruga	Street

Postbox

This is written *kutia postare nr.* in Albanian.

Postal codes

Albania has no postal code system.

Towns

The following list gives foreign-language alternative names for Albanian settlements:

Albanian	*English*	*Italian*	*German*
Durrësi		Durazzo	Durazzo
Gjirokastra		Argyrokastron	
Shkodra		Scutari	
Tiranë	Tirana		Tirana
Vlora		Valona	Valona

Administrative districts

Albania consists of 26 provinces. These are:

Berat
Dibrë
Durrës
Elbasan
Fier
Gjirokastër
Gramsh
Krujë
Kukës
Kolonjë
Korçë
Librazhd
Lushnjë
Lezhë
Mat
Mirditë
Pogradec
Pukë
Përmet
Sarandë
Shkodër
Skrapar
Tropojë
Tepelenë
Tiranë
Vlorë

Algeria
Al-Jazā'ir

Algeria is in the throes of a civil war. Mail deliveries may consequently be affected.

Official name: Democratic and Popular Republic of Algeria, al Jumhuriya al-Jazãiriya ad-Dimuqratiya ash-Shabiya
Area: 2 460 500 sq. km (949 753 sq. miles)
Population: 26 400 000
Capital: Alger (Algiers)
Currency: 1 Algerian Dinar (AD, DA) = 100 centimes
International telephone access code: 213

Languages

The official language is Standard Arabic. 16 other languages are spoken. The most widespread are: Algerian Saharan Spoken Arabic (100 000 speakers); Algerian Spoken Arabic (20 400 000 speakers); Chaouia (1 400 000 speakers); French (110 600 speakers) and Kabyle (2 537 000 speakers).

Address Format

Addresses written in Latin script are usually written in French and are similar in format to French addresses. Their format is:

Name
number[,]thoroughfare type[ ]Thoroughfare name
postal code[ ]SETTLEMENT

For example:

Said Mohamed
2, rue de l'Indépendance
16000 ALGER

Thoroughfare types are written starting with a lower-case letter. For lists of thoroughfare types and other address component information, please refer to the chapter on France.

Postbox

When written in Latin script, this is written as *Boite Postale*, abbreviated to *BP*.

Postal code

Postal codes consist of a block of 5 digits. The first two digits indicate the *wilaya* (department), the last three the delivery office.

Towns

The following list gives foreign language equivalents of Algerian town names:

Arabic	*English*	*French*	*German*
Alger	Algiers		Algier
Annaba		Bône	
Bejaia		Bougie	Bougie
Sétif			Setif
Skikda			Philippeville

American Samoa
São Paulo de Loanda

Official name: American Samoa
Area: 197 sq. km (76 sq. miles)
Population: 46 773
Capital: Pago Pago/Fago Togo
Currency: 1 United States Dollar (US$) = 100 cents
International telephone access code: 684

Languages

The official language is English (1 248 first-language speakers). Samoan is spoken by 38 700 people.

Addresses etc.

American Samoa is an unincorporated territory of the United States in the Pacific. It forms part of the United States' postal system. Its state code is AS and its postal code is 96799.

American Samoa is an archipelago including the islands of Tutuila, Aunu'u, Ofu, Olosega, Swain's, Tua and Rose. The name of the island may be included in the address.

Please refer to the chapter on the United States of America for further information.

Andorra

Until the beginning of 1993, Andorra was ruled jointly by the Spanish Bishop of Urgel and the President of France, making the country a co-principality. On 5th May 1993, Andorra became a sovereign nation, and as such, on 30 July 1993 became a member of the United Nations.

Official Names: Principality of Andorra, The Valleys of Andorra, Vallée d'Andorre, Valls d'Andorra, Princiupat d'Andorra
Area: 467 sq. km (180 sq. miles)
Population: 54 507
Capital: Andorra la Vella
Currency: 1 French franc (Fr) = 100 centimes and 1 Spanish peseta (Pta, Pa.) = 100 céntimos
International telephone access code: 376

Languages

The official language of Andorra is Catalan spoken by some 31 000 people. Castilian Spanish is spoken by 24 600 people, and French by 2 400 people.

Address Format

Addresses are written in the format:

Name
number[,]thoroughfare type[ ]Thoroughfare name
PARISH

For example:

H. Jean
2, avinguda Carlemany
ESCALDES ENGODANY

Thoroughfare types are usually written in Catalan and commence with a lower case letter. Please refer to the chapter on Spain for Catalan thoroughfare type information.

Postal code

Andorra has no postal code system.

Administrative districts

Andorra is divided into 7 parishes *(Parroquies)*. These are:

Andorra la Vella
Canillo

Encamp
Escaldes Engordany
Lamassana
Ordino
Sant Julia de Loria

Angola

Angola is militarily divided between the government in Luanda and the rebels of the UNITA movement. Mail distribution is consequently affected.

Official name: People's Republic of Angola, República Popular de Angola.
Area: 1 245 790 sq. km (480 875 sq. miles)
Population: 10 301 000
Capital: Luanda
Currency: 1 New Kwanza (ka, kz) = 100 Iweis
International telephone access code: 244

Languages

The official language is Portuguese (57 600 speakers). 40 other languages are spoken. The most widespread are: Chokwe (500 000 speakers); Kongo (1 144 000 speakers); San Salvador Kongo (1 500 000 speakers); Mbundu (3 000 000 speakers) and Umbundu (4 000 000 speakers).

Example address format

Sr. João Pembclc
Rua Frederik Engels 92 - 7° andar
LUANDA

Addresses will often be written in the ex-colonial language, Portuguese. They follow the Portuguese structure - thoroughfare types are written first and with a capital first letter, the house number is at the end of the street address string often followed by an indication of floor, stairwell etc. For a full description of thoroughfare types and other address components, please refer to the chapter on Portugal.

Postal codes

There is no postal code system in Angola.

Argentina

Official name: Argentine Republic, República Argentina
Area: 2 780 092 sq. km (1 073 115 sq. miles)
Population: 32 646 000
Capital: Buenos Aires
Currency: 1 Peso = 100 centavos
International telephone access code: 54

Languages

The official language is Spanish, spoken by 96% of the population. 24 other, mainly Indian languages are also spoken. The most widespread are: Mapudungun (40 000 speakers in the provinces of Neuquen, Rio Negro, Chubut, Buenos Aires and La Pampa); South Bolivian Quecha (850 000 speakers along the border with Bolivia and in Buenos Aires) and Santiago del Estero Quichua (75 000 speakers in Santiago del Estero province).

Example address format

Sr. José Perez
Montiel 13, 3° piso, Officina 12
5501 GODOY CRUZ
MENDOZA

Street addresses follow closely the Spanish structure - the thoroughfare type *calle* (street) is usually not written - other thoroughfare types are written with a lower-case first letter. The house number is at the end of the street address string often followed by an indication of floor, stairwell etc. For a full description of thoroughfare types and other address components, please refer to the chapter on Spain.

The address includes the province name. A full list, with abbreviations commonly used, is provided below:

Province	*Abbreviation*
Buenos Aires	BA
Capital Federal	CF
Catamarca	C
Chaco	CHO
Chubut	CHT
Córdoba	CBA
Corrientes	CTS
Entre Rios	ER
Formosa	F
Jujuy	J
La Pampa	LP
La Rioja	LR

Mendoza	MZA
Misiones	MS
Neuquen	N
Rio Negro	RN
Salta	S
San Juan	SJ
San Luis	SL
Santa Cruz	SC
Santa Fé	SF
Santiago del Estero	SE
Tierra del Fuego	TF
Tucumán	T

Postal codes

Postal codes consist of a block of 4 digits. The first digit indicates the region; the second digit the territory and the third the district.

Administrative Districts

Argentina has 24 provinces, which are included on the last line of addresses. A list of these abbreviations is provided above in the section "Example Address Format".

Armenia

Official name: Republic of Armenia, Haikakan Hanrapetoutioun
Area: 29 800 sq. km (11 500 sq. miles)
Population: 3 500 000
Capital: Yerevan
Currency: Dram
International telephone access code: 374

Languages

The national language is Armenian, with some 3 197 000 speakers. This is written in a unique script. There are 5 000 speakers of Assyrian Neo-Aramaic; 161 000 of Northern Azerbaijani and 58 000 speakers of Kurmanji. The Gypsy language, Lomavren, is also spoken.

Postal codes

Postal codes consist of a block of 6 digits. This is the same code that was used before the independence of Armenia from the Soviet Union. The first three digits indicate the regional centre, capital, town or district; the last three digits indicate the post office.

Towns

Armenian place-names should be used in preference to the Russian equivalents:

Armenian	*Russian*
Angeeghakot'	Angekhakot
Art'ik	Artik
Ch'arents'avan	Charentsavan
Dilijan	Dilizhan
Ejmiatsin / Yejmiadzin	Echmiadzin
Gyumri	Leninakan / Kumayri
Hoktemberyan	Oktemberyan
Hrazdan	Razdan
Ijevan	Idzhevan
Jermuk	Dzhermuk
K'ajaran	Kadzharan
Kapan	Kafan
Meghri	Megri
Sot'k'	Zod
Vanadzor	Kirovakan

Yerevan is written as *Jerewan* in German.

Australia

Official name: Commonwealth of Australia
Area: 7 692 300 sq. km (2 969 228 sq. miles)
Population: 16 850 540
Capital: Canberra
Currency: 1 Australian Dollar ($A) = 100 cents
International telephone access code: 61

Languages

The official language is English (15 682 000 speakers). 233 other languages are spoken, most by only a handful of people. The most widespread of these are: Kala Lagaw Ya (3-4 000 speakers); Kriol (10 000 speakers); Pitjantjatjara (2 500 speakers) and Torres Strait Creole (23 400 speakers).

Address format

Addresses are formatted as follows:

NAME
NUMBER[ ]THOROUGHFARE NAME[ ]THOROUGHFARE TYPE
SUBURB[ ]STATE CODE[ ]POSTAL CODE

For example:

MR N MANGLE
21 RAMSEY STREET
ERINSBURGH VIC 3001

The Australian post office prefers that the address is written in upper-case only, that it contain no punctuation, and that it should be on no more than 3 lines.

For lists of thoroughfare names, please refer to the chapter for the United Kingdom.

The state codes, with their postal code ranges, are:

State/Territory	*Code*	*Postal code range*
Australian Capital Territory	ACT	0200-0299 (postboxes and large users); 2600-2639 (street addresses)
New South Wales	NSW	1000-1999 (postboxes and large users); 2000-2599 (street addresses)
Northern Territory	NT	0900-0999 (postboxes and large users); 0800-0899 (street addresses)
Queensland	QLD	9000-9999 (postboxes and large users); 4000-4999 (street addresses)
South Australia	SA	5000-5799 (postboxes and large users);

		5800-5999 (street addresses)
Tasmania	TAS	7800-7999 (postboxes and large users); 7000-7499 (street addresses)
Victoria	VIC	8000-8999 (postboxes and large users); 3000-3999 (street addresses)
Western Australia	WA	6800-6999 (postboxes and large users); 6000-6799 (street addresses)

Postal codes

Postal codes consist of a block of 4 digits. The first digit indicates the state or territory; the second a zone and the final two the delivery office. Most municipalities, settlements or suburbs have a single own code. Postboxes have different postal codes to street addresses, and large users may also have a unique code. A company can therefore possibly have two codes. The mailing address (postbox/large user) should in these cases be used in preference to the street address.

Administrative Areas

Australia consists of 8 states and territories. Their codes (see above, section "Address Format") are used in addresses.

Australia administers the populated external territories of Christmas Island, Cocos (Keeling) Island and Norfolk Island, and the unpopulated external territories of The Ashmore and Cartier Islands, Australian Antarctic Territory, Coral Sea Island and Heard Island & McDonald Islands.

Austria
Österreich

Official Name: Republic of Austria, Republik Österreich
Area: 83 854 sq. km (32 368 sq. miles)
Population: 7 812 000
Capital: Wien (Vienna)
Currency: 1 Schilling (S, Sch) = 100 Groschen
International telephone access code: 43

Languages

German is the official language, spoken by 99% of the population. There are 300 000 speakers of Allemanisch; 22 000 speakers of Hungarian; 60 000 speakers of Serbo-Croatian; 30 000 speakers of Slovenian along the border with Slovenia and 500 speakers of Sinte Romani.

Company names

Where the *nature* of a company is mentioned in the company name this *precedes* the name of the company, thus:

Bäcker Schmidt

You will often, however, find these activity indications *after* the company name, thus:

Schmidt, Bäcker
Schmidt (Bäcker)

Austrian company names will also often contain the name of the *inhaber(in)* (owner), usually indicated by the abbreviation 'Inh.'.

Company types

The following company types may be found in Austrian company names:

AG (Aktiengesellschaft)
Einzelunternehmen
Genossenschaft
GmbH (also written Gesellschaft mbH) (Gesellschaft mit beschraenkter Haft)
GmbH & Co. KG
KG (Kommanditgesellschaft)
OHG (Offene Handelgesellschaft)

For the attention of

The words *zu Händen*, abbreviated to z.H. or z.Hd. mean 'For the attention of'.

Contact names

Austrians set great store by their titles, where they form part of the salutation (e.g. *Herr Doktor Schmidt*). When addressing an Austrian within a letter, the surname should be omitted where the title exists, for example:

Sehr geehrter Herr Doktor

Addresses

In company addresses the name of the company precedes the name of the contact. The house number follows the street name. The salutation of the person or the type of company comes on the top line alone. Thus:

Herrn
Günther Meyer
Beethovengasse 25
1020 WIEN

or

Bäcker Meyer
Herrn Mirgel
Klagenfurter Strasse 10
1000 WIEN

For post sent within Austria, the city name is written in mixed case.

The general rule is that the thoroughfare name and the thoroughfare type are written as one word, thus:

Hauptstrasse
Bahnhofstrasse

There are two important exceptions. If the thoroughfare name refers to the real name of a place (e.g. a town name, a castle name, a forest name, etc.) then there is a space between the thoroughfare name and the thoroughfare type, thus:

Wiener Strasse
Tyroler Allee

The second exception is where complete personal names are used. In these cases, each component of the name and each thoroughfare type are separated with hyphens. Note, however, that surnames only are not covered by this exception. Thus:

Kaiser-Wilhelm-Strasse
Albert-Einstein-Strasse

but

Beethovenstrasse
Einsteinstrasse

In streets beginning with prepositions or some adjectives ('Am', 'An', 'Alter', etc.) the preposition or adjective is followed by a space, thus:

Alter Marktstrasse

House numbers are usually hyphenated thus:

33-39

not

33/39

Thoroughfare types

Below is a list of the most commonly occurring thoroughfare types, with the abbreviated form(s) which you are most likely to find in address databases:

Allee	
Berg	
Boulevard	Bd
Bruch	
Bühl	
Chaussee	Ch
Damm	
Gasse	
Graben	
Hafen	
Hof	
Kamp	
Markt	
Platz	Pl
Ring	
Strasse	Str
Ufer	
Wall	
Weg	
Weide	

Other nouns, adjectives and prepositions commonly found in address databases

NB: German grammar rules governing articles, prepositions and adjectives are complex, and there is no need to explain them here. It is only necessary to be able to recognise them when and where they occur in addresses. For this reason a list without further explanation is provided. As a very general rule of thumb, the prepositions and adjectives listed may have one of the following endings added: nothing; e; er; em; en or es.

German	*English*
der/die/das/den/dem/des	the
ein/eine/eines/einen/einem/einer	a, an
und	and
bis	till, until, up to
für	for
von	of, from
zu, zu der (zur), zu dem (zum), nach	to, towards
bei, bei der/den/dem (beim)	near, at
an, an der/den/dem (am)	at, by, towards
auf, auf der/den/dem	on
in, in der/den/dem (im)	in
gegenüber	opposite, facing
nächst, neben, neben der/dem/den	next to
hinter, hinter der/den/dem	behind
vor, vor der/den/dem	before, in front of
zwischen, zwischen der/den/dem	between, amongst
über, über der/den/dem	over, above, beyond
unter, unter der/dem/den	under, beneath, below
mit	with
neu/neue	new
alt/alte	old
kurz/kurze/kurzen/kurzer/kurzem/kurzes (K.)	short
lang/lange/langen/langer/langem/langes (L./Lge.)	long
gross/grosse/grossen/grosser/grossem/grosses (G.)	large
klein/kleine/kleinen/kleiner/kleinem/kleines (K./Kl./Kle.)	small
nord	north
ost	east
süd	south
west	west
Sankt (St.)	saint
Industrieterrein, Industriegebiet	industrial estate

For addresses written in Slovenian, Serbo-Croat or Hungarian, please refer to the appropriate country chapter.

Postbox

This is written as Postfach (PF).

Postal codes

The postal code is written on the same line, and before, the name of the town.

Austrian postal codes consist of a block of 4 digits (the first digit cannot be a 0). These codes do not correspond well to administrative districts, as many towns have more than one code, and many codes refer to more than one municipality. Codes may refer to a whole town, a set of postboxes or an area centred on a post office within larger towns.

Towns

For the Slovenian-speaking minority along the border with Slovenia, the following equivalent town names exist:

German	*Slovenian*
Arnfels	Arvež
Arnoldstein	Podklošter
Bleiburg	Pliberk
Brückl	Mostič
Deutsch Goritz	Nova Goricia
Diex	Djekše
Ebenthal	Žrelec
Eberndorf	Dobria vas
Ebriach	Obirsko
Ehrenhausen	Emaž
Eibiswald	Ivnik
Eisenkappel	Žel. Kapla
Faak	Bače
Fehring	Borinje
Feistritz	Bistrica
Feldbach	Vrbna
Feldkirchen	Trg
Ferlach	Borovlje
Finkestein	Bekštajn
Förolach	Borlje
Fürnitz	Brnca
Gailtal	Zilja
Gallizien	Galicija
Gamlitz	Gomilica
Globasnitz	Globasnica
Goritz	Goricia
Grafenstein	Grabštanj

Graz	Gradec
Griffen	Grebinj
Grosswalz	Veliki Boč
Halbenrain	Obrajna
Hermagor	Šmohor
Jauntal	Podjuna
Jennersdorf	Ženavci
Keutschach	Hodiše
Klagenfurt	Celovec
Köttmannsdorf	Kotmaravas
Köstenberg	Kostanje
Krumpendorf	Kriva-Vrba
Kühnsdorf	Sinča vas
Lavamünd	Labot
Leibnitz	Lipnica
Leutschach	Lučane
Lichendorf	Lihovci
Loibltal	Brodj
Ludmannsdorf	Bilčovs
Maria Saal	GospaSveta
Mittertrixen	Sr. Trušnje
Möderndorf	Modrinja vas
Mogersdorf	Modinci
Moosburg	Možberk
Mureck	Cmurek
Neumarkt	Stankovcí
Niederdorf	Dolnja vas
Nötsch	Čajna
Oberdrosen	Straža
Oberhaag	Osek
Pischeldorf	Škofji Dvor
Poggersdorf	Pokrče
Pörtschach	Poreče
Pössnitz	Pesnica
Pustritz	Pustrica
Radkersburg	Radgorra
Reifnitz	Ribnica
Rosedd	Rožek
Rosental	Roz
Ruden	Ruda
St. Andrä	Št. Andraž
St. Jakob im Rosental	Št. Jakob v Rozu
St. Johann	Št. Janž
St. Margarethen	Šmarjeta
St. Stefan	Št. Stefan
St. Veit	Št. Vid
Schlossberg	Gradišče

Sicheldorf	Žetinci
Sittersdorf	Žitara vas
Spielfeld	Špilje
Tainach	Tinje
Tauka	Toka
Tröpolach	Dropole
Unterpurkla	Spodnja Purkla
Velden	Vrba
Vellach	Bela
Viktring	Vetrinj
Villach	Beljak
Völkermarkt	Velikovec
Vorderberg	Blače
Wernberg	Vernberk
Wölfnitz	Golovica
Zell Pfarre	Sele

For the Hungarian- and Croat-speaking minorities in the Burgenland region, the following equivalent town names exist:

German	*Hungarian*	*Croat*
Allersdorf		Ključarevac
Allersgraben		Širokani
Althodis		Stari Hodas
Antau		Otava
Baumgarten		Pajngert
Deutsch Minihof	Németlak	
Deutschkreuz	Sopronkeresztúr	
Drassburg		Rasporak
Durnbach		Vincet
Eisenstadt	Kismarton	
Frankenau		Frakanava
Frauenkirchen	Boldogasszony	
Gols	Gálos	
Grossmürbisch		Veliki Medveš
Grossmütschen		Mučindrof
Grosswarasdorf		Veliki Borištof
Güssing	Németújvár	
Guttenbach		Pinkovac
Hackerberg		Hakerberg
Heugraben		Žarnovica
Hornstein		Vorištan
Kaisersdorf		Kalištrof
Kittsee	Köpcsény	Gijeca
Kleinmütschen		Pervane
Kleinwarasdorf		Mali Borištof
Klingenbach		Klinpuh

Kroatisch Geresdorf		Gerištof
Kroatisch Minihof		Mjenovo
Kroatisch Tschantschendorf		Hrvatska Čenča
Langental		Longitolj
Lockenhaus	Léka	
Mattersburg	Nagymarton	
Mönchhof	Barátudvar	
Münchmeierhof		Marof
Neusiedl	Nezsider	
Nebersdorf		Šuševo
Neuberg		Nova Gora
Neudorf		Novo Selo
Nikitsch		Filež
Oberpodgoria		Podgorje
Oberpullendorf	Felsőpulya	
Oslip		Uzlop
Pama		Bijelo Selo
Pamhagen	Pomogy	
Parapatischberg		Parapatić Brig
Parndorf		Pandrof
Reinesdorf		Žamar
Rumpersdorf		Rupišće
Rust	Ruszt	
Schachendorf		Čajta
Schandorf		Čemba
Siegendorf		Cindorf
Sigless		Cikleš
Soitzzicken		Hrvatski Ciklijn
Stegersbach		Santalek
Steinbrunn		Štikapron
Stinatz		Stinjaki
Trausdorf		Trajštof
Unterpodgoria		Bošnjakov Brig
Unterpullendorf		Dolnja Pulja
Wallern im Burg	Valla	
Weiden		Bandol
Weingraben		Bajngrob
Wulkaprodersdorf		Vulkaprodrštof
Zagersdorf		Cogrštof
Zillingtal		Celindrof
Zuberbach		Sabara
Zurndorf	Zurány	

The following list gives other foreign language equivalents of Austrian town names:

German	*English*	*French*	*Spanish*	*Italian*	*Dutch*
Salzburg		Salzbourg	Salzburgo	Salisburgo	
Wien	Vienna	Vienne	Viena	Vienna	Wenen

Administrative Districts

Austria has 9 states (*Bundesländer*):

Bundesländ	*Abbrev.*	*Postal code areas*
Burgenland	Bgl	242, 2473-2475, 2491, 70-73, 740-741, 7422-7423, 743-747, 75, 838
Kärnten	Kä	90-92, 930-931, 9321-9322, 933-937, 94-96, 970-977, 9781, 98
Niederösterreich	NÖ	20-23, 240-241, 243-246, 247-2472, 248, 2490, 2492-2493, 25-28, 30-32, 330-332, 3331-3333, 334-339, 34-39, 430, 4392, 443, 4441, 4482
Oberösterreich	OÖ	3334-3335, 40-42, 431-438, 4391, 440-442, 4442-4443, 445-447, 4481, 4483-4484, 449, 45-49, 512-514, 521-528, 531, 536
Salzburg	Sbg	50, 510-511, 515-516, 520, 530, 532-533, 5340, 5342, 535, 54-57
Steiermark	Stm	7421, 80-82, 830-836, 84-89, 9323
Tirol	Tir	60-66, 9782
Vorarlberg	Vbg	67-69
Wien		1

The name of the province is never used in addresses.

Azerbaijan
Azarbaijchan

The territory of Nagorno-Karabakh and the areas immediately adjacent to it in the west of the country are held by Armenian separatists. Mail deliveries to these areas may consequently be affected.

Official name: Republic of Azerbaijan, Republik Azarbaijchan
Area: 86 600 sq. km (33 428 sq. miles)
Population: 7 236 000
Capital: Bakı (Baku)
Currency: 1 Manat = 100 gopik
International telephone access code: 994

Languages

The official language, North Azerbaijani, is spoken by some 6 069 453 people. Though this has been written officially in the Latin script since the breakup of the Soviet Union, many people still use Cyrillic script. Armenian is spoken in and around the disputed territory of Nagorno-Karanakh. There are 44 000 Avar-speakers; 2 000 Budukh-speakers (no written form); 24 000 Judeo-Tat-speakers; 1 500 Khinalugh-speakers; 6 000 Kryts-speakers (no written form); 20 000 Kurmanji-speakers (Kurdish); 171 400 Lezgi-speakers; 130 000 Talysh-speakers (speakers are bilingual in Azerbaijani); 22 000 Muslim-Tat-speakers (no written form); 13 000 Tsakhur-speakers and 4 200 Udi-speakers (no written form).

Postal codes

Postal codes consist of a block of 6 digits. This is the same code that was used before the independence of Azerbaijan from the Soviet Union.

Towns

Many settlements previously known by their Russian names have Azeri equivalents which should be used:

Azeri	*Russian*
Ağcabädı	Agdzhabedi
Agdaş	Agdash
Ağstafa	Akstafa
Ağsu	Akhsu
Älät	Alyat
Äli Bayramli	Ali-Bayramly
Bakı	Baku
Balakan	Belokany
Bänkä	Bank

Biläsuvar	Pushkino
Cälilabad	Dzhalilabad
Culfa	Dzhulfa
Daşkäzan	Dashkesan
Däviçi	Divichi
Füzuli	Fizuli
Gädäbäy	Kedabek
Gäncä	Kirovabad / Gyandzha
Göuçay	Geokchay
İmişli	Imishli
İsmayilli	Ismailly
Jiloy	Zhiloy
Kälbacar	Kelbadzhar
Kürdämir	Kyurdamir
Lacın	Lachin
Länkäran	Lenkoran
Massallı	Masally
Maştağa	Mashtaga
Mingäçevir	Mingechaur
Naxçıvan	Nakhichevan
Neftçala	Neftechala
Port-İliç	Port-Ilich
Qaxı	Kakhi
Qazax	Kazakh
Qazimämmäd	Kazi Magomed
Qonaqkänd	Khonakhkend
Quba	Kuba
Qusar	Kusary
Sabunçu	Sabunchi
Şäki	Sheki / Nukha
Salyan	Salyany
Şämäxi	Shemakha
Şamkır	Shamkhor
Siyäzän	Siazan
Sumqayıt	Sumgait
Şuşa	Shusha
Tovuz	Tauz
Ucar	Udzhary
Yardimb	Yardymly
Yevlax	Yevlakh
Xaçmaz	Khachmas
Xankändı	Stepanakert
Xanlar	Khanlar
Xudat	Khudat
Zängilän	Zengelan
Zaqatala	Zakately

Bahamas

Official name: The Commonwealth of the Bahamas
Area: 13 934 sq. km (5 378 sq. miles)
Population: 254 685
Capital: Nassau
Currency: 1 Bahamian Dollar (BA$, B$) = 100 cents
International telephone access code: 1

Languages

The official language is English. 86.6% of the population speaks Bahamas Creole English.

Example address format

Mr John Smith
P.O. Box N-1417
NASSAU, N.P.

General Delivery
Marsh Harbour PO
ABACO

The name of the island (or its abbreviation) may appear in the address after the town name. The island names are:

Abaco
Acklins
Andros
Berry Islands
Bimini
Cat Island
Crooked Island
Eleuthera
Exuma
Grand Bahama
Harbour Island
Inagua
Long Cay
Long Island
Mayaguana
New Providence
Ragged Island
Rum Cay
San Salvador (or Watling Island)

Postboxes

Postbox numbers are preceded by a sorting code, which may be N, GT, CB or FH.

Postal codes

The Bahamas have no postal code system.

Telephone numbers

All telephone numbers in The Bahamas have the area code 242.

Bahrain
Al-Bahrayn

Official name: State of Bahrain, Dawlat al-Bahrayn
Area: 678 sq. km (262 sq. miles)
Population: 531 000
Capital: Al Manāmah (Manama)
Currency: 1 Bahrain Dinar (BD) = 1000 fils
International telephone access code: 973

Languages

The official language is Standard Arabic. There are 300 000 speakers of Bahanra Spoken Arabic and 100 000 speakers of Gulf Spoken Arabic.

Postal code

Bahraini postal codes consist of a block of three or four digits. Those consisting of three digits refer to regions number 1 to 9. Those with four digits refer to regions 10-12.

Towns

Al Manāmah is known as *Manama* in English.

Bangladesh

Official name: People's Republic of Bangladesh, GaNa Prajãtantrï Bangaldesh
Area: 143 998 sq. km (55 583 sq. miles)
Population: 110 602 000
Capital: Dhaka
Currency: 1 Taka (TK) = 100 paisa
International telephone access code: 880

Languages

The official language is Bengali, with 100 000 000 speakers. 34 other languages are spoken. The most widespread of these are: Burmese (231 000 speakers); Chakma (260 577 speakers) and Sylhetti (5 000 000 speakers).

Example address format

Mr Ashraduddin Khan
Vill Genda
P.O. SAVAR
DHAKA - 1340

Postal codes

Bangladeshi postal codes consist of a block of 4 digits. The first two digits refer to the main post office in the district headquarters, the last two digits refer to the sub-post office.

Belarus

Official name: Republic of Belarus, Respublika Belarus
Area: 207 600 sq. km (80 134 sq. miles)
Population: 10 300 000
Capital: Minsk
Currency: 1 Belorussian Rouble = 100 kopec (parallelled with the Russian Rouble)
International telephone access code: 375

Languages

Most of the population speak Belorussian. There are large minorities of people speaking languages from other parts of the former Soviet Union.

Example address format

220050 MINSK-50
F.Skaryna propect 24
Kornilova S.I.

Note that the order of address lines in Belarus is the opposite to that used in Western Europe - the postal code and town comes first, then the street address, then the name of the person or company.

Postal codes

Postal codes consist of a block of 6 digits. The code used is that in use since before independence from the Soviet Union. The first three digits indicate the region, the last three the post office.

Towns

Many settlements have both Belorussian and Russian names. The Belorussian name should be used:

Belorussian	*Russian*
Asipovychy	Osipovichi
Babruysk	Bobruysk
Baranavichy	Baranovichi
Barysaw	Borisov
Chervyen	Cherven
Dobrush	Dobrush
Hlybokaye	Glubokoye
Homyel	Gomel
Horki	Gorki
Hrodna	Grodno
Kalinkavichy	Kalinkovichi

Krychaw	Krichev
Luninyets	Luninets
Mahilyow / Mahilyew	Mogilyov / Mogilyev
Maladzyechna	Molodechno
Marina Horka	Marina Gorka
Mazyr	Mozyr
Mavahrudak	Movogrudok
Navapolatsk	Novopolotsk
Pahachow	Rogachev
Pastavy	Postavy
Polatsk	Polotsk
Rechytsa	Rechitsa
Salihorsk	Soligorsk
Smarhon	Smorgon
Svyetlahorsk	Svetlagorsk
Vawkavysk	Volkovysk
Vilyeyka	Vileyka
Vitsyebsk	Vitebsk
Zhytkavichy	Zhitkovichi

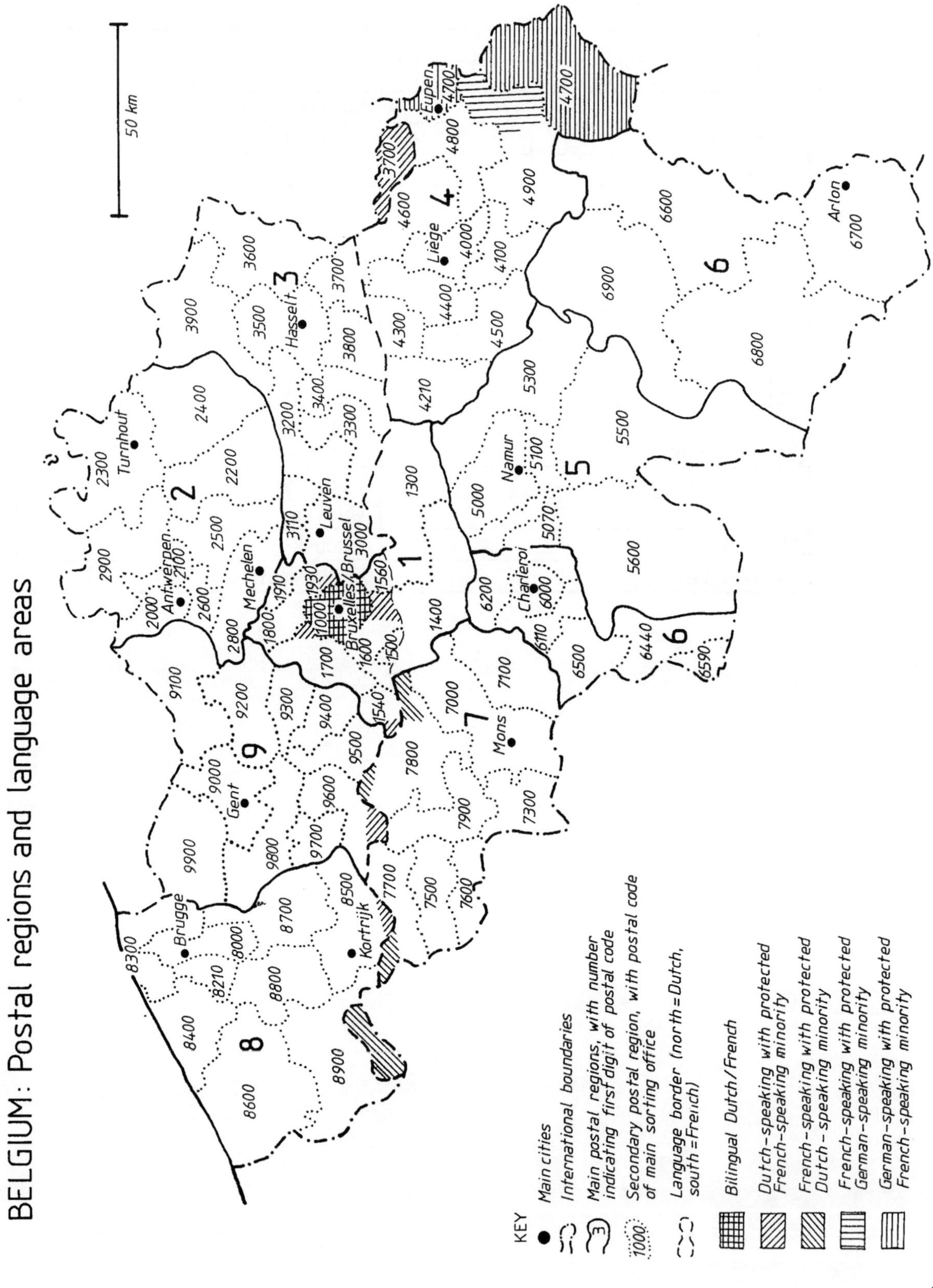
BELGIUM: Postal regions and language areas
50 km
KEY
Main cities
International boundaries
Main postal regions, with number indicating first digit of postal code
Secondary postal region, with postal code of main sorting office
Language border (north = Dutch, south = French)
Bilingual Dutch/French
Dutch-speaking with protected French-speaking minority
French-speaking with protected Dutch-speaking minority
French-speaking with protected German-speaking minority
German-speaking with protected French-speaking minority
Brugge
Kortrijk
Gent
Antwerpen
Turnhout
Mechelen
Leuven
Bruxelles/Brussel
Hasselt
Liège
Eupen
Namur
Charleroi
Mons
Arlon

98

Belgium
België/Belgique/Belgien

Official name: Kingdom of Belgium, Koninkrijk België, Royaume de Belgique, Königreich Belgien
Area: 30,519 sq. km (11,783 sq. miles)
Population: 9 978 681
Capital: Bruxelles, Brussel (Brussels)
Currency: 1 Belgian franc/frank = 100 centimes
International telephone access code: 32

Languages

Belgium has three official languages, Dutch, French and German. Luxembourgeois, a dialect of German, is spoken by about 14 900 in Luxembourg province near to the border of Luxembourg. The Dutch that Belgians speak is a distinctive dialect called Flemish, which is related to Dutch in the same way as British English and American English are related. Communications can be made in the Dutch of The Netherlands, but are much better received if in Flemish. Belgians are very language sensitive - you must bear this in mind always when communicating to or within Belgium. The country has a federal structure, and the number of inhabitants in each area (1991) is as follows:

Flemish-speaking area	5 768 925 (57.8%)
French-speaking area (excluding German language area)	3 189 711 (32.0%)
German-speaking area	66 000 (0.7%)
Brussels	954 045 (9.6%)

Brussels is officially a bilingual Flemish-French area, but in fact approximately 80 per cent of the population speak French, 20 per cent Flemish. A large number of people, especially amongst the Flemish population of Brussels, are bilingual.

Company names

In all three language areas, it is more correct, where the *nature* of a company is mentioned in its name, that this *precedes* the name of the company, thus:

Boulangerie Dupont
Bakkerij Janssens
Bäcker Schmidt

You will often, however, find these activity indications *after* the company name, thus:

Dupont, Boulangerie
Dupont (Boulangerie)
Janssens, Bakkerij

Janssens (Bakkerij)
Schmidt, Bäcker
Schmidt (Bäcker)

Company types

Company type indications will sometimes be present in both French and Flemish versions within the same name, thus:

Janssens NV/SA

or

NV Janssens SA

The following company types may be found in Belgian company names:

Flemish	*French*
Buitenlandse Vennootschap	Société Etrangère
BVBA (Besloten Vennootschap met Beperkte Aansprakelijkheid)	SPRL (Société Privée a Responsibilité Limitée)
Commanditaire Vennootschap op Aandelen	Société en Commandité par Actions
Coöperatieve Vennootschap	Société Cooperatieve
Eenmanszaak	Affaire Personnelle
Feitelijke Vereniging	Association de Fait
Gewone Commanditaire Vennootshap	Société en Commandité Simple
NV (Naamloze Vennootschap)	SA (Société Anonyme)
PVBA (Personenvernootschap met Beperkte Aansprakelijkheid)	SPRL (Sociéte de Personnes a Responsibilité Limitée)
SV (Samenwerkende Vennootschap)	SC (Société Cooperative)
Tijdelijke Handelsvereniging	Association Momentanée
VEG (Vennootschap bij Wijze van Eenvoudige Geldschieting)	SCS (Société en Commandite)
VGN (Vernootschap onder Gemeenschappelijke Naam)	SNC (Société en Nom Collectif)
VOF (Vennootschap onder Firma)	
VZW (Vereniging zonder Winstoogmerk)	ASBL (Association sans But Lucratif) (Indicates a Charity)

Contact names

Belgian personal names often contain prepositions, especially 'van de/van der/de la/du' which mean, literally 'of the'. Unlike The Netherlands, there is no rule for the capitalisation or writing of these prepositions. In the Flemish area, they are more often, though not exclusively, written with an upper case first letter. In some names these prepositions are written as one word with the rest of the surname, in others they are written as a separate word.

For Flemish speakers, the salutation which would be used on an address label is inappropriate for use within a letter.

Addresses

Structure:

Addresses will be written in French, Flemish or German, depending on the language of the region. In the bilingual regions, addresses may be written in either or both languages. Addresses should always be written in this format:

Recipient name
Thoroughfare[ ]number
postal code[ ]TOWN NAME

regardless of the language area. The order and format in which the thoroughfare name and thoroughfare type are written differ according to the language of the address. For example:

French language region

M. Emile Dubois
rue du Diamant 215
4800 VERVIERS

Flemish language region

Dhr. Hugo Degroot
Kerkstraat 112
3000 LEUVEN

German language region

Herr Helmut Müller
Bergstrasse 23
4700 EUPEN

There should be nothing written or typed beneath the last line of the address.

Street address

In the Flemish areas, the thoroughfare type part of the address is suffixed to the rest of the street address without a space. An exception exists in the address '*Steenweg op* name of town' or '*Steenweg naar* name of town'. For example:

Groenmolenstraat 5
Bergensesteenweg 7
Steenweg op Leuven 19

In the French language addresses, the thoroughfare type part of the street address is prefixed, with spaces between the words. For example:

> rue Montfort 8
> rue d'Arlon 98
> avenue de la Gare 4

In the German-speaking areas, the general rule is that the thoroughfare type part of the address is suffixed to the rest of the address, as in the Flemish areas. For example:

> Hauptstrasse 3

However, there are two important exceptions. If the thoroughfare name refers to the real name of a place (e.g. a town name, a castle name, a forest name, etc.) then there is a space between the thoroughfare name and the thoroughfare type. The second exception is where complete personal names are used. In these cases, each component of the name and each part of the street address string are separated with hyphens. Surnames *only* are *not* covered by this exception. Thus:

> Lüticher Strasse 9
> Ludwig-von-Beethoven-Strasse 15
> Beethovenstrasse 11

In streets beginning with prepositions or some adjectives ('Am', 'An', 'Alter' etc.), the preposition is followed by a space, thus:

> Alter Marktstrasse 3

In the French language regions, thoroughfare types should correctly begin with a lower case letter. In all three regions, prepositions like 'de la' and 'op' should also be written without a capital letter.

In bilingual areas, street addresses might be written with both the French thoroughfare type as a prefix and the Flemish thoroughfare type as a suffix. For example:

> rue du Beethovenstraat 12

This is unnecessary, and one may be removed.

If the address has a box number, add this after the address so:

> street name[ ]number[- bus]number (Flemish or German)

or

> street name[ ]number[- boite]number (French)

For example

> Bergstraat 15 - bus 19

rue d'Arlon 90 - boite 23

Thoroughfare types

Below is a list of the most commonly occurring thoroughfare types, with the abbreviated form(s) which you are most likely to find in address databases:

Flemish	*Abbreviations*
Allée	
Baan	Bn
Berg	Bg
Centrum	
Dal	
Dam	
Dijk	
Dreef	Dr
Dwarsstraat	
Dwarsweg	
Gracht	
Hof	
Kaai	
Kade	
Kanaal	
Laan	Ln
Lei	
Markt	Mkt
Park	Pk
Plantsoen	
Plein	Pl
Rui	
Singel	
Square	Sq
Steenweg	Stwg, Swg
Straat	Str
Straatweg	
Vaart	
Veld	
Vest	
Vliet	
Weg	
Wijk	

French	*Abbreviations*
allée	
avenue	ave
boulevard	bd, bld
canal	

centre	
champ	
chaussée	ch, chee
chemin	
clos	
cour	
digue	
impasse	imp
marché	
mont/montagne	mt
parc	
place	pl
quai	
quartier	
route	rte
Route National	RN
rue	r
square	sq
val/vallée	

German	*Abbreviations*
Allee	
Berg	
Boulevard	Bd
Bruch	
Chaussee	Ch
Damm	
Gasse	
Hafen	
Hof	
Kamp	
Markt	
Platz	Pl
Ring	
Strasse	Str
Ufer	
Wall	
Weg	
Weide	

Other nouns, adjectives and prepositions commonly found in address databases

Flemish

NB: The following abbreviations are used: (n) = neuter; (g) = gendered and plural. Abbreviated forms are given in brackets.

Flemish	*English*
het (sometimes 't) (n), de (g)	the
een	a, an
en	and
tot	till, until, up to
voor	for
van	of, from
op, naar	to, towards
bij	near, by
aan	on (sea, for example), at
aan de (a/d)	on (a river)
op	on
in	in
tegenover	opposite
naast	next to
achter	bchind
vóór	in front of
tussen	between
over	over
onder	under
met	with
nieuw (n) (nw.)/nieuwe (g) (nwe.)	new
oud (n)/oude (g)	old
kort (n) (K.)/korte (g) (Kte.)	short
lang (n) (L.)/lange (g) (Lge.)	long
groot (n) (G./Gt.)/grote (g) (G. or Gte.)	large
klein (n) (K./K1.)/kleine (g) (K. or Kle.)	small
noord	north
oost	east
zuid	south
west	west
sint (St.)	saint
Industriepark	industrial estate

French

NB: The following abbreviations are used: (m) = masculine form; (f) = feminine form; (pl) = plural form. Except where specified, the plural form of adjectives is the correctly gendered singular form followed by an 's'.

French	*English*
le (m)/la (f)/les (pl) (NB: le and la are written 1' before a vowel or an unaspirated h)	the
un (m)/une (f)	a, an
et	and
à/au (m)/à la (f)/aux (pl)	till, until, up to, to
pour	for
de (before a proper noun)/du (m)/de la, de 1' (f)/des (pl)	of, from
à	at
près de	by, near to
sur	on (a river, the sea)
dans	in
en face de	opposite
à côté de	next to
derrière	behind
devant	in front
entre	between
avec	with
sous	under
lès (occurs *only* in place names)	near
nouveau (m)/nouvelle (f)/nouveaux (m.pl.)/nouvelles (f.pl.)/nouvel (m, before a vowel or unaspirated h)	new
vieux (m, pl)/vieille (f)/vielles(f.pl.)/vieil (m, before (f.pl.)/vieil (m, before a vowel or an unaspirated h)	old
court (m) (Ct.)/courte (f) (Cte.)	short
long (m) (Lg.)/longue (f) (Lgue.)	long
grand (m) (Gr./Grd.)/grande (f) (Gr./Grde.)	large
petit (m) (P./Pt.)/petite (f) (P./Pte.)	small
nord	north
est	east
sud	south
ouest	west
saint (m) (St.)/sainte (f) (Ste.)	saint
Parc Industriel, Zone d'Activités (Z.A.C.), Zone Industrielle (Z.I.), Zone Artisanale (Z.A.)	industrial estate

German

NB: German grammar rules governing articles, prepositions and adjectives are complex, and there is no need to explain them here. It is only necessary to be able to recognize them when and where they occur in addresses. For this reason a list without further explanation is provided. As a very general rule of thumb, prepositions and adjectives may have one of the following endings added: nothing; -e; -er; -em; -en; or -es.

German	English
der/die/das/den/dem/des	the
ein/eine/eines/einen/einem/einer	a, an
und	and
bis	till, until, up to
für	for
van	of, from
zu, zu der (zur), zu dem (sum), nach	to, towards
bei, bei der/den/dem (beim)	near, at
an, an der/den/dem (am)	at, by, towards
auf, auf der/den/dem	on
in, in der/den/dem (im)	in
gegenüber	opposite, facing
nächst, neben, neben der/dem/den	next to
hinter, hinter der/den/dem	behind
vor, vor der/den/dem	before, in front of
zwischen, zwischen der/den/dem	between, amongst
über, über der/den/dem	over, above, beyond
unter, unter der/dem/den	under, beneath, below
mit	with
neu/neue	new
alt/alte	old
kurz/kurze/kurzen/kurzer/kurzem/kurzes (K.)	short
lang/lange/langen/langer/langem/langes (L./Lge.)	long
gross/grosse/grosser/grosser/grossem/grosses (G.)	large
klein / kleine / kleinen /kleiner/kleinem/kleines (K./Kl./Kle.)	small
nord	north
ost	east
süd	south
west	west
sankt (St.)	saint
Industrieterrein, Industriegebiet	industrial estate

Postbox

This is written as: *Postbus* (*PB*) in Flemish; *Boite Postale* (*BP*) in French; and *Postfach* (*PF*) in German.

Postal codes

All postal codes in Belgium have 4 numbers, the first digit being a number between 1 and 9. Not all numbers between 1000 and 9999 have been utilized for postal codes. No postal codes currently exist beginning with the digits 57, 58 or 59. The boundaries of the postal code regions correspond with the boundaries of the municipalities before fusion of some municipalities took place in 1975 and 1982. Postal codes correspond well to language regions. Postal codes are written before, and on the same line as, the town, thus:

3000 LEUVEN

The municipality named should be that which applied prior to fusion in 1975 and 1982.

In the cases of certain cities a second part of the postal code, indicating a sorting office within the main Postal code region is sometimes added after the town name. This is essential, especially in the case of postboxes, as without it delivery will be impossible. For example:

1080 BRUXELLES 8

Regional language can be determined on the basis of postal codes as follows:

Flemish

1500-3999, 8000-9999

Note: Postal code areas 1547, 1640, 1780, 1950, 1970, 3717, 3790, 8587 and 9600 have facilities for French-speaking minorities.

French

1300-1499, 4000-4699,4800-5699, 6000-7999

Note: Postal code areas 7700, 7780, 7850 and 7880 have facilities for Flemish-speaking minorities. Postal code areas 4950 and 4960 have facilities for German-speaking minorities.

German

4700-4799

Note: All of the German-language areas of Belgium have facilities for French-speaking minorities.

Brussels (Bilingual French-Flemish)

1000-1299

Towns

Towns are usually written in the address in capital letters.

Many towns in Belgium have more than one name - one Flemish, one French or one German and one French. Belgians are extremely language sensitive, and it is important to use the correct town name.

Town names consisting of more than one word are hyphenated with the exception of town names written in German in the German language area, and towns beginning with the words 'LE', 'LA', 'DE', 'HET', ' 'T' and ' 'S' where there is a space between this word and the next (other words in the same town name will be hyphenated). For example:

La Roche-en-Ardenne
Le Roux
's Gravenbrakel
De Panne
Sankt Vith
Saint-Vith

The following lists give the corresponding settlement names in the various languages. The first list gives the French equivalent for Flemish-speaking settlements; the second gives the Flemish and German equivalents for French-speaking settlements; the third gives the French equivalents for German-speaking settlements; and the fourth gives the alternatives for bilingual settlements. Finally, a list of corresponding town names in other languages is given. Some of the names refer to bilingual municipalities, although in these municipalities one language is recognized as being dominant. A postal code following the autochthonal name indicates to which settlement the alternatives refer, when more than one settlement of the same name exists.

Name equivalents for Flemish-language settlements

Flemish	*French*
Aalst (9300)	Alost
Antwerpen	Anvers
Baarle-Hertog	Baerle-Duc
Beert	Brages
Bever	Biévène
Borgloon	Looz
Brugge	Bruges
Dendermonde	Termonde
De Panne	Le Panne
Diets-Heur	Heur-le-Tiexhe
Diksmuide	Dixmude
Drongen	Tonchiennes
Dworp	Tourneppe
Eeklo	Ecklo

Galmaarden	Gammerages
Gent	Gand
Geraardsbergen	Grammont
Goetsenhoven	Gossoncourt
Helkijn	Helchin
Herk-de-Stad	Herck-la-Ville
Ieper	Ypres
Jeuk	Goyer
Kelmis	La Calamine
Kortrijk	Courtrai
Lauw	Lowaige
Leopoldsburg	Bourg-Léopold
Leuven	Louvain
Lier	Lierre
Mechelen	Malines
Mechelen-Bovelingen	Marlinne
Menen	Menin
Mesen	Messines
Moelingen	Mouland
Nieuwkerke	Neuve-Eglise
Nieuwpoort	Nieuport
Oostende	Ostende
Oudenaarde	Audenarde
Roeselare	Roulers
Ronse	Renaix
Rukkelingen-Loon	Roclenge-Looz
Rutten	Russon
Scherpenheuvel	Montaigu
's Gravenvoeren	Fouron-le-Comte
Sint-Genesius-Rode	Rhode-Saint-Genèse
Sint-Martens-Voeren	Fouron-Saint-Martin
Sint-Niklaas	Saint-Nicolas
Sint-Pieters-Kapelle	Saint-Pierre-Capelle
Sint-Pieters-Voeren	Fouron-Saint-Pierre
Sint-Stevens-Woluwe	Woluwe-Saint-Etienne
Sint-Truiden	Saint-Trond
Sluizen	Sluse (Limburg)
Spiere	Espierres
Spiere-Helkijn	Espierres-Helchin
Temse	Tamise
Tielt	Thielt
Tienen	Tirlemont
Tongeren	Tongres
Veulen	Fologne
Veurne	Furnes
Vilvoorde	Vilvorde
Vorsen	Fresin

Waasmont	Waasten
Walshoutem	Houtain-l'Evêque
Warneton	Waasten
Zoutleeuw	Léau

Name equivalents for French-language settlements

French	*Flemish*	*German*
Archennes	Eerken	
Arlon	Aarlen	
Ath	Aat	
Bassenge	Bitsingen	
Bassilly	Zullik	
Bastogne	Bastenaken	
Bas-Warneton	Neerwaasten	
Beauverchain	Bevekom	
Bettincourt	Bettenhoven	
Bierghes	Bierk	
Bois-de-Lessines	Lessenbos	
Bombaye	Bolbeek	
Braine-l'Alleud	Eigenbrakel	
Braine-le-Château	Kasteelbrakel	
Braine-le-Comte	's Gravenbrakel	
Clabecq	Klabbeek	
Comines	Komen	
Deux-Acren	Twee Akren	
Dottignies	Dottenijs	
Ellezelles	Elzele	
Enghien	Edingen	
Flobecq	Vloesberg	
Genappe	Genepiën	
Ghislenghien	Gellingen	
Glons	Glaaien	
Grez-Doiceau	Graven	
Halle	Hal	
Hannut	Hannuit	
Henri-Chapelle	Hendrik-Kapelle	
Hombourg	Homburg	
Hoves	Hove (Hainault)	
Huy	Hoei	
Ittre	Itter	
Jauche	Geten	
Jodoigne	Geldenaken	
Jodoigne-Souveraine	Opgeldernaken	
Jurbise	Jurbeke	
La Hulpe	Terhulpen	
Lanaye	Ternaaien	

L'Ecluse	Sluizen (Brabant)	
Lessines	Lessen	
Liège	Luik	
Limbourg	Limburg	
Lincent	Lijsem	
Linsmeau	Linsmeel	
Lixhe	Lieze	
Marcq	Mark	
Mélin	Malen	
Mouscron	Moeskroen	
Namur	Namen	
Nivelles	Nijvel	
Oisquercq	Oostkerk	
Ollignies	Woelingen	
Oreye	Oerle	
Othée	Elch	
Otranges	Wouteringen	
Papignies	Papegem	
Pellaines	Pellen	
Perwez	Perwijs	
Petit-Enghien	Lettelingen	
Piétrain	Petren	
Racour	Raatshoven	
Rebecq-Rognon	Roosbeek (Brabant)	
Roclenge-sur-Geer	Rukkelingen-aan-de-Jeker	
Rosoux-Crenwick	Roost-Krenwik	
Russeignies	Rozenaken	
Saintes	Sint-Renelde	
Saint-Jean-Geest	Sint-Jans-Geest	
Saint-Remy-Geest	Sint-Remigius-Geest	
Silly	Opzullik	
Soignies	Zinnik	
Steenkerque	Steenkerke	
Tourinnes-la-Grosse	Deurne (Brabant)	
Tournai	Doornik	
Trognée	Tubeke	
Visé	Wezet	
Waimes		Weismes
Waremme	Borgworm	
Warsage	Weerst	
Wauthier-Braine	Woutersbrakel	
Wavre	Waver	
Wihogne	Nudorp	
Zétrud-Lumay	Zittert-Lummen	

Name equivalents for German-language settlements

German	*French*
Amel	Amblève
Büllingen	Bullange
Bütchenbach	Butgenbach
Sankt Vith	Saint-Vith

Name equivalents for Bilingual settlements

French	*Flemish*
Bruxelles	Brussel

Name equivalents in other European languages

Autochthone	*English*	*German*	*Spanish*	*Italian*
Antwerpen	Antwerp		Amberes	Anversa
Arlon		Arel		
Bastogne		Bastenaken		
Brugge	Bruges	Brügge	Brujas	Bruges
Bruxelles, Brussel	Brussels	Brüssel	Bruselas	Brusselle
Gent	Ghent		Gante	Gand
Ieper	Ypres	Ypern	Ipres	
Kortrijk	Courtrai		Courtrai	
Leuven	Louvain	Löwen	Lovaina	Lovagno
Liège		Lüttich	Lieja	Liegi
Mechelen	Malines	Mecheln	Malinas	Malines
Menen	Menin			
Oostende	Ostend	Ostende		Ostenda
Zeebrugge	Zeebruges	Zeebrügge		

The following municipalities (with their postal codes) are majority Flemish speaking with a protected French-speaking minority. Note that in this and the following lists the status of the municipalities are established by law and do not necessarily represent the true proportion of speakers within them.

1547 Bever
3717 Herstappe
1950 Kraainem
9600 Ronse
1640 Sint-Genesius-Rode
8587 Spiere-Helkijn (includes Spier and Helkijn)
3790 Voeren (includes Moelingen, 's-Gravenvoeren, Sint-Martens-Voeren, Sint-Pieters-Voeren, Remersdaal and Teuven)
1780 Wemmel
1970 Wezembeek-Oppem

The following municipalities are majority French speaking with a protected Flemish-speaking minority:

7780 Comines-Warneton (includes Ploegsteert, Warneton, Bas-Warneton, Comines and Houtem)
7850 Enghien (includes Petit-Enghien and Marcq)
7880 Flobecq
7700 Mouscron (includes Luingne, Herseaux and Dottignies)

The following municipalities are majority French speaking with a protected German-speaking minority:

4960 Malmedy (includes Bevercé, and Bellevaux-Ligneuville)
4950 Waimes (includes Faymonville and Robertville)

The following municipalities are majority German speaking with a protected French-speaking minority:

4770 Amel (includes Heppenbach and Meyerode)
4760 Büllingen (includes Rocherath and Manderfeld)
4790 Burg-Reuland (includes Thommen and Reuland)
4750 Bütgenbach (includes Elsenborn)
4700 Eupen (includes Kettenis)
4720 Kelmis (includes Hergenrath and Neu-Moresnet)
4710 Lontzen (includes Walhorn)
4730 Raeren (includes Hauset and Eynatten)
4780 Sankt-Vith (includes Recht, Crombach Lommersweiler amd Schoenberg)

Brussels

Brussels is a bilingual area, with some 80 per cent of the population speaking French, the rest having Flemish as a mother tongue. Virtually all of the Flemish-speaking minority speak French, but mailing indiscriminately in French is not well received. It is therefore essential that mailings are sent and other communications made in the language of the respondent, not the language of the area.

Bruxelles and Brussel are used interchangeably. In the interests of consistency, use either one or 'Brussels' within the database and output Bruxelles or Brussel according to the language of the recipient. Alternatively, using 'Brussels' is acceptable (and better received than either of the alternatives to a speaker of the 'other' language), especially in business-to-business mailings.

Brussels consists of 19 municipalities. Addresses will often use the French or Flemish municipality name, or a version of the name 'Brussels'. The municipality names in the correct language of the address should be used. The municipalities are, listed here with the French version first, for no particular reason, and with their postal codes:

1070 Anderlecht
1160 Auderghem/Oudergem
1080 Berchem-Sainte-Agathe/Sint-Agatha-Berchem
1000 Bruxelles/Brussel
1040 Etterbeek

1140 Evere
1190 Forest/Vorst
1080 Ganshoren
1050 Ixelles/Elsene
1090 Jette
1080 Koekelberg
1080 Molenbeek-Saint-Jean/Sint-Jans-Molenbeek
1060 Saint-Gilles/Sint-Gillis
1030 Saint-Josse-ten-Noode/Sint-Joost-ten-Node
1030 Schaerbeek/Schaarbeek
1180 Uccle/Ukkel
1170 Watermael-Boitsfort/Watermaal-Bosvoorde
1200 Woluwe-Saint-Lambert/Sint-Lambrechts-Woluwe
1150 Woluwe-Saint-Pierre/Sint-Pieters-Woluwe

Administrative districts

Belgium is a federal state with a bewildering number of administrative layers based on geographical area and language community. It has 10 provinces split into 41 *arrondissements.* Fortunately they should never be used in addresses. The provinces are all unilingual, although some will contain some municipalities where there are facilities for a language minority. The provinces with their abbreviations, languages and *arrondissements* are as follows:

Antwerpen (Antw.) (Flemish speaking. French name: Anvers)
- Antwerpen
- Mechelen
- Turnhout

Brabant Wallon (Bt.W.) (French speaking. Flemish name: Waals Brabant)
- Nivelles

Hainault (Ht.) (French speaking. Flemish name: Henegouwen)
- Ath
- Charleroi
- Mons
- Soignes
- Thuin
- Tournai

Liège (Lg.) (French and German speaking. Flemish name: Luik; German name: Lüttich)
- Huy
- Liège
- Verviers
- Waremme

Limburg (Limb.) (Flemish speaking. French name: Limbourg)
- Hasselt
- Maaseik
- Tongeren

Luxembourg (Lux.) (French speaking. Flemish name: Luxemburg)
- Arlon
- Bastogne

Marche-en-Famenne
Neufchâteau
Virton
Namur (Nam.) (French speaking. Flemish name: Namen)
Dinant
Namur
Philippeville
Oost Vlaanderen (O.-V1.) (Flemish speaking. French name: Flandre-Orientale)
Aalst
Dendermonde
Eeklo
Gent
Oudenaarde
Sint-Niklaas
Vlaams Brabant (Vl.-Bt.) (Flemish speaking. French name: Brabant-Flamand)
Leuven
Vilvoorde
West Vlaanderen (W.-V1.) (Flemish speaking. French name: Flandre-Occidental)
Brugge
Diksmuide
Ieper
Kortrijk
Oostende
Roeselare
Tielt
Veurne

Belize
Belice (Spanish)

Official name: Belize
Area: 22 963 sq. km (8 864 sq. miles)
Population: 196 000
Capital: Belmopan
Currency: 1 Belize Dollar (Bz$) = 100 cents
International telephone access code: 501

Languages

The official language is English (55 998 second-language speakers). There are 55 051 speakers of Belize Creole English; 12 274 speakers of Garífuna; 9 000 speakers of Kekchí; 5 800 speakers of Maya; 7 000 speakers of Mopán; 5 763 speakers of Platdietsch and 80 477 speakers of Spanish.

Example address format

Mr John Smith
45 Barracuda Drive
SAN PEDRO
AMBERGRIS CAYE

The address is usually written in English. In the above case, an island name is included in the address. In other cases the name of the village or town is sufficient.

Postal codes

Belize has no postal code system.

Benin

Official name: Republic of Benin, République du Benin
Area: 112 622 sq. km (43 472 sq. miles)
Population: 4 883 000
Capital: Porto Novo
Currency: 1 CFA Franc (CFAFr) = 100 centimes
International telephone access code: 229

Languages

The official language is French (16 700 speakers). 50 other languages are spoken. The most widespread of these are: Aja-Gbe (360 000 speakers); Bariba (342 000 speakers); Fon-Gbe (1 400 000 speakers); Gun-Gbe (320 000 speakers) and Yoruba (465 000 speakers).

Example address format

M. Abou Kodjo
03 BP 1000
COTONOU

Any address written in a non-native language will be written in French. Deliveries are made only to post office boxes (*Boite Postale*, or *BP*). These box numbers are preceded with a number to indicate the post office where the box is located as follows:

01	Recette Principale
02	Gbègamey
03	Jericho
04	Cadjèjhoun
05	Akpakpa
06	PK 3
07	Sainte Rita
08	Pri Postal

The box number may be followed by the name of the post office.

Postbox

This is written as *Boite Postale*, or *BP*.

Postal codes

Benin has no postal code system.

Bolivia

Official name: Republic of Bolivia, República de Bolivia
Area: 1 098 580 sq. km (424 052 sq. miles)
Population: 7 356 000
Capital: La Paz
Currency: 1 Bolivano (Bs) = 100 centavos
International telephone access code: 591

Language

The official languages are Spanish (3 483 700 speakers), Quechua (2 898 983 speakers of two different forms) and Aymará (1 785 000 speakers). Spanish is not as dominant as in other South-American countries and Indian-language addresses will be found in databases.

42 other languages are spoken. The most widespread of these are: Chiquitano (30 000 speakers) and German (160 000 speakers).

Address Format

Addresses are written in the following format:

Recipient name
{thoroughfare type[]}Thoroughfare name[,]house number
SETTLEMENT

For example:

Sra Ana Jimenez
calle Sucre, 76
LA PAZ

The address may also be written without the comma after the thoroughfare name.

When addresses are written in Spanish, *calle*, the Spanish word for street, is rarely written. The Spanish thoroughfare type, when included, is written before, and separately from, the thoroughfare name. It should be written with the first letter in lower case.

Addresses may also be found written in Quechua or Aymará.

Postal codes

Bolivia currently has no postal code system.

Bosnia-Hercegovina
Bosnia i Hercegovina

Bosnia has been ravaged by civil war, and although currently at peace, there is still great tensions between the Serbs, Croats and Muslims. The country is divided into the Serb Republika Srbska and the Muslim and Croat federation, and there is little co-operation between the two regions. The currency of Croatia is widely used in the Croat region. Postal services are inevitably disrupted.

Official name: Republic of Bosnia-Hercegovina, Republika Bosnia i Hercegovina
Area: 51 129 sq. km (19 736 sq. miles)
Population: 4 364 574
Capital: Sarajevo
Currency: 1 Dinar (D, Dn) = 100 paras
International telephone access code: 387

Languages

Most of the population speak Serbo-Croatian. Serbs use the Cyrillic script, Croats the Latin script. Given the ethnic tensions within the country, choosing the correct script and dialect for each correspondent is essential. There are also speakers of Vlach Romani.

Address format

Addresses are written as follows:

Name
Thoroughfare[ ]number
postal code[ ]SETTLEMENT

For example

Nedim Zec
Skenderija 23
71000 SARAJEVO

Postal codes

The postal codes used consist of a block of 5 digits and are still those of the former Yugoslavia. Postal codes begin with the numbers 7, 80 or 88. The first two digits indicate the postal region, the last three the post office.

Botswana

Official name: Republic of Botswana
Area: 581 730 sq. km (224 711 sq. miles)
Population: 1 347 000
Capital: Gabarone
Currency: 1 Pula (P, Pu) = 100 thebes
International telephone access code: 267

Languages

The official language is English. Tswana (1 070 000 speakers) is also a national language. 28 other languages are spoken. The most widespread are: Afrikaans (20 000 speakers); Gabake-Ntshori (20 000 speakers); Kalanga (160 000 speakers); Kgalagadi (35 000 speakers) and Yeye (20 000 speakers).

Example address format

Name
P.O. Box 231
HUKUNTSI
Via Lobatse

Deliveries in Botswana are through postboxes, post offices or private bags. The last line in the example above gives the name of the postal town through which the letter is channelled.

Postal codes

Botswana has no postal code system

Brazil
Brasil

Official name: Federative Republic of Brazil, República Federativa do Brasil
Area: 8 511 965 sq. km (3 285 618 sq. miles)
Population: 151 381 000
Capital: Brasília
Currency: 1 Cruzeiro (Cr$) = 100 centavos
International telephone access code: 55

Languages

Brazil's official language is Portuguese, spoken by a large majority of the population. 194 other languages are known to exist, including large numbers of Indian languages. The most widespread of these are: Amapá Creole (25 000 speakers); Baniwa (5 460 speakers); Guajajára (10 000 speakers); Guaraní (5 000 speakers); Kaingáng (18 000 speakers); Kaiwá (15 000 speakers); Plautdietsch (5 955 speakers); Sataré-Mawé (9 000 speakers); Terêna (15 000 speakers); Ticuna (12 000 speakers); Xavánte (8 000 speakers) and Yanomámi (9 000 speakers).

Address format

Addresses are written in the format:

> Salutation
> Name
> Thoroughfare type[ ]Thoroughfare Name[,]number{[,]apartment etc. indicators}
> postal code[ ]SETTLEMENT[-]STATE CODE

For example:

> Sr.
> Manuel Paes de Carvalho
> Rua São Luis 3, 2º andar
> 12003-213 BELÉM - PA

Postal codes may also be found on the last line of an address by themselves (i.e. under the line containing the settlement name and state).

Larger cities are divided into neighbourhoods (*barrios*) which may be found in addresses.

The planned city of Brasilía has no street names. It is divided into sectors (*setores*, *SBN*), which are in turn divided into *quadras* (*Q*) and then into *blocos*. These indicators are used in addresses as, for example:

Departamento Polícia
SBN 2 - Quadra 23 - Bloco 7 - 1° andar
79800-122 BRASÍLIA - DF

The states and their abbreviations are:

State	*Abbreviation*
Acre	AC
Alagoas	AL
Amapá	AP
Amazonas	AM
Bahia	BA
Ceará	CE
Distrito Federal	DF
Espirito Santo	ES
Goiás	GO
Maranhão	MA
Mato Grosso	MT
Mato Grosso do Sul	MS
Minas Gerais	MG
Pará	PA
Paraíba	PB
Paraná	PR
Pernambuco	PE
Piauí	PI
Rio de Janeiro	RJ
Rio Grande do Norte	RN
Rio Grande do Sul	RS
Rondônia	RO
Rorâima	RR
Santa Catarina	SC
São Paulo	SP
Sergipe	SE
Tocantins	TO

For thoroughfare and other address component information, please refer to the chapter on Portugal.

Postbox

The word for postbox is *caixo postal*, abbreviated to *CP*.

Postal codes

Postal codes (*Codificacao de Enderecamento Postal*) consists of 8 digits in the format:

99999[-]999

The first digit indicates the region, the second a sub-region, the third a sector, the fourth a sub-sector, the fifth a part of a sub-sector, and the numbers after the hyphen indicate the point of delivery.

Towns

Brasilía is usually written as *Brasilia* in English; São Paulo as *Sao Paulo*.

Administrative Districts

Brazil is divided into 27 states. Their abbreviations are used in addresses. Please see the section "Address Format" above.

Brunei
Negara Brunei Darussalam

Official name: State of Brunei Darussalam, Negara Brunei Darussalam
Area: 5 765 sq. km (2 225 sq. miles)
Population: 268 000
Capital: Bandar Seri Begawan
Currency: 1 Brunei Dollar (Br$) = 100 sen
International telephone access code: 673

Languages

The official language is Malay. English is also used nationally. 14 other languages are spoken. The most widespread are: Brunei (250 000 speakers); Mandarin Chinese (15 000 speakers); Min Nan Chinese (10 000 speakers); Iban (15 000 speakers); Tutong 1 (15 000 speakers) and Tutong 2 (15 000 speakers).

Example address format

Mr P.H. Ibrahim
5 Simpang 271,
JALAN KOTA BATU
MUARA 4284

There are 8 postal districts. These are:

Bandar Seri Begawan
Bangar
Belait
Brunei-Muara
Kuala Belait
Muara
Seria
Tutong

Postal codes

Brunei postal codes consist of a block of 4 digits. The first two digits indicate the district, the last two the postman's delivery route.

Bulgaria
Bălgarija

Official name: Republic of Bulgaria, Republika Bălgarija
Area: 110 994 sq. km (42 855 sq. miles)
Population: 8 989 165
Capital: Sofiya (Sofia)
Currency: 1 Lev (Lv) = 100 stotinki. The plural of lev is leva, the singular of stotinki is stotinka.
International telephone access code: 359

Languages

Bulgarian is the official language spoken by 85% of the population. Turkish is spoken by 9% of the population and Romani by 2%. There are also 1 000 Gheg Albanian-speakers; 6 000 Crimean Turkish-speakers; 12 000 Gagauz-speakers and some Macedonian is spoken on the borders of Montenegro, Serbia and Greece.

Addresses

Addresses are written in the following format:

Recipient name
Thoroughfare[ ]number
postal code[ ]TOWN NAME

For example:

Dr Tzantcho Gantchev
Dimo Hadjidimov 6
1606 SOFIA

Postal codes

Postal codes consist of a block of 4 digits. The first digit indicates the zone, the second the area and the last two the locality.

Towns

Sofiya, the capital, is known as Sofia in English, Dutch and French, and Sofía in Spanish.

Administrative districts

Bulgaria has 9 *oblasts*:

Burgas

Lovech
Haskovo
Montana
Plovdiv
Ruse
Sofiya - City
Sofiya - Province
Varna

Burkina Faso

Official name: Republic of Burkina Faso, République de Burkina Faso
Area: 274 200 sq. km (105 870 sq. miles)
Population: 8 776 000
Capital: Ouagadougou
Currency: 1 CFA Franc (CFAFr) = 100 centimes
International telephone access code: 226

Languages

The official language is French. 70 other languages are spoken. The most widespread of these are: Malba Birifor (108 000 speakers); Bissa (400 000 speakers); Southern Bobo Madaré (150 000 speakers); Bwamu (140 000 speakers); Northern Dagara (287 000 speakers); Dogon (138 000 speakers); Fulfulde (1 038 000 speakers); Gourmanchéma (359 000 speakers); Jula (1 000 000 speakers); Kasem (100 000 speakers); Koromfé (151 000 speakers); Lobi (285 500 speakers); Lyélé (225 000 speakers); Marka (200 000 speakers); Mòoré (4 500 000 speakers); Southern Nuni (150 000 speakers) and Songai (122 700 speakers).

Example address format

M. Issa SANOU
BP 784
OUAGADOUGOU 01

Any address written in a non-native language will be written in French. Deliveries are made only to post office boxes (*Boite Postale*, or *BP*). For larger settlements, their name may be followed by a two-digit sorting-code. As in French, the surname of the person being addressed is usually written in upper case.

Postbox

This is written as *Boite Postale*, or *BP*.

Postal codes

There is no postal code system in Burkina Faso.

Burundi

Burundi is stricken with civil war. Mail distribution may consequently be affected in some areas.

Official name: Republic of Burundi, Republika y'Uburundi
Area: 27 834 sq. km (10 744 sq. miles)
Population: 5 472 000
Capital: Bujumbura
Currency: 1 Burundi Franc (BuFr, FBu) = 100 centimes
International telephone access code: 257

Languages

The national languages are French, and Rundi (spoken by some 4 600 000 speakers). Hima is also spoken by a small number of people.

Example address format

M. André Bucuri
B.P. 258
BUJUMBURA

Any address written in a non-native language will be written in French. Deliveries are made only to post office boxes (*Boite Postale*, or *BP*).

Postbox

This is written as *Boite Postale*, or *BP*.

Postal codes

Burundi has no postal code system.

Cameroon
Cameroun

Official name: Republic of Cameroon, République du Cameroun
Area: 475 439 sq. km (183 519 sq. miles)
Population: 12 700 000
Capital: Yaoundé
Currency: 1 CFA Franc (CFAFr) = 100 centimes
International telephone access code: 237

Languages

The official languages of Cameroon are English and French. There are 277 other languages spoken. The most widespread of these are: Ewondo (577 700 speakers); Fulfulde (668 700 speakers) and Cameroon Pidgin (2 000 000 speakers, mainly as a second language).

Example address format

M. Pierre Marie
BP 6000
YAOUNDE

Any address written in a non-native language will be written in French or English. Deliveries are made only to post office boxes (*Boite Postale*, or *BP* in French).

Postbox

This is written as *Boite Postale*, or *BP* in French.

Postal codes

Cameroon has no postal code system

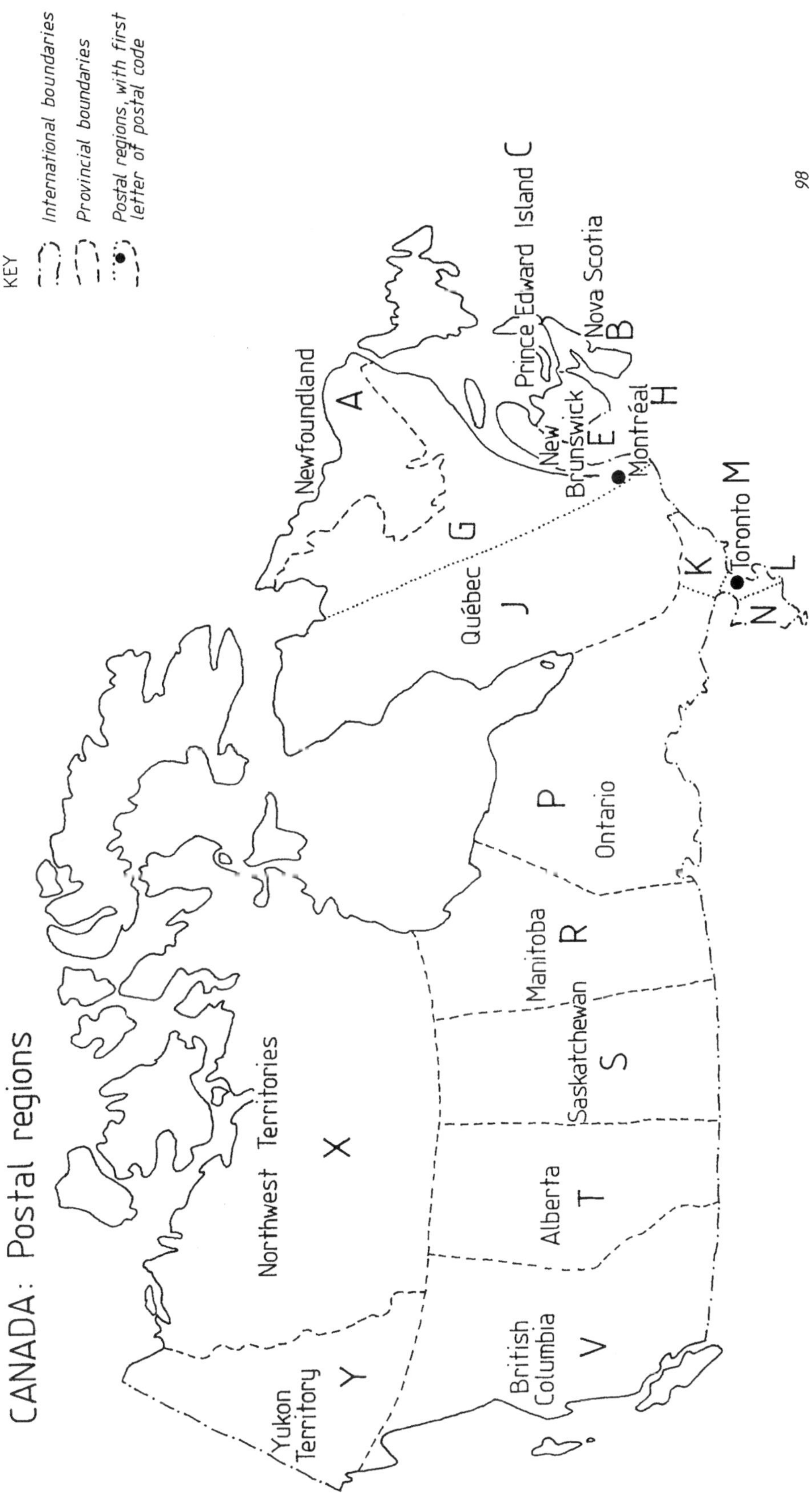
CANADA: Postal regions
KEY
International boundaries
Provincial boundaries
Postal regions, with first letter of postal code
Yukon Territory
Y
Northwest Territories
X
British Columbia
V
Alberta
T
Saskatchewan
S
Manitoba
R
Ontario
P
Québec
J
G
Newfoundland
A
New Brunswick
E
Prince Edward Island C
Nova Scotia
B
Montréal
H
K
Toronto M
L
N
98

Canada

Official name: Canada
Area: 9 970 610 sq. km (3 849 672 sq. miles)
Population: 27 296 859
Capital: Ottawa
Currency: 1 Canadian Dollar (C$, Can$) = 100 cents
International telephone access code: 1

Languages

Canada is officially bilingual English (spoken as a mother language by 14 122 770 Canadians) and French (6 200 000 mother-language speakers). Approximately 16% of Canadians are bilingual (slightly more than half of these live in Québec province). The province of Québec has been officially French-speaking only since 1977, though some 18% of the population of Québec is English-speaking (mainly living in Montréal, the Ottawa Valley and the Eastern Townships near the Ontario border). In Québec, legislation demands that all advertising material be sent in French unless your contact has made a written request to receive it in English. The province of New Brunswick is bilingual. The other provinces and territories are mainly English-speaking but officially bilingual. There are, however, significant minorities speaking English in Québec and French in the other provinces. These speakers are accorded the same rights regardless of where in Canada they live.

There are some 23 000 French speakers in Alberta, 20 000 in British Colombia, 27 000 in Manitoba, 230 000 in New Brunswick, 2 000 in Newfoundland, 1 000 in Northwest Territories, 23 000 in Nova Scotia, 340 000 in Ontario, 4 000 in Prince Edward Island, 6 000 000 in Québec, 10 000 in Saskatchewan and 500 in Yukon.

Québecois differs from Metropolitan French and this needs to be taken into account in mailings. Canadian English differs in its colloquialisms and spelling from both US English and British English.

There are at least 60 first-nation (Indian, Métis and Inuit) languages spoken by about 182 000 people in Canada. Many of these are spoken by few people and in some cases are threatened with extinction as they are not spoken by younger natives of these tribes. Addresses are unlikely to be encountered in these languages. The most widely spoken of these languages are Western Cree (35 000 speakers in North Central Manitoba, Saskatchewan and Alberta); Eastern Canadian Inuktitut (14 000 speakers west of Hudson Bay, and east through Baffin Island, Québec and Labrador); and Western Ojibwa (35 000 speakers from Lake Superior westwards and north-westward into Saskatchewan)

Contact Names

Since 1980, married women in Québec have been required to retain their maiden name. Those women married before 1980 have been allowed to choose between their husband's name and their maiden name. Children may take the surname of either their mother or their father, or a hyphenated version of both. This has obvious implications for database management and deduplication.

Company names

For French company names, it is more correct, where the *nature* of a company is mentioned in its name, that this *precedes* the name of the company, thus:

Boulangerie Dupont

You will often, however, also find these activity indications *after* the company name, thus:

Dupont, Boulangerie
Dupont (Boulangerie)

Addresses

The Canadian Post Office prefers that addresses are formatted to contain:

- Only upper case
- No punctuation
- Standard abbreviations

The format is:

RECIPIENTS NAME AND/OR TITLE
DEPARTMENT/BUILDING NAME
COMPANY NAME
NUMBER[ ]THOROUGHFARE
SETTLEMENT[ ]PROVINCE CODE[ ]POSTAL CODE

For example:

Mr J. Smith
14 Greenman Drive Apt. 103
KINGSTON ON K7M 7T5

should be written

MR J SMITH
14 GREENMAN DR APT 103
KINGSTON ON K7M 7T5

Unit or apartment number follows the street type. If more space is required, this information can be moved to a line above.

The postal code is placed on the same address line as the settlement and province, and is separated from the province by two spaces. If the total length of this line is greater than 40, the Canadian Post Office prefers that the postal code is moved (left-justified) to the line beneath.

The province codes to be used in addresses are:

Province/Territory	*Code*
Alberta	AB
British Columbia	BC
Manitoba	MB
New Brunswick	NB
Newfoundland	NF
Northwest Territories	NT
Nova Scotia	NS
Ontario	ON
Prince Edward Island	PE
Québec	QC
Saskatchewan	SK
Yukon Territory	YT

On 1 April 1999, Northwest Territories will be split. A new territory, Nunavut, occupied mainly by Inuit, will be created from the Eastern half.

Addresses may be written in French or English regardless of the majority language of the area concerned.

Street address

In the French language addresses, the thoroughfare type part of the street address is prefixed, with spaces between the words. For example:

rue Montfort 8
rue d'Alberta 98
avenue de la Gare 4

In the French language regions, thoroughfare types should correctly begin with a lower case letter. Prepositions like 'de la' should also be written without a capital letter.

Thoroughfare types

The Canadian Post Office prefers that thoroughfare types are written as standard abbreviations. This is required to profit from discounted mail rates but will reduce the quality of the address layout in the eyes of the recipient. The official abbreviations ("symbols") are:

Thoroughfare Type	*Required Abbreviation*
ABBEY	ABBEY
ACRES	ACRES

ALLÉE	ALLÉE
ALLEY	ALLEY
AUTOROUTE	AUT
AVENUE (English)	AVE
AVENUE (French)	AV
BAY	BAT
BEACH	BEACH
BEND	BEND
BOULEVARD (English)	BLVD
BOULEVARD (French)	BOUL
BY-PASS	BYPASS
BYWAY	BYWAY
CAMPUS	CAMPUS
CAPE	CAPE
CARRÉ	CAR
CARREFOUR	CARREF
CENTRE (English)	CTR
CENTRE (French)	C
CERCLE	CERCLE
CHASE	CHASE
CHEMIN	CH
CIRCLE	CIR
CIRCUIT	CIRCT
CLOSE	CLOSE
COMMON	COMMON
CONCESSION	CONC
CORNERS	CRNRS
CÔTE	CÔTE
COUR	COUR
COURT	CRT
COVE	COVE
CRESCENT	CRES
CROISSANT	CROIS
CROSSING	CROSS
CUL-DE-SAC	CDS
DALE	DALE
DELL	DELL

DIVERSION	DIVERS
DRIVE	DR
ÉCHANGEUR	ÉCH
END	END
ESPLANADE	ESPL
ESTATES	ESTATE
EXPRESSWAY	EXPY
EXTENSION	EXTEN
FARM	FARM
FIELD	FIELD
FOREST	FOREST
FREEWAY	FWY
FRONT	FRONT
GARDENS	GDNS
GATE	GATE
GLADE	GLADE
GLEN	GLEN
GREEN	GREEN
GROUNDS	GRNDS
GROVE	GROVE
HARBOUR	HARBR
HEIGHTS	HTS
HIGHLANDS	HGHLDS
HIGHWAY	HWY
HILL	HILL
HOLLOW	HOLLOW
ÎLE	ÎLE
IMPASSE	IMP
ISLAND	ISLAND
KEY	KEY
KNOLL	KNOLL
LANDING	LANDNG
LANE	LN
LIMITS	LMTS
LINE	LINE
LINK	LINK
LOOKOUT	LKOUT

LOOP	LOOP
MALL	MALL
MANOR	MANOR
MAZE	MAZE
MEADOW	MEADOW
MEWS	MEWS
MONTÉE	MONTÉE
MOOR	MOOR
MOUNT	MOUNT
MOUNTAIN	MTN
ORCHARD	ORCH
PARADE	PARADE
PARC	PARC
PARK	PK
PARKWAY	PKY
PASSAGE	PASS
PATH	PATH
PATHWAY	PTWAY
PINES	PINES
PLACE (English)	PL
PLACE (French)	PLACE
PLATEAU	PLAT
PLAZA	PLAZA
POINT	PT
PORT	PORT
PRIVATE	PVT
PROMENADE	PROM
QUAY	QUAY
RANG	RANG
RANGE	RG
RIDGE	RIDGE
RISE	RISE
ROAD	RD
ROND POINT	RDPT
ROUTE	RTE
ROW	ROW
RUE	RUE

RUELLE	RLE
RUN	RUN
SENTIER	SENT
SQUARE	SQ
STREET	ST
SUBDIVISION	SUBDIV
TERRACE	TERR
TERASSE	TSSE
THICKET	THICK
TOWERS	TOWERS
TOWNLINE	TLINE
TRAIL	TRAIL
TURNABOUT	TRNABT
VALE	VALE
VIA	VIA
VIEW	VIEW
VILLAGE	VILLGE
VISTA	VISTA
VOIE	VOIE
WALK	WALK
WAY	WAY
WHARF	WHARF
WOOD	WOOD
WYND	WYND

Other nouns, adjectives and prepositions commonly found in address databases

NB: The following abbreviations are used: (m) = masculine form; (f) = feminine form; (pl) = plural form. Except where specified, the French plural form of adjectives is the correctly gendered singular form followed by an 's'.

French	*English*
le (m)/la (f)/les (pl) (NB: le and la are written l' before a vowel or an unaspirated h)	the
un (m)/une (f)	a, an
et	and
à/au (m)/à la (f)/aux (pl)	till, until, up to, to
pour	for
de (before a proper noun)/du (m)/de la, de l' (f)/des (pl)	of, from

à	at
près de	by, near to
sur	on (a river, the sea)
dans	in
en face de	opposite
à côté de	next to
derrière	behind
devant	in front
entre	between
avec	with
sous	under
lès (occurs *only* in place names)	near
nouveau (m)/nouvelle (f)/nouveaux (m.pl.)/nouvelles (f.pl.)/nouvel (m, before a vowel or unaspirated h)	new
vieux (m, pl)/vieille (f)/vielles(f.pl.)/vieil (m, before (f.pl.)/vieil (m, before a vowel or an unaspirated h)	old
court (m) (Ct.)/courte (f) (Cte.)	short
long (m) (Lg.)/longue (f) (Lgue.)	long
grand (m) (Gr./Grd.)/grande (f) (Gr./Grde.)	large
petit (m) (P./Pt.)/petite (f) (P./Pte.)	small
nord	north
est	east
sud	south
ouest	west
saint (m) (St.)/sainte (f) (Ste.)	saint

Postbox

This is written as *Boite Postale* (*BP*) in French.

Postal codes

Canada has around 700 000 postal codes, one for every 40 people. Postal codes in Canada are formed as follows:

A9A[ ]9A9

Each character must be printed in capital letters.

The part of the postal code before the space is called the "Forward Sortation Area". The part after the space is called the "Local Delivery Unit".

The first character of the code represents the province or part of province (Ontario and Québec only) covered by the code:

First Letter	*Area Covered*
A	Newfoundland
B	Nova Scotia
C	Prince Edward Island
E	New Brunswick
G	Eastern Quebec
H	Metropolitan Montréal
J	Western Ontario
K	Eastern Ontario
L	Central Ontario
M	Metropolitan Toronto
N	South-western Ontario
P	Northern Ontario
R	Manitoba
S	Saskatchewan
T	Alberta
V	British Columbia
X	Northwest Territories
Y	Yukon Territory

The first digit of the postal code cannot therefore be D, F, I, O, Q, U, W or Z.

The letters W and Z are not used at all in the Forward Sortation Area (first part of code). The letters D, F, I, O, Q and U are not used in any part of the postal code.

A digit between 1 and 9 in the second position indicated an urban postal code, serviced by letter carriers or community mail boxes. A "0" indicates a rural postal code serviced by rural route drivers and/or postal outlets.

The third character describes the exact area covered of a city, town or other geographical area.

In urban areas, the Local Delivery Unit may indicate a single street side, a single building or a large-user. In rural areas, these three digits identify a specific settlement.

Towns

Use the correct language form for the person being addressed, especially in Québec province. For French language names, respect diacritic marks - use Montréal rather than Montreal, Québec rather than Quebec and so on.

In the Northwest Territories and Northern Québec, a number of towns have both English/French names and an Inuit name. In some cases, the official name has reverted to the Inuit name, and this trend is set to accelerate when Nunavet is created in 1st April 1999. In the table below, where the Inuit name is the official one, it has been marked with an asterisk (*):

French/English	*Inuit*
Arctic Bay	Tununirusiq
Bellin / Payne	* Kingirsuk
Cambridge Bay	* Ikaluktutiak
Cape Dorset	Kinngait
Chesterfield Inlet	* Igluligaarjuk
Coppermine	* Kugluktuk
Coral Harbour	* Salliq
Eskimo Point	* Arviat
Fort-Chimo	* Kuujjuaq
Frobisher Bay	* Iqaluit
George River	* Kangiqsualujjuaq
Gjoa Haven	Oqsuqtooq
Hall Beach	* Sanirajak
Igloolik	Iglulik
Inoucdjouac	* Inukjuak
Koartak / Koartac	* Quaqtaq
Lake Harbour	* Kimmirut
Loks Land	Takuligjuaq
Maricourt / Wakeham	* Kangiqsujuaq
Notre-Dame-d'Ivugivic	* Ivujuvik
Notre-Dame-de-Koartac	* Quaqtaq
Pelly Bay	Aqvilikjuaq
Port Brabant	* Tuktoyaktuk
Port Burwell	* Killiniq
Port Harrison	* Inukjuak
Port-Nouveau-Québec	* Kangiqsualujjuaq
Poste-de-la-Baleine	* Kuujjuaraapik
Resolute	* Qausuittuq
Saglouc / Sugluk	* Salluit
Spence Bay	* Taloyoak / Taluqjuak / Taluqjuaq

Administrative districts

Canada consists of 10 provinces and 2 territories. These are:

Alberta
British Columbia
Manitoba
New Brunswick
Newfoundland
Northwest Territories (territory)
Nova Scotia
Ontario
Prince Edward Island
Québec
Saskatchewan

Yukon (territory)

On 1st April 1999, Northwest Territories will be split. A new territory, Nunavut, occupied mainly by Inuit, will be created from the Eastern half.

Cape Verde
Cabo Verde

Official name: Republic of Cape Verde, República de Cabo Verde
Area: 4 033 sq. km (1 557 sq. miles)
Population: 386 000
Capital: Praia
Currency: 1 Escudo (CVEsc) = 100 centavos
International telephone access code: 238

Languages

The official language is Portuguese. There are 300 000 speakers of Upper Guinea Crioulo. Balanta and Mandyak are also spoken.

Example address format

Sr. João Cabral
Rua Serpa Pinto 33
PRAIA

Addresses will often be written in Portuguese. They follow the Portuguese structure - thoroughfare types are written first and with a capital first letter, the house number is at the end of the street address string often followed by an indication of floor, stairwell etc. For a full description of thoroughfare types and other address components, please refer to the chapter on Portugal.

Postal codes

There is no postal code system in Cape Verde.

Central African Republic
République Centrafricaine

Official name: Central African Republic, République Centrafricaine
Area: 622 984 sq. km (240 535 sq. miles)
Population: 3 039 000
Capital: Bangui
Currency: 1 CFA Franc (CFAFr) = 100 centimes
International telephone access code: 236

Languages

The official language is French (9 000 speakers). 67 other languages are spoken. The most widespread are: Banda-Bambari (183 000 speakers); Banda-Banda (102 000 speakers); Mid-Southern Banda (100 000 speakers); South Central Banda (150 000 speakers); Bokoto (130 000 speakers); Kano-Katsina-Bororo Fulfulde (156 000 speakers); Gbaya-Bossangoa (176 000 speakers); Northwest Gbaya (200 000 speakers); Southwest Gbaya (164 000 speakers); Manza (220 000 speakers); Sango (350 000 speakers) and Yakoma (100 000 speakers).

Example address format

M. Antoine Olonga
BP 352
BANGUI

Any address written in a non-native language will be written in French. Deliveries are made only to post office boxes (*Boite Postale*, or *BP*).

Postbox

This is written as *Boite Postale*, or *BP*.

Postal codes

The Central African Republic has no postal code system.

Chad
Tchad

Official name: Republic of Chad, République du Tchad
Area: 1 284 640 sq. km (495 871 sq. miles)
Population: 5 678 000
Capital: N'Djamena
Currency: 1 CFA Franc (CFAFr) = 100 centimes
International telephone access code: 235

Languages

The official languages are French (3 000 speakers) and Standard Arabic. 125 other languages are spoken. The most widespread of these are: Chadian Spoken Arabic (754 590 speakers); Bilala (136 629 speakers); Daza (282 281 speakers); Gulay (163 271 speakers); Yerwa Kanuri (100 000 speakers); Maba (120 000 speakers); Marba (124 357 speakers); Masana (109 093 speakers); Mundang (160 000 speakers); Musey (100 000 speakers) and Sar (183 471 speakers).

Example address format

M. Mbaigoto Laougossou
BP 238
SARH

Any address written in a non-native language will be written in French. Deliveries are made only to post office boxes (*Boite Postale*, or *BP*).

Postbox

This is written as *Boite Postale*, or *BP*.

Postal codes

Chad has no postal code system.

Towns

Ndjamena is also known as *Fort Lamy* in English and German.

Chile

Official name: Republic of Chile, República de Chile
Area: 756 626 sq. km (292 058 sq. miles)
Population: 13 600 000
Capital: Santiago
Currency: 1 Chilean Peso (Ch$) = 100 centavos
International telephone access code: 56

Languages

The official language is Spanish. Other languages are: Central Aymara (899 speakers); Huilliche (3 000 speakers); Kawesqar (10 speakers); Mapudungin (400 000 speakers); Rapa Nui (2 200 on Easter Island, 300 in mainland Chile) and Yámana (4 speakers).

Address Format

Addresses are written in the following format:

> Recipient name
> {thoroughfare type[]}Thoroughfare name[,]house number{[,]floor etc. indicators}
> SETTLEMENT{[ ]sorting code}

For example:

> Sra Ana Jimenez
> calle Iquique, 34, 2º piso
> SANTIAGO 1

When addresses are written in Spanish, calle, the Spanish word for street, is rarely written. The Spanish thoroughfare type, when included, is written before, and separately from, thc thoroughfarc name. It should be written with the first letter in lower case. For further information about address components, please refer to the chapter on Spain.

A single-digit sorting code may be found in Santiago addresses.

Postbox

The word for postbox is *Casilla Postal*, sometimes abbreviated to *Casilla* or *CP*.

Postal codes

Chile currently has no postal code system

China (People's Republic of)
Zhongguo

Official name: People's Republic of China, Zhonghua Renmin Gongheguo
Area: 9 597 000 sq. km (3 704 000 sq. miles)
Population: 1 133 682 501
Capital: Beijing (Peking)
Currency: 1 Renminbi Yuan (RMBY, \$, Y) = 10 jiao = 100 fen
International telephone access code: 86

Languages

The official language is Mandarin Chinese (836 000 000 speakers). China has 205 languages. 55 official minority nationalities are recognized. The most widespread of these languages are: Bouyei (2 000 000 speakers); Gan Chinese (20 580 000 speakers, no written form); Hakka Chinese (25 725 000 speakers); Jinyu Chinese (45 000 000, no written form); Min Bei Chinese (10 290 000 speakers), Min Nan Chinese (25 725 000 speakers); Wu Chinese (77 175 000 speakers); Xiang Chinese (36 015 000, no written form); Yue Chinese (Cantonese, 46 305 000 speakers); Peripheral Mongolian (2 713 000 speakers); Uyghur (7 214 431 speakers) and Southern Zhuang (4 000 000 speakers).

English is still widely spoken in Hong Kong Special Administrative Region, though its importance is already decreasing.

Example address format

95 Yong An Road
Beijing Friendship Hospital
100050 BEIJING

Postal codes

Postal codes consist of a block of 6 digits. The first two digits indicate the province, the third the postal area, the fourth the city and county and the final two the delivery region.

Colombia

There is a continuing civil war in Colombia. Mail deliveries may consequently be affected.

Official name: Republic of Colombia, República de Colombia
Area: 1 140 105 sq. km (440 080 sq. miles)
Population: 33 392 000
Capital: Bogotá
Currency: 1 Colombian Peso (Col$) = 100 centavos
International telephone access code: 57

Languages

The official language is Spanish. 78 other, mainly Indian, languages are spoken. The most widespread of these are: Cuaiquer (20 000 speakers); Cubeo (6 000 speakers); Embera-Baudó (5 000 speakers); Emberá-Catío (15 000 speakers); Emberá-Chamí (11 000 speakers); Northern Embará (15 000 speakers); Guahibo (15 000 speakers); Guambiano (9 000 speakers); Ica (5 272 speakers); Inga (10 000 speakers); Jungle Inga (5 000 speakers); Kogui (5 000 speakers); Páez (68 467 speakers); Wayuu (150 000 speakers) and Western Caribbean Creole English (15 000 speakers).

Address Format

Addresses are written in the following format:

Salutation
Recipient name
{thoroughfare type[]}Thoroughfare name[,]house number{[,]floor etc. indicators}
SETTLEMENT{[,]PROVINCE[ ]sorting code}

For example:

Sra
Ana Jimenez
calle Maria, 42, 1º piso
MEDALLÍN, ANT 1

When addresses are written in Spanish, calle, the Spanish word for street, is rarely written. The Spanish thoroughfare type, when included, is written before, and separately from, the thoroughfare name. It should be written with the first letter in lower case.

For further information about address components, please refer to the chapter on Spain.

A single-digit sorting code may be found in addresses in the larger cities.

The province name may be included for addresses for smaller settlements. The provinces, with standard abbreviation, are:

Province	*Abbreviation (if different)*
Amazonas	
Antioquia	ANT
Arauca	
Atlántico	ATL
Bolívar	BOL
Boyaca	BOY
Caldas	CAL
Caquetá	CAQ
Casanare	
Cauca	
César	
Chocó	
Córdoba	CORD
Cundinamarca	CUND
Distrito Especial	DE
Guainía	
Huila	HUIL
La Guajira	GUIJARA
Magdalena	MAG
Meta	
Nariño	NAR
Norte de Santander	NS
Putumayo	
Quindio	QUIND
Risaralda	RIS
San Andrés y Providencia	SAN ANDRES
Santander	SANT
Sucre	
Tolima	TOL
Valle del Cauca	VALLE
Vaupés	
Vichada	

Postbox

The word for postbox is *Apoartado Aéro* or *AA*.

Postal codes

Colombia currently has no postal code system.

Towns

Bogotá and Medallín are usually written without the accents in English.

Administrative Regions

One of the 32 region names may be found in addresses. Please see the section 'Address Format'.

Comoros
Comores

The Comoros are an archipelago consisting of the three islands of Njazidja (Grand Comore), Nzwani (Anjouan) and Mwali (Mohéli). The fourth island in the archipelago, Mayotte, elected to remain part of France when the Comoros became independent from that country in 1975.

At the time of going to press, both Nzwany and Mwali have declared unilateral independence from Comoros with the aim of re-uniting with France. Some fighting has ensued. Mail deliveries may consequently be affected.

Official name: Federal Islamic Republic of the Comoros, Jumhuriyet al-Qumur al-Itthadiyah al-Islamiyah.
Area: 1 862 sq. km (719 sq. miles)
Population: 503 000
Capital: Moroni
Currency: 1 Comorian Franc (CFr) = 100 centimes
International telephone access code: 269

Languages

The official languages are Arabic and French (1 700 speakers). 97% of the population speak Comorian. There are some speakers of Shigazidja Comorian on Njazidja, and 700 people speak Malagasy.

Example address format

M. Mohamed Ahmed
BP 350
MORONI

Any address written in a non-native language will be written in French. Deliveries are made only to post office boxes (*Boite Postale*, or *BP*).

Postbox

This is written as *Boite Postale*, or *BP*.

Postal codes

Comoros has no postal code system.

Congo (People's Republic of - Brazzaville)

Official name: People's Republic of the Congo, République Populaire du Congo
Area: 341 945 sq. km (132 000 sq. miles)
Population: 2 271 000
Capital: Brazzaville
Currency: 1 CFA Franc (CFAFr) = 100 centimes
International telephone access code: 242

Languages

The official language is French (28 000 speakers). 59 other languages are spoken. The most widespread of these are: Kongo (836 000 speakers); Lingala (300 000 speakers) and Munukutuba (1 156 800 speakers).

Example address format

M. Joseph Mbemba
12, rue Kakamoueka
IMPFONDO

Any address written in a non-native language will be written in French. The house number precedes the thoroughfare, and the thoroughfare type commences with a lower-case letter. For more information on thoroughfare types and other address components, please see the chapter on France.

Postbox

This is written as *Boite Postale*, or *BP*.

Postal codes

Congo has no postal code system.

Congo (Democratic Republic of - Kinshasa)

Democratic Republic of Congo is the new (1997) name for Zaire.

Official name: Democratic Republic of Congo
Area: 2 234 585 sq. km (905 365 sq. miles)
Population: 37 900 000
Capital: Kinshasa
Currency: 1 Zaire (Z) = 100 makuta (singular likuta) (It is likely that the name of the currency will soon change)
International telephone access code: 243

Languages

221 languages are spoken in the Democratic Republic of Congo, with a complex geographical pattern. The official language is French. Widespread languages include: Alur (500 000 speakers); Bangala (3 500 000 second-language speakers); Kituba (4 200 000 speakers); Kongo (1 000 000 speakers); Lendu (750 000 speakers); Lingala (8 400 000 speakers); Luba-Kasai (6 300 000 speakers); Luba-Shaba (1 505 000 speakers); Nandi (903 000 speakers); Ngbaka (750 000 speakers); Shi (654 000 speakers); Songe (1 000 000 speakers); Zaire Swahili (9 100 000 second-language speakers); Tetela (750 000 speakers) and Zande (730 000 speakers).

Example address format

M. Pasteur Mashala Kashama Kashale
B.P. 7948
KINSHASA 1

Addresses are likely to be written in French Deliveries are to postboxes.

Postbox

This is written as *Boite Postale*, or *BP*.

Postal codes

Democratic Republic of Congo has no postal code system.

Costa Rica

Official name: Republic of Costa Rica, República de Costa Rica
Area: 51 022 sq. km (19 694 sq. miles)
Population: 3 160 000
Capital: San José
Currency: 1 Costa Rican Colón (CR¢) = 100 céntimos
International telephone access code: 506

Languages

The official language is Spanish. Other languages spoken are: Boruca (5 speakers); Bribri (6 000 speakers); Cabécar (3 000 speakers); Yue Chinese (4 500 speakers); Maléku Jaíka (365 speakers); Platdietsch (100 speakers); Teribe (5 speakers) and Western Caribbean Creole English (55 100 speakers).

Address Format

Addresses are written in the following format:

> Recipient name
> {thoroughfare type[]}Thoroughfare name[,]house number{[,]floor etc. indicators}
> postal code[ ]SETTLEMENT

For example:

> Sra Ana Jimenez
> calle Limón, 17, 3° piso
> 1001 San José

The postal code is sometimes written to the right of the settlement name.

When addresses are written in Spanish, calle, the Spanish word for street, is rarely written. The Spanish thoroughfare type, when included, is written before, and separately from, the thoroughfare name. It should be written with the first letter in lower case.

For other address element information, please refer to the chapter on Spain.

Postbox

The word for postbox is *Case Postale*, abbreviated to *CP*.

Postal codes

The postal codes consist of a block of 4 digits. The first digit indicates the postal region, the middle two digits the delivery centre and the final digit the post office.

Croatia
Hrvatska

Croatia retook control of the previously rebel-held territory of Slovonia on 15th January 1998. The mail delivery problems that were being experienced in this area should now be resolved.

Official name: Republic of Croatia, Republika Hrvatska
Area: 56 540 sq. km (21 825 sq. miles)
Population: 4 600 000
Capital: Zagreb
Currency: Kuna (HRK)
International telephone access code: 385

Languages

Language use is heavily nationalistically influenced. Most of the population speak the official language, Croatian, or, still in some areas, Serbian. There are 1 000 speakers of Istriot on the Western coast of the Istrian Peninsula, in the towns of Rovinj and Vodnjan; 297 000 Italian-speakers; 1 000 Istro-Romanian speakers in the Northeast Istrian Peninsula in Žejane and a few villages to the south; and some 100 000 speakers of Venetian.

Address Format

Addresses are formatted in this way:

Name
thoroughfare name [ ]number
postal code[ ]SETTLEMENT

For example:

Ben Kovac
Jurilja 87
10 000 ZAGREB

Postal codes

The postal codes consist of 5 digits in the format:

99[ ]999

A new postal code system has been devised - up until recently the code used was that from the former Yugoslavia. The code can commence with a number between 1 and 5.

The first two digits indicate the district, the third indicates the zone and the last two the post office. A code ending '000' is for the district capital. A code ending '00' or '0' is for a large town. A code ending '010' or '090' is for a town with more than two delivery offices. A code ending '001' refers to a postbox.

The districts are as follows:

10	Zagreb/Zagrebacka
20	Dubrovacko-Neretvanska
21	Splitsko-Dalmatinska
22	Sibenska
23	Zadarsko-Kninski
31	Osjecko-Baranjska
32	Vukovarsko-Srijemska
33	Viroviticko-Podravska
34	Pozesko-Slavonska
35	Brodsko-Posavska
40	Medimurska
42	Varazdinska
43	Bjelovarsko-Bilogorska
44	Sisacko-Moslavacka
47	Karlovacka
48	Koprivnicko-Krizevacka
49	Krapinsko-Zagorska
51	Primorsko-Goranska
52	Istarska
53	Licko-Senjska

Towns

The following list gives other-language equivalents of Croatian place-names:

Croatian	*German*	*Italian*	*Istro-Romanian*
Baboći		Babici	
Bašanija		Bassania	
Brdo		Collalto	
Brtonigla		Verteneglio	
Buje		Buie	
Bužinija		Buzinia	
Čepić		Cepici	
Dajla		Daila	
Dubrovnik		Ragusa	
Gamboči		Gambozzi	
Grožnjan		Grisignano	
Jasenovik			Sucodru
Juricani		Giurizzani	
Kaldanija		Caldania	
Karlobag		Carlopago	

Karlovac	Karlstadt		
Karšete		Carsette	
Kastel		Castelvenere	
Kraljevica		Buccari	
Kućibreg		Cucibrech	
Lovrečica		San Lorenzo	
Lucija		Santa Lucia	
Marija na Krasu		Madonna di Carso	
Marušići		Marusici	
Merišće		Merischie	
Momjan		Momiano	
Murine		Morno	
Nova Vas		Villa Nova	Noselo
Novigrad		Cittanova	
Opatija	Abbazia	Abbazia	
Oprtalj		Portole	
Pelegrin		San Pelegrino	
Petrovija		Petrovia	
Poreč		Parenzo	
Pula		Pola	
Rijeka	Fiume	Fiume	
Rovinj		Rovigno	
Rovinjsko Selo		Villa di Rovigno	
Savudrija		Salvore	
Senj		Segna	
Šibenik		Sebenico	
Split		Spalato	
Šterna			
Triban		Tribano	
Umag		Umago	
Valica		Valizza	
Vilanija		Villania	
Vodnjan		Dignano	
Zadar		Zara	
Zagreb	Agram	Zagabria	
Zambratija		Zambrattia	
Žminj		Gimino	

Cuba

Official name: Republic of Cuba, República de Cuba
Area: 110 860 sq. km (42 792 sq. miles)
Population: 10 603 000
Capital: La Habana (Havana)
Currency: 1 Cuban Peso (Cub$) = 100 centavos
International telephone access code: 53

Language

The official language, spoken by all native Cubans, is Spanish.

Example address format

Sr. Héctor Garcia Marizá
Ponce 8818 entre San Antonio y Mireles
CP 11900 CIUDAD DE LA HABANA

Calle, the Spanish word for street, is rarely written. The Spanish thoroughfare type, when included, is written before, and separately from, the thoroughfare name. It should be written with the first letter in lower case.

The postal code is preceded by the letters CP. The settlement name is written in upper case.

For further address-component information, please refer to the chapter on Spain.

Postal codes

Postal codes consist of a block of 5 digits.

Towns

La Habana is known as *Havana* in English and *La Havane* in French.

Cyprus
Kypros (Greek); Kibris (Turkish)

Cyprus has since the summer of 1974 been militarily divided between the Turkish and Greek Cypriot communities.

Official name: Republic of Cyprus, Kypriaki Dimokratia, Kibris Cumhuriyeti
Area: 9 251 sq. km (3 572 sq. miles)
Population: 695 000 (1989 estimate for the whole island)
Capital: Lavkosia (Nicosia)
Currency: 1 Cyprus pound = 100 cents
International telephone access code: 357 (please refer to section "Telephone Numbers", below)

Languages

Greek is spoken by 73 per cent of the population, Turkish by 23 per cent. There are small minorities speaking Cypriot Spoken Arabic and Armenian. English is common. The Greek Cypriot dialect is different from that spoken in Greece itself.

Address Format

Addresses in Cyprus are written in the following format:

Name
Title
Company
house number[,]Thoroughfare name
postal code[ ]SETTLEMENT

For Example:

Stavros Stavropoulos
98, Alkamenou
8034 PAPHOS

Addresses written in Latin script are often written in English.

For certain large users a street address is not necessary - a name, code and town name suffice:

Department of Postal Services
1900 NICOSIA

As the district name is now included in the postal code, writing it in the address is no longer necessary.

Postal codes

Postal codes (for both areas) are formed by a block of 4 digits starting with a number between 1 and 9. The first digit of the code indicates the district as follows:

Lefkosia (Nicosia)	1, 2
Lemesos (Limassol)	3, 4
Ammoschostos (Famagusta)	5
Larnaca	6, 7
Pafos (Paphos)	8
Kyreneia	9

Post Offices containing postboxes have their own codes and these codes should be used for the relevant postboxes.

Towns

Note that alternative spellings, translated from Greek script, are being introduced locally. So, for example, *Ayios* will become *Agios*, *Paphos* will become *Pafos*, and *Yeorysios* will become *Georgios*.

The following list gives foreign language equivalents of Cypriot town names. Those settlements whose names are preceded by an asterisk (*) are in the Turkish Cypriot-controlled section of the country. Where more than one Turkish name exists next to a Greek name, the names refer to different settlements with the same Greek name:

Greek	*Turkish*	*English*	*German*
Aghirda	* Ağirdağ		
Agridhaki	* Alemdağ		
Akanthou	* Tatlisu		
Akhyritou	* Güvercinlik		
Aloa	* Athlılar		
Ambelikou	* Bağlıköy		
Ammoschostos	* Gazimağusa	Famagusta	
Angastina	* Aslanköy		
Angolemi	* Taşpinar		
Ardhana	* Ardahan		
Argaki	* Akçay		
Arnadhi	* Kuzucuk		
Arsos	* Yiğitler		
Artemi	* Arıdami		
Asha	* Pasaköy		
Asomatos	* Özhan		

Athna	* Düzce		
Avgalidha	* Kurtuluş		
Avlona	* Gayretköv		
Ayia	* Dilekkaya		
Ayia Marina	* Gürpınar		
Ayia Trias	* Sipani		
Ayios Amvrosios	* Esentepe		
Ayios Andronikos	* Topçuköy * Yeşilköy		
Ayios Epiktitos	* Catalköy		
Ayios Ermolaos	* Şirinevler		
Ayios Evstathios	* Zeybekköy		
Ayios Iakovos	* Altınova		
Ayios Khariton	* Ergenekon		
Ayios Nikolaos	* Yamacköy		
Ayios Seryios	* Yeniboğazici		
Ayios Symeon	* Avtepe		
Ayios Theodhoros	* Cayırova		
Ayios Vasilios	* Türkeli		
Ayios Yeoryios	* Karaoğlanoğlu * Aygün		
Bellapais	* Beylerbeyri		
Bey Keuy	* Beyköy		
Boghaz	* Boğaz		
Chatos	* Serdalı		
Dhavlos	* Kaplıca		
Dhiorios	* Tepebaşı		
Elea	* Doğancı		
Ephtakomi	* Yedikonuk		
Epikho	* Cihangir		
Exometokhi	* Düzova		
Gaidhouras	* Korkuteli		
Galatia	* Mehmetcik		
Galinporni	* Kaleburnu		
Gastria	* Kalecik		
Geunyeli	* Gönyeli		
Ghaziveran	* Gaziveran		

Goupes	* Çamlıca		
Gypsos	* Akova		
Kalogrea	* Baçeli		
Kalokhorio	* Çamlıköy * Kalkanlı		
Kalopsidha	* Çayönü		
Kalyvakia	* Kalavaç		
Kanli	* Kanlıköy		
Kambyli	* Hisarköy		
Karakoumi	* Karakum		
Karavas	* Alsancak		
Karavostasi	* Gemikonaği		
Karmi	* Karaman		
Karpasha	* Karpaşa		
Kato Dhikomo	* Aş. Dikmen		
Kato Kopia	* Zümrütköy		
Kato Zodhia	* Aş. Bosranci		
Kharcha	* Karaağac		
Kilanemos	* Esenköy		
Klepini	* Arapköy		
Knodhara	* Gönendere		
Kokkina	* Erenköy		
Koma tou Yialou	* Kumyalı		
Komi Kebir	* Büyükkonuk		
Kondea	* Türkmenköy		
Kondemenos	* Kılıçaslan		
Kormakiti	* Koruçam		
Kornokipos	* Görneç		
Korovia	* Kuruova		
Kourou Monastir	* Çukurova		
Koutsovendis	* Güngör		
Kridhia	* Kilitkaya		
Kyrenia	* Girne		
Kythrea	* Degirmenlik		
Jrini	* Pınarbaşi		
Kouklia	* Köprülü		
Kyra	* Mevlevi		

Lapathos	* Boğaziçi		
Lapithos	* Lapta		
Larnaca			Larnaka
Larnaka	* Kozan		
Lefka	* Lefke		
Lefkosia		Nicosia	Nikosia
Lefkoniko	* Geçitkale		
Lemesos		Limmasol	
Leonarisso	* Ziyamet		
Limnia	* Mormenekse		
Limnitis	* Yesilırmak		
Livadhia	* Sazlıköy		
Louroujina	* Akıncılar		
Loutros	* Bademliköy		
Lysi	* Akdoğan		
Lythrangomi	* Boltaşlı		
Makrasyka	* Incirli		
Mandres	* Hamitköy * Ağillar		
Marathovouno	* Ulukışla		
Masara	* Şahinlar		
Melounda	* Mallıdag		
Melousha	* Kırıkkale		
Mia Milea	* Haspolat		
Milea	* Yıldırım		
Monarga	* Boğaztepe		
Mora	* Meriç		
Morphou	* Güzelyurt		
Mousoulita	* Kurudere		
Myrtou	* Çamlıbel		
Neokhorio	* Minareliköy		
Neta	* Taşlica		
Nikitas	* Güneşköy		
Orga	* Kayalar		
Orta Keuy	* Ortaköy		
Ovgoros	* Ergazi		
Pafos		Paphos	

Palekythro	* Balıkesir		
Panagra	* Geçitköy		
Pano Dhikomo	* Yu. Dikmen		
Pano Zodhia	* Yu. Bostancı		
Pergamos	* Beyarmudu		
Peristerona	* Alaniçi		
Petra	* Taşköy		
Petra tou Dhiyeni	* Yeniceköy		
Patriki	* Tuzluca		
Philia	* Serhadköy		
Phlamoudi	* Mersinlik		
Photta	* Dağyolu		
Phterykha	* Malatya		
Pileri	* Göçeri		
Platani	* Çinarli		
Platanisso	* Balalan		
Prastio	* Aydınköy * Dörtyol		
Psilatos	* Sütlüce		
Pyrga	* Pirhan		
Pyroi	* Gaziler		
Rizokarpaso	* Dipkarpaz		
Sandalaris	* Sandallar		
Selemani	* Süleymaniye		
Sinda	* Inönü		
Sisklipos	* Akçiçek		
Skylloura	* Yilmazköy		
Spathariko	* Otüken		
Strongylos	* Turunçlu		
Styllos	* Mutluyaka		
Sykhari	* Kaynakköy		
Syngrasis	* Sınırüsktü		
Syrianokhori	* Yayla		
Tavros	* Pamuklu		
Temblos	* Zeytinlik		
Thermia	* Doğanköy		
Trakhoni	* Demirhan		

Trapeza	* Besparmak		
Tremetousha	* Erdemli		
Trikomo	* Iskele		
Trypimeni	* Tirmen		
Tymbou	* Kırklar		
Varisha	* Sirinköy		
Varosha	* Maraş		
Vasilia	* Karşiyaka		
Vathylakkas	* Derince		
Vatili	* Vadili		
Vavilas	* Güzelyali		
Vitsadha	* Pınarlı		
Vokolidha	* Bafra		
Voni	* Gökhan		
Vouno	* Taşkent		
Yenagra	* Nergisli		
Yerani	* Turnalar		
Yerolakkos	* Alayköy		
Yialousa	* Yenierenköy		

Telephone numbers

The international country code for Cyprus is 357, but settlements in the Turkish controlled area are reached via Turkey, international code 90. In these latter cases, dial 90-5-area code-subscriber's number.

Czech Republic
Českà Republika

Official name: Czech Republic, Českà Republika
Area: 78 864 sq. km (30 441 sq. miles)
Population: 10 362 000
Capital: Praha (Prague)
Currency: 1 Koruna (Kcs) = 100 halẽř
International telephone access code: 420

Languages

Czech is spoken by most of the population. There are 200 000 speakers of Romani, 200 000 speakers of German, concentrated along the border with Germany, and some 50 000 Polish-speakers.

Address format

Addresses are formatted as follows:

Salutation
Name
thoroughfare type[ ]Thoroughfare name[ ]number
postal code[ ]SETTLEMENT{[ ]sorting code}

For example:

Pan
Vaclav Havel
ul. Praha 12
267 88 BRNO 2

Two spaces should be left between the postal code and the settlement name.

The sorting code (following the city name) is used for addresses in larger cities.

Postal codes

Postal codes (*Postovni Smerovaci Cisla* or *PSC* in Czech) are formed from five digits in the following format:

999[ ]99

This code is still that used before the splitting of Czechoslovakia into the Czech Republic and Slovakia on 1st January 1993. Czech addresses all have postal codes commencing with numbers 1, 2, 3, 4, 5, 6 and 7.

Towns

The following list provides foreign-language versions of Czech settlement names:

Czech	*English*	*German*	*Italian*
Benešov		Deutsch Beneschau	
Borovany		Forbes	
Břeclav		Lundenburg	
Brno		Brünn	
Černá		Schwarzbach	
Česke Budějovice		Budweis	
Česke Krumlov		Krumau	
Cheb		Eger	
Chlum		Humwald	
Chvalsiny		Kalsching	
Dolni Dvŏriště		Unter Haid	
Frymburk		Friedberg	
Halámky		Witschkoberg	
Hodonín		Göding	
Hořice		Höritz	
Horni Dvŏriště		Ober Haid	
Horni Planá		Ober Plan	
Horni Vltavice		Over Moldau	
Hradec Králové		Königgrätz	
Hustopeče		Auspitz	
Jihlava		Iglau	
Kaplice		Kaplitz	
Karlovy Vary		Karlsbad	
Kraslice		Graslitz	
Křištanov		Christianburg	
Lanžhot		Landshut	
Lednice		Eisgrub	
Liberec		Reichenberg	
Litoměřice		Leitmeritz	
Malonty		Meinetschlag	
Mikulov		Nikolsburg	
Nová Bištřice		Neubistritz	
Nové Hrady		Gratzen	
Olomouc		Olmütz	
Ondřejev		Andreasburg	
Pardubice		Pardubitz	
Polná		Stein	
Praha	Prague	Prag	Praga
Přerov		Prerau	
Plzeň		Pilsen	
Rožmberk		Rosenberk	
Strobnice		Strobnitz	

Světlik		Kirschschlag	
Teplice		Teplitz	
Trhove Sviny		Schweinitz	
Trutnov		Trautenau	
Valtice		Feldsberg	
Větřini		Wettern	
Vranov		Frein	
Volary		Wallern	
Vyšší Brod		Hohenfurth	
Znojmo		Znaim	

Administrative Units

The Czech Republic consists of the following regions, which are not used in addresses:

Jihočeský
Jihomoravský
Praha
Severočeský
Severomoravský
Středočeský
Východočeský
Západočský

Denmark
Danmark

Official name: Kingdom of Denmark, Kongeriget Danmark
Area: 43 093 sq. km. (16 638 sq. miles)
Population: 5 146 469
Capital: København (Copenhagen)
Currency: 1 krone = 100 øre
International telephone access code: 45

Languages

The official language, Danish, is spoken by 98 per cent of the population. Faroese is spoken in the Faeroe Islands by 47 000 people. German is spoken by a minority of 23 000 in North Slesvig (Sydjylland) along the German border. There are 40 000 speakers of Greenlandic (Inuktitut) in Greenland. A distinctive Danish dialect called Jutish is spoken by a small number of people near to the western end of the border with Germany. Each inhabitant of the village of Rudbøl is reputed to speak 5 languages - Danish, German, North Frisian, Low Saxon and Jutish.

Company Types

The following company types may be found in Danish company names:

AMBA
Aktieselskab (A/S)
Interessentskab (I/S)
Andelsselskab
Fond

Addresses

Addresses are written in this format:

Recipient name
Thoroughfare[ ]number
postal code[ ]TOWN NAME{[ ]SORTING CODE}

for example:

Torben Raldorf
Tietgensgade 137
1004 KØBENHAVN V

The Postal code should be separated from the town name by two spaces.

The thoroughfare type is suffixed to the thoroughfare name without a space. As with other Scandinavian languages, the definite article does not appear as a separate word but as a suffix (-en) at the end of the word.

Thoroughfare types

Thoroughfare types are usually suffixed to the thoroughfare name. However, in some cases these words can stand on their own, for example when the thoroughfare name is a real noun, such as a person's name. In this case it starts with an upper-case letter. So

Tietensgade

but

Sankt Knuds Gade

This is a list of thoroughfare types:

allé
anlæg
bakken
banen
bastion
boulevard
bro
broen
buen
dammen
dossering
gaard
gade
gangen
gård
get
grænsen
have
havn
høj
højen
holmen
huset
kær
kræmten
længen
marken
parken
passagen
plads
siden

stien
stræde
svinget
toften
torv
vangen
varden
vej
vey
vænge

Other nouns, adjectives and prepositions commonly found in address databases:

NB: the following abbreviations are used: g = gendered, n = neuter, s = singular, pl = plural.

den, det	the (but only when followed by an adjective preceding a noun. Otherwise -en (gendered) or -et (neuter) is added to the end of the noun. So, for example, vej =road, den store vej = the big road, but ...vejen
en, et	a, an
og	and
til	till, until, up to
for, til	for
af	of
fra	from
mod, imod	to, towards
i nærheden af	near, by
på	on
i	in
overfor	opposite
ved siden af	next to
bagefter	behind
foran	in front of
mellem	between
over	over
under	under
med	with
ny (g s), nyt (n s), nye (pl)	new
gammel (g s), gammelt (n s), gamle (pl)	old
kort (s), korte (pl)	short
lang (g s), langt (n s), lange (pl)	long
stor (g s), stort (n s), store (pl)	big

lille (s), små (pl)	small
nord	north
øst	east
syd	south
vest	west
Sankt	Saint

(NB: When used with nouns, the words for north, south, east and west are prefixed without a space to the noun to which they refer, e.g. Sydgade = South Street.)

Postbox

This is written as Postboks, abbreviated to PB.

Postal codes

Postal codes in Denmark and Greenland are composed of a block of 4 digits (the first digit cannot be a 0). It should be separated from the town name which follows it by 2 spaces. Copenhagen, Frederiksberg and Odense have a suffix (sorting code) to the town name to indicate the area of the town served or the region. The suffixes are as follows:

N	North
S	South
Ø	East
V	West
NV	North-West
NO	North-East
SV	South-West
SO	South-East
K	Central (København)
C	Central (Odense, Århus and Frederiksberg)

The postal codes of larger communities end in '00' or '000'.

Postal codes for Greenland can be distinguished as they begin with the numbers 39. Postal codes for the Faeroe Islands have 3 digits only. If you use the international sorting code, use FR for addresses in the Faeroe Islands rather than DK.

Provincial communities usually have a single postal code for the whole borough. Smaller towns (Esbjerg, Odense, Ålborg, Århus, Vejle and København N, NV, S, SV and Ø) distinguish different areas by postal code, whilst København K and V, and Frederiksberg C have different postal codes for some streets.

Postbox numbers 1001-1029 in København are in area K, 1501-1529 in area V. In Odense C, postbox numbers have the postal code 5100 as opposed to 5000; in Ålborg postbox numbers have the postal code 9100 as opposed to 9000; and in Århus C postbox numbers have the postal code 8100 as opposed to 8000.

Certain large mail users have their own postal code in Denmark.

Towns

The following list gives foreign language equivalents of Danish town names:

Danish	*English*	*French*	*German*	*Spanish*	*Italian*	*Dutch*
Aabenraa / Åbenrå			Apenrade			
Augustenborg			Augustenburg			
Bov			Bau			
Dybbøl			Düppel			
Gråsten			Gravenstein			
Haderslev			Hadersleben			
Højer			Hoyer			
København	Copenhagen	Copenhague	Kopenhagen	Copenhague	Copenhagen	Kopenhagen
Kruså			Krusau			
Løgumkloster			Lügumkloster			
Nordborg			Nordburg			
Sønderborg			Sonderburg			
Tinglev			Tinglef			
Tønder			Tondern			
Varnæs			Warnitz			
Vojens			Woyens			

Administrative districts

Denmark has 14 counties *(Amter)* and 2 municipalities *(Staden).*

Counties

Århus
Bornholm
Frederiksborg
Fyn
København
Nordjylland
Ribe
Ringkøbing
Roskilde
Sønderjylland
Storstrøm
Vejle
Vestsjælland
Viborg

Municipalities

København
Odense

Djibouti
Jumhouriyya Djibouti

Official name: Republic of Djibouti, Jumhouriyya Djibouti
Area: 23 200 sq. km (8 958 sq. miles)
Population: 541 000
Capital: Djibouti
Currency: 1 Djibouti Franc (DF, DjFr) = 100 centimes
International telephone access code: 253

Languages

The official language is Djibouti Arabic, spoken by 11% of the population. Afar is spoken by 55%, Somali by 33%.

Example address format

M. Farah Ismaël
BP 32
DJIBOUTI

Any address written in a non-native language will be written in French. Deliveries are made only to post office boxes (*Boite Postale*, or *BP*).

Postbox

This is written as *Boite Postale*, or *BP*.

Postal codes

Djibouti has no postal code system.

Dominica

Official name: Commonwealth of Dominica
Area: 751 sq. km (290 sq. miles)
Population: 86 000
Capital: Roseau
Currency: 1 East Caribbean Dollar (EC$) = 100 cents
International telephone access code: 1

Languages

The national language is English. The Dominican English dialect is spoken. 96% of the population speak Lesser Antillean Creole French. An estimated 70% of the population speak no other language. Standard French is understood by no more than 10% of the population.

Example address format

M. Alvin Thomas
Bay Front
ROSEAU

Postal codes

Dominica has no postal code system.

Telephone numbers

All telephone numbers in Dominica have the area code 809.

Dominican Republic
República Dominicana

Official name: Dominican Republic, República Dominicana
Area: 48 442 sq. km (18 699 sq. miles)
Population: 7 384 000
Capital: Santo Domingo
Currency: 1 Dominican Peso (RD$, DR$) = 100 centavos
International telephone access code: 1

Language

Spanish, the official language, is spoken by some 87% of the population. About 2% speak Haitian Creole French. There is a community of 8 000 Samaná English speakers on the Samaná Peninsula.

Address Format

Addresses are written in the following format:

Recipient name
{thoroughfare type[]}Thoroughfare name[ ]house number
postal code[ ]SETTLEMENT

For example:

Sra Ana Jimenez
C/ Duarte 26
0100 SANTO DOMINGO

When addresses are written in Spanish, calle (or C/), the Spanish word for street, may not be written. The Spanish thoroughfare type, when included, is written before, and separately from, the thoroughfare name. It should be written with the first letter in lower case.

For further information about address components, please refer to the chapter on Spain.

Postal codes

These consist of a block of 4 digits.

Telephone numbers

All telephone numbers in Dominican Republic have the area code 809.

Ecuador

Official name: Republic of Ecuador, República del Ecuador
Area: 270 699 sq. km (104 490 sq. miles)
Population: 10 607 000
Capital: Quito
Currency: 1 Sucre (Su, S/.) = 100 centavos
International telephone access code: 593

Language

Spanish, the official language, is spoken by 77% of the population. Around 19% of the population speak American Indian languages, mainly several forms of Quichua (1 470 000 speakers). Others are Achuar-Shiwiar, Chachi, Cofán, Colorado, Cuaiquer, Secoya, Shuar, Siona, Tetete, Waorani and Záparo. Many of these people do not speak a second language. These people are found mainly in the Andes and the Amazon basin areas.

Address Format

Addresses are written in the following format:

Recipient name
{thoroughfare type[]}Thoroughfare name[ ]house number
POSTAL CODE
SETTLEMENT

For example:

Sr. Rigoberto Martinez
Alfonso Villagómez 1545
H0103C
RIOBAMBA

When addresses are written in Spanish, *calle*, the Spanish word for street, is rarely written. The Spanish thoroughfare type, when included, is written before, and separately from, the thoroughfare name. It should be written with the first letter in lower case.

For further information about address components, please refer to the chapter on Spain.

Postal codes

The newly implemented code has the pattern

A9999A

The first character indicates the province, the first two digits the canton, the last two digits the commune and the final character the postbox or delivery area.

Egypt
Misr

Official name: Arab Republic of Egypt, Jumhuriya Misr al-Arabiya
Area: 1 001 449 sq. km (386 559 sq. miles)
Population: 55 980 000
Capital: Cairo
Currency: 1 Egyptian Pound (E£, LE) = 100 piastres
International telephone access code: 20

Language

The national language, Arabic, is spoken in a number of forms by most people. Some 100 000 people speak Kenuzi-Dongola, 200 000 speak Nobiin and 5 000 speak Siwi, a Berber dialect.

Address Format

Addresses are written in the following format:

Recipient name
number[ ]Thoroughfare name[ ]District name
Province
postal code

Addresses written in Latin script will often be written in English.

Postal codes

The postal code consists of a block of 5 digits. The first indicates the region, the second the governorate, the third the quality of service and the last two the delivery area or post office.

Towns

The following list gives foreign language equivalents of Egyptian town names:

Arabic	*English*	*French*	*German*
Aswân	Aswan	Assouan	Assuan
Asyût		Assiout	Assiut
Bûr Saîd	Port Said	Port-Saïd	Port Said
Dumyât	Damietta	Damiette	Damietta
El Gîza	Giza	Guizeh	Giseh
El Iskandarîya	Alexandria	Alexandrie	Alexandria
El Khârga		Kharge	Kharga
El Qâhira	Cairo	Le Caire	Kairo

El Suweis	Suez	Suez	Sues
El Uqsur	Luxor		Luxor
Isna			Esna
Qena			Kene
Salûm			Sollum
Sîwa			Siwa
Zagazig			Sagasig

Administrative areas

Province names will be found in addresses. The provinces are:

Alexandria
Aswân
Asyût
Béhéra
Beni Suef
Cairo
Daqahlîlîa
Dumîat
El Ahman
El Bahr
Fayûm
Gharbîa
Giza
Ismailîa
Kafr El Sheikh
Matrûh
Menufîa
Minîa
North Sinaï
Port Said
Qena
Qualiubîa
Red Sea
Sharqîa
Sinaï
Sohâg
Sud Sinaï
Suez
Wâdi El Guedîd

El Salvador

Official name: Republic of El Salvador, República de El Salvador
Area: 21 476 sq. km (5 418 000sq. miles)
Population: 5 418 000
Capital: San Salvador
Currency: 1 Colón (ES¢) = 100 centavos
International telephone access code: 503

Language

About 92% of the population speak the official language, Spanish. There are some 12 000 speakers of Kekchí (also known as Quecchí or Cacché); 37 000 speakers of Lenca in the town of Chilango and 20 speakers of Pipil (or Nahuat).

Address Format

Addresses are written in the following format:

> Recipient name
> {thoroughfare type []}Thoroughfare name[ ]house number
> SETTLEMENT
> PROVINCE[ ]POSTAL CODE

For example:

> Sr. Juan Castillo
> Col. Santa Lucia - PJE. 6 - N°. 29
> ILOPANGO
> SAN SALVADOR 01702

The word *Col.* (*Colonia*, meaning "section") may be used instead of a thoroughfare type.

Calle, the Spanish word for street, is rarely written. The Spanish thoroughfare type, when included, is written before, and separately from, the thoroughfare name. It should be written with the first letter in lower case.

For further information about address components, please refer to the chapter on Spain.

Postal codes

The postal code consists of a block of 5 digits. The first two digits indicate the department, the third the locality and the last two the delivery office.

Equatorial Guinea
Guinea Ecuatorial

Official name: Republic of Equatorial Guinea, República de Guinea Ecuatorial.
Area: 26 016 sq. km (10 042 sq. miles)
Population: 360 000
Capital: Malabo
Currency: 1 CFA Franc (CFAFr) = 100 centimes
International telephone access code: 240

Languages

The national language, Spanish, is spoken by some 2.3% of the population. Fang is spoken by 75% of the population. Other languages are Balenque, Benga, Bube, Crioulo, Krio, Ngumba, Ngumbi, Seki and Yasa.

Example address format

Ignacio Nguema
Apartado 36
MALABO

Any address written in a non-native language will be written in Spanish. Deliveries are made only to post office boxes (*Apartado*).

Postbox

This is written as *Apartado.*

Postal codes

Equatorial Guinea has no postal code system.

Eritrea

Area: 124 000 sq. km (47 876 sq. miles)
Population: 3 677 000
Capital: Asmera (Asmara)
Currency: 1 Birr = 100 cents
International telephone access code: 355

Languages

English is the national language but spoken by few as a first language. There are 450 000 speakers of Afar; 120 000 of Bedawi; 70 000 of Bilcn (in and around the town of Keren); 140 000 of Kunama; 63 000 of Nara; 144 000 of Saho; 683 000 of Tigré and 1 900 000 of Tigrinya.

The official language is Djibouti Arabic, spoken by 11% of the population. Afar is spoken by 55%, Somali by 33%.

Example address format

Mr Samuel Habte
Awet Street 4
ASMARA

Any address written in a non-native language will be written in English.

Postal codes

Eritrea has no postal code system.

Towns

Asmera is known as *Asmara* in English and German.

Estonia
Eesti

Official name: Republic of Estonia, Eesti Vabariik
Area: 45 100 sq. km (17 409 sq. miles)
Population: 1 600 000
Capital: Tallinn
Currency: 1 Kroon = 100 cents
International telephone access code: 372

Languages

The official language, Estonian, is spoken by about 62% of the population. Russian is spoken by 30% and Ukrainian by 1.4%. Belorussian, Finnish, Latvian, Lithuanian, Chuvash, Tatar and Romani are also spoken.

Address format

Addresses are formatted as follows:

Name
Thoroughfare[ ]number
POSTAL CODE[ ]SETTLEMENT

For example:

Esto Lotta
Narvasaare 17
EE1965 TALINN

Postal codes

Postal codes consist of the letters 'EE' followed by a block of 4 digits. The digits commence with numbers between 0 and 3.

Towns

The following list gives German equivalents of Estonian town names:

Estonian	*German*
Kuressaare	Ahrensburg
Narva	Narwa
Paldiski	Baltischport
Pärnu	Pernau
Rakvere	Wesenberg
Tallinn	Reval
Tapa	Taps

Tartu	Dorpat
Valga	Walk
Viljandi	Fellin
Võru	Werro

Ethiopia
Ityopiya

Official name: People's Democratic Republic of Ethiopia, Ye Etiyop'iya Hizbawi Dimokrasiyawi Ripublik
Area: 1 251 282 sq. km (483 123 sq. miles)
Population: 53 131 000
Capital: Addis Abeba (Addis Ababa)
Currency: 1 Ethiopian Birr (Br) = 100 cents
International telephone access code: 251

Languages

The national languages are English and Amharic, with 15 000 000 speakers.

81 other languages are spoken in Ethiopia. The geographical distribution of these languages is complex. The other main languages are Aari (109 000 speakers); Afar (450 000 speakers); Agaw (350 000 speakers); Awngi (490 000 speakers); Gamo-Gofa-Dawro (781 000 speakers); Gedeo (500 000 speakers); Gurage (East) (493 000 speakers); Gorage (North) (104 000 speakers); Gorage (West) (890 000 speakers); Hadiyya (1 000 000 speakers); Kaficho (500 000 speakers); Kambaata (1 000 000 speakers); Komso (200 000 speakers); Libido (100 000 speakers); Oromo, Borana-Arsi-Guji (3 809 000 speakers); Oromo, Qotu (2 142 000 speakers); Oromo, West Central (about 8 000 000 speakers); Sidamo (1 500 000 speakers); Somali (2 050 000 speakers); Tigrinyi (4 150 000 speakers); Wolaytto (2 000 000 speakers) and Yemsa (500 000 speakers).

Example address format

Mr Teka Lemma
P.O. Box 5020
JIMMA

Postal codes

Ethiopia has no postal code system.

Towns

Addis Abeba is known as *Addis Ababa* in English.

Faeroe Islands
Faerøerne (Danish)

Area: 1 400 sq. km (540 sq. miles)
Population: 47 449
Capital: Tórshavn
Currency: 1 Danish Krone (Dkr) = 100 øre
International telephone access code: 298

Addresses

Addresses are written in this format:

Recipient name
Thoroughfare[ ]number
postal code[ ]SETTLEMENT NAME

for example:

Torben Raldorf
Argirgade 1
100 TÓRSHAVN

The Postal code should be separated from the town name by two spaces.

Postal codes

The mail system for the Faeroe Islands is administered by Denmark. Unlike Danish postal codes, Faeroes Island postal code consist of a block of 3 digits, the first digit being a number between 1 and 9.

Postboxes in the capital, Tórshavn, have a separate postal code (110). Each settlement has its own postal code except Argir, which has two.

Fiji
Viti

Official name: Republic of Fiji
Area: 18 333 sq. km (7 076 sq. miles)
Population: 748 000
Capital: Suva
Currency: 1 Fiji Dollar (F$) = 100 cents
International telephone access code: 679

Languages

10 languages are spoken on Fiji's 844 islands. The national languages are English and Fijian. Hindi has official status. Fijian (Standard and Western) is spoken by 46.2% of the population. 48.6% of the population speak Hindi. There are 500 speakers of Gone Dau on the Gone and Dau Islands; 5 300 speakers of Kiribati; 16 000 speakers of Lau on Lau, Nayau, Lakeba, Oneata, Moce, Komo, Namuka, Kabara, Vulaga, Ogea and Vatoa Islands; 2 500 speakers of Rotuman on Rotuma. Lomaiviti is spoken on Koro, Makogai, Levuka, Ovalau, Batiki, Nairai and Gau. Namosi-Naitasiri-Serua is spoken in south-central Viti-Levu, Namosi, Serua and Naitasiri provinces.

Example address format

Mr. Raman Dass
72 Batiki Street
SUVA

Mr. Epeli Toroca
GPO Box 96
RAKI RALI

Addresses written in a non-native language will be written in English. For more information on thoroughfare types and other address components, please refer to the chapter on United Kingdom.

Postal codes

Fiji has no postal code system.

FINLAND: Postal areas and language regions

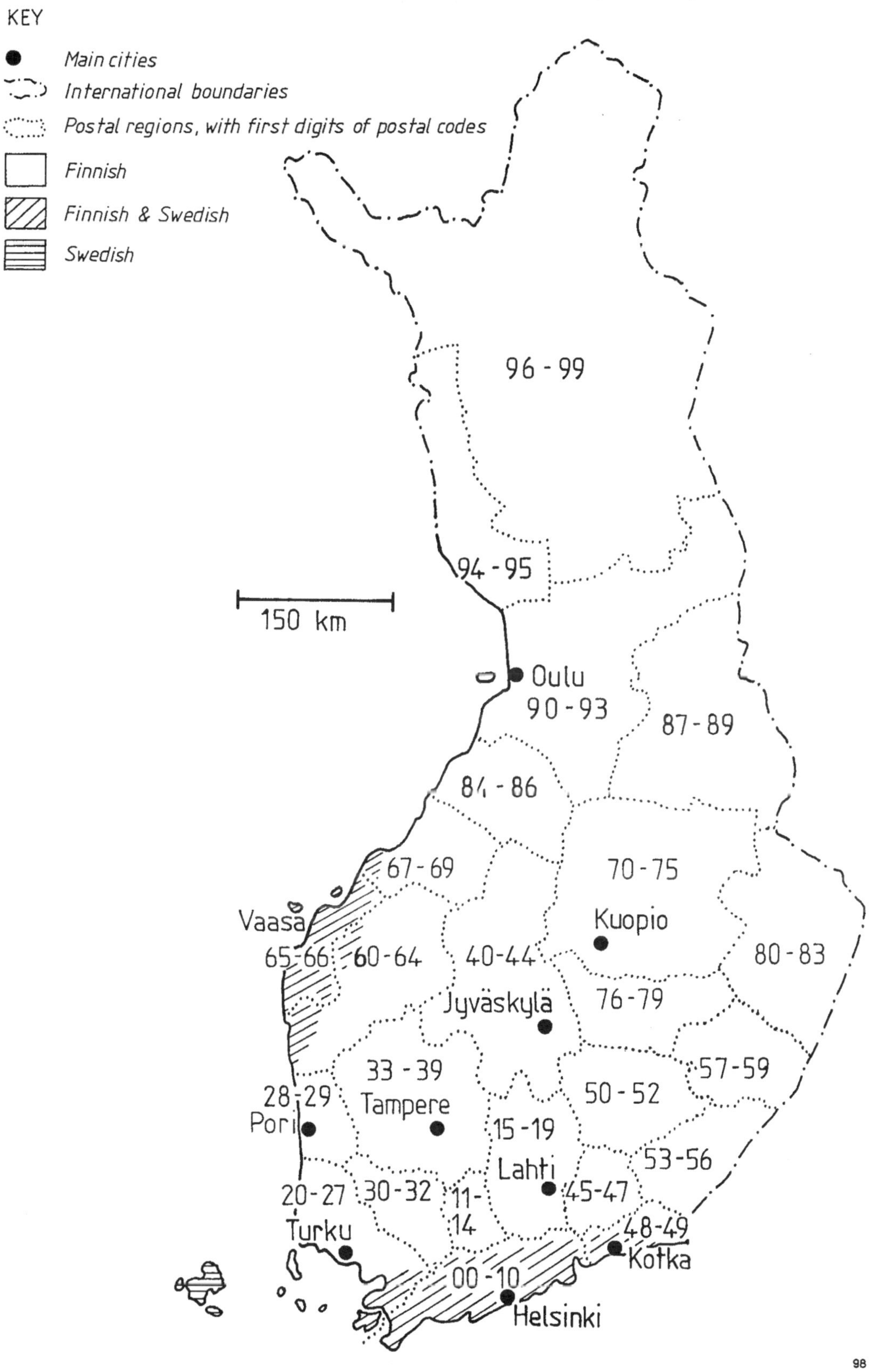

98

Finland

Suomi (Finnish); Finland (Swedish)

Official name: Republic of Finland, Suomen Tasavalta
Area: 338 145 sq. km (130 559 sq. miles)
Population: 5 029 002
Capital: Helsinki/Helsingfors
Currency: 1 Markka (Finnmark, FMk) = 100 penniä
International telephone access code: 358

Languages

Finland has two official languages: Finnish, spoken by 94 per cent of the population; and Swedish, spoken by 6 per cent. Some 22 900 of the Swedish speakers inhabit the Åland Islands, where they form 95 per cent of the population. The Swedish speakers are concentrated in two areas, along the southern coast between Helsinki and Hangö, and along the western coast between Pori and Jakobstad.

There are 24 municipalities that are unilingually Swedish, 17 with a Swedish majority and 23 where the minority is Swedish (in all cases, the municipality must contain at least 3000 people or 8 per cent of the population as Swedish speakers to be declared bilingual). The names of the relevant municipalities are listed in the towns section of this chapter.

There are 10 000 speakers of Karelian in northern Finland close to the Russian border; 4-6 000 speakers of Romany and 7 000 speakers of three dialects of Saami in northern Finland, especially around the town of Utsjoki. There are also scattered speakers of Livvi.

Company types

The following company type indications will be identified in address databases:

KY (usually followed by the name of the owner)
Osuuskunta (co-operative association)
OY (Osakeyhtiö - limited liability company)
RY

Addresses

Finnish addresses are written in this format:

Recipient name
Thoroughfare[ ]number
[ ]
postal code[ ]TOWN NAME {[ ]sorting code}

for example:

Mikka Herttua
Haanvuorentie 34

49420 HAMINA 2

The Finnish Post Office prefer addresses to follow a fixed six-line pattern with blank lines where necessary so that each component of an address will always fall on the same line:

Name
Company Name
Street Address
blank line
postal code[ ]SETTLEMENT NAME
Country name

There should be two spaces between the postal code and the settlement name.

In multilingual areas street addresses can be given in either language.

Ja is the Finnish word for 'and'.

In Finnish, articles do not exist as separate words but are added as endings to the words to which they refer. There is no separate word for Saint in Finnish.

Please refer to the chapter on Sweden for information on Swedish.

Thoroughfare types

Please refer to the chapter on Sweden for thoroughfare lists in Swedish.

Below is a list of the most commonly occurring thoroughfare types in Finnish, with the abbreviated form(s) which you are most likely to find in address databases. Finnish, one of Europe's most complex languages, has 16 cases, and appropriate declensions are added at the ends of words, including words indicating thoroughfare types.

Finnish	*Abbreviation*	*Translation*
Bulevardi, Bulevard		Avenue
Esplanadi		Esplanade
Gatan, Gate, Gata	Gt., G.	Street
Katu		Street
Kuja		Alley (cul-de-sac)
Portti		Gate
Rinne		Street
Tie		Street
Vägen, Väg	V.	Road

There is no rule governing hyphenation in street addresses.

Postbox

This is written as *Posti Loaero* (*PL*) in Finnish, *Box* in Swedish.

Postal codes

Postal codes are composed of a block of 5 digits. These are written on the same line, and before, the town name. The first 2 digits of the postal code indicate the area of Finland covered (the sorting office). The next two digits indicate the area within this region (on the basis of municipality/village or suburb). The last digit can be a 0 (ordinary postal code) or a 1 (postbox).

In larger towns a sorting code following the town name may be found. For example:

02361 ESPOO 36

The Finnish Post Office prefers that this sorting code, which is included in the postal code, not be used.

Some isolated areas do not have door-to-door postal deliveries, and these areas are served, especially for newspaper deliveries, by buses. These delivery lines have postal codes ending in 899.

In many towns in Finland, different streets, and different house numbers within those streets, belong to different postal code areas. These can be identified only by reference to the *Postinumeroluettelo* (Postal code book) under the heading *Postiosoitehakemistot Kadunnimistöineen*.

Towns

As Finland is a bilingual country, many settlements have both a Finnish and a Swedish name. The following list gives the alternative names for these settlements:

Unilingually Swedish-speaking municipalities

Swedish	*Finnish*
Houtskär	Houtskari
Larsmo	Luoto
Malax	Maalahti
Mariehamn	Maarianhamina
Maxmo	Maksamaa
Närpes	Närpiö

Other unilingually Swedish-speaking municipalities are:

Brändö

Eckerö
Finström
Föglö
Geta
Hammarland
Iniö
Jomala
Kökar
Korsnäs
Kumlinge
Lemland
Lumparland
Saltvik
Sottunga
Sund
Vårdö
Västanfjärd

Municipalities with a Swedish-speaking majority

Swedish	*Finnish*
Ekenäs	Tammisaari
Ingå	Inkoo
Jakobstad	Pietersaari
Karis	Karjaa
Korpo	Korpoo
Korsholm	Mustasaari
Kronoby	Kruunupyy
Nagu	Nauvo
Oravais	Oravainen
Pargas	Parainen
Pemå	Pemaja
Sibbo	Sipoo
Tenala	Tenhola
Vörå	Vöyri

Other municipalities with a Swedish-speaking majority are:

Dragsfjärd
Kemiö
Liljendal

Municipalities with a Swedish-speaking minority

Finnish	*Swedish*
Espoo	Esbo
Hanko	Hangö
Helsinki	Helsingfors
Kaskinen	Kaskö

Kauniainen	Grankulla
Kirkkonummi	Kyrkslätt
Kokkola	Karleby
Kristiinankaupunki	Kristinestad
Lohja	Lojo
Loviisa	Lovisa
Myrskylä	Mörskom
Pyhtää	Pyttis
Porvoo	Borgå
Ruotsinpyhtää	Strömfors
Särkisalo	Finby
Siuntio	Sjundeå
Turku	Åbo
Uusikaarlepyy	Nykarleby
Vaasa	Vasa
Vantaa	Vanda

Other municipalities with a Swedish-speaking minority are:

Lapinjärvi
Pohja
Porvoon

Other settlements

Finnish	*Swedish*
Ähtäri	Etseri
Ähtävä	Esse
Ahvenkoski	Abborfors
Anttila	Andersböle
Artjärvi	Artsjö
Askainen	Villnäs
Degerby UL	Nylands Degerby
Emäsalo	Emsalö
Enontekiö	Enontekis
Eurajoki	Euraåminne
Fiskari	Fiskars
Hailuoto	Karlö
Hamari	Hammars
Hämeenkyrö	Tavastkyro
Hämeenlinna	Tavastehus
Hamina	Fredrikshamn
Hangonkylä	Hangöby

Hanko Pohjoinen	Hangö Norra
Härkäpää	Härpe
Heikinkylä	Hindersby
Heinlahti	Heinlax
Hiittinen	Hitis
Hinthaara	Hindhår
Hyvinkää	Hyvinge
Iisalmi	Idensalmi
Ikaalinen	Ikalis
Ilola	Illby
Ilomantsi	Ilomants
Inari	Enare
Ingermaninkylä	Ingermansby
Isojoki	Storå
Isokyrö	Storkyro
Jakari	Jackarby
Järvenpää	Träskända
Jepua	Jeppo
Jokioinen	Jockis
Joroinen	Jorois
Kaarenkylä	Karsby
Kaarina	St. Karins
Kajaani	Kajana
Kalkkiranta	Kalkstrand
Kälviä	Kelviå
Kankkila	Kanböle
Karijoki	Bötom
Karjalohja	Karislojo
Karkkila	Högfors
Kaunislahti	Grundsjö
Kaustinen	Kaustby
Kerava	Kervo
Kerkko	Kerko
Kiila	Kila
Kimito	Kemiö
Kirkniemi	Gerknäs
Koivulahti	Kvevlax

Kokemäki	Kumo
Kolppi	Kållby
Koskenkylän Saha	Forsby Såg
Köyliö	Kjulo
Kujala	Gränden
Kulloo	Kullo
Kulloonkylä	Kulloby
Kuninkaankylä	Kungsböle
Kustavi	Gustavs
Lahti	Lahtis
Laihia	Laihela
Lapinkylä	Lappböle
Lappeenranta	Villmanstrand
Lappohja	Lappvik
Lappträsk	Lapinjärvi
Lapua	Lappo
Lapväärtti	Lappfjärd
Lielahti TL	Lielax
Lieto	Lundo
Liminka	Limingo
Lohtaja	Lochteå
Luoma	Bobäck
Martinkylä	Mårtensby
Masala	Masaby
Meltolan Sairaala	Mjölbolsta Sjukhus
Menkarvia	Sastmola
Metsälä	Ömossa
Mikkeli	St. Michel
Mustio	Svartå
Naantali	Nådendal
Nedervetil	Ala-Veteli
Nikkilan Sairaala	Nickby Sjukhus
Noormarkku	Norrmark
Nousiainen	Nousis
Oitmäki	Oitbacka
Oravaisten Tehdas	Oravais Fabrik
Oulu	Uleåborg

Paattinen	Patis
Paimio	Pemar
Paippinen	Paipis
Päivölä	Solberg
Pännäinen	Bennas
Pämäinen	Pärnäs
Pellinki	Pellinge
Pernajan Vanhakylä	Gammelby
Perniö	Bjärnå
Piikiö	Pikis
Pikkala	Pickala
Pinjainen	Billnäs
Pirkkala	Birkala
Pohjankuru	Skuru
Pomarkku	Påmark
Pori	Björneborg
Porlammi	Porlom
Pornainen	Borgnäs
Pukaro	Pockar
Purola	Svartbäck
Raahe	Brahestad
Raippaluoto	Replot
Raisio	Reso
Rauma	Raumo
Ruotsinkylä	Svenskby
Rymättylä	Rimito
Sannainen	Sannäs
Sauvo	Sagu
Savonlinna	Nyslott
Siipyy	Sideby
Siltakylä	Broby
Sulva	Solf
Suurpellinki	Storpellinge
Tähtelä	Täkter
Taivassalo	Tövsala
Talma	Tallmo
Tampere	Tammerfors

Teerijärvi	Terjärv
Tesjoki	Tessjö
Teuva	Östermark
Tiukka	Tjöck
Tolkkinen	Tolkis
Tornio	Torneå
Tuusula	Tusby
Ulvila	Ulvsby
Upinniemi	Obbnäs
Uusikaupunki	Nystad
Vähäkyrö	Lillkyro
Valko	Valkom
Vehralahti	Veckelax
Veikkaala	Veikars
Veteli	Vetil
Vihti	Vichtis
Virkkala	Virkby
Virrat	Virdois
Voolahti	Vålax
Ylitornio	Överthomeå

The predominant language of the Åland islands (Ahvenanmaan lääni) is Swedish.

Finns often use abbreviations to indicate certain towns, such as HKI for Helsinki and MH for Mariehamn. If you find these in a database or directory, the equivalents are given in the *Postinumero-luettelo* under the heading *'Vahvistetut Nimilyhenteet'*.

Administrative districts

Finland has 12 provinces *(Lääni)*. They are not used in addresses. They are as follows:

Åland (Ahvenanmaa)
Häme
Keski-Suomi
Kuopio
Kymi
Lappi
Mikkeli
Oulu
Pohjois-Karjala
Turku-Pori
Uusimaa

Vaasa

Telephone numbers

All telephone numbers in Finland have ten digits, including the area code.

FRANCE: Postal regions and language areas

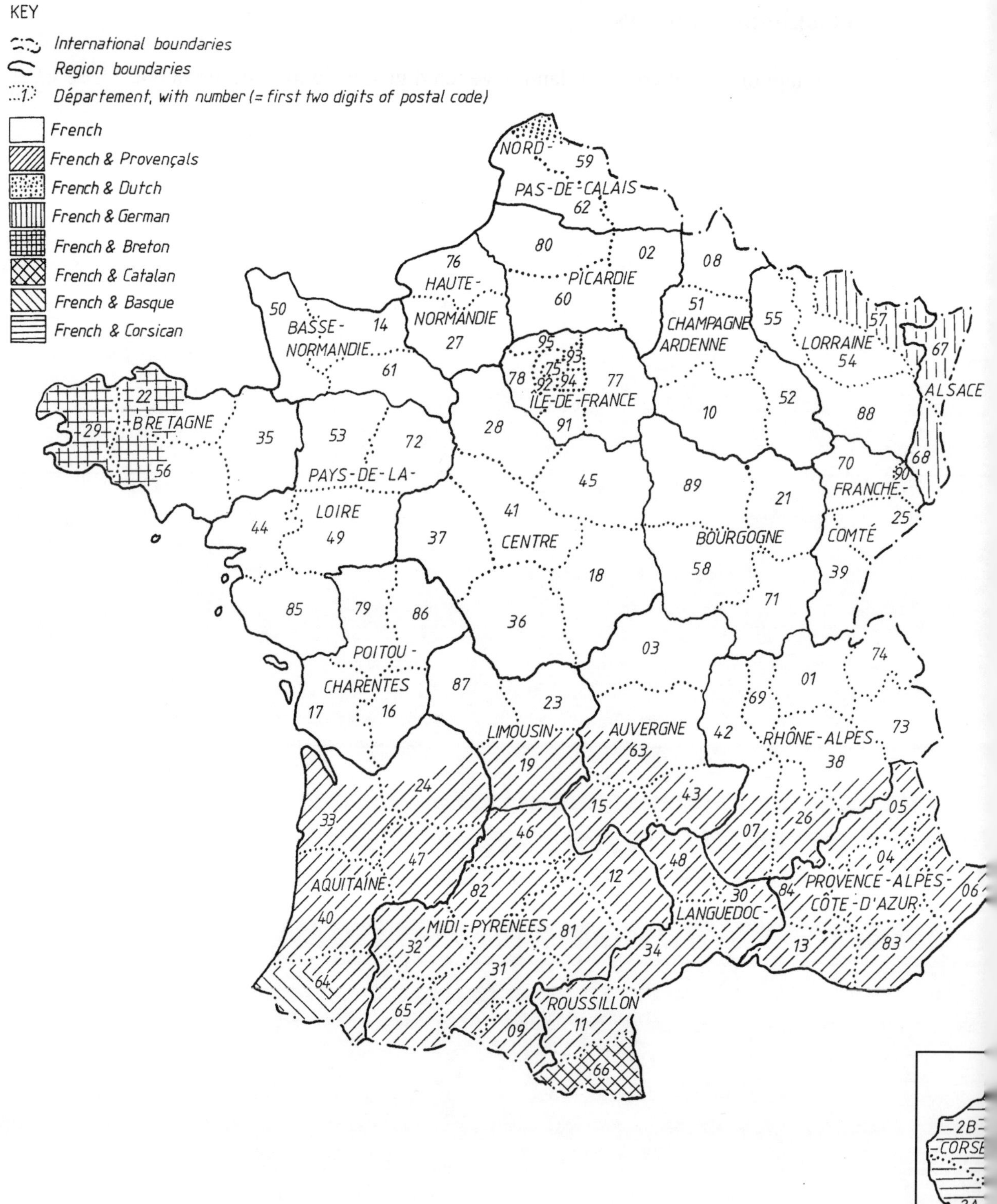

France

Official name: Republic of France, République Française.
Area: 543 965 sq.km. (210 026 sq. miles)
Population: 56 614 493
Capital: Paris
Currency: 1 French franc = 100 centimes
International telephone access code: 33

Languages

French is the only official language of France. Few people do not speak French, but only 87 per cent of the population speak French as a mother tongue. Along France's borders a number of people speak other languages - Alsatian (German, in various dialects) in Alsace-Lorraine on the border with Germany; Letzebuergesch on the border with Luxembourg; Flemish in the north on the Belgian border; Provençals (Occitan - in the dialects of Avergnat, Franco-Provençal, Gascon, Languedocien, Limousin and Provençals) in the south; Catalan in the south near the Spanish border; and Basque in the south-west on the Spanish border. Breton is still spoken in Brittany. In Corsica Corsican, a dialect of Italian, is spoken. There are significant numbers of people speaking these languages:

Alsatian : 2.6%
Basque : 0.1%
Breton : 0.9%
Catalan : 0.5%
Corsican : 0.5%
Flemish : 0.1%
Provençals : 3%

Caló (Iberian Romany) and Romani are spoken by some 30-60 000 people in France.

France is a highly unitary state, and these languages are rarely given more than a passing recognition that they exist. It is highly unusual (but not impossible) to come across addresses written in any language other than French.

For the attention of

This is written *A l'Attention du* in French.

Contact names

Contact names are usually written first name first, last name last, but this is also often reversed. Surnames are usually written in upper case in addresses.

Company names

It is more correct, where the *nature* of the company is mentioned in its name, that this *precedes* the name of the company, thus:

Boulangerie Lalosse et Cie.

You will often, however, find these activity indications *after* the company name, thus:

Lalosse, Boulangerie
Lalosse (Boulangerie)

Equally, articles are often put in brackets after the name of the company, so:

Le Centre

becomes

Centre (Le)

This is also the case with initials. Thus:

Boulangerie J. Dumalin
becomes

Dumalin (Boulangerie J.)

STE in a company name is an abbreviation of *Société* (company).

Company Types

These company types will often be found in address databases:

Affaire personelle
SA (Sociéte Anonyme)
Sarl (Société a responsibilité limitée)

Addresses

Addresses are rarely written in any language other than French. Addresses are usually written in this format:

First name[ ]LAST NAME
COMPANY NAME
number[ ]thoroughfare type[ ]Thoroughfare name
postal code[ ]TOWN NAME{[ ]SORTING CODE}

or

First name[ ]LAST NAME
COMPANY NAME
number[,]thoroughfare type[ ]Thoroughfare name
postal code[ ]TOWN NAME{[ ]SORTING CODE}

For example

Mme Marie PAGE
A.C.T. BOULANGERIE
23 rue de Grenell
75700 PARIS CÉDEX

or

Mme Marie PAGE
A.C.T. BOULANGERIE
23, rue de Grenell
75700 PARIS CÉDEX

The French Post Office prefers that the address is written without the comma between the house number and the thoroughfare.

It is usual for the surnames of French people, and company names, to be written in upper case.

If the address has a box number, add this after the number:

number[boite]number[ ]thoroughfare type[ ]Thoroughfare name

You will also find indications of the staircase or building in which the inhabitant lives:

[Escalier No.]number

or

[Bâtiment]number

The number might also be followed by the words *bis* or *ter*.

Numbers may be written as follows:

1-4
1/4
1 à 4 (1 to 4), or
1 et 4 (1 and 4)

The thoroughfare type part of the address is prefixed to the thoroughfare name with a space between the words. For example:

7 rue Amiens
123 avenue de la Gare

It is more accurate to write the thoroughfare types in lower case, as above.

Building indicators

Indicator	*Abbreviation*	*English*
apartement	app.	Apartment
bâtiment	bat.	Building
immeuble	imm.	Building
maison		House
résidence	res., rés.	Residence
villa	vla	Villa

Thoroughfare types

Below is a list of the most commonly occurring thoroughfare types, (with the abbreviated forms which you are most likely to find in address databases:

Thoroughfare	*Abbreviation*
allée	all.
avenue	av., ave.
boulevard	bld., bd.
centre	
champ	
chaussée	ch., chee., chs.
chemin	
clos	
cour	
domaine	dom.
faubourg	fg.
impasse	imp.
marché	
mont/montagne	mt
parc	
passage	pas., pass.
place	pl.
quai	
quartier	qu., qrt., qua.
rond-point	rpt.
route	rte.
Route Nationale	RN
rue	r.
ruelle	
square	sq.
traverse	tra.
val/vallée	

Other nouns, adjectives and prepositions commonly found in address databases:

NB: The following abbreviations are used (m) = masculine form; (f) = feminine form; (pl) = plural form. Except where specified, the plural form of adjectives is the correctly gendered singular form followed by an 's'.

le (m)/la (f)/les (pl) (NB: le and la are written l' before a vowel or an unaspirated h)	the
un (m)/une (f)	a, an
et	and
à/au (m)/à la (f)/aux (pl)	till, until, up to, to
pour	for
de (before a proper noun)/du (m)/de la, de l' (f)/des (pl)	of, from
à	at
près de	by, near to
sur	on (a river, the sea)
dans	in
en face de	opposite
à côté de	next to
derrière	behind
devant	in front
entre	between
avec	with
sous	under
lès (occurs *only* in place names)	near
nouveau (m)/nouvelle (f)/nouveaux(m.pl.)/nouvelles (f.pl.) /nouvel (m, before a vowel or unaspirated h)	new
vieux (m, pl)/vieille (f)/vielles (f.pl.)/vieil (m, before a vowel or an unaspirated h)	old
court (m) (Ct.)/courte (f) (Cte.)	short
long (m) (Lg.)/longue (f) (Lgue.)	long
grand (m) (Gr./Grd.)/grande (f) (Gr./Grde.)	large
petit (m) (P./Pt.)/petite (f) (P./Pte.)	small
nord	north
est	east
sud	south
ouest	west
saint (m) (St.)/sainte (f) (Ste.)	saint
Parc Industriel Zone d'Activités (Z.A.C.) Zone Industrielle (Z.I.) Zone Artisanale (Z.A.) Centre Commercial (C.C.)	Industrial Estate

Note that prepositions are written in lower case in addresses.

Postbox

This is written as *Boite Postale*, abbreviated to *BP*.

Postal codes

Postal codes consist of a block of 5 digits. They are always placed before and on the same line as the town name. The first two digits are the *département* number. Where the *département* number is less than 10 it is preceded by 0, for example 05. *Département* 2A has postal codes beginning with 200 and 201, *département* 2B has postal codes beginning with 202 and 206. The *préfecture* (capital) of each *départment* has as its last three digits 000.

Most communes have their own unique postal code number. However, some scattered rural communities have more than one code. 32 cities have more than one distribution office and therefore more than one code. These, with their codes, are:

Aix-en-Provence	13090, 13100
Ajaccio	20000, 20090
Amiens	80000, 80080, 80090
Angers	49000, 49100
Bastia	20200, 20600
Bordeaux	33000, 33100, 33200, 33300, 33800
Cergy	95000,95800
Clermont-Ferrand	63000, 63100
Dunkerque	59140, 59240, 59640
Fort-de-France	97200, 97234
Grenoble	38000, 38100
Le Havre	76600, 76610, 76620
Le Mans	72000, 72100
Lille	59000, 59800
Limoges	87000, 87100, 87280
Metz	57000, 57050, 57070
Montpellier	34000, 34070, 34080, 34090
Mulhouse	68100, 68200
Nancy	54000, 54100
Nantes	44000, 44100, 44200, 44300
Nice	06000, 06100, 06200, 06300
Nîmes	30000, 30900
Orléans	45000, 45100

Paris (16th arrondissement)	75016, 75116
Perpignan	66000, 66100
Rennes	35000, 35200, 35700
Rouen	76000, 76100
Saint-Étienne	42000, 42100
Strasbourg	67000, 67100, 67200
Toulon	83000, 83100, 83200
Toulouse	31000, 31100, 31200, 31300, 31400, 31500
Tours	37000, 37100, 37200

Five *communes* have two codes with different names for the same *commune:*

Antibes: 06600 Antibes and 06160 Juan les Pins
Cannes: 06400 Cannes and 06150 Cannes la Bocca
Meudon: 92190 Meudon and 92360 Meudon la Forêt
Saint-Denis: 93200 Saint-Denis and 93210 La Plaine-Saint-Denis
Saint-Maurs-des-Fossés: 94100 Saint-Maur-des-Fosses and 94210 La Varenne-Saint-Hilaire

Three cities (Paris with 20, Lyon with 9 and Marseilles with 16) are split into *arrondissements.* These have their own postal codes, the number of the *arrondissement* being the last two digits of the postal code (with the exception of the Paris 16th *arrondissement,* with 2 codes - 75016 and 75116).

Large companies, town halls and so on can have their own unique postal code. In these cases the town name is followed by the word CÉDEX, thus:

75910 PARIS CÉDEX

The word CÉDEX may itself be followed by a number:

75910 PARIS CÉDEX 19

Military bases need no street address, but the town name is followed by either AIR (air-force base), NAVAL (naval base) or ARMÉES (army base).

There are 6 000 main post offices serving the 36 000 *communes.* Before 1989, where the recipient did not live in the same *commune* as that in which the main post office was situated, both *communes* had to be named, thus:

Monsieur Durand
12, rue des Rossignols
Villemoisson-sur-Orge
91360 Epinay-sur-Orge

Since 1989 this is no longer necessary, though they may still be found in addresses. Now the code is that of the main post office, but the *commune* is that of the recipient, so:

Monsieur Durand
12, rue des Rossignols
91360 Villemoisson-sur-Orge

Postal codes beginning with 97 belong to France's Overseas *départements* and territories.

Postal codes beginning with 98 belong to the independent state of Monaco.

Towns

All town names consisting of more than one word are hyphenated, with the exception of those beginning with 'LE', 'LA' or 'LES', where there is a space between this word and the next. All other words within a town name beginning with one of these words will be hyphenated, for example:

La Ferté-Vidame
Le Château-d'Oléron

The following lists give corresponding settlement names in different languages. Although the French language names are usually used by the French Post Office, some of the regional languages have their own names for towns in their regions. They are used by the speakers of the appropriate languages and, therefore, can be used by you if so desired.

French	*Breton*
Auray	Alre
Bain-de-Bretagne	Baen
Baud	Baod
Belle-Isle-en-Terre	Berac'h
Blain	Blaen
Bourbriac	Boulvriag
Callac-de-Bretagne	Kallag
Cancale	Konkaver
Carhaix-Plouguer	Karaez
Carnac	Karnag
Châteaubourg	Kastell-Jiron
Châteaubriant	Kastell-Briant
Châteaulin	Kastellin
Cléguérec	Klegereg
Clisson	Klison
Concarneau	Konk-Kerne
Crozon	Kroazon
Dinard	Dinarzh
Fouesnant	Fouenan

Fougeray	Felgerieg
Fougères	Foujera
Gouarec	Gwareg
Guéméné-Penfao	Gwenvenez-Pennfao
Guéméné-sur-Scorff	Ar-Gemene
Guer	Gael
Guérande	Gwenrann
Guimiliau	Gwimilio
Guingamp	Gwengamp
Hennebont	An-Herbont
Huelgoat	An-Uhel-Goad
Josselin	Josilin
Jugon	Pl-Yugon
L'Aber-Wrec'h	An-Enez-Werc'h
La Baule-Escoublac	Ar Baol-Skoubleg
La Guerche-de-Bretagne	Ar C'herch
Lamballe	Lambal
Landerneau	Landerne
Lanester	Lannarster
Lanmeur	Lanveur
Lannion	Lanuon
Le Conquet	Konk-Leon
Le Faou	Ar-Faou
Le Faouët	Ar-Faoued
Le Folgoët	Ar-Folgoad
Le Mont-Saint-Michel	Menez-Mikael-Ar-Mor
Locronan	Lokorn
Lorient	An-Oriant
Loudéac	Loudieg
Louvigné	Louvigneg
Mallestroit	Malastreg
Martigné-Ferchaud	Marzineg
Maure-de-Bretagne	Maour
Montfort	Monforz
Morlaix	Montroulez
Nantes	Naoned
Paimpol	Pempoull
Paimboeuf	Pembro
Penmarch	Penn-Marc'h
Perros-Guirec	Perroz
Pipriac	Prispinag
Plélan-le-Grand	Ploulan-Vraz
Plessé	Plousei
Pleyben	Pleiben
Plöermel	Plouarzel
Plouay	Pouskorv
Ploudalmézeau	Gwetalmeze

Plouescat	Ploueskad
Plougastel-Daoulas	Plougastell-Daoulas
Pontchâteau	Pont-ar-C'hastell
Pont-Croix	Pont-e-Kroaz
Pontivy	Pondivi
Pont-L'Abbé	Pont-n-Abad
Portsall	Porsall
Questembert	Kistreberzh
Quiberon	Kiberon
Quimper	Kemper
Quimperlé	Kemperle
Quintin	Kintin
Rennes	Roazon
Rezé	Reydied
Rohan	Roc'han
Roscoff	Rosgo
Saint-Aubin-d'Aubigné	Sant-Albin-an-Hiliber
Saint-Brieuc	Sant-Brieg
Sainte-Anne-d'Auray	Ker-Anna
Saint-Etienne-de-Montluc	Sant-Stevan
Saint-Guénole	Sant-Gwerole
Saint-Jean-Brévelay	Sant-Yec'han-Brevele
Saint-Malo	Sant-Malo
Saint-Nazaire	Sant-Nazer
Saint-Philbert-de-Grand-Lieu	Sant-Filiber
Saint-Pol-de-Léon	Kastell-Paol
Saint-Quay-Portrieux	Plouc'ha-Sant-Ke
Saint-Thégonnec	Sant-Tegoneg
Scaër	Skaer
Trégastel	Tregastell
Tréguier	Langreger
Vannes	Gwened
Vertou	Gwerzhav
Vitré	Ar C'hantreg

French	*Basque*
Adour	Aturri
Aldudes	Aldude
Ance	Arhantze
Anglet	Angelu
Aramits	Aramitze
Ascain	Azkaine
Aussurucq	Altürükü
Autevielle	Autile
Bayonne	Baiona
Bearn	Biarno
Biarritz	Miarritze

Bidart	Bidarte
Bigorre	Bigorra
Bordeaux	Bordele
Boucau	Bokale
Cambo-les-Bains	Kanbo
Carresse	Karrese
Cize	Garazi
Dax	Akize
Escos	Ezkoze
Espiute	Azpilda
Eysus	Isuazi
Feas	Inhasi
Geronce	Jeruntze
Geus	Ustasu
Guéthary	Getaria
Guinarthe	Ginarthe
Hasparren	Hazparne
Hendaye	Hendaia
Iholdy	Iholdi
Iraty	Irati
Josbaigt	Josibaia
La Rhune	Larrun
Landes	Landak / Landes
Lanne	Landa
Larrau	Larrañe
Lescun	Laskun
Lichos	Lixoze
Lourdes	Lurda
Marseille	Marseilla
Mauléon-Soule	Maule
Meritein	Meritiñe
Mixe	Amikuze
Monein	Muneiñe
Mont-de-Marsan	Mendi-Marzana
Nabas	Nabarzi
Narbonne	Narbona
Navarrenx	Nabarrenkose
Nice	Niza
Oloron	Olorue
Oloron-Sainte-Marie	Olorue
Orthez	Ortheze
Pau	Paue
Saint-Etienne-de-Baïgorry	Baigorri
Saint-Goein	Sangueiñe
Saint-Jean-de-Luz	Donibane-Lohizone
Saint-Jean-Pied-de-Port	Donibane-Garazi
Saint-Palais	Donapaleu

Saint-Pée-sur-Nivelle	Senpere
Saint-Vincent-de-Tyrosse	San Bisentse
Sainte-Engrâce	Santa Grazi
Salies	Saliese
Sare	Sara
Sauveterre	Sauvatèrre
Sus	Xütxe
Tarbes	Aturbe / Tarbe
Tardets	Atharratze
Tarnos	Ternose
Toulouse	Tolosa
Ustaritz	Uztaritze

French	*Catalan*
Banyuls-sur-Mer	Banyuls de la Marenda
Bompas	Bompàs
Canet-en-Rousillon	Canet de Roselló
Cerbère	Cervera de la Marenda
Collioure	Cotlliure
Elne	Elna
Ille-sir-Têt	Illa
Le Perthus	El Pertús
Perpignan	Perpinyà
Port-Barcarès	El Bacarès
Port-Vendres	Portvendres
Rivesaltes	Ribesaltes
Sorède	Sureda
Saint Cyprien	Sant Cebrià de Roselló
Saint Estève	Sant Esteve del Monestir
Saint Lautent-de-la-Salanque	Sant Llorenç de la Salanca
Thuir	Tuïr
Toulouges	Toluges

French	*Provençals*
Adour	La Dor
Agde	Agte
Aix-en-Provence	Ais
Arcachon	Arcaishon
arles	Arle
Arnaud-Bernard	Naut Bernat
Aspe	Aspa
Astafort	Astahòrt
Auch	Aush
Aurillac	Orlhac
Auvilar	Lo Vilar
Auzeville	Ausevila
Avignon	Avinhon

Barcelonette	Barceloneta
Bayonne	Baiona
Bethmale	Vath Mala
Beziers	Besièrs
Bigorre	Bigòrre
Blagnac	Blanhac
Blaye	Blaia
Bordeaux	Bordèu
Boucau	Bocau
Brive	Briva
Cahors	Caurs
Canezac	Canesac
Cannes	Canas
Capestang	Capestanh
Carcassone	Carcassona
Carmaux	Cramauç
Cazaux	Casaus
Cintegabelle	Cintagabèla
Clermont-Ferrand	Clarmont
Cordes	Còrda
Dax	D'Acs
Escanecrabe	Escana-craba
Fau-Montagne	Fau Montanha
Foix	Foish
Forgues	Hòrgas
Gaillac	Galhac
Garonne	Garona
Gascogne	Gasconha
Gedre	Gèdra
Grenoble	Grasanòbol
Gueret	Garait
Herault	Erau
Landes	Lanas
Lauragais	Lauragués
Laymont	Laimont
Le Puy	Lo Puèg
le Mirail	Le Miralh
Lectoure	Leitora
Leucate	Laucate
Limoges	Lemòtges
Lombez	Lombés
Lot	Òlt
Lourdes	Lorda
Luz	Lutz
Marseillan	Marselhan
Marseille	Marselha
Matabiau	Mata-Buòu

Millau	Milhau
Mont-de-Marsan	Lo Mont
Montauban	Montalban
Montesquiou	Montesquieu
Montpellier	Montpelhier
Muret	Murèth
Narbonne	Narbona
Nice	Niça
Oloron	Auloron
Ororon-Sainte-Marie	Auloron
Orthez	Ortès
Pamiers	Màmias
Pampalonne	Pamparona
Paris	París
Paulinet	Paurinet
Perigueux	Peirigús
Perpignan	Perpinhan / Perpinyá
Plagnole	Planhòla
Puyslaurens	Puèglaurenç
Quillan	Quilhan
Ramonville	Ramonvila
Rebirechioulet	Revira-shiulet
Rieumes	Rieumas
Rieux	Rieus
Rodez	Rodés
Salies	Salias
Sauveterre	Sauvatèrra
Savès	Savés
Saint Chignan	Sanch Inhan
Saint Gaudens	Sant Gaudenç
Saint Girons	Saint Gironç
Saint Jean de Jeannes	Sant Joan de Joanas
Tarbes	Tarba
Toulon	Tolon
Toulouse	Tolosa
Ustou	Ustó
Uzeste	Usèsta
Valence	Valença
Ventadour	Ventadorn
Villefranche	Vilafranca

French	*Corsican*
Ajaccio	Aiacciu
Asco	Ascu
Aullene	Auddè
Belogdere	Belgudè

Bocognano	Bucugnà
Bonifacio	Bonifaziu
Calinzana	Calenzana
Cargese	Carghjese
Corte	Corti
Coti-Chiavari	Coti Chjavari
Fiumorbo	Fiumorbu
Galéria	Galeria
Guagno-les-Bains	Guagnu
L'Ile-Rousse	L'Isula
Piana	A Piana
Pianottoli	Pianottuli
Pedicorte	Piedicorti
Porto	A Sarrera
Porto-Vecchio	Porti Vechju
Propriano	Prupia
San Lorenzo	San Lorenzu
Santa Maria Siché	Santa Maria Sicchè
Santo Pietro di Tenda	Santu Petru di Tenda
Sartène	Sarte
Sermano	Sermanu
Soccia	A Soccia
Venaco	Venacu
Vero	Veru
Vico	Vicu
Vivario	Vivariu

French	*English*	*German*	*Spanish*	*Italian*	*Dutch*
Abbeville					Abbegem
Aire-sur-la-Lys					Ariën aan de Leie
Armentières					Armentiers
Arques					Arken
Arras					Atrecht
Audresselles					Oderzele
Audruicq					Ouderwijk
Avesnes-sur-Helpe					Avenne-aan-de-Helpe
Avignon				Avignone	
Bailleul					Belle
Bavay					Bavik
Belfort		Beffert			
Bergues					Sint-Winoksbergen
Bitche		Bitsch			
Bouchain					Boesem
Boulogne-sur-Mer					Bonen
Bourbourg					Broekburg
Bouvines					Bovingen
Caëstre					Kaaster
Calais					Kales
Cambrai					Kamerijk

Cassel					Kassel
Cernay		Sennheim			
Chateau-Salins		Salzburgen			
Châtenois		Kestenholz			
Comines					Komen
Condé-sur-l'Escaut					Konde
Coudekerque					Koudekerke
Coudekerque-Branche					Nieuw-Koudekerke
Craywick					Kraaiwijk
Creutzwald		Kreuzwald			
Delle		Dattenried			
Dijon				Digione	
Dompierre-sur-Authie					Sint-Pieters-aan-de-Otie
Dompierre-sur-Authie					Sint-Pieters-aan-de-Helpe
Douai					Dowaai
Doullens					Dorland
Dunkerque	Dunkirk	Dünkirchen	Dunquerque		Duinkerke
Eperleques					Sperleke
Esquelbecq					Ekelsbeke
Esquerdes					Zwerde
Estaires					Stegers
Estrée-Blanche					Strate
Fauquembergues					Valkenberg
Flêtre					Vleteren
Fleurbaix					Vloerbeek
Grande-Synthe					Groot-Sinten
Gravelines					Gravelingen
Guines					Giezene
Guise					Wieze
Guebwiller		Gebweiler			
Haguenau		Hagenau			
Halluin					Halewijn
Hazebrouck					Hazebroek
Hem					Ham
Hesdin					Heusden
Houtkerque					Houtkerke
La Madeleine					Berkem
Laires					Laren
Lapoutroie		Schnierlach			
Le Doulieu					Zoeterstede
Le Quesnoy					Kiezenet
Lille				Lilla	Rijsel
Lyon				Lione	
Marbaix					Maarbeke
Marc-en-Baroeul					Marke
Marseille				Marsiglia	
Maubeuge					Mabuse
Menton				Mentone	
Merck-Saint-Liévin					Merkenes
Merville					Mergem
Mons-en-Pévèle					Pevelenberg
Montreuil-sur-Mer					Monsterole

Morbecque					Morbeke
Moustier-en-Fagne					Veemunster
Mulhouse		Mülhausen			
Narbonne				Narbona	
Nice		Nizza	Niza	Nizza	
Nieppe					Niepkerke
Orchies					Oorschie
Outreau					Wabingen
Oye-Plage					Ooie
Paris	Paris	Paris	Parìs	Parigi	Parijs
Pecquencourt					Vissershoven
Perpignan				Perpignano	
Quaëdypre					Kwaadieper
Renescure					Ruischeure
Réty					Reetseke
Rexpoëde					Rekspoede
Ribeauville		Rappoltsweiler			
Rinxent					Erningsem
Roncq					Ronk
Roubaix					Robeke
Sailly-sur-la-Lys					Zelleken
Sainghin-en-Mélantois					Singem
Saint-Amand-les-Eaux					Sint-Amands-aan-de-Skarpe
Saint-Louis		Sankt Ludwig			
Saint-Omer					Sint-Omaars
Saint-Momelin					Sint-Mommelins (Oudmunster)
Saint-Quentin					Sint-Kwintens
Saint-Ricquier					Sint-Rikiers
Saint-Venant					Papingem
Sainte-Marie-aux-Mines		Markirch			
Samer					Sint-Wulmaars
Sangatte					Zandgate
Sarrebourg		Saarburg			
Sarreguemines		Saargemünd			
Saverne		Zabern			
Seclin					Siekelin
Sélestat		Schlettstadt			
Steenbecque					Steenbeke
Strasbourg		Straßburg	Estrasburgo	Strasburgo	Straatsburg
Tarascon				Tarascona	
Thérouanne					Terenburg
Thiennes					Tienen
Thionville		Diedenhofen			
Toulouse				Tolosa	
Tourcoing					Torkonje
Tournehem-sur-la-Hem					Doornem
Valenciennes					Valensijn
Wambrechies					Wemmersijs
Warneton					Waasten
Wasselonne		Wasselnheim			
Wintzenheim		Winzenheim			

Wissant					Witsant / Witzand
Wissembourg		Weißenburg			
Zutkerque					Zuidkerke
Zuydcoote					Zuidcote

Administrative districts

France is divided into 22 *régions,* 102 *départements* (6 of which are overseas) and around 36 000 communes (municipalities). The *départements* are numbered, and these numbers are important because they appear in the postal codes. Initially these numbers were assigned by alphabetical order, but since the first classification some changes have been made which have altered this order.

Départements

Département	*Region*
01 Ain	Rhône-Alpes
02 Aisne	Picardie
2A Corse-du-Sud	Corse
2B Haute-Corse	Corse
03 Allier	Auvergne
04 Alpes-Haute-Provence	Provence - Alpes - Côte-d'Azur
05 Hautes-Alpes	Provence - Alpes - Côte-d'Azur
06 Alpes-Maritimes	Provence - Alpes - Côte-d'Azur
07 Ardèche	Rhône-Alpes
08 Ardennes	Champagne-Ardenne
09 Ariège	Midi-Pyrénées
10 Aube	Champagne-Ardenne
11 Aude	Languedoc-Roussillon
12 Aveyron	Midi-Pyrénées
13 Bouches-du-Rhône	Provence - Alpes - Côte-d'Azur
14 Calvados	Basse-Normandie
15 Cantal	Auvergne
16 Charente	Poitou-Charentes
17 Charente Maritime	Poitou-Charentes
18 Cher	Centre
19 Corrèze	Limousin
20 (see 2A and 2B)	
21 Côte d'Or	Bourgogne
22 Côte d'Armor (previously Côte-du-Nord)	Bretagne
23 Creuse	Limousin
24 Dordogne	Aquitaine
25 Doubs	Franche-Comté
26 Drôme	Rhône-Alpes
27 Eure	Haute Normandie
28 Eure-et-Loire	Centre
29 Finistère	Bretagne
30 Gard	Languedoc-Roussillon

31 Haute Garonne	Midi-Pyrénées
32 Gers	Midi-Pyrénées
33 Gironde	Aquitaine
34 Hérault	Languedoc-Roussillon
35 Ille-et-Villaine	Bretagne
36 Indre	Centre
37 Indre-et-Loire	Centre
38 Isère	Rhône-Alpes
39 Jura	Franche-Comté
40 Landes	Aquitaine
41 Loir-et-Cher	Centre
42 Loire	Rhône-Alpes
43 Haute Loire	Auvergne
44 Loire-Atlantique	Pays de la Loire
45 Loiret	Centre
46 Lot	Midi-Pyrénées
47 Lot-et-Garonne	Aquitaine
48 Lozère	Languedoc-Roussillon
49 Maine-et-Loire	Pays de la Loire
50 Manche	Basse-Normandie
51 Marne	Champagne-Ardenne
52 Haute-Marne	Champagne-Ardenne
53 Mayenne	Pays de la Loire
54 Meurthe-et-Moselle	Lorraine
55 Meuse	Lorraine
56 Morbihan	Bretagne
57 Moselle	Lorraine
58 Nièvre	Bourgogne
59 Nord	Nord Pas-de-Calais
60 Oise	Picardie
61 Orne	Basse Normandie
62 Pas-de-Calais	Nord Pas-de-Calais
63 Puy-de-Dôme	Auvergne
64 Pyrénées Atlantiques	Aquitaine
65 Hautes Pyrénées	Midi-Pyrénées
66 Pyrénées-Orientales	Languedoc-Roussillon
67 Bas-Rhin	Alsace
68 Haut-Rhin	Alsace
69 Rhône	Rhône-Alpes
70 Haute Saône	Franche-Comté
71 Saône-et-Loire	Bourgogne
72 Sarthe	Pays de la Loire
73 Savoie	Rhône-Alpes
74 Haute Savoie	Rhône-Alpes
75 Paris	Ile-de-France
76 Seine-Maritime	Haute-Normandie
77 Seine-et-Marne	Ile-de-France

78 Yvelines	Ile-de-France
79 Deux-Sèvres	Poitou-Charentes
80 Somme	Picardie
81 Tarn	Midi-Pyrénées
82 Tarn-et-Garonne	Midi-Pyrénées
83 Var	Provence - Alpes - Côte-d'Azur
84 Vaucluse	Provence - Alpes - Côte-d'Azur
85 Vendée	Pays de la Loire
86 Vienne	Poitou-Charentes
87 Haute Vienne	Limousin
88 Vosges	Lorraine
89 Yonne	Bourgogne
90 Belfort	Franche-Comté
91 Essonne	Ile-de-France
92 Hauts-de-Seine	Ile-de-France
93 Seine-Saint-Denis	Ile-de-France
94 Val-de-Marne	Ile-de-France
95 Val-d'Oise	Ile-de-France

Postal codes commencing '99' are special postal codes for Paris.

These form the French Overseas' Territories/*Départements*:

970 Guadeloupe Cédex
971 Guadeloupe
972 Martinique
973 Guyane Française (French Guiana)
974 Réunion
975 Saint-Pierre-et-Miquelon
976 Mayotte
985 Mayotte Cédex
987 Polynésie Française (French Polynesia)
988 Nouvelle-Calédonie (New Caledonia)

Régions

Alsace
Aquitaine
Auvergne
Basse-Normandie
Bourgogne
Bretagne
Centre
Champagne-Ardenne
Corse
Franche-Comté
Haute-Normandie
Ile-de-France

Languedoc-Roussillon
Limousin
Lorraine
Midi-Pyrénées
Nord - Pas-de-Calais
Pays de la Loire
Picardie
Poitou - Charentes
Provence - Alpes - Côte-d'Azur
Rhône-Alpes

Telephone numbers

France changed its telephone number system on 18th October 1996. Every number, including code, now consists of 10 digits. Each subscribers number now has 8 digits and a two digit area code, 01, 02 , 03, 04 or 05.

The zone Paris/Ile de France *(départements* 75-Paris, 77-Seine-et-Marne, 78-Yvelines, 91-Essonne, 92-Hauts-de-Seine, 93-Seine-Saint-Denis, 94-Val-de-Marne and 95-Val d'Oise) has retained the area code 01.

02 covers western France (Normandie, Bretagne, Pays-de-la-Loire and part of Centre).

03 covers northern and eastern France - Picardie, Pas-de-Calais, Champagne-Ardenne, Lorraine, Alsace and parts of Bourgogne and Franche-Comté.

04 covers south-western France - Poitou-Charentes, Aquitaine and parts of Centre and Midi-Pyrenées

05 covers south-eastern France - Auvergne, Rhône-Alpes, Provence, Côte-d'Azur, Languedoc, Roussillón and part of Midi-Pyrenées.

The correct area code can be identified on the basis of the first two digits of the telephone number for numbers outside the Île-de-France 01 region as below. Numbers within the Paris region remain unchanged.

First 2 digits of subscriber's number (outside Île-de-France region)	*New area code*
20	03
21	03
22	03
23	03
24	03
25	03
26	03
27	03
28	03

29	03
31	02
32	02
33	02
34	05
35	02
37	02
38	02
39	02
40	02
41	02
42	04
43	02
44	03
45	05
46	05
47	02
48	02
49	05
50	04
51	02
53	05
54	02
55	05
56	05
57	05
58	05
59	05
60	03
61	05
62	05
63	05
65	05
66	04
67	04
68	04
69	04
70	04
71	04
72	04
73	04
74	04
75	04
76	04
77	04
78	04
79	04

80	03
81	03
82	03
83	03
84	03
85	03
86	03
87	03
88	03
89	03
90	04
91	04
92	04
93	04
94	04
95	04
96	02
97	02
98	02
99	02

French Guiana
Guyane Française

French Guiana is a *département* of France. It forms part of the French mail system.

Area: 90 909 sq. km (35 091 sq. miles)
Population: 130 000
Capital: Cayenne
Currency: 1 French Franc (Ffr) = 100 centimes
International telephone access code: 594

Languages

French Guiana has ten languages. The official language is French. 50 000 people speak French Guianese, a French-based Creole. Other languages are Arawak (150-200 speakers); Hakka Chinese; Emerillon (200 speakers); Caribbean Javanese; Kalihna (1 200 speakers); Palikúr (600 speakers); Wayampi (400 speakers) and Wayana (200 speakers).

Address formats

Please refer to the chapter on France for address information.

Postal codes

All French Guianan postal codes commence with the digits 973.

French Polynesia
Polynésie Française

French Polynesia is an overseas territory of France. It forms part of the French mail system. It includes the Maruqesas Islands, Gambier Islands, Austral Islands, Tuamotu Archipelago, Tahiti and the Society Islands.

Area: 3 941 sq. km (1 521 sq. miles)
Population: 200 000
Capital: Papeete
Currency: 1 French Franc (Ffr) = 100 centimes
International telephone access code: 689

Languages

The official languages are French, having 15 338 first-language speakers, and Tahitian, with 117 000 speakers. The other 7 languages are Austral (8 000 people in the Austral Islands); Hakka Chinese (19 200 people); Mangareva (1 600 people in the Gambier Islands and on Mangareva Island); North Marquesan (3 400 people in the Marquesas Islands); South Marquesan (2 100 people in the Marquesas Islands); Rapa (400 people on Rapa Island) and Tuamotuam (14 400 on Tuamotu and Tahiti).

Address formats

Please refer to the chapter on France for address information.

Postal codes

All French Polynesia postal codes commence with the digits 987.

Gabon

Official name: Gabonese Republic, République Gabonaise
Area: 267 667 sq. km (103 319 sq. miles)
Population: 1 079 000
Capital: Libreville
Currency: 1 CFA Franc (CFAFr) = 100 centimes
International telephone access code: 241

Languages

The official language is French. There are 40 languages spoken in Gabon, and the geographical spread is complex. The main languages are Fang (427 000 speakers); Mbere (110 000 speakers); Myene (35-69 000 speakers) and Njebi.

Example address format

M. Jean Makaya
B.P. 4462
LIBREVILLE

Any address written in a non-native language will be written in French. Deliveries are made only to post office boxes (*Boite Postale*, or *BP*).

Postbox

This is written as *Boite Postale*, or *BP*.

Postal codes

Gabon has no postal code system.

Georgia
Sakartvelos

The province of Abkhazia to the north-west of Georgia has been administered by Abkhaz rebels since 1993. Mail to this area may consequently be affected.

Official name: Republic of Georgia, Sakartvelos Respublika
Area: 69 700 sq. km (26 900 sq. miles)
Population: 5 400 000
Capital: T'bilisi
Currency: Lari
International telephone access code: 995

Languages

The geographical spread of Georgia's 10 languages is very complex. Georgian is the official language, spoken by 3 900 000 people (72%). Abkhaz is spoken by 101 000 (2%) in Abkhazia (north-west Georgia); Mingrelian by 500 000 (9.3%) in western Georgia; Osetin by 160 000 (3%) in South Ossetia. Other languages include Assyrian Neo-Aramaic, Bats (in Zemo-Alvani); Judeo-Georgian; Laz, Svan (in northern Georgia) and Urum.

Example address format

26, avenue D, Agmachenebeli
380002 T'BILISI

Postal codes

Postal codes consist of a block of 6 digits. This is the same code that was used before the independence of Georgia from the Soviet Union.

Towns

T'bilisi is known as *Tiflis* in German.

The following cities have changed their names since independence:

Old name	*New name*
Gegechkori	Martvili
Makharadze	Ozurgeti
Ordzhonikidze	Kharagouli
Tsakhaya	Senaki
Tsulukidze	Khoni

Georgian place names should be used in preference to their Russian equivalents:

Georgian	*Russian*
Akhali Ap'oni	Novyy Afon
Akhalk'alak'i	Akhalkalaki
Akhalts'ikhe	Akhaltsikhe
Bagdadi	Mayakovskiy
Bat'umi	Batumi
Bichvint'a	Pitsunda
Borjomi	Borzhomi
Chiat'ura	Chiatura
Dushet'i	Dusheti
Gudauta	Gudaut'a
Gurjaani	Gurdzhaani
Jvari	Dzhvari
Khoni	Tsulikidze
K'obulet'i	Kobuleti
K'ut'aisi	Kutaisi
Mts'khet'a	Mtskheta
Och'amch'ira	Ochamchira
P'ot'i	Poti
Rust'avi	Rustavi
Samtredia	Samtrediya
Senak'i	Senaki
Sighnaghi	Signakhi
Sokhumi	Sukhumi
T'bilisi	Tbilisi
T'elavi	Telavi
T'et'ri-Tsqaro	Tetri-Tskaro
Tqibuli	Tkibuli
Tqvarch'eli	Tkvarcheli
Tsit'eli-Tsqaro	Tsiteli-Tskaro
Tsqaltubo	Tskhaltubo
Zest'ap'oni	Zestafoni

In Abkhazia, Abkhazian equivalents exist for Georgian place names:

Georgian	*Abkhazian*
Gudaut'a	Gudawta
Och'amch'ira	Ochamchära
Sokhumi	Aq'wa

GERMANY: Postal regions and language areas

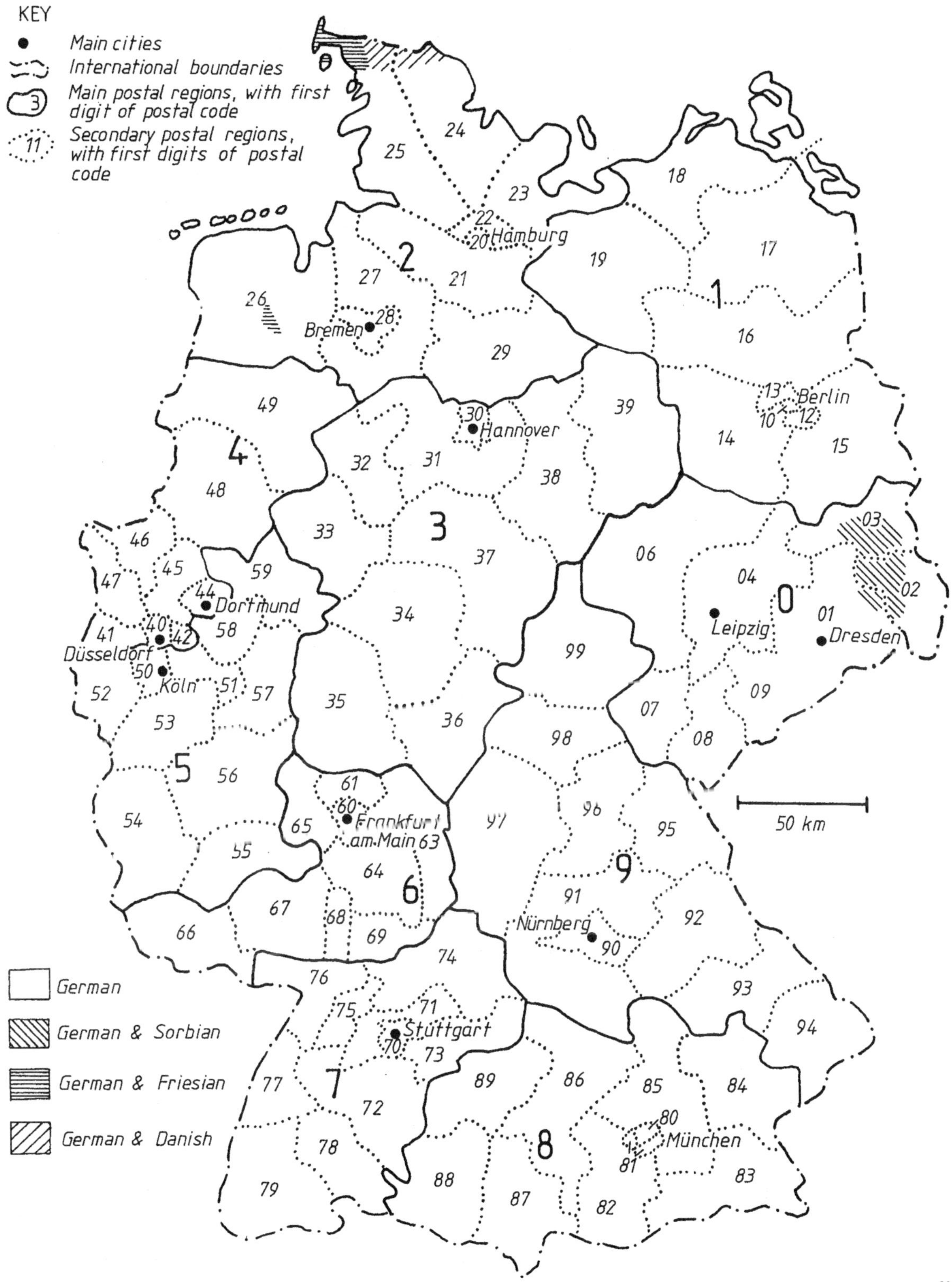

98

Germany
Bundesrepublik Deutschland

Official name: Federal Republic of Germany, Bundesrepublik Deutschland
Area: 356 945 sq. km. (137 817 sq. miles)
Population: 80 293 000
Capital: Berlin
Currency: 1 Deutschmark = 100 Pfennig
International telephone access code: 49

Languages

German is the official language, spoken by 98 per cent of the population. There are several dialects of German spoken: Allemannisch (similar to Alsatian spoken in France); Bavarian in Bavaria; Frankish (similar to German spoken in Belgium and to Letzebuergesch); Low German; Mainfränkisch; Low Saxon; Standard German and Swabian). Sorbian, also known as Wendish and Lusation, is a Slavic language spoken in Lusatia, which is a small area in the south-east of the former East Germany. There are some 70 000 speakers of two dialects: Upper Sorbian (around the city of Bautzen), resembling Czech; and Lower Sorbian, spoken around Cottbus, resembling Polish.

Frisian (21 000 speakers in the mutually unintelligible forms of North and East Frisian) is spoken in an area around Saterland, postal codes 26640-26689 and around Emden and Oldenburg. In Nord Friesland (near to the Danish border) it is spoken on the peninsula of Sylt (postal code area 25960-25999) except in the far north around List, where Danish is spoken. It is spoken on the islands of Föhr (except around Wyk and Nieblum); Amrum and Helgoland (postal code areas 27450-27499). It is also spoken along the coastal postal code areas 25890-25959 and 25800-25889. There is a "mainland" dialect and an "island" dialect, and other dialects between villages within these main areas.

Other minority languages include Danish in Jutland (50 000 speakers); Letzebuergesch around Bitburg near to the Luxembourg border and Romani.

Company names

It is more correct to place the words indicating the *nature* of a company in front of the name of the company, thus:

> Bäcker Klaus Schmidt

You will, however, often find these activity indications *after* the company name, thus:

> Klaus Schmidt, Bäcker
> Klaus Schmidt (Bäcker)

German company names will also often contain the name of the *inhaber(in)* (owner), usually indicated by the abbreviation *Inh*.

Company Types

The following company types may be recognized in German company names:

AG (Aktiengesellschaft)
Ausländische Rechtsform
BGB Gesellschaft
EG (Eintragener Verein)
Einzelfirma
Einzelunternehmen
Genossenschaft
GmbH (also often written Gesellschaft mbH) (Gesellschaft mit beschraenker Haft
GmbH & Co.
GmbH & Co. KG
GmbH & Co. OHG
KG (Kommanditgesellschaft)
KGaA (Kammanditgesellschaft auf Aktien)
OHG (Offene Handelsgesellschaft)
Stiftung

For the Attention Of

The words *zu Händen,* abbreviated to z.H. or z.Hd. mean 'For the attention of'.

Addresses

In company addresses the name of the company precedes the name of the contact. The house number follows the street name. The salutation of the person or the type of company comes on the top line alone. Thus:

Salutation
Contact name
Thoroughfare[ ]number
[ ]
postal code[ ]SETTLEMENT

or

Company
Salutation[ ]Contact name
Thoroughfare[ ]number
[ ]
postal code[ ]SETTLEMENT

For example

Herrn
Günther Meyer
Goethestraße 25

20002 HAMBURG

or

Bäcker Meyer
Herrn Mirgel
In der Raste 10

53001 BONN

Where the company name is a personal name, the word *Firma* may be used in the address thus:

Firma
Hans Meyer
In der Raste 10

53001 BONN

A blank line should always be printed above the line containing the postal code.

The general rule is that the thoroughfare name and the thoroughfare type are written as one word, thus:

Hauptstraße
Bahnhofstraße

There are two important exceptions. If the thoroughfare name refers to the real name of a place (e.g. a town name, a castle name, a forest name, etc.) or to a surname ending in *-er* then there is a space between the thoroughfare name and the thoroughfare type, thus:

Mainzer Straße
Hamburger Allee
Durer Straße

The second exception is where complete personal names are used. In these cases, each component of the street name is separated with a hyphen. Note, however, that surnames only are not covered by this exception. Thus:

Kaiser-Wilhelm-Straße
Albert-Einstein-Straße

but

Beethovenstraße
Einsteinstraße

In street names beginning with prepositions or some adjectives ('Am', 'An', 'Alter', etc.) the preposition or adjective is followed by a space, thus:

Alter Marktstraße

Thoroughfare types

Below is a list of the most commonly occurring thoroughfare types, with the abbreviated form(s) which you are most likely to find in address databases:

Thoroughfare type	*Abbreviation*
Allee	
Berg	
Boulevard	Bd
Bruch	
Bühl	
Chaussee	Ch
Damm	
Gasse	
Graben	
Hafen	
Hof	
Kamp	
Markt	
Platz	Pl
Ring	
Strasse	Str
Ufer	
Wall	
Weg	
Weide	

Other nouns, adjectives and prepositions commonly found in address databases

NB: German grammar rules governing articles, prepositions and adjectives are complex, and there is no need to explain them here. It is only necessary to be able to recognise them when and where they occur in addresses. For this reason a list without further explanation is provided. As a very general rule of thumb, the prepositions and adjectives listed may have one of the following endings added: nothing; -e; -er; -em; -en or -es.

der/die/das/den/dem/des	the
ein/eine/eines/einen/einem/einer	a, an
und	and

bis	till, until, up to
für	for
von	of, from
zu, zu der (zur), zu dem (zum), nach	to, towards
bei, bei der/den/dem (beim)	near, at
an, an der/den/dem (am)	at, by, towards
auf, auf der/den/dem	on
in, in der/den/dem (im)	in
gegenüber	opposite, facing
nächst, neben, neben der/dem/den	next to
hinter, hinter der/den/dem	behind
vor, vor der/den/dem	before, in front of
zwischen, zwischen der/den/dem	between, amongst
über, über der/den/dem	over, above, beyond
unter, unter der/dem/den	under, beneath, below
mit	with
neu/neue	new
alt/alte	old
kurz/kurze/kurzen/kurze /kurzem/kurzes (K.)	short
lang/lange/langen/langer/langem/langes (L./Lge.)	long
gross/grosse/grossen/grosser/grossem/grosses (G.)	large
klein/kleine/kleinen/kleiner/kleinem/kleines (K./Kl./Kle.)	small
nord	north
ost	east
süd	south
west	west
Sankt (St.)	saint
Industrieterrein, Industriegebiet	industrial estate

Postbox

This is written as *Postfach* followed by a number of digits in this pattern:

Postfach XX XX XX

Postboxes have their own postal codes, referring to the location of the post office where the box is situated, not of the company itself.

Postal codes

The postal code (*Postleitzahl* or *PLZ*) is written on the same line, and before, the name of the town.

The 4-digit postal code, valid since 1961, was changed on 1 July 1993. The old 4-digit postal code corresponded to a municipality.

The new postal codes contain 5 digits, and begin with any digit between 0 and 9. The first digit indicates the area of Germany in which the address is situated:

0 = Dresden/Leipzig
1 = Berlin
2 = Hamburg
3 = Hannover
4 = Düsseldorf/Essen
5 = Köln/Bonn
6 = Frankfurt
7 = Stuttgart
8 = München
9 = Nürnberg/Erfurt

The second digit indicates a smaller region within this area.

The third digit indicates a city, a part of a city, or a municipality.

The last two digits are split into three categories, each indicating (a) postboxes; (b) large users (receiving on average more than 2,000 letters per working day); and (c) groups of residences/businesses.

So, for example, a postal code may be built up as follows:

39	Region
390	Musterhausen
39001-39058	Post boxes
39060-39078	Large users
39080-39097	Deliveries (residences/businesses)
391	Bischofstadt

etc.

Postbox users now have two postal codes, one referring to their post box (for letters), the other referring to their street address (for packages etc.). Large users may have a third postal code. Any database containing German addresses will need to be able to store three postal codes per company.

The international sorting codes W- and O- (indicating respectively West and East Germany) have been replaced by the single international sorting code D-.

The delivery office number (the number which followed the town name, e.g. 2000 Hamburg 46) is no longer used.

Sorbian, a Slavic language, will be encountered in the following postal code areas:

01916, 01917, 01920, 02625, 02627, 02633, 02692, 02694, 02699, 02906, 02943, 02957, 02959, 02977, 02979, 02991, 02997, 02999, 03042-03055, 03042, 03044, 03058, 03096, 03099, 03130, 03139, 03149, 03172, 03185, 03197, 03205, 03222, 03226, 15907, 15913.

Towns

In the Sorbian-speaking area in the south-eastern part of the former East Germany, most towns and villages have both a German and a Sorbian name. The following list shows the corresponding names with their postal code areas:

German	*Sorbian*	*Postal code*
Arnsdorf	Warnoćicy	02633
Auritz	Wuricy	02627
Babow	Bobow	03099
Bärenbrück	Barbuk	03185
Baruth	Bart	02627
Bärwalde	Bjerwald	02999
Basabkwitz	Bozankecy	02625
Baschütz	Bošecy	02627
Bautzen	Budyšin	02625
Belgern	Běla Hora	02627
Belten	Bełošin	03226
Binnewitz	Bónjecy	02627
Birkau	Breza	02633
Bloaschütz	Blohasecy	02627
Blösa	Brězow	02627
Bluno	Bluń	02979
Bocka	Bokowc	01920
Bolbritz	Bolborcy	02627
Bornitz	Boranecy	02627
Boxberg	Hamor	02943
Brahmow	Brama	03096
Brehmen	Brěmjo	02694
Brieschko	Brěžki	02997
Briesen	Brjazyna	03096
Briesing	Brězynka	02694
Brießnitz	Brězecy	02627
Brohna	Bronjo	02627
Brösa	Brězyna	02694
Brösang	Brězynka	02633
Bröthen	Brětnja	02979
Buchwalde	Bukonjna	02694

Burg	Bórk	02979
Burg	Borkowy	03096
Burghammer	Bórkhamor	02979
Burgneudorf	Nowa Wjes	02979
Buscheritz	Bóšericy	02633
Byhleguhre	Běla Gora	15913
Byhlen	Bělin	15913
Calau	Kalawa	03205
Camina	Kamjenej	02627
Caminau	Kamjenej	02699
Canitz-Christina	Konjecy	02627
Cannewitz	Kanecy	01920
Cannewitz	Skanecy	02627
Caseritz	Kozarcy	01920
Caßlau	Koslow	02699
Coblenz	Koblicy	02633
Cölln	Chelno	02627
Commerau	Komorow	02694
Commerau bei Königswartha	Komorow p Rakec	02699
Cortnitz	Chortnica	02627
Cosul	Kózły	02692
Cottbus	Chośebuz	03042-03055
Crosta	Chróst	02694
Crostwitz	Chróśćicy	01920
Cunnewitz	Konjecy	01920
Dahlitz	Dalic	03099
Dahlowitz	Dalicy	02694
Dahren	Darin	02633
Daranitz	Torońca	02627
Dauban	Dubo	02906
Denkwitz	Dźenikecy	02692
Diehmen	Demjany	02633
Dissen	Dešno	03096
Döberkitz	Debrikecy	02627
Doberschau	Dobruša	02692
Doberschütz	Dobrošecy	02694
Doberschütz bei Neschwitz	Dobrošicy p Njeswačidło	02699

Dobranitz	Dobranecy	02633
Döbschke	Debiškow	02633
Döhlen	Delany	02627
Dörgenhausen	Němcy	02979
Drachhausen	Hochoza	03185
Drauschkowitz	Družkecy	02633
Drehna	Tranje	02999
Drehnow	Drjenow	03185
Drehsa	Droždźij	02627
Dreikretscham	Haslow	02633
Dreistern	Tři Hwězdy	02633
Dreiweibern	Tři Žony	02999
Dretschen	Drječin	02633
Drewitz	Drjejce	03197
Driewitz	Drěwcy	02999
Droben	Droby	02699
Dubrauke	Dubrawka	02627
Dubring	Dubrjenk	02997
Dürrbach	Dyrbach	02906
Dürrwicknitz	Wěteńca	01920
Ebendörfel	Bělšecy	02692
Eichow	Dubje	03099
Entenschenke	Kača Korčma	02699
Eulowitz	Jiłocy	02692
Eutrich	Jitk	02699
Fehrow	Prjawoz	03096
Fleißdorf	Ługi	03226
Forst	Baršć	03149
Förstgen	Dołha Boršć	02906
Friedersdorf	Bjedrichecy	02999
Gablenz	Jabłońk	02953
Gaußig	Huska	02633
Gebelzip	Hbjelsk	02627
Geierswalde	Lejno	02991
Geißlitz	Kislica	02694
Glaubnitz	Hłupońca	01920
Gleina	Hlina	02694

Glinzig	Glinsk	03099
Gnaschwitz	Hnašecy	02692
Göbeln	Kobjelń	02694
Göda	Hodźij	02633
Golenz	Holca	02633
Gränze	Hrańca	01920
Gröditz	Hrodźišćo	02627
Großbrösern	Přezdrěń	02627
Großdönschütz	Debsecy	02692
Groß Düben	Dźěwin	02959
Großdubrau	Wulka Dubrawa	02694
Großkunitz	Chójnica	02692
Groß Neida	Wulka Nydej	02979
Großpostwitz	Budestecy	02692
Groß Särchen	Wulke Ždźary	02999
Groß Saubernitz	Zubornica	02627
Großwelka	Wulki Wjelkow	02627
Grötsch	Grožišćo	03185
Grubditz	Hrubоćicy	02627
Grubschütz	Hrubjelčicy	02692
Grünbusch	Haj	02627
Guben	Gubin	03172
Guhra	Hora	02699
Guhrow	Gory	03096
Gulben	Gołbin	03099
Günthersdorf	Hunćericy	02633
Guttau	Hučina	02694
Haasow	Hažow	03058
Haide	Hola	02957
Halbendorf	Brežowka	02959
Halbendorf, Spree	Połpica, Sprjewa	02694
Heinersbrück	Most	03185
Hermsdorf	Hermanecy	02999
Hochkirch	Bukecy	02627
Höflein	Wudwor	01920
Holscha	Holešow	02699
Holschdubrau	Holešowska Dubrawka	02699

Horka	Hórki	01920
Hornow	Lěšće	03130
Horscha	Hóršow	02906
Hoske	Hózk	02997
Hoyerswerda	Wojerecy	02977
Jannowitz	Janecy	02633
Jänschwalde	Janšojce	03197
Jänschwalde Ost	Janšojce podzajtšo	03197
Jauer	Jawora	01920
Jauernick	Jawornik	02627
Jenkwitz	Jenkecy	02627
Jeschütz	Ješicy	02694
Jeßnitz bei Puschwitz	Jaseńca p Bóšicy	02699
Jeßnitz, Gebirge	Jaseńca, Horiny	02627
Jetscheba	Jatřob	02694
Johannisbad	Janska kupjel	01920
Johnsdorf	Jeńšecy	02699
Kamenz	Kamjenc	01917
Kaschel	Košla	02906
Kaschwitz	Kašecy	01920
Katschwitz	Kоćica	02633
Kaupen	Kupy	02957
Kauppa	Kupoj	02694
Keula	Kulowc	02997
Kleinbautzen	Budyšink	02627
Kleinbrösern	Přezdrěńk	02627
Kleindöbschütz	Małe Debsecy	02692
Kleinförstchen	Mala Boršć	02633
Kleingaußig	Mała Huska	02633
Kleinhänchen	Mały Wosyk	01920
Kleinholscha	Mały Holešow	02699
Kleinkunitz	Chójnička	02692
Klein Loitz	Łojojc	03130
Klein Oelsa	Wolešnica	02906
Klein Partwitz	Bjezdowy	02979
Kleinpraga	Mala Praha	02633
Klein Radisch	Radšowk	02906

Kleinsaubernitz	Zubornička	02694
Kleinseidau	Zajdow	02627
Kleinseitschen	Źičeńk	02633
Kleinwelka	Mały Wjelkow	02627
Klitten	Klětno	02906
Klix	Klukš	02694
Knappenrode	Hórnikecy	02979
Koblenz	Koblicy	02999
Kohlwesa	Kolwaz	02627
Kolkwitz	Gołkojce	03099
Königswartha	Rakecy	02699
Kopschin	Kopšin	01920
Kotitz	Kotecy	02627
Kotten	Koćina	02997
Kreba	Chrjebja	02906
Kreckwitz	Krakecy	02627
Kringelsdorf	Krynhelecy	02943
Krimnitz	Kśimnice	03222
Krinitz	Krónica	02699
Kronförstchen	Kříwa Boršš	02627
Kubschütz	Kubšicy	02627
Kumschütz	Kumšicy	02627
Kunersdorf	Kosobuz	03099
Kuppritz	Koporcy	02627
Laske	Łask	01920
Lauske	Łusč	02627
Lehde	Lědy	03222
Lehn	Lejno	02627
Lehndorf	Lejno	01920
Leipe	Lipje	03226
Leutwitz	Lutyjecy	02633
Liebegast	Lubhozdź	02997
Liebon	Liboń	02633
Lieske	Lěskej	02694
Limberg	Limbark	03099
Lippen	Lipiny	02999
Lippitsch	Lipič	02699

Lissahora	Liša Hora	02699
Litschen	Złyčin	02999
Litten	Lětoń	02627
Lobendorf	Łobožice	03226
Loga	Łahow	02633
Lohsa	Łaz	02999
Lömischau	Lemišow	02694
Lomsche bei Luppa	Łomsk p Łupoj	02694
Lomske	Łomsk	02699
Löschau	Lešawa	02627
Lubachau	Lubochow	02627
Lübben	Lubin	15907
Lübbenau	Lubnjow	03222
Luga	Łuh	02699
Luppa	Łupoj	02694
Luppedubrau	Łupjanska Dubrawka	02694
Luttowitz	Lutobč	02627
Malschwitz	Malešecy	02694
Maltitz	Malećicy	02627
Margarethenhütte	Margarećina Heta	02694
Märkischheide	Wusoka	03226
Maukendorf	Mučow	02979
Maust	Hus	03185
Mehltheuer	Lubjenc	02627
Merzdorf	Žylowk	03042
Meschwitz	Mječicy	02627
Milkel	Minakał	02699
Milkersdorf	Gornej	03099
Milkwitz	Miłkecy	02627
Miltitz	Miłoćicy	01920
Mönau	Manjow	02999
Mortka	Mortkow	02999
Mücka	Mikow	02906
Mühlrose	Miłoraz	02959
Mulkwitz	Mułkecy	02959
Muschelwitz	Myšecy	02633
Müschen	Myšyn	03096

Nardt	Narć	02979
Naundorf	Njabožkojce	03226
Naußlitz	Nowoslicy	01920
Nebelschütz	Njebjelčicy	01920
Nechern	Njechorń	02627
Nedaschütz	Njezdašecy	02633
Neschwitz	Njeswačidło	02699
Neubloaschütz	Nowe Błohašecy	02633
Neubornitz	Nowe Boranecy	02627
Neu Brohna	Nowe Bronjo	02627
Neu Buchwalde	Nowa Bukojna	02999
Neudiehmen	Nowe Dejany	02633
Neudorf	Nowa Wjes	02906
Neudorf	Nowa Wjes	02997
Neudorf bei Königswartha	Nowa Wjes p Rakecy	02699
Neudorf bei Neschwitz	Nowa Wjes p Njeswačidsło	02699
Neudörfel	Nowa Wjeska	01920
Neudörfel	Nowa Wjeska	02694
Neudorf, Spree	Nowa Wjes, Sprjewja	02694
Neuendorf	Nowa Wjas	03185
Nouhof	Nowy Dwór	01920
Neujeßnitz	Nowa Jaseńca	02699
Neukuppritz	Nowe Koporcy	02627
Neulauske	Nowy Łusč	02699
Neumalsitz	Nowe Małsecy	02625
Neupurschwitz	Nowe Poršicy	02627
Neupuschwitz	Nowe Bóšicy	02699
Neusärchen	Nowe Zdžarki	02694
Neustadt	Nowe Město	02979
Neustädtel	Nowe Město	01920
Neuwiese	Nowa Łuka	02979
Niedergurig	Delnja Hórka	02694
Niederkaina	Delnja Kina	02625
Niederuhna	Delni Wunjow	02627
Niesky	Niska	02906
Niethen	Něćin	02627
Nochten	Wochozy	02943

Nostitz	Nosaćicy	02627
Nucknitz	Nuknica	01920
Oberförstchen	Hornja Boršć	02633
Obergurig	Hornja Hórka	02692
Ober Prauske	Hornje Brusy	02906
Oberuhna	Horni Wunjow	02627
Oehna	Wownjow	02625
Oppitz	Psowje	02699
Ostro	Wotrow	01920
Pannewitz, Taucher	Banecy, Tuchor	01916
Panschwitz-Kuckau	Pančicy-Kukow	01920
Papitz	Popojce	03099
Paßditz	Pozdecy	02633
Peitz	Picnjo	03185
Petershain	Hóznica	02906
Pielitz	Splósk	02627
Pietzschwitz	Běčicy	02633
Piskowitz	Pěskecy	01920
Pließkowitz	Plusnikecy	02694
Plotzen	Błócany	02627
Pommritz	Pomorcy	02627
Prautitz	Prawoćicy	01920
Preilack	Pśiłuk	03185
Preititz	Přiwćicy	02627
Preske	Praskow	02633
Preuschwitz	Přišecy	02692
Prischwitz	Prěčecy	02633
Purschwitz	Poršicy	02627
Puschwitz	Bóšicy	02699
Quartitz	Chwaćicy	02694
Quoos	Chasow	02699
Rabitz	Rabocy	02627
Rachlau	Rachlow	02627
Rachlau	Rachlow	02997
Rackel	Rakojdy	02627
Räckelwitz	Worklecy	01920
Raddusch	Raduš	03226

Radewiese	Radowiza	03135
Radibor	Radwor	02627
Ralbitz	Ralbicy	01920
Rattwitz	Ratarjecy	02625
Rauden	Rudej	02999
Reichwalde	Rychwałd	02943
Reuthen	Ruśi	03130
Riegel	Roholń	02999
Rieschen	Zrěšin	02627
Rodewitz	Rodecy	02627
Rohne	Rowno	02959
Rosenthal	Róžant	01920
Ruben	Rubyn	03096
Ruhethal	Wotpočink	02694
Saalau	Salow	02997
Sabrodt	Zabrod	02979
Saccassne	Zakaznja	03096
Sagar	Zagor	02957
Salga	Załhow	02694
Salzenforst	Słona Boršc	02627
Sandförstgen	Borštka	02627
Särchen	Zdźar	02694
Saritsch	Zarěč	02633
Särka	Žarki	02627
Saspow	Zaspy	03044
Säuritz	Žricy	01920
Scheckwitz	Šekecy	02627
Schleife	Slepo	02959
Schlungwitz	Słónkecy	02692
Schmeckwitz	Smječkecy	01920
Schmerlitz	Smjerdźaca	01920
Schmochtitz	Smochćicy	02627
Schmogrow	Smogorjow	03096
Schönau	Corny	01920
Schönhöhe	Šejnejda	03185
Schwarzadler	Čorny Hodler	02627
Schwarzaußlitz	Čorne Noslicy	02692

Schwarze Pumpe	Carna Plumpa	03139
Schwarzkolim	Čorny Chołmc	02991
Schweinerden	Swinjarnja	01920
Sdier	Zdźěr	02694
See	Jězor	02906
Seidewinkel	Židźino	02979
Seitschen	Žičeń	02633
Semmichau	Semichow	02633
Siebitz	Zejicy	01920
Siebitz	Dźiwoćicy	02633
Singwitz	Dźěžnikecy	02692
Soculahora	Sokolca	02627
Sollschwitz	Sulšecy	02633
Sollschwitz	Sulšecy	02997
Soritz	Sowrjecy	02627
Sornßig	Žornosyki	02627
Spittel	Špikały	02627
Spittwitz	Spytecy	02633
Spohla	Spale	02979
Spreetal	Sprjewiny Doł	02979
Spreewiese	Lichań	02694
Spreewitz	Šprjejcy	02979
Spremberg	Grodk	03130
Sprey	Sprjowje	02943
Steindörfel	Trjebjenća	02627
Steinitz	Šćeńca	02999
Stiebitz	Sćijecy	02625
Storcha	Baćoń	02633
Stradow	Tšadow	03226
Straupitz	Pšupc	15913
Striesow	Strjažow	03096
Strohschütz	Stróžišćo	02627
Suschow	Zušow	03226
Tätzschwitz	Ptačecy	02991
Tauer	Turjej	03185
Techritz	Ćěchorjecy	02692
Teichhäuser	Haty	01920

Temritz	Ćěmjercy	02627
Terpe	Terpje	03139
Tiegling	Tyhelk	02999
Trebendorf	Trjebin	02959
Truppen	Trupin	02699
Tschaschwitz	Casecy	01920
Übigau	Wbohow	02699
Uhyst	Delni Wujězd	02999
Vetschau	Wětošow	03226
Wadelsdorf	Zakrjejc	03130
Waditz	Wadecy	02627
Wartha	Stróža	02694
Wartha	Stróža	02999
Wawitz	Wawicy	02627
Weicha	Wichowy	02627
Weidlitz	Wutołčicy	02633
Weigersdorf	Wukrančicy	02906
Weißenberg	Wóspork	02627
Weißig	Wysoka	02627
Weißkeißel	Wuskidź	02957
Weißkollm	Běly Cholmc	02999
Weißnaußlitz	Běłe Noslicy	02633
Weißwasser	Běła Woda	02943
Wendischbaselitz	Serbske Pazlicy	01920
Werben	Wjerbno	03096
Weskow	Wjaska	03130
Wessel	Wjesel	02699
Wetro	Wětrow	02699
Wittichenau	Kulow	02997
Wolfshain	Śisej	03130
Wuischke bei Hochkirch	Wuježk p Bukecy	02627
Wuischke bei Weißenberg	Wuježk p Wóspork	02627
Wurschen	Worcyn	02627
Zahsow	Cazow	03099
Zeißig	Ćisk	02979
Zerkwitz	Cerkwica	03222
Zerna	Sernjany	01920

Zerre	Drětwa	02979
Zescha	Šešow	02699
Zieschütz	Cyžecy	02627
Zimpel-Tauer	Cympł Turjo	02906
Zischkowitz	Čěškecy	02633
Zockau	Cokow	02633
Zscharnitz	Čornecy	02633
Zschillichau	Čelchow	02694
Zschorna	Čornjow	02627

In North Friesland, near the border with Denmark, settlements may have a German, Frisian and/or Danish name:

German	*Frisian*	*Danish*
Bredstedt	Bräist	Bredsted
Dannewerk		Danevirke
Eckernförde		Ekernførde
Flensburg		Flensborg
Friedrichstadt		Frederiksstad
Glücksburg		Lyksborg
Groß-Wihe		Store Vi
Handewitt		Hanved
Husum	Hüsem	Husum
Kappeln		Kappel
Klixbüll		Klægsbøl
Niebüll	Naidbel	Nibøl / Nybøl
Norderbrarup		Nøorre Brarup
Schlei		Slien
Schwesing		Svesing
Süder-Lügum		Sønder Løgum
Viöl		Fjolde
Westerland	Wästerlönj	Vesterland
Wyk	Bi de Wik	Vyk

The following list gives foreign language equivalents of German city names.

NB: Towns ending in -burg in German are usually written ending in *-bourg* or *-burgo* in French and Italian respectively.

German	*English*	*French*	*Spanish*	*Italian*	*Dutch*
Aachen	Aix-la-Chappelle	Aix-la-Chapelle	Aquisgrán	Aquisgrana	Aken
Augsburg		Augsbourg			
Berlin	Berlin		Berlín	Berlino	Berlijn
Brandenburg		Brandebourg			
Braunschweig	Brunswick	Brunswick			
Breisach		Brisach			
Bremen	Brême			Brema	
Coburg		Cobourg			
Dresden		Drèsde		Dresda	
Duisburg		Duisbourg			
Flensburg		Flensbourg			
Frankfurt am Main	Frankfurt	Francfort		Francoforte	Frankfort aan de Main
Frankfurt an der Oder		Francfort			
Freiburg		Fribourg		Friburgo	
Hamburg	Hamburg	Hambourg	Hamburgo	Amburgo	
Hannover		Hanovre			
Kassel		Cassel			
Kleve	Cleves	Clèves			
Koblenz	Coblenz	Coblence	Coblenza		
Köln	Cologne	Cologne	Colonia	Colonia	Keulen
Konstanz	Constance	Constance		Constanza	
Leipzig				Lipsia	
Lübeck				Lubecca	
Lüneburg		Lunebourg			
Magdeburg		Magdebourg			
Mainz		Mayence	Maguncia		
München	Munich	Munich	Munich	Monaco (di Baviera)	
Nürnberg	Nuremberg	Nuremberg		Norimberga	Neurenberg
Oldenburg		Oldenbourg			
Regensburg		Ratisbonne			
Saarbrücken		Sarrebruck			
Saarlouis		Sarrelouis			
Speyer		Spire			
Stuttgart				Stoccarda	
Trier		Trèves	Tréveris		
Würzburg		Wurzbourg			
Zweibrücken		Deux-Ponts			

Settlement names in Germany will often contain a suffix indicating geographical position such as *am Rhein* or *bei Kamenz.* The new postal codes incorporate this information and the Bundepost refers that such suffixes are not used in addresses except where two settlements of the same name have the same postal code. The *Postleitzahlenbuch,* published by the Bundespost, gives the preferred written form for each settlement.

Administrative districts

Germany has 16 states *(Bundesländer)* split into 36 regions *(Regierungsbezirke).* These names are not used in addresses. In the following list, the English translations are given in brackets:

State	*Region*
Baden-Württemberg	Freiburg Karlsruhe Stuttgart Tubingen
Bayern (Bavaria)	Mittelfranken Niederbayern Oberbayern Oberfranken Oberpfalz Schwaben Unterfranken
Berlin	
Brandenburg	
Bremen	
Hamburg	
Hessen (Hesse)	Darmstadt Giessen Kassel
Mecklenburg-Vorpommern (Mecheleberg Pomerania)	
Niedersachsen (Lower Saxony)	Braunschweig Lüneburg Hannover Weser-Ems
Nordrhein-Westfalen (North Rhine-Westphalia)	Arnsberg Detmold Düsseldorf Köln Münster
Rheinland-Pfalz (Rhineland-Palatinate)	Koblenz Pfalz Trier
Saarland	
Sachsen (Saxony)	
Sachsen-Anhalt (Saxony-Anhalt)	
Schleswig-Holstein	
Thüringen (Thuringia)	

Ghana

Official name: Republic of Ghana
Area: 238 537 sq. km (92 100 sq. miles)
Population: 15 616 000
Capital: Accra
Currency: 1 Cedi (¢) = 100 pesewas
International telephone access code: 233

Languages

The national language is English.

71 other languages are spoken in Ghana. The geographical distribution of these languages is complex. The main languages are Abron (606 600 speakers); Ahanta (100 000 speakers); Akan (7 000 000 speakers); Anyin (200 000 speakers); Awutu (100 000 speakers); Birifor (100 000 speakers); Bissa (119 100 speakers); Buli (100 000 speakers); Dagaari (501 000 speakers); Dagbani (540 000 speakers); Éwé (1 615 000 speakers); Ga-Adangme-Krobo (1 125 900 speakers); Gonjo (250 000 speakers); Gua (156 000 speakers; Gurenne (526 000 speakers); Kasem (100 000 speakers); Konkomba (400 000 speakers); Kusaal (500 000 speakers); Mampruli (226 800 speakers); Ntcham (100 000 speakers); Nzema (285 800 speakers); Sehwi (200 000 speakers); Sisaala (20 000 speakers) and Wasa (175 000 speakers).

Example address format

Mr John Aka
P.O. Box 1234
ACCRA

There are no street deliveries in Ghana.

Postal codes

Ghana has no postal code system.

Greece
Ellás

Official name: Hellenic Republic, Elliniki Dimokratia
Area: 131 957 sq. km. (50 949 sq. miles)
Population: 10 264 156
Capital: Athínai (Athens)
Currency: 1 Drachma (Dr) = 100 leptae
International telephone access code: 30

Languages

Greek *(Demotiki)* is the official language, spoken by 95 per cent of the population. It is written in Greek script, though it is often found transcribed into Latin script. Other languages spoken are Macedonian (2 per cent), Turkish (1 per cent) and Albanian (1 per cent). There are some 200 000 (2%) speakers of Pontic (a form of Greek unintelligible to speakers of Standard Greek) in the suburbs between Athens and Peiraeus Katerini); 30 000 speakers of Bulgarian; 62 000 speakers of Romanian in the two dialects of Macedo and Megleno, 1 000 speakers of Romani and 300 speakers of Tsakonian.

Company Types

The following company types may be found in Greek addresses:

AE (Anonymous Eteria - limited liability)
Atomiki Epihirisi (sole proprietorship)
EPE (Eteria Periorismeris Efthinis - limited liability)

Addresses

Addresses have the following structure:

Contact name or Business name
Thoroughfare[ ]number
postal code[ ]TOWN NAME

For example:

George Larsis
Alkamenou 37
117 80 ATHÍNAI

The postal code should be separated from the settlement name by two spaces.

Postal codes

Postal codes consist of 5 digits. They are written on the same line (the last line) and before the town name in the following format:

999[ ]99

for example:

145 63 Athens
546 45 Thessaloniki

The first two digits indicate the prefecture of large town (more than 50 000 inhabitants), the third digit is a '0' to indicate a large town; the last three figures give the post office or destination.

Towns

Macedonian is spoken by some 180 000 inhabitants of the province of Macedonia, around Thessaloníki. Some settlements have both Greek and Macedonian names:

Greek	*Macedonian*
Édhessa	Voden
Flórina	Lerin
Kastoría	Kostur
Kilkís	Kuskuš
Polipotamos	Nered
Sérrai	Serres
Thessaloníki	Salonika / Solun
Véroia	Ber

The following list gives foreign language equivalents of Greek town names:

Greek	*English*	*French*	*German*	*Spanish*	*Italian*	*Dutch*
Athínai	Athens	Athènes	Athen	Atenas	Atene	Athene
Iráklion	Candia		Heraklion			
Kérkira	Corfu	Corfou	Korfu			
Khalkís	Chalcis					
Khaniá	Canea	La Canée	Chania			
Kórinthos	Corinth					
Patrai	Patrae		Patras		Patrasso	
Piraiévs	Piræus		Piräus	Pireo	Pireo	Piraeus
Ródos	Rhodes		Rhodos	Rodas	Rodi	Rhodos
Sparti	Sparta					
Thessaloníki	Salonica	Salonique	Saloniki	Tesalónica	Salonicco	Thessalonica

Administrative districts

Greece has 9 regions *(Dhiamerisma)* plus Greater Athens and 52 departments *(Nomoi)*. They are not used in addresses and are listed below with the English translation in brackets:

Region	*Department*
Aegean Islands	Khíos
	Kikládhes
	Lésvos
	Sámos
	Sporádhes
Athinai (Athens)	
Iónioi Nísoi	Kefalliniá
	Kérkira (Corfu)
	Levkás
	Zákinthos
Ípiros (Epirus)	Árta
	Ioánnina
	Préveza
	Thesprotia
Kríti (Crete)	Iráklion
	Khaniá
	Lasíthi
	Réthimnon
Makedhonía (Macedonia)	Dráma
	Flórina
	Grevená
	Imathía
	Kastoría
	Kaválla
	Khalkidhíki
	Kilkís
	Kozáni
	Pangaíon óros
	Pélla
	Piería
	Sérrai
	Thessaloníki
Pelopónnisos (Peloponnes)	Akhaïa
	Argolís
	Arkadhía
	Ilía
	Kórinthos
	Lakonía
	Messinia
Sterea Ellás-Évvoia	Aitolía-Akarnania

	Attiki
	Evritanía
	Évvoia
	Fokís
	Fthiótis
	Voíotía
Thessalía (Thessaly)	Kardhítsa
	Lárisa
	Magnisía
	Tríkkala
Thráki (Thrace)	Évros
	Rodhópi
	Xánthi

Greenland

Kalaalit Nunaat (Greenlandic), Kalâtdlit-Nunât (Inuit), Grønland (Danish)

Greenland is a self-governing Island Region of Denmark but relies on Denmark for its foreign affairs.

Official name: Greenland
Area: 2 175 600 sq. km (839 781 sq. miles)
Population: 55 533
Capital: Nuuk
Currency: 1 Danish krone (Dkr) = 100 øre
International telephone access code: 299

Languages

The official languages are Danish (7 830 speakers) and Inuktitut (Greenlandic) (40 000 speakers), an Inuit (Eskimo) language.

Addresses

Addresses are written in this format:

Recipient name
Thoroughfare[ ]number
postal code[ ]SETTLEMENT NAME

for example:

Torben Raldorf
Inuitgade 1
3900 NUUK

The Postal code should be separated from the town name by two spaces.

The address may be written in Greenlandic, Inuit or Danish.

Postal codes

Greenland belongs to the Danish postal system and, like Denmark, all its postal codes consist of a block of 4 digits placed before and on the same line as the settlement name. All Greenland postal codes begin with the number 39. Each settlement has its own postal code.

Towns

The following list gives corresponding settlement names in two of Greenland's languages:

Greenlandic	*Danish*	*Postal code*
Aasiaat	Egedesminde	3950
Ammassalik	Angmagssalik	
Ikerasassuaq	Prins Christian Sund	3924
Ilulissat	Jacobshavn	3952
Ittoqqortoormiit	Scoresbysund	3980
Kangerlussuaq	Søndre Strømfjord	3910
Kangaatsiaq	Kangatsiak	
Kangersuatsiaq	Prøven	
Kangillinnguit	Grønnedal	3930
Maniitsoq	Sukkertoppen	3912
Nunap Isua	Kap Farvel	
Nuuk	Godthåb	3900
Nuusuaq	Kraulshavn	
Paamiut	Frederikshåb	3940
Pituffik / Uummanaq	Dundas	3970
Qaanaaq	Thule	3971
Qaqortoq	Julianehåb	3920
Qasigiannguit	Christianshåb	3951
Qeqertarsuaq	Godhavn	3953
Sisimut	Holsteinsborg	3911
Uummannaq	Umanak	

Telephone numbers

Greenland telephone numbers have no area codes.

Grenada

Official name: State of Grenada
Area: 344 sq. km (133 sq. miles)
Population: 100 000
Capital: St George's
Currency: 1 East Caribbean Dollar (EC$) = 100 cents
International telephone access code: 1

Languages

The national language is English. Some 43 000 people speak Less Antillean Creole English. There are scattered pockets of speakers of Less Antillean Creole French.

Example address format

Mr Tom Brown
ST. GEORGE'S

Postal codes

Grenada have no postal code system.

Telephone numbers

All telephone numbers in Grenada have the area code 809.

Guadeloupe

Guadeloupe is a *département* of France. It forms part of the French mail system. There are two large islands, Basse Terre and Grande Terre. It also includes the islands of the Saintes group, Marie Galante, Desirade, St Barthelemy and most of St Martin.

Area: 1 779 sq. km (687 sq. miles)
Population: 346 000
Capital: Basse Terre
Currency: 1 French Franc (Ffr) = 100 centimes
International telephone access code: 590

Languages

The official language is French, though 97% of the population speak Lesser Antillean Creole French.

Address formats

Please refer to the chapter on France for address information.

Postal codes

All Guadeloupe postal codes commence with the digits 971, or 970 for *Cédex* addresses.

Guam

Official name: Guam
Area: 541 sq. km (209 sq. miles)
Population: 138 000
Capital: Agaña
Currency: 1 United States Dollar (US$) = 100 cents
International telephone access code: 1

Languages

English, spoken by 28 800 people and Chamorro, spoken by 62 500 people are the official languages.

Addresses etc.

Guam is an unincorporated territory of the United States in the Pacific. It forms part of the United States' postal system. Its state code is GU and its postal codes fall in the range 96910-31.

Guam includes the island of Chuuk.

Please refer to the chapter on the United States of America for further information.

Guatemala

Official name: Republic of Guatemala, República de Guatemala
Area: 108 889 sq. km (42 031 sq. miles)
Population: 9 718 000
Capital: Guatemala City
Currency: 1 Quetzal (Q) = 100 centavos
International telephone access code: 502

Languages

The official language is Spanish, with 4 673 000 speakers.

Guatemala has 50 other languages, many of them Mayan dialects. The most important are Central Cakchiquel (132 200 speakers); Kekchi (335 800 speakers); Central Mam (100 000 speakers); Northern Mam (155 800 speakers); Southern Mam (125 000 speakers); Central Quiché (216 910 speakers); Eastern Quiché (100 000 speakers) and West Central Quiché (250 000 speakers).

Address format example

Sr. Raúl Rivera
18 calle 5-60, Z.I.
09001- QUETZALTENANGO

Many thoroughfares are numbered, as in the example above.

When addresses are written in Spanish and the thoroughfare has a name rather than a number, *calle*, the Spanish word for street, is rarely written. The Spanish thoroughfare type, when included, is written before, and separately from, the thoroughfare name. It should be written with the first letter in lower case.

For additional information on address components, please refer to the chapter on Spain.

Postal codes

The postal code (*Codigo Postal* or *CP*) consists of a block of 5 digits. The first two digits indicate the department, the middle digit the delivery method and the final two digits the delivery office.

Guernsey

Guernsey consists of the Channel Islands of Guernsey, Alderney, Sark and Herm. It is a Crown Dependency, and therefore not part of the United Kingdom of Great Britain and Northern Ireland. Except in matters of foreign affairs and defence, it is effectively an independent nation, and its inhabitants are fiercely proud of their status. The words 'United Kingdom', 'Great Britain' or 'England' should not be used in addresses - it is better to use 'Channel Islands'.

Area:	Guernsey:	65 sq. km (25 sq. miles)
	Alderney:	7.9 sq. km (3 sq. miles)
	Sark:	5.5 sq. km (2.1 sq. miles)
	Herm:	2 sq. km. (0.8 sq. miles)

Population:	Guernsey:	55 482
	Alderney:	2 000
	Sark:	420
	Herm with Jethou:	107

Capital: Guernsey: St. Peter Port
Alderney: St. Anne's

Currency: 1 Pound Sterling (£) = 100 pence.
International telephone access code: 44

Languages

English is the official language. A Norman patois, which has no written form, is spoken in some parishes.

Company names, contact names, addresses, postbox, towns

L

To a great extent, the same rules and formats apply as in the United Kingdom. The settlement name used is usually that of the parish. These parishes are:

Castel
Forest
St Andrew's
St Martin's
St Peters in the Wood
St Peter Port
St Sampson's
St Saviour's
Torteval
Vale

The name of the island (Guernsey, Alderney, Herm and Sark) is also written. The address is therefore structured as follows:

Contact name
{Job Title}
Company Name
number[ ]Thoroughfare name[ ]Thoroughfare type
PARISH
Island
POSTAL CODE

Postal codes

A postal code system was introduced into Guernsey only in June 1993. Each postal code begins with the letters GY. The format of the code is:

[GY]9[ ]9AA

for example

GY2 2BT

Guinea-Bissau
Guiné-Bissau

Official name: Republic of Guinea-Bissau, República da Guiné-Bissau
Area: 36 125 sq. km (13 948 sq. miles)
Population: 1 000 000
Capital: Bissau
Currency: 1 Guinea-Bissau Peso (GBP, PG) = 100 centavos
International telephone access code: 245

Languages

The official language is Portuguese.

There are 22 other languages spoken in Guinea-Bissau. Their geographical spread is complex. The most widely spoken are: Balanta (270 000 speakers); Upper Guinea Crioulo (a Creole based on Portuguese) (150 000 speakers); Fulfulde (180 000 speakers); Madinka (119 000 speakers); Mandyak (125 000 speakers) and Papel (97 000 speakers).

Example address format

Sra. Celina Soares das Gama
Rua Justino Lopes 12C
1000 BISSAU

Any address written in a non-native language will be written in Portuguese. The rules for Portuguese addresses will be followed - thoroughfare type first with an upper case first letter followed by thoroughfare name then number. For more information on thoroughfare types and other address components, please refer to chapter on Portugal.

Postal codes

These consist of a block of 4 digits.

Guinea
Guinée

Official name: Republic of Guinea, République de Guinée
Area: 246 000 sq. km (94 974 sq. miles)
Population: 7 800 000
Capital: Conakry
Currency: 1 Guinea Franc (GFr) = 100 cauris
International telephone access code: 224

Languages

The official languages are French and Fuuta Jalon with 2 550 000 speakers

There are 28 other spoken languages in Guinea. Their geographical spread is complex. The most widely spoken are: Northern Kissi (286 500 speakers); Maninka (1 816 000 speakers); Susu (800 000 speakers); Toma (143 800 speakers) and Yalunka (146 800 speakers).

Example address format

M. Diallo Alpha
B.P. 2345
CONAKRY

Any address written in a non-native language will be written in French. Deliveries are made only to post office boxes (*Boite Postale*, or *BP*).

Postbox

This is written as *Boite Postale*, or *BP*.

Postal codes

Guinea has no postal code system.

Guyana

Official name: Cooperative Republic of Guyana
Area: 214 969 sq. km (82 978 sq. miles)
Population: 800 000
Capital: Georgetown
Currency: 1 Guyana Dollar (G$) = 100 cents
International telephone access code: 592

Languages

The official language is English.

There are 13 other languages spoken in Guyana. The most widely spoken is Guyanese (an English-based Creole) with 650 000 speakers.

Example address format

M. Clyde Hamlet
Post Office Corporation
GEORGETOWN

Any address written in a non-native language will be written in English.

Postal codes

Guyana has no postal code system.

Haiti

Official name: Republic of Haiti, République d'Haiti
Area: 27 750 sq. km (10 712 sq. miles)
Population: 6 286 000
Capital: Port-au-Prince
Currency: 1 Gourde (G, Gde) = 100 centimes
International telephone access code: 509

Languages

French is the official language. However, the language spoken by almost the whole population is Haitian Creole French. 95% of the population understand no other language.

Example address format

M. Roland Rémy
rue Samba 1
6120 DELMAS 29

Addresses are written in French. For information about thoroughfare types and other address formats, please refer to the chapter on France.

Postal codes

Postal codes consist of a block of 4 digits. The first digit refers to the department, the second to the district, the third to the commune and the fourth to the part of the commune.

Honduras

Official name: Republic of Honduras, República de Honduras
Area: 112 088 sq. km (43 266 sq. miles)
Population: 5 105 500
Capital: Tegucigalpa
Currency: 1 Lempira (L, La) = 100 centavos
International telephone access code: 504

Languages

The official language is Spanish. There are 75 000 speakers of Garífuna, 11 000 speakers of English, 10 000 speakers of Mískito, and small numbers of speakers of Lenca, Pech, Sumo and Tol.

Example address format

Sr. Juan C. Martel
CM1102 LA LAJAS, COMAYAGUA

Postal codes

The postal codes consist of 6 alphanumeric characters. The first two digits refer to the department, the third to the category of post office and the last three the points of delivery.

Hungary
Magyarország

Official name: Republic of Hungary, Magyar Köztársaság
Area: 93 031 sq. km (35 919 sq. miles)
Population: 10 375 000
Capital: Budapest
Currency: 1 Forint = 100 fillér .
International telephone access code: 36

Languages

Hungarian is the official language, spoken by 98% of the population. Romany (1 per cent), German (1 per cent) and Slovak (1 per cent) are also spoken. There are smaller numbers of speakers of Romanian, Serbo-Croatian. There are some 5 000 Slovenian-speakers living in the area called Slovensko Raba, where the borders of Austria, Slovenia and Hungary meet.

Company names

A word indicating the *nature* of the company always follows the name of the company. The indication of legal company status follows this. So, for example:

Kovács Pékség Kft.

meaning Smith's Bakers Ltd. The main legal types found are Kft. (or KFT.) and BT.

Contact names

Contact names are always written with the surname first followed by the first name, without a comma separating them.

Addresses

Addresses may be written in one of the following formats, both of which are in common use and both of which are correct:

Recipient name
postal code[ ]TOWN NAME
Thoroughfare name[ ]thoroughfare type[ ]number

For example:

Nagy Sándor
1022 BUDAPEST
Hermann Ottó út 2

The alternative form is:

Recipient name
TOWN NAME
Thoroughfare name[ ]thoroughfare type[ ]number
postal code

For example:

Industrila Developments AB
BUDAPEST
Kavics utca 13
1025

When the address is split into more than one apartment, this can be indicated by showing the floor number in roman numerals, followed by a slash and then the apartment number in this way:

Kavics utca 13 II /3

The slash can be replaced by the word *em*, meaning floor, and the apartment number can be followed by the word *ajtó,* meaning door, in this way:

Kavios utca 13 II em 3 ajtó

In letters to destinations outside Hungary posted within Hungary, it is normal to put an "X" on its own on the line beneath the postal code (where the street address is normally found):

Graham Rhind
P. van Leeuwen Laan 32
3012 WILSELE
X
Belgium

This "X" may be found in address databases originating or data-entered in Hungary.

Thoroughfare types

The thoroughfare type should always be written starting with a lower case letter, and it is written after and separately from the street name. The most commonly occurring thoroughfare types, with their abbreviated forms, are:

árok
dűlő
fasor
kert
körönd
körút (krt.)

köz
lejtő
lépcső
liget
mező
park
rakpart (rpt.)
sétány
sor
sugárút
tér
tere
út
utca (u.)
útja

The genitive forms tere and útja occur where the street name is in the plural, such as Roses Street (*útja*) or Heroes Square (*tere*). The types *árok, dűlő, kert, lejtő, lépcső, liget, mező, park* and *sor* can also be street names, as in the English Park Lane or Court Street, but their position in the address will always make clear whether it is a thoroughfare name (with a capital letter) or a thoroughfare type (without a capital letter).

Postbox

Postbox is written *Postafiók*, usually shortened to *p.f.*, *P.f.*, *Pf.* or *pf.*

Nouns and prepositions commonly found in address databases

In Hungarian, adjectives are added as suffixes to nouns and can therefore not be identified as separate words.

Hungarian	*English*
a (before a consonant), az (before a vowel)	the
egy	a, an
és	and
új	new
öreg/regi	old
észak	north
kelet	east
dél	south
nyugat	west
Szent (Szt.)	Saint (St.)

Postal codes

Postal codes consist of a block of 4 numbers, written either before the town name or on their own on the last line of the address. They are sometimes written with spaces between each number.

Postal codes for Budapest always begin with a 1. The second and third digits indicate the district, whilst the last digit is determined by the post office.

Towns

Budapest is often abbreviated to Bp. in addresses. Many towns, particularly along the border with Austria where there is a small German-speaking minority, have German equivalents:

Hungarian	*German*
Alsósyölnök	Unterzeming
Bozsok	Poschendorf
Bucsu	Butsching
Csörötnek	Schriedling
Doymat	Großmucken
Felsöcsatár	Oberschilding
Gasztony	Gösting
Horvátlövő	Kroat. Schütyen
Jakabháza	Jakobshof
Kondorfa	Krottendorf
Köszeg	Güns
Magzarlak	Ung. Minihof
Narda	Nahring
Pinkamindszent	Alleheiligen
Pornóapäti	Pernau
Rábafüzes	Raabfidisch
Rábatótfalu	Windischdorf
Rátót	Neustift
Rönök	Radling
Sopron	Ödenburg
Sopronköhida	Strafanstalt
Szakonzfalu	Eckersdorf
Szentgotthárd	St. Gotthard
Szentpéterfa	Prostrum
Szombathely	Sternamanger
Vaskeresztes	Großdorf
Vasszentmihály	Raab-Michael
Velem	St. Veit

In the Slovenian-speaking area, the following settlements have alternative names:

Hungarian	*Slovenian*
Alsószölnök	Dolnji Senik
Apátistvánfalva	Števanovci
Farkasfa	Farkašovci
Felsőszölnök	Gornji Senik
Kétvölgy	Dve dolini
Orfalu	Andovci
Permise	Verice
Rábatótfalu	Slovenska ves
Ritkaháza	Ritkarovci
Szakonyfalu	Sakalovci
Szentgotthárd	Monošter

Croat-speakers, in some villages along the border with Burgenland in Austria use the following alternative names:

Hungarian	*Croat*
Alsócsatár	Dolnji Čatar
Felsőcsatár	Gornji Čatar
Horvátkimle	Hrvatska Kemlja
Horvátlövő	Hrvatske Šice
Horvátsidány	Židan
Kisnarda	Mala Narda
Kópháza	Koljnof
Nagynarda	Velika Narda
Ólmod	Plajgor
Peresznye	Prisika
Szentpéterfa	Petrovo Selo
Tomord	Temerje
Und	Unda

Administrative districts

Hungary has 20 counties *(Megye)*. They are not used in addresses. They are listed below:

Bács-Kiskun
Baranya
Békés

Borsod-Abaúj-Zemplén
Budapest
Csongrád
Fejér
Györ-Moson-Sopron
Hajdú-Bihar
Heves
Jász-Nagykun-Szolnok
Komárom-Esztergom
Nógrád
Pest
Somogy
Szabolcs-Szatmár-Bereg
Tolna
Vas
Veszprém
Zala

Iceland
Ísland

Official name: Republic of Iceland, Lýoveldio Ísland
Area: 103 000 sq. km (39 769 sq. miles)
Population: 259 000
Capital: Reykjavík (Reykjavik)
Currency: 1 Krónur (Kr, SK) = 100 aurar
International telephone access code: 354

Languages

Icelandic is spoken by 100 per cent of the population.

Contact names

Care must be taken when addressing Icelanders as members of the same family will have different surnames. Surnames are still formed from the name of the father followed by *dottír* for females and *son* for males. Thus Eirík and Rutar, son and daughter respectively of Magnus Jonsson will be Eirík Magnusson and Rutar Magnusdottír. For this reason, Icelandic telephone directories are ordered on the basis of first names.

Addresses

Addresses are written in the following format:

Contact name
Street name[ ]number
postal code[ ]TOWN NAME

For example:

Jon Jonsson
Einimel 80
107 REYKJAVIK

The thoroughfare type is suffixed to the thoroughfare name without a space, as in, for example:

Holtagata 5

Below is a list of the most commonly occurring thoroughfare types:

barð
borg
braut

byggð
fell
gata
gerði
götu
grund
hagi
háls
hjalli
hlíð
holt
land
lundur
melur
múli
nes
sel
sendi
siða
strætii
tangitún
teigur
torg
tún
vangur
vegi
vegur
vellir

Postbox

This is written as *Pósthólf*, abbreviated to *Ph.*

Postal codes

Postal codes are formed of a block of 3 digits. Street addresses and postboxes have different postal codes for the larger settlements (Akureyri, Gardabaer, Hafnarfjörður, Keflavík, Kópavogur, Reykjavík, Selfoss, Seltjarnarnes and Vestmannaeyjar)

Towns

The capital of Iceland, *Reykjavík is* generally known as *Reykjavik* (without the accent on the final i) in most other European languages. It is known as *Reikiavik* in Spanish.

Administrative districts

Iceland has 8 regions:

Asturlandskjördæmi
Midvesturlandskjördæmi
Nordurlandskjördæmi eystra
Nordurlandskjördæmi vestra
Reykjaneskjördæmi
Reykjavík
Sudurlandskjördæmi
Vestfjardakjördæmi

They are not used in addresses.

India
Bhārat (Hindi)

Official name: Republic of India, Bhārat
Area: 3 166 829 sq. km (1 222 369 sq. miles)
Population: 889 700 000
Capital: New Delhi
Currency: 1 Indian Rupee (Re, Rs) = 100 paisa
International telephone access code: 91

Languages

India has 407 languages. 16 of these are national languages. These are: Assamese (14 604 000 speakers in Assam, Meghalaya and Arunchal Predesh), written in Bengali script; Bengali (67 200 000 speakers in West Bengal and neighbouring states, written in Bengali script); English; Gujarati (43 312 000 speakers in Gujarat, Maharashtra, Rajasthan, Karnataka and Madhya Pradesh), written in Gujarati script; Hindi (180 000 000 speakers throughout northern India), written in Devanagari script; Kannada (33 663 000 speakers in Karnataka, Andhra Pradesh, Tamil Nadu and Maharashtra), written in Kannada script; Kashmiri (4 161 000 speakers in Jammu & Kashmir, Punjab, Uttar Pradesh, Delhi and Kashmir Valley), written in a Persian-based script; Malayalam (33 667 000 speakers in Karala, Laccadive Islands and neighbouring states), written in Mayalalam script; Maldivian (5 035 speakers on Minicoy Island in the Laccadive Islands), written in Tana script; Marathi (64 783 000 speakers in Maharachtra and neighbouring states), written in Devanagari script; Oriya (30 158 000 speakers in Orissa, Bihar, West Bengal, Assam and Andhra Pradesh), written in Oriya script; Panjabi (25 690 000 speakers in Punjab, Haryana, Delhi, Rajasthan, Jammu and Kashmir; Sindhi (2 678 000 speakers in Gujarat, Maharashtra, Rajasthan, Andhra Pradesh, Bihar, Delhi, Madhya Pradesh, Orissa, Tamil Nahu and Uttar Pradesh), written in Arabic and Gurumukhi scripts; Tamil (58 597 000 speakers in Tamil Nadu and neighbouring states), written in Tamil script; Telugu (66 318 000 speakers in Andhra Pradesh and neighbouring states), written in Telugu script; Urdu (45 733 000 speakers in Jammu & Kashmir and by Muslims spread throughout India), written in Arabic script.

Example address format

Mr. I.K. Taneja
Flat 100
Triveni Appartments
Pitampur
NEW DELHI 110034

Addresses written in a non-native language will be written in English.

The address may contain the state name. The constituent states of India, with their common abbreviations, are:

Andaman & Nicobar	AN
Andhra Pradesh	AP
Arnuchal Pradesh	AR
Assam	AS
Bihar	BR
Chandigarh	CHD
Daman & Diu	DD
Delhi	DEL
Dadra & Nagar Haveli	DNH
Goa	GOA
Gujarat	GUJ
Himachal Pradesh	HP
Haryana	HR
Jammu & Kashmir	JK
Kerala	KER
Karnataka	KRN
Lakshadweep	LKP
Maharashtra	MAH
Meghalaya	MEG
Mizoram	MIZ
Manipur	MNP
Madhya Pradesh	MP
Nagaland	NLD
Orissa	OR
Pondicherry	PDY
Punjab	PU
Rajasthan	RAJ
Sikkim	SKM
Tamil Nadu	TN
Tripura	TRP
Uttar Pradesh	UP
West Bengal	WB

Postal codes

Indian postal codes consist of a block of 6 digits. The first two indicate the state, the third the sorting centre and the last three a large town, a group of post offices or a delivery office.

Towns

Bombay is now correctly known as *Mumbai*. Calcutta is known as *Kalkutta* in German. Panjim is known in English as *Goa* and Puna as *Poona.*

Indonesia

The former Portuguese colony of East Timor has been occupied and annexed by Indonesia but the authority of Indonesia over this province is not recognized by the international community.

Official name: Republic of Indonesia, Republik Indonesia
Area: 1 906 240 sq. km (735 809 sq. miles)
Population: 184 796 000
Capital: Jakarta
Currency: 1 Indonesian Rupiah (Rp) = 100 sen
International telephone access code: 62

Languages

A huge number of languages are spoken on the 6 000 inhabited islands of Indonesia. 256 are spoken on Irian Jaya; 17 on Java and Bali; 82 on Kalimantan (Borneo); 128 in Maluku; 63 in Nusa Tenggara; 114 on Sulawesi and 52 on Sumatra.

The national language is Bahasa Indonesian, spoken by 17-30 000 000 as a mother language and a further 140 000 000 as a second language. Javanese is widely spoken (75 200 000 speakers). The former colonial language of Dutch is still understood by some.

Example address format

Tn. N. Suprapto
73, Jalan Cilaki
BANDUNG 40115

Postbox

This is called *Kotak Pos* in Indonesia.

Postal code

The postal code consists of a block of 5 digits.

Iran
Īrān

Official name: Islamic Republic of Islam, Jomhori-e-Islami-e-Īrān
Area: 1 648 000 sq. km (636 128 sq. miles)
Population: 59 600 000
Capital: Tehrān (Teheran)
Currency: 1 Iranian Rial (Ris, RI) = 100 dinars
International telephone access code: 98

Languages

There are 68 languages spoken in Iran. The main ones are Mesopotamian Arabic (1 200 000 speakers); South Azerbaijani (13 000 000 speakers) (also called Turkic); Western Farsi, the national language (25 300 000 speakers); Gilaki (3 265 000 speakers); Kurdish (3 250 000 speakers); Luri (4 280 000 speakers); Mazanderani (3 265 000 speakers) and Turkmen (1 000 000 speakers).

The use of Kurdish is highly discouraged by the Iranian authorities.

Example address format

Dr. Ali Shariati Ave.
Company Name
Bldg. No. 2
No. 797
16314 TEHERAN

Postal codes

The postal code consists of a block of 5 digits. The first digit is the forwarding code, the second the region, the third the district, the fourth the part of the district and the final digit is the delivery zone.

Towns

Tehrān is known as *Teheran* in English, French and German.

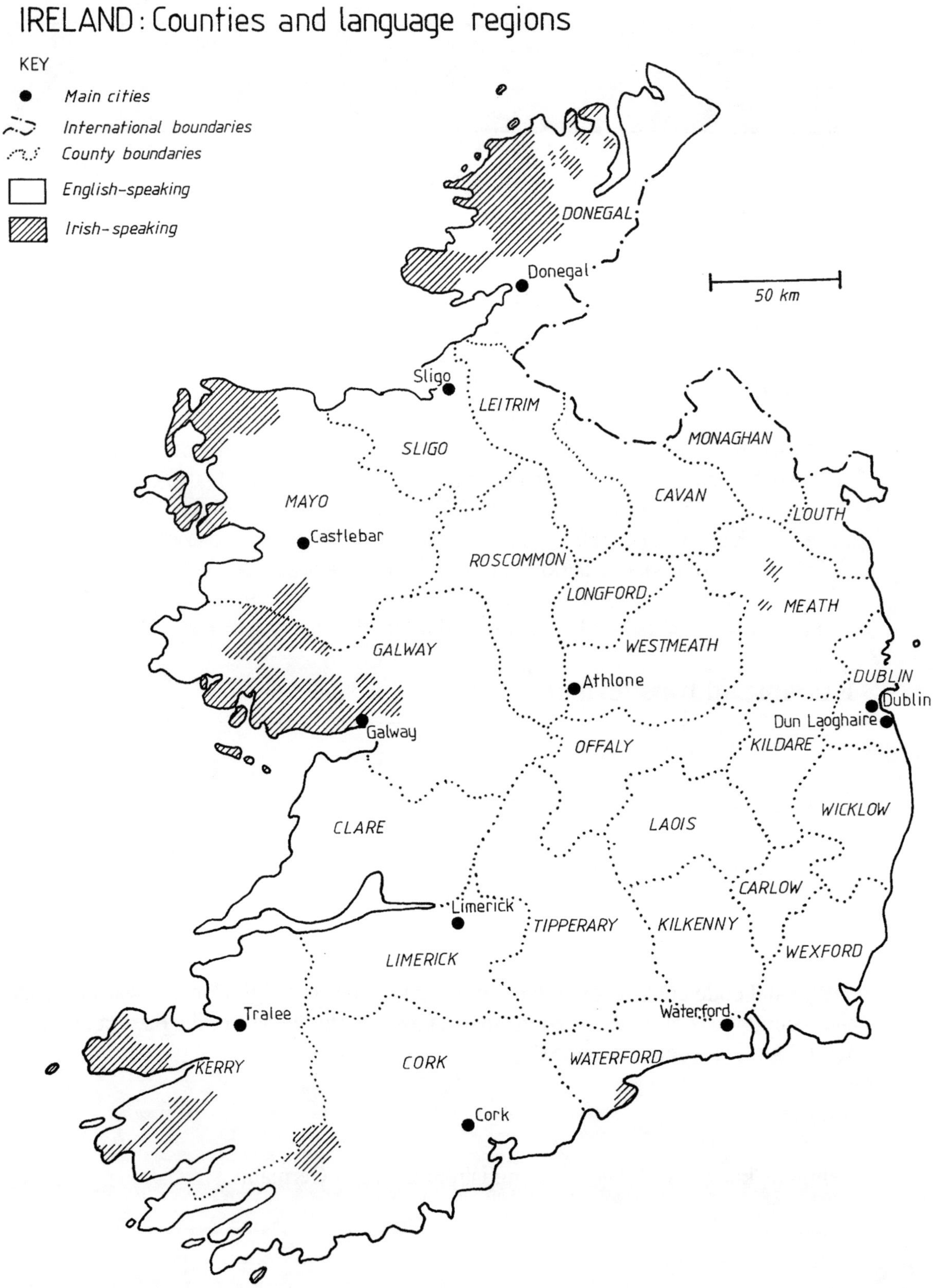
IRELAND: Counties and language regions
KEY
Main cities
International boundaries
County boundaries
English-speaking
Irish-speaking
50 km
DONEGAL
Donegal
Sligo
LEITRIM
SLIGO
MONAGHAN
MAYO
CAVAN
LOUTH
Castlebar
ROSCOMMON
LONGFORD
MEATH
GALWAY
WESTMEATH
Athlone
DUBLIN
Dublin
Dun Laoghaire
Galway
OFFALY
KILDARE
WICKLOW
CLARE
LAOIS
CARLOW
Limerick
TIPPERARY
KILKENNY
WEXFORD
LIMERICK
Waterford
Tralee
KERRY
CORK
WATERFORD
Cork

98

Ireland, Republic of
Éire

Official name: Republic of Ireland, Eire
Area: 70 283 sq. km (27 136 sq. miles)
Population: 3 525 719
Capital: Dublin
Currency: Irish pound/punt = 100 pence
International telephone access code: 353

Languages

Ireland has two official languages: English, spoken by 95 per cent of the population, and Irish (Gaelic) spoken by the remaining 5 per cent. The Irish speakers are mainly to be found in *An Ghaeltacht*, areas to the west and south-west of the country.

Contact Names

The surnames of the Irish may differ within a family (more so amongst speakers of Irish). In the name *Sean O'Fearghail*, the 'O' indicates "the lineage of". For a daughter, this would become *ni'Fearghail*. This is used whether single or married, as her status as daughter does not change. A married woman using her husband's name may use *Ui'Fhearghail* meaning "wife of". However, this form changes before a vowel or as a genitive making recognition for non-Irish-speakers difficult - for example, *Seán Mac Anna* (son), *Áine nic Anna* (daughter), *Máire bean Mhic Anna* (wife). Amongst English-speakers, the people in this last example would be known as *Seán McCann, Áine McCann* and *Máire McCann.*

Company names

In English, words indicating the *nature* of a company, when forming part of the company name, will always follow the name of the company, either after a comma or in brackets, thus:

> John Smith, Bakers
> John Smith (Bakers)

In Irish, this is reversed to become "Bakery of Smith" (with the name written in the genitive form):

> Bacus Mhic Ghabann

Company types

The following company types will be identified in Irish address databases:

Co-op (Co-operative)
Comhlucht Poibli Teoranta (CPT - Irish form of "PLC")
Friendly Society
Ltd (private limited company)
Partnership
PLC (Public Limited Company)
Public Corporation
Public Unlimited Company
Teoranta (Teo. - Irish form of "Limited")

Addresses

Addresses are written in the following formats:

Recipient name
number[ ]Street name
TOWN NAME{[ ]sorting code}
{County name}

or

Recipient name
number[,]Street name
TOWN NAME{[ ]sorting code}
{County name}

For example:

Mr Gerard Carey
45 O'Connell Street
DUBLIN 1

County names are not required for county towns.

The thoroughfare type is written after and separately from the thoroughfare name in English. In Irish the thoroughfare type is written before and separately from the thoroughfare name (with the exception of when the thoroughfare name is an adjective - thus Golden Lane is *Ór Lána*). Note also that Irish real names in addresses will change in their Irish form as dictated by rules governing the genitive case. Thus:

McDermott Tower

is

Túr Mhic Dhiarmada

in Irish. Another example:

O'Connell Street

is

Sráid Uí Chonaill

Non Irish-names will be unaffected:

Churchill Terrace

is

Ardán Churchill

Similar rules apply to place-names within street address strings.

In *An Ghaeltacht* (Irish-speaking areas) the law dictates that addresses are written in Irish only.

Building Indicators

Below is a list of commonly occurring building indicators, with the abbreviated form(s), which you are most likely to find in address databases:

English	*Abbreviation*	*Irish*
Apartments		Leithlanna
Buildings	Blgs	Foirgnimh
Cottages		Iostáin
Dwelling		Teaghais
Farm		Feirm
Flatlets		Mionárasáin
Flats		Árasáin
Hall		Halla
House(s)	Hse(s)	Teach (Tithe)
Lodge		Lóiste
Maison(n)ettes		Teaghaiseáin
Manor		Mainéar
Mansions		Árais
Penthouse		Díonteach
Tower		Túr
Villas		Bailtíní

Thoroughfare types

Below is a list of commonly occurring thoroughfare types, with the abbreviated form(s), which you are most likely to find in address databases:

English	*Abbreviation*	*Irish*
Alley		Scabhat

Arcade		Stuara
Arch		Áirse
Avenue	Ave.	Ascaill
Bank		Bruach
Bar		Barra
Behereen		Bóithrín
Boulevard	Bd.	Búlbhard
Bow		Bogha
Brae		Brí
Bridge		Droichead
Centre	Ctr.	
Chambers		
Circus		
Close		Clós
Colonnade		Colúnra
Coppice		Rosán
Copse		Rosán
Court	Ct.	Cúirt
Crescent	Cr.	Corrán
Croft		Croit
Cross		Crosaire
Dale		Gleanntán
Dell		Gleannán
Demesne		Diméin
Dene		Fothair
Diamond		Diamont
Dingle		Cumairín
Dock(s)		Duga(í)
Downs		Mulláin
Drive		Céide
Drove		
Dunes		Dumhcha
Estate		Eastát
Extension		Síneadh
Farm		Feirm
Field		Gort
Gardens		Gairdíní
Garth		Goirtín
Gate		Geata
Glade		Ceapach
Glebe		Gléib
Glen		Gleann
Grange		Gráinseach
Green		Faiche
Grove		
Guard		Garda
Haggard		Iothlainn

Hamlet		Gráig
Harbour		Calafort
Heath		Fraoch
Heights		Arda
Hill		Cnoc
Inns		Óstaí
Island		Oileán
Junction		Gabhal
Lands		Fearann
Lane		Lána
Lawn		Plásóg
Lott(s)		Scair(eanna)
Mall		Meal
Mardyke		Mairdíog
Market	Mkt.	Margadh
Mart		Marglann
Mead		Móinéar
Meadow		Cluain
Mews		Eachlann
Moor		Móinteán
Mount		Cnocán
Orchard		Úllord
Oval		Ubhchruth
Parade		Paráid
Park		Páirc
Passage		Pasáiste
Path		Cosán
Place	Pl.	Plás
Pound		Póna
Promenade		Promanáid
Quarter(s)		Ceathrú
Quay		Cé
Rise		Ard
Road	Rd.	Bóthar
Route	Rte.	
Row		Rae
Shambles		Seamlas
Side		Taobh
Slip		Caolbhealach
Spinney		Roschoill
Square	Sq.	Cearnóg
Steps		Céimeanna
Strand		Trá
Street	St.	Sráid
Terrace		Ardán
Third		Trian
Track		Raon

Vale		Gleann
Valley		Gleann
View		Radharc
Village		Sráidbhaile
Walk		Siúlán
Way		Bealach
Wood(s)		Coill(te)
Yard	Yd.	Clós

NB: The abbreviation for Saint commonly written in the same way as that used for Street, 'St.', though correctly Saint, as a contraction, is abbreviated without the full stop.

Other nouns, adjectives and prepositions commonly found in address databases for Gaelic

NB: note that the casing of Gaelic does not follow the logic used by other Indo-European languages such as English. The first letter of a real noun does not necessarily start with a capital letter, whilst a capital letter may appear in the second or third position of a word otherwise in lower case. For example *Teach an tSagairt*. These indicate letters ("eclipsing letters" added to the front of an existing word (which retains its case) in certain grammatical situations. Though no hard and fast rules can be given, it is usually the case that in words beginning with the following letters the first letter is in lower case, the second (or third) is in upper case thus: bhF, bP, dT, gC, mB, nD. E.g.. "Heights Road" is *Br na nArda*, "Trees Road" is *Br na gCrann.*

Prepositions in Irish change according to their position and combination with other words. Many do not have English equivalents. Where identifiable, they should be written in lower case.

There is no indefinite article ("a", "an").

Irish	*English*
an, a' (na for plural nouns)	the
Cúl-	Back
Cuar-	Circular
Cros-	Cross
Thoir	East
Oirthearach	Eastern
An Chéad	First
Tosaigh	Front
Mór	Great
Laistigh	Inner
Beag	Little

Íochtarach (or Íocht.)	Lower
Príomh-	Main
Láir	Middle
Míleata	Military
Nua	New
Thuaidh	North
Sean-	Old
Lasmuigh	Outer
Cúil	Rear
An Dara	Second
Theas	South
An Tríú	Third
Uachtarach (or Uacht.)	Upper
Thiar	West
Iartharach	Western
Saint	Naomh

Postbox

This is written as P.O. Box, Post Office Box, PO Box, or Postbox in English, *Bosca Poist* in Irish.

Postal codes

Ireland has no postal code system. Dublin addresses, however, will often contain a numeric sorting code (between 1 and 24), written after and on the same line as the town name. This code is always numeric with the single exception of the code "6W'.

Towns

Town names may be found in Gaelic, although they will more often be in English. The list below gives corresponding settlement names in English and Irish. The towns marked with an asterisk in the first list are in *An Ghaeltacht*, and their Irish names should therefore be used as preference. As Ireland has no postal codes, and the county is usually given in the address, the county in which the settlement is located is given.

English	*Gaelic*	*County*
Abbeyfeale	Mainistil na Féile	Limerick
Abbeyleix	Mainistir Laoise	Laois
* Achill Sound	Gob an Choire	Mayo
* Annagry	Anagaire	Donegal
Ardmore	Aird Mhór	Waterford
Arklow	An tlnbhear Mór	Wicklow
Askeaton	Eas Géitine	Limerick
Athenry	Baile Átha an Ri	Galway
Athlone	Átha Luain	Westmeath
Athy	Baile Átha Í	Kildare
Balbriggan	Baile Brigín	Dublin
Ballaghaderreen	Bealach an Doírín	Roscommon
Ballina	Béal an Átha	Mayo
Ballinasloe	Beal Átha na Sluaighe	Galway
* Ballingeary	Béal Átha an Ghaorthaidh	Cork
Ballinrobe	Baile an Róba	Mayo
Ballinskelligs	Baile an Sceilg	Kerry
Ballydavid	Baile na nGall	Kerry
* Ballyferriter	Baile an Fheirtéaraigh	Kerry
Ballyhaunis	Béal Átha hAmhnais	Mayo
Ballymakeera	Baile Mhic Ire	Cork
Ballymote	Baile an Mhotá	Sligo
Ballyshannon	Béal Átha Seanaidh	Donegal
* Ballyvourney	Baile Bhuirne	Cork
Baltinglass	Bealach Conglais	Wicklow
Bantry	Beanntraí	Cork
* Barna	Bearna	Galway
* Belmullet	Béal an Mhuirthead	Mayo
Belturbet	Béal Tairbirt	Cavan
* Binghamstown	An Geata Mór	Mayo
Birr	Biorra	Offaly
Blarney	An Bhlarna	Cork
Borris	An Buiríos	Carlow
Boyle	Mainastir na Búille	Roscommon
Bray	Bré	Wicklow

* Bunbeg	An Bun Beag	Donegal
Bunclody	Bun Clóidí	Wexford
Buncrana	Bun Chranncha	Donegal
Bundoran	Bun Dobhráin	Donegal
* Burtonport	Ailt an Chorráin	Donegal
Cahir	An Chathair	Tipperary
Cahirsiveen	Cathair Saidhbhín	Kerry
Callan	Callainn	Kilkenny
Cappoquin	Ceapach Choinn	Waterford
Carlow	Ceatharlach	Carlow
* Carna	Cárna	Galway
Carndonagh	Carn Domhnach	Donegal
* Carraroe	An Cheathrú Rua	Galway
* Carrick	An Charraig	Donegal
Carrickmacross	Carraig Mhachaire Rois	Monaghan
* Carrigart	Carraig Airt	Donegal
Cashel	Caiseal	Tipperary
Castlebar	Caisleán an Bharraigh	Mayo
Castlecomer	Caisleán an Chomair	Kilkenny
Castleisland	Oileán Chiarraí	Kerry
Castlerea	An Caisleán Riabhach	Roscommon
Cavan	An Cabhán	Cavan
Clara	Clóirtheach	Offaly
Claremorris	Clár Chlainne Mhuiris	Mayo
* Cloghan	An Clochán	Donegal
Clonakilty	Cloich na Coillte	Cork
* Clonbur	An Fhairche	Galway
Clones	Cluian Eios	Monaghan
Clonmel	Cluain Meala	Tipperary
Cóbh	An Cóbh	Cork
* Coelea	Cuil Aodha	Cork
Cong	Conga	Mayo
Cork	Corcaigh	Cork
* Costelloe	Casla	Galway
* Crolly	Croithli	Donegal
Croom	Cromadh	Limerick
Crosmolina	Crois Mhaoilíona	Mayo

Crosshaven	Bun an Tábhairne	Cork
* Dingle	An Daingean	Kerry
Donegal	Dún na nGall	Donegal
* Doochary	An Duchcharaid	Donegal
* Dooega	Dumha Éige	Mayo
* Downings	Dúnaibh	Donegal
Drogheda	Droichead Átha	Louth
Dublin	Baile Átha Cliath	Dublin
Dundalk	Dún Dealgan	Louth
Dungarvan	Dún Garbhan	Waterford
* Dungloe	An Clochán Liath	Donegal
Dunleer	Dún Léire	Louth
Dunmanway	Dún Mánmhaí	Cork
Dunmore	Dún Mór	Galway
* Dunquin	Dún Chaoin	Kerry
Edenderry	Éadan Doire	Offaly
Ennis	Inis	Clare
Enniscorthy	Inis Córthaidh	Wexford
Ennistimon	Inis Díomáin	Clare
* Falcarragh	An Fál Carrach	Donegal
Fermoy	Mainistir Fhear Maí	Cork
Fethard	Fiodh Ard	Tipperary
* Fintown	Baile na Finne	Donegal
Foynes	Faing	Limerick
Galway	An Ghaillimh	Galway
* Geesala	Gaoth Sáile	Mayo
* Glenamoy	Gleann na Muaidhe	Mayo
* Glencolumbkille	Gleann Cholm Cille	Donegal
Glengarriff	An Gleann Garbh	Cork
* Glinsk	Glinsce	Galway
Gorey	Guaire	Wexford
Gort	An Gort	Galway
* Gortahork	Gortan Choirce	Donegal
* Gortmore	An Gort Mór	Galway
* Gowla	Gabhla	Galway
Graiguenamanagh	Gráig na Manach	Kilkenny
Granard	Gránard	Longford

Greystones	Na Clocha Liatha	Wickford
* Gweedore	Gaoth Dobhair	Donegal
Headford	Áth Cinn	Galway
Hospital	An tOspigéal	Limerick
Inishcrone	Inis Crabhann	Sligo
* Inverin	Indreabhán	Galway
Julianstown	Baile Iúiliáin	Meath
Kanturk	Ceann Toirc	Cork
Kells	Ceanannus Mór	Meath
* Kilcar	Cill Charthaigh	Donegal
Kildare	Cill Dara	Kildare
Kilkee	Cill Chaoi	Clare
Kilkenny	Cill Chainnigh	Kilkenny
* Kilkieran	Cill Ciaráin	Galway
Killala	Cill Ala	Mayo
Killaloe	Cill Dalua	Clare
Killarney	Cill Áirne	Kerry
Killorglin	Cill Orglan	Kerry
Killybegs	Na Cealla Beaga	Donegal
Kilmallock	Cill Mocheallog	Limerick
Kilrush	Cill Rois	Clare
Kingscourt	Coill an Chollaigh	Cavan
Kinsale	Cionn tSáile	Cork
Leenan	An Líonan	Mayo
Letterkenny	Leitir Ceanainn	Donegal
Limerick	Luimneach	Limerick
Lisdoonvarna	Lios Dúin Bhearna	Clare
Lismore	Lios Mór	Waterford
Listowel	Lios Tuathail	Kerry
Longford	An Longfort	Longford
Loughrea	Baile Locha Riach	Galway
* Maam	Mám	Galway
Macroom	Maigh Chromtha	Cork
Malahide	Mullach Íde	Dublin
Mallow	Mala	Cork
Manorhamilton	Cluainín	Leitrim
Maynooth	Maigh Nua	Kildare

Millstreet	Sráid an Mhuilinn	Cork
Milltown Malbay	Sráid na Cathrach	Clare
Mitchelstown	Baile Mhisteála	Cork
Moate	An Móta	Westmeath
Mohill	Maothail	Leitrim
Monaghan	Muineachán	Monaghan
Mountmellick	Móinteach Mílic	Laois
Mountrath	Maighean Rátha	Laois
* Moycullen	Maigh Cuilinn	Galway
Mullingar	An Muileann gCearr	Westmeath
Naas	An Náa	Kildare
Navan	An Uaimh	Meath
Nenagh	An tAonach	Tipperary
Newcastle West	An Caisleán Nua	Limerick
Newmarket	Áth Trasna	Cork
New Ross	Ros Mhic Thriúin	Wexford
Oldcastle	An Seanchaisleán	Meath
Oughterard	Uachtar Ard	Galway
Portlaoise	Port Laoise	Laois
Portumna	Port Omma	Galway
Raphoe	Ráth Bhoth	Donegal
Rathdrum	Ráth Droma	Wicklow
Rathkeale	Ráth Caola	Limerick
Ráth Luire	An Ráth	Cork
Rathmelton	Ráth Mealtain	Donegal
Rathnew	Ráth Naoi	Wicklow
* Reananaree	Re na nDoiri	Cork
* Recess	Straith Salach	Galway
* Ring	An Rinn	Waterford
Roscrea	Ros Cré	Tipperary
Roscommon	Ros Comáin	Roscommon
* Rosmuck	RosMuc	Galway
* Rossaveal	Ros an Mhil	Galway
Rosslare	Calafort Ros Láir	Wexford
* Screeb	Scriob	Galway
Skerries	Na Sceirí	Dublin
Skibereen	An Sciobairín	Cork

Sligo	Sligeach	Galway
Swords	Sord	Dublin
Tarbert	Tairbeart	Kerry
Templemore	An Teampall Mór	Tipperary
Thomastown	Baile Mhic Andáin	Kilkenny
Thurles	Durlas	Tipperary
Tipperary	Tiobraid Árann	Tipperary
Tralee	Trá Lí	Kerry
Tramore	Trá Mhór	Waterford
Trim	Baille Átha Troim	Meath
Tuam	Tuaim	Galway
Tubbercurry	Tobar an Choire	Sligo
Tulla	An Tulach	Clare
Tullamore	Túlach Mhór	Offaly
Tullow	An Tulach	Carlow
* Ventry	CeannTra	Kerry
Waterford	Port Láirge	Waterford
Westport	Cathair na Mart	Mayo
Wexford	Loch Garman	Wexford
Wicklow	Cill Mhantáin	Wicklow
Youghal	Eochaill	Cork

Dublin is known as *Dublino* in Italian.

Administrative districts

Ireland has 4 provinces and 26 counties. Note that only part of the province of Ulster is within the Irish Republic. Counties are usually mentioned in the address, preceded by the abbreviation 'Co ', short for 'County', as Ireland has no postal codes.

Province	*County*
Connaught	Galway
	Leitrim
	Mayo
	Roscommon
	Sligo
Leinster	Carlow
	Dublin
	Kildare
	Kilkenny
	Laois
	Longford

	Louth
	Meath
	Offaly
	Westmeath
	Wexford
	Wicklow
Munster	Clare
	Cork
	Kerry
	Limerick
	Tipperary
	Waterford
Ulster	Cavan
	Donegal
	Monaghan

The remaining 6 counties of Ulster (Antrim, Armagh, Down, Fermanagh, Londonderry and Tyrone) form Northern Ireland, a constituent region of the United Kingdom.

Isle of Man

The Isle of Man is a Crown Dependency within the British Commonwealth. It is not part of the United Kingdom of Great Britain and Northern Ireland. Except in matters of foreign affairs and defence, it is effectively an independent nation, and its inhabitants are fiercely proud of their status. Do not use the words 'United Kingdom', 'Great Britain' or 'England' in the address.

Area: 572 sq. km (221 sq. miles)
Population: 64 282
Capital: Douglas
Currency: Manx pound (equivalent of Pound Sterling) = 100 pence
International telephone access code: 44

Languages

English is spoken. Manx, a Celtic language, is still spoken by 50 people as a second language.

Company names, contact names, addresses, postbox

The same rules and formats apply as in the United Kingdom.

Postal codes

A postal code system was introduced into the Isle of Man only in early 1994. It follows the same structure and format as United Kingdom postal codes. Each postal code begins with the letters IM. The format of the code is:

[IM]9[ ]9AA

for example

IM2 2BT

Israel
Yisr'el (Hebrew), Isrā'īl (Arabic)

Mail for the Palestine authority areas (West Bank and Gaza Strip) are routed through Israel.

Official name: State of Israel, Medinat Israel
Area: 20 770 sq. km (8 017 sq. miles)
Population: 5 240 000
Capital: Jerusalem
Currency: 1 New Israeli Shekel (NIS) = 100 agorot
International telephone access code: 972

Languages

Israel counts 31 languages. The national languages are Hebrew (4 510 000 speakers), written in Hebrew script; and Arabic (about 1 600 000 speakers in 6 different forms), written in Arabic script.

Example address format

Ploni Almoni
17 Jaffa Road
94142 JERUSALEM

Postal codes

Postal codes consist of a block of 5 digits.

Towns

The following list gives foreign language equivalents of Israeli town names:

Hebrew	*English*	*French*	*German*
Akko	Acre	Acre	Akre
Elat			Eylat
Nazerat	Nazareth		Nazareth
Tel Aviv-Yafo	Tel Aviv-Jaffa	Tel Aviv-Jaffa	Tel Aviv-Jaffa
Teverya	Tiberias		

ITALY: Provinces, postal regions and language areas

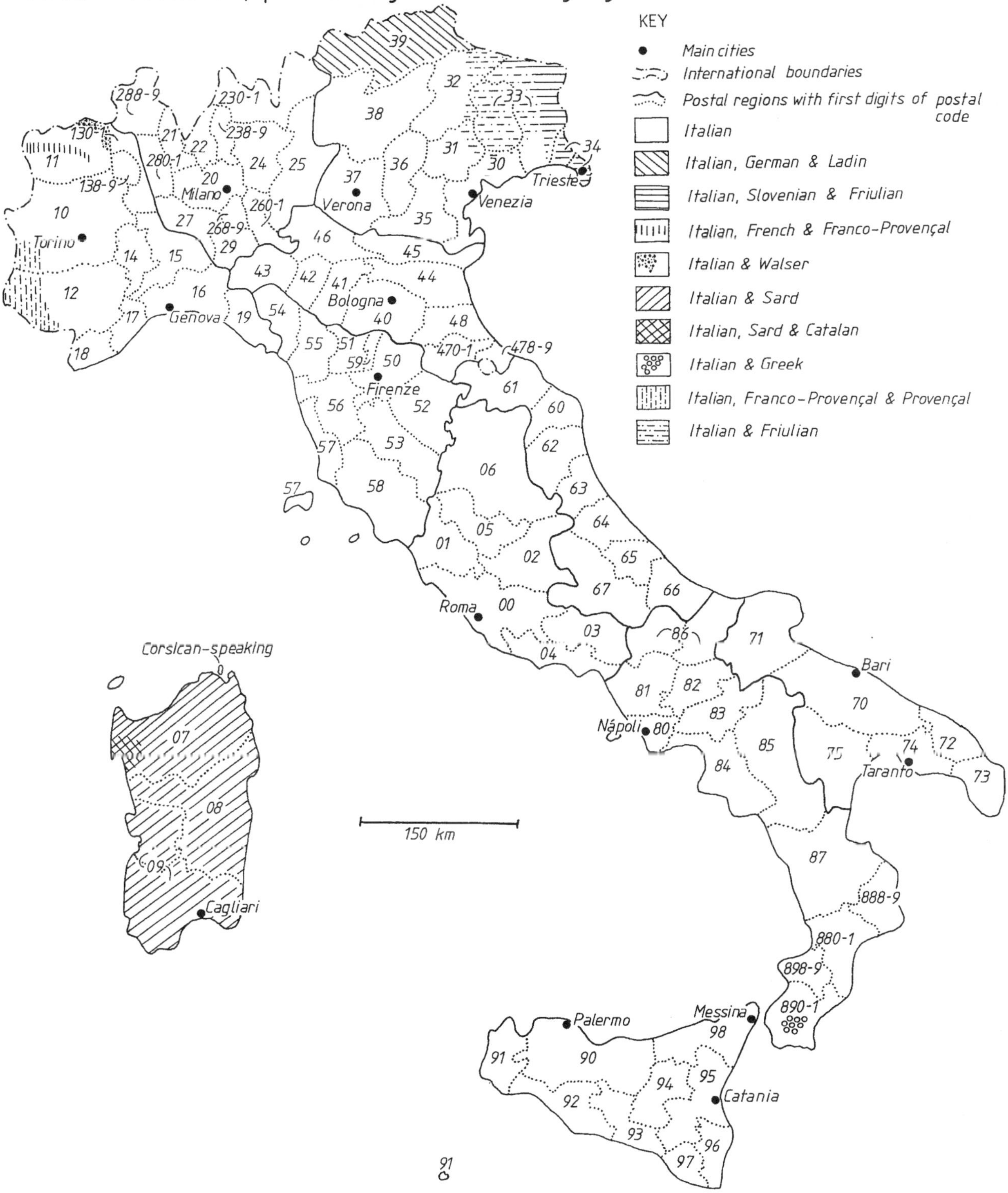

Italy
Italia

Official name: Italian Republic, Repubblica Italiana
Area: 301 277 sq. km (116 324 sq. miles)
Population: 57 103 833
Capital: Rome (Rome)
Currency: 1 Italian Lira (L, Lit, £) = 100 centesimi (no longer in circulation)
International telephone access code: 39

Languages

Italian, the official language, is spoken by 94 per cent of the population. Other languages are Sard (2 per cent, spoken in Sardinia in four distinct forms); Rhaetian (or Ladin, spoken by about 30 000 people, mainly in South Tyrol); German (also spoken in South Tyrol by some 225 000 people); French (spoken by 100 000 people in Piedmont in the Aosta Valley); Friulian (600 000 speakers - a Rhaetian dialect, spoken in Friuli-Venezia-Giulia; Catalan (21 629 speakers in Alghero on Sardinia); Slovene (by 100 000 people in Trieste and Friuli-Venezia-Giulia); Croat, (3 500 speakers); Greek (20 000 speakers) and Albanian (80 000 speakers) (all mainly spoken in southern Italy).

There are 2 230 speakers of Cimbrian (a Germanic dialect) in Trentino-Alto-Adige; 3 400 speakers of Walser, a dialect of German, in the Piedmont and Valle d'Aosta mountain villages of Alagna, Pedemonte, Rimella, Gressoney Saint Jean and Gressoney la Trinité; 270 000 speakers of Franco-Provençal and Provençal (in the Aosta Valley and other valleys of upper Piedmont); 1 900 speakers of Mócheno, a Germanic language, in the villages of Palú, Gereut and Fierozzo in the Valle del Fersina and 21 000 speakers of three forms of Romani. Corsican is spoken on the island of Maddalena off the north-east coast of Sardinia. Ligurian, an Italian dialect, is spoken by some 1 800 000 people in Liguria; Lombard, also an Italian dialect, by some 8 600 000 people in Lombardy, and similarly Sicilian is spoken by 4 700 000 people on Sicily and Venetian by 2 100 000 people around Venetia.

The South Tyrol, Südtirol in German, Alto Adige or Bolzano in Italian (postal code area 39) has a population of 433 229 (1981), of which 66 per cent (and increasing) are German speakers, 30 per cent (and decreasing) Italian speakers and 4 per cent Ladins-speakers (Rhaeto-Romanche). It became an autonomous region in January 1995. The inhabitants of this area are highly language-sensitive. It is important to mail in the right language.

For the Attention Of

This is written *A.C.A.* (*Alla Cortese Attenzione)* or simply as *Cortese* in Italian. One may also use *All' Attenzione d'* before a vowel, *All' Attenzione del* before a male name or *All' Attenzione della* before a female name.

Company names

In Italy it is more correct, where the *nature* of a company is mentioned in its name, that this *precedes* the name of the company, thus:

Fornaio Luigi

Company types

The following company types may be recognized in Italian company names:

Associazione
Azienda
Consorzio
Ente Morale
ICDP
Municipale
Municipale Assicurazioni
Società
SA (Società Anonima)
SapA (Società in accomandita per Azioni)
Sas (Società in accomandita semplice)
Società Individuale
Società Consortile
Società Cooperativa
Società di Fatto
Società Estera
SnC (Società in nome Collettivo)
SpA (Società per Azioni)
SrL (Società a responsabilità Limitata)

Addresses

Italian addresses are written in this format:

Recipient name
thoroughfare type[ ]Thoroughfare name[ ]number
postal code[ ]TOWN[ ]PROVINCE ABBREVIATION

or

Recipient name
thoroughfare type[ ]Thoroughfare name[,]number
postal code[ ]TOWN[ ]PROVINCE ABBREVIATION

For example:

Sig. Giovanni Masci
via Garibaldi 27
47037 RIMINI FO

or

Sig. Giovanni Masci
via Garibaldi, 27
47037 RIMINI FO

The province abbreviation may also be found written between brackets, but the Italian Post Office prefer that no punctuation is used in the address.

The thoroughfare type is written before and separately from the thoroughfare name. The thoroughfare type should be written with the first letter in lower case. Italian addresses may give the kilometre number of a house or company on long or inter-city routes rather than house numbers.

Building Indicators

Below is a list of the most commonly occurring building indicators, with the abbreviated form(s) which you are most likely to find in address databases:

Italian	*Abbreviation*	*English*
Casa	Ca., Ca'	House
Chiesa		Church
Municipio		Town Hall
Stazione		Station

Thoroughfare types

Below is a list of the most commonly occurring thoroughfare types, with the abbreviated form(s) which you are most likely to find in address databases:

accesso	
androne	
archivolto	
arco	
bacino	
baglio	
bastioni	
belvedere	
borghetto	
borgo	
calata	
calle	

campazzo	
campiello	
campo	
chiasso	
clivo	
colle	
contrada	c.^{da}
corte	
cortile	
corso	c, cso, c.^{so}
diramazione	
discesa	
fondamenta	
frazione	fraz, fr
galleria	
giardino	
gradinata	
gradini	
isola	
largo	lgo
lungo	
lungofiume (*fiume* can be replaced with the name of a river, such as *lungarno* or *lungo Po*)	
lungolago (*lago* can be replaced with the name of a lake)	
lungomare (*mare* can be replaced with the name of a sea)	
molo	
mura	
parco	
passaggio	
passeggiata	
passetto	
passo	
piazza	p, p.^{za}
piazzale	p.^{le}
piazzetta	
poggio	
ponte	
porta	
portici	
quadrato	
quartiere	
ramo	
rampa	
rio	
rione	

ripa	
riviera	
rotonda	
ruga	
salita	
scala	
scalinata	
scalo	
sentiero	
sito	
sottopassaggio	
sottoportico	
spianata	
strada	
strada comunale	
strada privata	
strada provinciale	
Strada Statale, Superstrada	SS (national route with km number)
strada vicinale	
stradella	
stradone	
traversa	
valle	
varco	
via	v
viale	vie, vl
vialetto	
vico	
vicoletto	
vicolo	
viuzzo	
volta	

Other nouns, adjectives and prepositions commonly found in address databases

NB: The form which certain common words take in Italian depends on a number of factors such as the gender of the following word, whether the next word is the definite article, whether the first letter of the next word is a vowel or a consonant, and whether that consonant is a z, gr, ps or an s+consonant. As this is rather complex, no explanation is given for each form but, where more than one form exists, each form is given.

il/i/l'/gli/lo/la/le	the
un/uno/una/un'	a, an
e	and
fino a, sino a	till, until
per	for
di	of
del/dei/dell'/degli /dello/della/delle	of the
per, a, in	to, towards
al/allo/alla/ai/agli/alle	towards the
presso, vicino a, accanto a	near, by, next to
su/sullo/sulle/sui/sugli/sulle	on (sea, a river), over
sul/sulla/sullo/sulle/sugli/sui	on the
in	in
nel/nello/nella/negli/nei/nelle	in the
in faccia a, di fronte (a), dirimpetto (a)	opposite
dietro, dopo, addietro, didietro	behind
davanti a, dinanzi a	in front of
fra, tra	between
sotto	under
sopra	over
con	with
nuovo, nuova, nuovi, nuove	new
vecchio, vecchia, vecchi, vecchie	old
corto, corta, corti, corte	short
lungo, lunga, lunghi, lunghe	long
grande, grandi	large
piccolo, piccola, piccoli, piccole	small
nord, del nord, settentrionale	north
est, dell'est, orientale	east
ovest, dell'ovest, occidentale	west
sud, del sud, meridionale	south
San (masculine), Santa (feminine), Sant' (before a vowel), Santo (before a masculine name beginning with a z, ps or s+consonant; e.g., Santo Stefano) (abbreviated to S., St., Sta.)	Saint
Zona Industriale	industrial estate

Postbox

This is written as *Casella Postale*, abbreviated to *CP*.

Postal codes

Postal codes *(il Codice di Avviamento Postale* (C.A.P.)) consist of a block of 5 digits, and are highly correlated with administrative districts.

Eight new provinces were created in 1995 (Biella, Crotone, Lecco, Lodi, Prato, Rimini, Verbano-Cúsio-Ossola and Vibo Valentia). Between 1995 and 1st October 1997, these new provinces shared postal codes with neighbouring provinces. From 1st October 1997, new postal codes were assigned to these new provinces, reproducing the good postal code/province fit which had previously existed. In the case of seven of these new provinces (excepting Prato), the new codes have as a third digit 8 or 9 rather than the 0 or 1 common in the rest of Italy.

The first digit of the postal code indicates one of 10 large postal zones. These do not correspond to Italy's provinces but the borders of the postal zones do follow the borders of the regions.

The first two numbers indicate the postal province. Italy has 95 administrative provinces and 92 postal provinces. The 8 number strings which are *not* found at the beginning of postal codes are as follows:

49, 68, 69, 76, 77, 78, 79, 99

In four cases, two provinces share the same first two digits:

09 - Cagliari and Oristano
33 - Pordenone and Udine
34 - Gorizia and Trieste
86 - Campobasso and Isernia.

Where the third, fourth and fifth numbers are 100 or 900, this indicates the capital of the province, which always has the same name as the province. In the cases of the provinces which share a postal code, this number is attributed to Cagliari, Udine, Trieste, and Campobasso. The third digit of the postal code can be 1, 3, 5, 7 or 9 if the postal code refers to the provincial capital; 0, 2, 4, 6 or 8 for other towns. In one case, postal code 30170, the third digit is a one but it does not refer to a regional capital.

Some of these provincial capital cities, and a single non-capital city (Mestre) are exceptions in as much as they themselves are split into further zones with postal codes on street level, where the last three digits fall between 101 and 199 or between 901 and 999. These cities are as follows:

00100 Roma
06100 Perugia
09100 Cagliari
10100 Torino
16100 Genova
19100 La Spezia
20100 Milano
24100 Bergamo
25100 Brescia
28900 Verbania
30100 Venezia
30170 Mestre
34100 Trieste

35100 Padova
37100 Verona
40100 Bologna
50100 Firenze
56100 Pisa
57100 Livorno
60100 Ancona
65100 Pescara
70100 Bari
80100 Napoli
84100 Salerno
89100 Reggio Calabria
90100 Palermo
95100 Catania
98100 Messina

Other cities, municipalities and large villages are indicated with the last three digits of the postal code falling between 001 and 099 or 801 and 899.

Please refer to the section on "Administrative Districts" for a list of postal codes per province.

The independent state of San Marino, region code SM, has the postal code 47031.

The independent state of Vatican City, has the postal code 00120.

Towns

The following lists gives alternative town names. The first list is for the bilingual Italian-/German-speaking area of South Tyrol. It is important in this area to use the German place names for German speakers.

Postal code	*Italian*	*German/Rhaetischian*
39030	Acerato	Ahornach
39050	Aica di Fié	Volser Aicha
39040	Aldino	Aldein
39040	Alpe di Siusi	Seiser Alpe
39010	Andriano	Andrian
39040	Anterivo	Altrei
39030	Anterselva	Antholz
39057	Appiano Strada Vino	Eppan Weinstrasse
39050	Auna di Sopra	Oberinn
39050	Auna Inferiore	Unterinn
39010	Avelengo	Hafling
39050	Avigna	Afing
39036	Badia	Abtei
39040	Barbiano	Barbian
39100	Bolzano	Bozen

39010	Borgo Vittoria	Meran Sinich
39030	Braies	Prags
39041	Brennero	Brenner
39042	Bressanone	Brixen
39051	Bronzolo	Bronzoll
39031	Brunico	Bruneck
39030	Cadipietra	Steinhaus in Ahrntal
39010	Caines	Kuens
39052	Caldaro Strado Vino	Kaltern Weinstrasse
39040	Campodazzo	Atzwang
39040	Campo di Trens	Freienfeld
39032	Campo Tures	Sand in Taufers
39053	Cardano	Kardaun
39056	Carezza al Lago	Karersee
39020	Castelbello Ciardes	Kastelbell Tschars
39010	Castelfirmiano	Sigmundskron
39040	Castelrotto	Kastelruth
39040	Cauria	Gfrill
39020	Cengles	Tschengels
39010	Cermes	Tscherms
39030	Chienes	Kiens
39043	Chiusa	Klausen
39043	Chiusa d'Isarco	Klausen
39020	Coldrano	Goldrain
39030	Colfosco in Badia	Kolfuschg
39054	Collalbo	Klobenstein
39040	Colle Isarco	Gossensass
39050	Collepietra	Steinegg
39050	Cologna	Glaning
39050	Contrada Val d'Ega	Eggental
39050	Cornaiano	Girlan
39050	Cornedo	Karneid
39040	Cortaccia Strada Vino	Kurtatsch Weinstrasse
39040	Cortina Strada Vino	Kurtinig Weinstrasse
39033	Corvara in Badia	Kurfar
39020	Curon Venosta	Graun im Vinschgau
39034	Dobbiaco	Toblach
39044	Egna	Neumarkt
39040	Eores	Afers
39030	Falzes	Pfalzen
39050	Fie'allo Sciliar	Vols am Schlern
39040	Fontanefredde	Kaltenbrunn
39045	Fortezza	Franzensfeste
39040	Funes	Villnoss
39010	Gargazzone	Gargazon
39020	Glorenza	Glurns
39043	Gudon	Gufidaun

39021	Laces	Latsch
39050	La Costa di Laives	Seit bei Leifers
39022	Lagundo	Algund
39040	Laion	Lajen
39055	Laives	Leifers
39011	Lana d'Adige	Lana a.d. Etsch
39023	Lasa	Laas
39020	Laudes	Laatsch
39040	Lauregno	Laurein
39030	La Valle	Wengen Pederoa
39030	La Villa in Badia	Stern in Abtei
39040	Lazfons	Laztfons
39030	Longega	Zwischenwasser
39030	Longiarú	Campill
39040	Luson	Lusen
39030	Lutago	Luttach
39040	Magré Strada Vino	Margreid Weinstrasse
39024	Malles Venosta	Mals
39030	Marebbe	St. Vigil Enneberg
39040	Mareta	Mareit
39020	Marlengo	Marling
39020	Martello	Martell
39020	Mazia	Matsch
39040	Meles	Meleins
39010	Meltina	Molten
39012	Merano	Meran
39035	Monguelfo	Welsberg
39040	Montagna Alto Adige	Montan
39020	Montechiaro	Lichtenberg
39020	Montefranco in Venostia	Freiberg Vinschgau
39040	Monte San Pietro	Petersberg
39020	Monte Santa Caterina	Katharinaberg
39010	Monte San Vigilio	Vigiljoch
39013	Moso in Passiria	Moos in Passeier
39020	Morter in Val Martello	Morter
39010	Nalles	Nals
39025	Naturno	Naturns
39040	Naz Sciaves	Natz Schabs
39056	Nova Levante	Welschnofen
39050	Nova Ponente	Deutschnofen
39040	Olmi	Holen
39040	Ora	Auer
39020	Oris	Eyers
39046	Ortisei	St. Ulrich Groden
39020	Parcines	Partschins
39010	Pavicolo	Pawigl
39030	Perca	Percha

39030	Piccolino	Pikolein
39050	Pineta di Laives	Steinmannwald
39020	Planeil	Planol
39010	Plan in Passiria	Pfelders
39040	Ponte Gardena	Waidbruck
39050	Pontenova	Birchabruck
39014	Postal	Burgstall
39050	Prato all'Isarco	Blumau
39026	Prato allo Stelvio	Prad
39030	Predoi	Prettau
39040	Preveis	Proves
39040	Pruno di Stilves	Elzenbaum
39040	Racines	Ratschings
39030	Rasun di Sotto	Niederrasen
39040	Redagno	Radein
39054	Renon	Ritten
39027	Resia all'Adige	Reschen
39040	Ridanna	Ridnaun
39010	Rifiano	Riffian
39037	Rio di Pusteria	Muhlbach
39031	Riscone	Reischnach
39030	Riva in Valle	Rain in Taufertal
39037	Rodengo	Rodeneck
39040	Salorno	Salurn
39010	Saltusio	Saltaus
39038	San Candido	Innichen
39030	San Cassiano in Badia	St. Kassian
39010	San Felice Val di Non	St. Felix
39050	San Genesio	Jenesien
39050	San Giacomo di Laives	St. Jakob bei Bozen
39030	San Giacomo in Valle Aurina	St. Jakob in Ahrntal
39030	San Giovanni in Valle Aurina	St. Johann in Ahrntal
39015	San Leonardo in Passiria	St. Leonhard in Passeier
39030	San Lorenzo di Sebato	St. Lorenzen in Pustertal
39040	San Lugano	St. Lugano
39030	San Martino Badia	St. Martin Thurn
39030	San Martino in Casies	St. Martin Gsies
39010	San Martino in Passiria	St. Martin in Passeier
39057	San Michele Appiano	Eppan
39050	San Nicoló in Val d'Ega	Untereggen
39010	San Nicoló Ultimo	St. Nikolaus Ulten
39050	Sant'Ottilia in Renon	Lengtein am Ritten
39010	San Pancrazio	St. Pankraz
39050	San Paolo Appiano	St. Pauls
39040	San Pietro Laion	St. Peter Lajen

39030	San Sigismondo	St. Sigmund
39047	Santa Cristina Valgardena	St. Christina Groden
39010	Santa Geltrude in Ultimo	St. Gertraud in Ulten
39040	Sant'Andrea in Monte	St. Andra bei Brixen
39016	Santa Valburga Ultimo	St. Walburg Ulten
39010	Sant'Orsola in Passiria	Schweinsteg
39050	Sant'Ottilia in Renon	Lengstein am Ritten
39050	San Valentino in Campo	Gummer
39020	San Valentino Mutta	St. Valentin a.d. Heide
39058	Sarentino	Sarntal
39017	Scena	Schonna
39030	Selva dei Molina	Muhlwald
39048	Selva di Val Gardena	Wolkestein in Groden
39010	Senale	Unsere Liebe Frau in Walde
39020	Senales	Schnals
39030	Sesto in Pusteria	Sexten
39028	Silandro	Schlanders
39040	Siusi	Seis am Schlern
39020	Sluderno	Schluderns
39029	Solda	Sulden
39040	Stange	Stanghe
39020	Stava	Staben
39020	Stelvio	Stilfs
39059	Soprabolzano	Oberbozen
39020	Tarces	Tartsch
39020	Tarres	Tarsch
39020	Tel	Toll
39031	Teodone	Dietenheim
39030	Terento	Terenten
39018	Terlano	Terlan
39040	Termeno Strada Vino	Tramin Weinstrasse
39010	Tesimo	Tisens bei Lana
39050	Tires	Tiers
39019	Tirolo di Merano	Tirol bei Meran
39040	Trodena	Truden
39020	Tubre	Taufers im Munstertal
39016	Ultimo	Ulten
39051	Vadena	Pfatten
39010	Valas	Flaas
39030	Valdaora	Olang
39049	Val di Vizze	Pfitsch
39040	Valgiovo	Jaufental
39030	Valle Aurina	Ahrntal
39030	Valle di Casies	Gsies
39010	Valtina	Walten
39030	Vandoies	Vintl

39050	Vanga	Wangen
39040	Varna	Vahrn
39040	Velturno	Feldthurns
39010	Verano	Voran
39039	Villabassa	Niederdorf
39043	Villandro	Villanders
39030	Villa Ottone	Uttenheim
39040	Villnoss	Funes
39010	Vilpiano	Vilpian
39049	Vipiteno	Sterzing
39040	Vizze	Pfitsch

For the Slovenian- and Friulian-speaking minorities in north-east Italy, the following equivalent town names exist:

Italian	*Slovenian*	*Friulian*
Aquileia	Oglej	
Aquilinea	Žavlje	
Artegna	Ratenj	
Attimis	Ahten	
Aurisina	Nabrežina	
Basivizza	Bazovica	
Benecia Centrale	Srednja Benečija	
Bisiacaria	Laško	
Campeglio	Čampej	
Campoformido		Cjampfuarmit
Camporosso	Žabnice	
Capriva	Kopriva	
Carso Goriziano	Goriški Kras	
Cave del Predil	Rabelj	
Cervignano	Červinjan	
Chiusaforte	Kluže	
Cividale del Friuli	Čedad	Cividat
Collio	Goriška Brda	
Cormons	Krmin	
Doberdò del Lago	Doberdob	
Dogna	Dunja	
Dolegna del Collio	Dolenje	
Drenchia	Dreka	
Duino-Aurisina	Devin-Nabrežina	

Faedis	Fojda	
Fusine	Bela Peč	
Germona	Gumin	Glemone
Gorizia	Gorica	Gurizze
Gradisca	Gradišče	
Grado	Gradež	
Grimacco	Grmek	
Latisana		Latisane
Lucinico	Ločnik	
Lusavera	Bardo	
Malborghetto-Valbruna	Naborjet-Ovčja	
Moggio Udine	Mužac	
Moimacco	Mojmak	
Monfalcone	Tržič	Monfalcon
Monrupino	Repentabor	
Monteaperta	Viškorša	
Montenars	Gorjani	
Muggia	Milje	
Nimis	Neme	
Pontebba	Tablja	
Pordenone		Pordenon
Portogruaro		Puartgruar
Premariacco	Premarjag	
Prepotto	Prapotno	
Prosecco	Prosek	
Pulfero	Podbonesac	
Raccolana	Reklana	
Resia	Rezija	
Resiutta	Na Bili	
Ronchi dei Legionari	Ronke	
Sagrado	Zagraj	
San Croce	Križ	
San Dorligo della Valle	Dolina	
San Floriano del Collio	Števerian	
San Leonardo	Sveti Lenart	
San Pietro al Natisone	Špeter Slovenov	
San Vito		San Vit

Savogna	Sovodnje	
Savogna d'Isonzo	Sovodnje ob Soči	
Sgonico	Zgonik	
Spilimbergo		Spilumberc
Stolvizza	Solbica	
Stregna	Srednje	
Stupizza	Štupica	
Taipana	Tipana	
Tarcento	Čenta	Tarcint
Tarvisio	Trbiž	
Tolmezzo		Tumiec
Torreano	Tavorjana	
Trieste	Trst	
Turriaco	Turjak	
Uccea	Učja	
Udine	Viden	Udin
Ugovizza	Ukve	
Valbruna	Ovčja vas	
Val Canale	Kanalska dolina	
Valli del Natisone	Nadiške Doline	
Valli del Torre	Terske doline	
Vas Tarvisio	Trbiž	
Venzone	Pušja Vas	
V. Opicina	Opčine	

Arberesh, a dialect of Albanian, spoken by 80-100 000 people in several pockets in the provinces of Avellino, Potenza, Taranto, Cosenza, Catanzaro and Palermo, stems from Albanian-speaking migrants of the 15th century. Their names for local settlements are:

Italian	*Arbaresh (Albanian)*
Acquaformosa	Firmoza
Barile	Barilli
Campomarino	Kemarini
Caraffa di Cantanzaro	Garfara
Carfizzi	Karfici
Casavecchio di Puglia	Kazallveqi
Castroregio	Kasternexhi
Cavallerizzo	Kajverici
Cervicati	Cervikati
Cerzeto	Qana

Chieuti	Qefti
Civita	Cifti
Eianina	Ejanina
Falconara Albanese	Fallkunara
Firmo	Ferma
Frascineto	Frasnita
Ginestra	Xhinestra
Lungro	Ungra
Macchia Albanese	Maqi
Maschito	Mashqiti
Mezzoiuso	Munxifsi
Mongrassano	Mungrasana
Montecilfone	Munxhfuni
Palazzo Adriano	Pallaci
Pallagorio	Puheriu
Piana degli Albanesi / Piana dei Greci	Hora e Arbereshevet
Plataci	Pllatani
Portocannone	Portkanuni
San Basile	Shen Vasili
San Benedetio Ullano	Shen Benedhiti
San Cosmo Albanese	Strighari
San Costantino Albanese	Shen Kostadini
San demetrio Corone	Shen Mitri
San Giacomo di Cerzeto	Shen Japku
San Giorgio Albanese	Mbuzati
San Martino di Finita	Shen Murtiri
San Marzano di San Giuseppe	Shen Marcani
San Nicola dell'Alto	Shen Kolli
San Paolo Albanese	Shen Pali
Santa Caterina Albanese	Picilia
Santa Cristina Gela	Sendahstina
Santa Sofia d'Epiro	Shen Sofia
Spezzano Albanese	Spixana
Ururi	Ruri
Vaccarizzo Albanese	Vakarici
Vena di Maide	Vina
Villa Badessa	Badhesa

Franco-Provençal is spoken in fourteen valleys of Western Piedmont, in the provinces of Torino and Cuneo (postal codes beginning 10 and 12). The Franco-Provençal names for local settlements are:

Italian	*Franco-Provençal*
Acceglio	Acelh
Aisones	Aison
Angrogna	Engroèha

Argentera	L'Argentièra
Bagnolo	Banhoèl
Bardonecchia	Bardonèicha
Bellino	Blins
Bernezzo	Bernes
Bibiana	Bubiana
Bibbio Pellice	Boèbi
Borgo San Dalmazzo	Lo Borg
Boves	Boèves
Bricherasio	Briqueràs
Briga Alta	Briga Auta
Brondello	Brondel
Brossasco	Brossasc
Busca	Buscha
Campiglione e Fenile	Campilhon e Fënil
Canosio	Chanoeias
Cantalupa	Chantaloba
Caraglio	Caralh
Cartignano	Cartinhan
Casteldelfino	Chasteldelfin
Castellar	Castlar
Castelmagno	Chastelmanh
Celle Macra	Celes
Chiomonte	Chaumont
Chiusa Pesio	La Chusa
Clavière	Clavièra
Crissolo	Crissòl
Demonte	Demont
Dronero	Droníer
Entracque	Entraiga
Exilles	Insilha
Fenestrelle	Fenestrella
Frabosa Soprana	Frabosa Sobrana
Frabosa Sottana	Frabosa Sotana
Frassino	Fraise
Frossasco	Frossasc
Gailoa	Gaiòla
Inverso Pinasca	Ënvèrs de Pinacha
Isasca	Isascha
Limone	Limon
Luserna San Giovanni	Lusèrna e San Jan
Lusernetta	Lusërnëtta
Macra	L'Alma e l'Albaré
Marmora	La Marmo
Martignana	Martinhana
Massello	Massèl
Melle	Lo Mel

Moiola	Moiòla
Montemale	Montmal
Monterosso	Montros
Oncino	Oncin
Oulx	Ols
Paesana	Paisana
Pagno	Panh
Perosa Argentina	Peirosa
Perrero	Prié
Peveragno	Poranh
Piasco	Lo Piasc
Pietraporzio	Peirapòrc
Pinasca	Pinacha
Pomaretto	Pomaret
Pontechianale	Pont e la Chanel
Porte	La Porta
Pragelato	Pratjalat
Prali	Pral
Pramollo	Pramòl
Prarostino	Prarustin
Prazzo	Pras
Rifreddo	Rifred
Rittana	Ritana
Roaschia	Roascha
Robilante	Robilant
Roccabruna	La Ròcha
Roccaforte Mondovì	Ròcafòárt
Roccasparvera	La Ròca
Roccavione	Rocavion
Roletto	Rolèi
Roure	Rore
Salza de Pinerolo	Salsa
Sambuco	Sambuc
Sampéyre	San Pèire
San Damiano Macra	San Damian
San Germano	San German
San Pietro	San Piere
San Secondo di Pinerolo	Ceisond
Sauze d'Oulx	Sause
Sauze di Cesana	Sause de Cesana
Sestrière	Sestrièra
Stroppo	Estròp
Torre Pellice	La Tor
Usseaux	Useaò
Valdieri	Vaudier
Valgrana	Valgrana
Valloriate	Valaoria

Venasca	Venascha
Vernante	Vërnant
Vignolo	Vinhoèl
Villar Pellice	Vilar
Villar Perosa	Li Vialar
Villar San Costanzo	Lo Vilar
Vinadio	Vinai

Italian town names in other languages:

Italian	*English*	*French*	*German*	*Spanish*	*Dutch*
Alessandria		Alexandrie			
Ancona		Ancône			
Aosta		Aoste			
Bergamo		Bergame			
Bologna	Bologne	Bologne		Bolonia	
Carrara		Carrare			
Catánia		Catane			
Como		Côme			
Cremona		Crémone			
Firenze	Florence	Florence	Florenz	Florencia	Florence
Genova	Genoa	Gênes	Genua	Génova	Genua
Gorízia			Görz		
Ivrea		Ivrée			
Livorno	Leghorn	Livourne			
Lucca		Lucques			
Mantova	Mantua	Mantoue	Mantua	Mantua	
Messina		Messine			
Milano	Milan	Milan	Mailand	Milán	Milaan
Modena		Modène			
Nápoli	Naples	Naples	Neapel		Napels
Novara		Novare			
Padova	Padua	Padoue	Padua	Padua	
Palermo		Palerme			
Parma		Parme			
Pavia		Pavie			
Pinerolo		Pignerol			
Pisa		Pise			
Piacenza		Plaisance			
Ravenna		Ravenne			
Roma	Rome	Rome	Rom	Roma	Rome
Savona		Savone	Savona		
Siena	Sienna	Sienne	Siena	Siena	
Siracusa	Syracuse				
Táranto		Tarente			
Tarvisio			Tarvis		
Torino	Turin	Turin	Turin	Turin	Turijn
Trento		Trente	Trient	Trento	
Treviso		Trévise			
Trieste			Triest		
Venezia	Venice	Venise	Venedig	Venecia	Venetië
Vercelli		Verceil			
Verona		Vérone			
Vicenza		Vicence			

Administrative districts

The correct abbreviation for the province in which an address is located should be included after and on the same line as the town name. Though these are often written between brackets, no brackets should be printed in the address.

Italy has 103 provinces *(Provincie)*(8 were added in 1995) in 20 regions *(Regioni).* Five of these regions (Valle d'Aosta, Trentino-Alto Adige, Friuli Venezia-Giulia, Sardegna and Sicilia) have special autonomy for ethnic, historical and/or peripheral reasons. The others have "ordinary" autonomy. Every province is named after its capital city.

The eight new provinces are Biella, Crotone, Lecco, Lodi, Prato, Rimini, Verbano-Cúsio-Ossola and Vibo-Valentia.

In the five cases where two provinces share the same first two postal code digits, these are marked with an asterisk. The provinces and regions are listed below with the English translation in brackets:

Province	*Postal code*	*Postal abbreviation*	*Region*
Agrigento	92	AG	Sicilia (Sicily)
Alessandria	15	AL	Piemonte (Piedmont)
Ancona	60	AN	Marche
Aosta	11	AO	Valle D'Aosta
Arezzo	52	AR	Toscana (Toscany)
Ascoli Piceno	63	AP	Marche
Asti	14	AT	Piemonte (Piedmont)
Avellino	83	AV	Campania
Bari	70	BA	Puglia
Belluno	32	BL	Veneto
Benevento	82	BN	Campania
Bergamo	24	BG	Lombardia (Lombardy)
Biella	138, 139	BI	Piemonte (Piedmont)
Bologna	40	BO	Emilia-Romagna
Bolzano-Bozen	39	BZ	Trentino-Alto Adige
Brescia	25	BS	Lombardia (Lombardy)
Brindisi	72	BR	Puglia
* Cagliari	09010-09017, 0902, 0903, 0904, 09070 (shared with Oristano) 09072 (shared with Oristano), 09080, 09100	CA	Sardegna (Sardinia)
Caltanissetta	93	CL	Sicilia (Sicily)
* Campobasso	8601-8604, 86100	CB	Molise
Caserta	81	CE	Campania

Catania	95	CT	Sicilia (Sicily)
Catanzaro	880, 881	CZ	Calabria
Chieti	66	CH	Abruzzo
Como	22	CO	Lombardia (Lombardy)
Cosenza	87	CS	Calabria
Cremona	260, 261	CR	Lombardia (Lombardy)
Crotone	888, 889	KR	Calabria
Cuneo	12	CN	Piemonte (Piedmont)
Enna	94	EN	Sicilia (Sicily)
Ferrara	44	FE	Emilia-Romagna
Firenze	50	FI	Toscana (Toscany)
Foggia	71	FG	Puglia
Forlì-Cesena	470, 471	FO	Emilia-Romagna
Frosinone	03	FR	Lazio
Genova	16	GE	Liguria
* Gorizia	3407, 3417	GO	Friuli-Venezia Giulia
Grosseto	58	GR	Toscana (Toscany)
Imperia	18	IM	Liguria
* Isernia	8607, 8608, 8609, 86170	IS	Molise
L'Aquila	67	AQ	Abruzzo
La Spezia	19	SP	Liguria
Latina	04	LT	Lazio
Lecce	73	LE	Puglia
Lecco	238, 239	LC	Lombardia (Lombardy)
Livorno	57	LI	Toscana (Toscany)
Lodi	268, 269	LO	Lombardia (Lombardy)
Lucca	55	LU	Toscana (Toscany)
Macerata	62	MC	Marche
Mantova	46	MN	Lombardia (Lombardy)
Massa-Carrara	54	MS	Toscana (Toscany)
Matera	75	MT	Basilicata
Messina	98	ME	Sicilia (Sicily)
Milano	20	MI	Lombardia (Lombardy)
Modena	41	MO	Emilia-Romagna
Napoli	80	NA	Campania
Novara	280, 281	NO	Piemonte (Piedmont)
Nuoro	08	NU	Sardegna (Sardinia)
* Oristano	09070 (shared with Cagliari), 09071, 09072 (shared with Cagliari), 09073-09079, 0908, 0909, 09170	OR	Sardegna (Sardinia)
Padova	35	PD	Veneto
Palermo	90	PA	Sicilia (Sicily)
Parma	43	PR	Emilia-Romagna
Pavia	27	PV	Lombardia (Lombardy)
Perugia	06	PG	Umbria
Pesaro e Urbino	61	PS	Marche

Pescara	65	PE	Abruzzo
Piacenza	29	PC	Emilia-Romagna
Pisa	56	PI	Toscana (Toscany)
Pistoia	51	PT	Toscana (Toscany)
* Pordenone	33030 (shared with Udine), 33070, 33073-33079, 3308, 3309, 33170	PN	Friuli-Venezia Giulia
Potenza	85	PZ	Basilicata
Prato	59	PO	Toscana (Toscany)
Ragusa	97	RG	Sicilia (Sicily)
Ravenna	48	RA	Emilia-Romagna
Reggio (di) Calabria	890, 891	RC	Calabria
Reggio (nell') Emilia	42	RE	Emilia-Romagna
Rieti	02	RI	Lazio
Rimini	478, 479	RN	Emilia-Romagna
Roma	00	RM	Lazio
Rovigo	45	RO	Veneto
Salerno	84	SA	Campania
Sassari	07	SS	Sardegna (Sardinia)
Savona	17	SV	Liguria
Siena	53	SI	Toscana (Toscany)
Siracusa	96	SR	Sicilia (Sicily)
Sondrio	230, 231	SO	Lombardia (Lombardy)
Taranto	74	TA	Puglia
Teramo	64	TE	Abruzzo
Terni	05	TR	Umbria
Torino	10	TO	Piemonte (Piedmont)
Trapani	91	TP	Sicilia (Sicily)
Trento	38	TN	Trentino-Alto Adige
Treviso	31	TV	Veneto
* Trieste	3401, 3410, 3411, 3412, 3413, 3414, 3415, 3416, 3418, 3419, 34062	TS	Friuli-Venezia Giulia
* Udine	3301, 3302, 33030 (shared with Pordenone), 33031-33039, 3304, 3305	UD	Friuli-Venezia Giulia
Varese	21	VA	Lombardia (Lombardy)
Venezia	30	VE	Veneto
Verbano-Cúsio-Ossola	288, 289	VB	Piemonte (Piedmont)
Vercelli	130, 131	VC	Piemonte (Piedmont)
Verona	37	VR	Veneto
Vibo-Valentia	898, 899	VV	Calabria
Vicenza	36	VI	Veneto
Viterbo	01	VT	Lazio

Ivory Coast
Côte d'Ivoire

Official name: Republic of Ivory Coast, République de la Côte d'Ivoire
Area: 322 462 sq. km (124 503 sq. miles)
Population: 12 100 000
Capital: Yamoussoukro
Currency: 1 CFA Franc (CFAFr) = 100 centimes
International telephone access code: 225

Languages

The official language is French, with 17 470 speakers. 72 other languages are spoken. The most widespread of these are: Anyin (610 000 speakers); Attié (381 000 speakers); Baule (2 130 000 speakers); Dan (800 000 speakers); Central Guéré (317 500 speakers); Guro (332 100 speakers); Jula (1 470 000 speakers) and Cebaara Senoufo (862 000 speakers).

Example address format

M. Paul Kouakou
03 BP 500
ABIDJAN 03

Any address written in a non-native language will be written in French. Deliveries are made only to post office boxes (*Boite Postale*, or *BP*). A sorting code is written both before the postbox number and after the settlement name.

Postbox

This is written as *Boite Postale*, or *BP*.

Postal codes

Ivory Coast has no postal code system.

Jamaica

Official name: Jamaica
Area: 10 957 sq. km (4 229 sq. miles)
Population: 2 445 000
Capital: Kingston
Currency: 1 Jamaican Dollar (J$) = 100 cents
International telephone access code: 1

Languages

The official language is English, though 94% of the population speak Western Caribbean Creole English.

Example address format

For Kingston:

> Mr James Garner
> 2 Cargill Avenue
> KINGSTON 10

For other areas:

> Ms Sandra Chin
> Dumfries District
> Morant Bay
> ST THOMAS

Address will be written in English. Kingston has a 1- or 2-digit sorting code written to the right of the city name.

Postal code

Jamaica have no postal code system.

Telephone numbers

All telephone numbers in Jamaica have the area code 876.

Japan
Nihon (Nippon)

Official name: Japan, Nippon
Area: 377 728 sq. km (145 803 sq. miles)
Population: 123 156 678
Capital: Tokyo
Currency: 1 Yen (¥, Y) = 100 sen
International telephone access code: 81

Languages

Japan counts 15 languages. Apart from Japanese, most are spoken by only a very small number of people, mainly on the Ryukyu Islands. Japanese is the mother language of 96% of the population. Korean is spoken by 0.5%. Okinawan is spoken by some on Okinawa.

Example address format

7-4, Marunouchi 3-chome
Naku-ku,
Nagoya-shi
AICI
460-9124

(Since the new postal code has been introduced on 2nd February 1998, the Japanese post office allows the postal code to be written on the top line of the address, as follows:

460-9124
7-4, Marunouchi 3-chome
Naku-ku,
Nagoya-shi
AICI)

The words *ken*, *fu* or *to* indicate a province. *Ku* indicates a ward within a city. The word *chome* indicates a division within this ward which is numbered. A *gaiku* is a block divided into *ban* and *jukyo bango*. The house number before the thoroughfare indicates the block number followed by the house number. The number order is therefore essential, even if it appears illogical. A third number may indicate an apartment within a house.

Postal code

Postal codes consist of seven digits in the following format:

999[-]9999

This code was introduced on February 2nd 1998. Before that postal codes had three or five digits. These old postal codes may still be found in address databases. The new seven-digit codes have been created by adding two or four digits to the end of the existing three- or five-digit code.

Jersey

Jersey is a British Crown Dependency and therefore is not part of the United Kingdom of Great Britain and Northern Ireland. Except in matters of foreign affairs and defence, it is effectively an independent nation, and its inhabitants are fiercely proud of their status. The words 'United Kingdom', 'Great Britain' or 'England' should not be used in addresses; it is better to use 'Channel Islands'.

Area: 116.2 sq. km (44.8 sq. miles)
Population: 82809
Capital: St. Helier
Currency: 1 Pound Sterling (£) = 100 pence
International telephone access code: 44

Languages

The official languages of Jersey are English and French. Though most people speak English, a dialect of Norman-French is still spoken by some people. This patois has no written form.

Company names, contact names, addresses, postbox

The same rules and formats apply as in the United Kingdom.

Postal codes

A postal code system was introduced into Jersey only in June 1993. It follows the same structure and format as United Kingdom postal codes. Each postal code begins with the letters JE and has the format:

[JE]9[ ]9AA

for example

JE2 2BT

Jordan
Al'Urdun

Official name: Hashemite Kingdom of Jordan, al Mamlaka al Urduniya al Hashemiyah
Area: 96 188 sq. km (37 129 sq. miles)
Population: 3 943 000
Capital: Amman
Currency: 1 Jordan Dinar = 1 000 fils
International telephone access code: 962

Languages

The national language is Standard Arabic. There are 44 280 (1.2%) speakers of Adyghe; 700 000 (17.8%) speakers of Levantine Bedawi Spoken Arabic; 50 000 (1.3%) speakers of Najdi Spoken Arabic and 3 500 000 (88.7%) speakers of South Levantine Spoken Arabic.

Example address format

Rajai Bashitti
4 str. Nicola Ghaneimeh Jabal
LUWEIBSEH-ALABDALY
AMMAN 11191

Postal code

The postal code consists of a block of 5 digits. The first indicates the region, the second the department, the third a zone, the fourth a sector and the last a unit (quarter or village).

Towns

The following list gives foreign language equivalents of Jordanian town names:

Arabic	*English*	*German*
Al'Aqabah		Akabah
Ammān	Amman	Ammân

Kazakhstan

Official name: Republic of Kazakhstan, Kazak Respublikasy
Area: 2 717 300 sq. km (1 048 878 sq. miles)
Population: 16 700 000
Capital: Akmola (since 10th December 1997. Before that, Almaty (Alma-Ata))
Currency: 1 Rouble (R) = 100 kopecks
International telephone access code: 7

Languages

The official language, Kazakh, is spoken by some 40% of the population. Russian is spoken by most of the remaining inhabitants. There are also speakers of German, Uyghur and Romani.

Example Address Format

474211 KAZAKHSTAN
AKMOLINSKAYA
Kourgaljinski
Ourkendé
M. Iskakovay

Note that the order of address lines in Kazakhstan is the opposite to that used in Western Europe - the postal code and town comes first, then the street address, then the name of the person or company.

Postal codes

Postal codes consist of a block of 6 digits. This is the same code that was used before the independence of Kazakhstan from the Soviet Union. The first three digits indicate the department, the fourth the zone (region), the fifth the sector and the last the business or post office of the centre of the department.

Kenya

Official name: Republic of Kenya, Jamhuri ya Kenya
Area: 564 162 sq. km (217 766 sq. miles)
Population: 25 241 000
Capital: Nairobi
Currency: 1 Kenyan Shilling (KSh) = 100 cents
International telephone access code: 254

Languages

61 languages are spoken in Kenya. The geographical distribution of these languages is complex. The official languages are English (mainly spoken as a second language) and Swahili (about 12 000 000 first- and second-language speakers). Other widely spoken languages include Bukusu (565 000 speakers); Embu (429 000 speakers); Gikuya (5 347 000 speakers); Giryama (551 000 speakers); Gusii (1 582 000 speakers); Kalenjin (2 248 123 speakers); Kamba (2 448 302 speakers); Luo (3 185 000 speakers); Luyia (3 083 083 speakers); Maasai (453 000 speakers) and Meru (1 305 000 speakers).

Example address format

Mr Akech Amin
P.O. Box 71587
00108-KAJIADO

Addresses will usually be a postbox number and will be written in English.

Postal codes

The postal code consists of a block of 5 digits. The first digit indicates the postal region, the second and third the regional distribution centre and the final two the delivery office.

Kiribati

Official name: Republic of Kiribati
Area: 717 sq. km (277 sq. miles)
Population: 71 100
Capital: Bairiki
Currency: 1 Australian Dollar ($A) = 100 cents
International telephone access code: 686

Languages

97.2% of the population speak Kiribati, the national language. There are a small number of English-speakers.

Example address format

Rui Tofiakai
St John Bosco
Betio
TARAWA

Postal codes

Kiribati has no postal code system.

Kuwait
Dowlat al Kuwait

Official name: State of Kuwait, Dowlat al Kuwait
Area: 17 818 sq. km (6 878 sq. miles)
Population: 1 200 000
Capital: Al Kuwayt (Kuwait City)
Currency: 1 Kuwait Dinar (KD) = 1 000 fils
International telephone access code: 965

Languages

The national language is standard Arabic. About 500 000 people speak Gulf Spoken Arabic. There are 3 537 speakers of Mehri.

Example address format

Hamad Abdullah Hussein
Al-Sabbahiya, Parcelle 4
Street 3, Building 11
54404 KUWAIT AL-SABBAHIYA

or

Hamad Abdullah Hussein
Al-Sabbahiya
PO Box 48001
54551 KUWAIT AL-SABBAHIYA

Postal codes

Postal codes consist of a block of 5 digits. The first indicates the sector, the second the zone and the last three the postbox, large user or delivery address.

Towns

Al Kuwayt is known as *Kuwait* in English and *Koweit* in French.

Kyrgyzstan

Official name: Republic of Kyrgyzstan, Kyrgyz Respublikasy
Area: 198 500 sq. km (76 621 sq. miles)
Population: 4 400 000
Capital: Bichkek (Bishkek, Frunze)
Currency: 1 Rouble (R) = 100 kopecks
International telephone access code: 996

Languages

The official language, Kyrgyz, is spoken by 2 448 220 people. There are also some 916 000 Russian-speakers, 550 000 Northern Uzbeck-speakers and 109 000 Ukrainian-speakers. The second indigenous language of Kyrgyzstan, Dungan, has 38 000 speakers.

Example Address Format

720001 BICHKEK-1
Avenue Tchuy, 227
Department of State

Note that the order of address lines in Kyrgyzstan is the opposite to that used in Western Europe - the postal code and town comes first, then the street address, then the name of the person or company.

Postal codes

Postal codes consist of a block of 6 digits. This is the same code that was used before the independence of Kyrgyzstan from the Soviet Union. The first three digits indicate the town or provincial centre, the final three the main post office of towns and villages.

Laos
Lao

Official name: Lao People's Democratic Republic, Sathanalat Paxathipatai Paxaxon Lao
Area: 236 800 sq. km (91 405 sq. miles)
Population: 4 410 000
Capital: Vientiane
Currency: 1 Kip (Kp) = 100 at
International telephone access code: 856

Languages

Laos counts 92 languages, most spoken by a few thousand people in isolated villages. The official language, Lao, is spoken by 3 000 000 people. Other main languages are Eastern Bru (64 000 speakers); Hmong (250 000 speakers); Kantu (50 000 speakers); Khmu (389 694 speakers); Kuy (64 000 speakers); Phu Thai (128 000 speakers); Phuan (96 000 speakers); Sô (102 000 speakers) and Tai Nüa (120 000 speakers).

Example Address Format

Khamsing Sengdeth
14, rue That louang
0116 XAYSETHA

Addresses not written in Lao or another native language will be written in French.

Postal codes

Postal codes consist of a block of 4 digits. The first two digits indicate the province, the last two the delivery office.

Latvia
Latvija

Official name: Republic of Latvija, Latvijas Republika
Area: 64 600 sq. km (24 900 sq. miles)
Population: 2 700 000
Capital: Riga
Currency: 1 Lats = 100 Santims
International telephone access code: 371

Languages

The national language, Latvian, is spoken by some 1 394 000 people, or 51.6% of the population. Some 32% (861 600) of the population have Russian as their mother language. There are also 105 000 Belorussian-speakers; 3 000 Estonian-speakers; 35 000 Lithuanian-speakers; 57 000 Polish-speakers; 8 000 Baltic Romani-speakers; 5 000 Tatar-speakers and 78 000 Ukrainian-speakers.

Yiddish is also spoken. Latvia is home to Europe's most endangered language, Liv, spoken by only 15-20 speakers in 8 coastal villages west of Kolkasrags.

Example address format

Aldis Ziemelis
5 Miesniescu Street
RIGA-50, LV-1050

The postal code is written to the right of the city name. Riga also has a sorting number indicating the post office. This number is duplicated within the postal code.

Postal codes

Postal codes consist of a block of 4 digits, usually preceded by *LV-*. The first two indicate the routing area, the last two the post office.

Towns

The following list gives German equivalents of Latvian town names:

Latvian	*German*
Aizpute	Hasenput
Bauska	Bauske
Daugavpils	Dünaburg
Ilukste	Iluxt
Jekabpils	Jakobstadt
Jelgava	Mitau
Kuldiga	Goldingen

Liepaja	Libau
Ludza	Ludsen
Rezekne	Rositten
Talsi	Talsen
Tukums	Tuckum
Valka	Walk
Valmiera	Wolmar
Ventspils	Windau

Lesotho

Official name: Kingdom of Lesotho
Area: 30 355 sq. km (11 720 sq. miles)
Population: 1 801 000
Capital: Meseru
Currency: 1 Loti (plural Maloti) (M, LSM) = 100 lisente
International telephone access code: 266

Languages

The official languages are English and Sotho (1 493 000 speakers). There are 248 000 Zulu-speakers.

Example address format

Mr Peter Makara
P.O. Box 500
MASERU

Deliveries are only to postboxes. Addresses not in a native language will be written in English.

Postal codes

Lesotho has no postal code system.

Libya
Lībiyā

Official name: Socialist People's Libyan Arab Jamahiriya, al-Jamahiriyah al-Libya al- Shabiya al-Ishtirakiya
Area: 1 758 610 sq. km (678 823 sq. miles)
Population: 4 450 000
Capital: Tarābulus (Tripoli)
Currency: 1 Libyan Dinar (LD) 1 000 millemes
International telephone access code: 218

Languages

The national language is Standard Arabic. Libyan Spoken Arabic is spoken by about 96% of the population. 9 other languages are spoken by the remaining inhabitants.

Example address format

Mohamed Ali Khalifa
Av. Al Ghazaly 12
TRIPOLI

Postal codes

Libya has no postal code system.

Towns

The following list gives foreign language equivalents of Libyan town names:

Arabic	*English*	*French*	*German*
Ajdābiyah			Adjedabia
Al Khums		Homs	Homs
Benghāzi	Benghazi		Bengasi
Darnah			Derna
Ghudāmis			Ghadames
Marsá Susah	Apollonia		
Marsūq			Mursuk
Misrātah			Misurata
Sabhah			Sebha
Shahhāt	Cyrene		Kyrene
Suluq			Soluk
Surt		Suri	Syrte

Tarābulus	Tripoli	Tripoli	Tripolis
Ţubruq	Tobruk		Tobruk
Ţulmaythah			Tolmeta
Zuwārah			Zuara

Liechtenstein

Liechtenstein is a small German-speaking country sandwiched between Switzerland and Austria. As with many small European countries, Liechtenstein tends more towards one of its neighbours, Switzerland, than to the other. Addresses for Liechtenstein will usually be found mixed into lists for Switzerland. They can be recognised by their postal codes.

Official name: Principality of Liechtenstein, Fürstentum Liechtenstein
Area: 160 sq. km (61.8 sq. miles)
Population: 28 777
Capital: Vaduz
Currency: 1 Swiss franc (Sfr, SwF) = 100 centimes. (The principality belongs to the Swiss economic area).
International telephone access code: 41

Languages

German is spoken by 93 % of the population. A dialect of Alemannish is widely spoken. There are also 800 Italian speakers.

Company names, contact names, street addresses, postbox

The same rules and formats apply as in Germany, Austria and German-speaking Switzerland.

Postal codes

Postal codes consist of a block of 4 numbers. Liechtenstein forms part of the postal system of Switzerland. The towns with their postal codes are listed below:

Balzers	9496
Bendern	under 9487 Gamprin-Bendern
Eschen	9492
Gamprin-Bendern	9487
Mäls	under 9496 Balzersi
Mauren FL	9493
Nendeln	9485
Planken	under 9494 Schaan
Ruggell	9491
Schaan	9494
Schaanwald	9486
Schellenberg	9488
Triesen	9495
Triesenberg	9497
Vaduz	9490

Administrative districts

Liechtenstein is composed of 11 communes.

Lithuania
Lietuva

Official name: Republic of Lithuania, Lietuvos Respublika
Area: 65 200 sq. km (25 167 sq. miles)
Population: 3 700 000
Capital: Vilnius
Currency: 1 Litas (plural Litu) = 100 cents
International telephone access code: 370

Languages

2 905 000 people speak the official language, Lithuanian (written using the Roman alphabet). There are also 63 000 Belorussian-speakers; 4 200 Latvian-speakers; 258 000 Polish speakers; 344 000 Russian-speakers; 5 100 Tatar-speakers and 45 000 Ukrainian-speakers. Romani is also spoken and there are 535 speakers of Karaim.

Address format

Name
Thoroughfare name[ ]house number{[-]apartment number}
City[ ]postal code

For example:

Algis Kantautas
Filaretu 98-13
Vilnius 2006

The postal code may also be found written to the left of the city name as follows:

Algis Kantautas
Filaretu 98-13
2006 Vilnius

Note that thoroughfare names are usually written without thoroughfare type indications - an exception is when an adjective is used, as is:

Donelaicio gatvė = Main Street

Thoroughfare types, when written, are written with the first letter in lower case.

Many smaller villages have no street names and only a house number is used along with the name of the street.

Thoroughfare types

Below is a list of the most commonly occurring thoroughfare types for Lithuania:

Lithuanian	*English*
alėja	Avenue
gatvė	Street
prospektas	Avenue

These indicators are not usually used in addresses (see section "Address format") and may change form according to their usage, thus:

Donelaicio Gatvė = Main Street
Donelaicio skersgatvis = Small Street near Main Street

Postal codes

This consists of a block of 4 digits. The first two indicate the routing territory, the last two the route.

Towns

The following list gives German equivalents of Lithuanian town names:

Lithuanian	*German*
Birzai	Birsche
Klajpeda	Memel
Panevezys	Ponewesch
Siauliai	Schaulen
Taurage	Tauroggen
Telšiai	Telsche
Vilnius	Wilna

Luxembourg
Lëtzebuerg

Official name: Grand Duchy of Luxembourg, Grand-Duché de Luxembourg
Area: 2,586 sq. km. (999 sq. miles)
Population: 389 800
Capital: Luxembourg
Currency: 1 Luxembourg franc (LFr)= 100 centimes (equal to the Belgian franc). Luxembourg forms part of the Belgian economic area.
International telephone access code: 352

Languages

The official language is Letzebuergesch, a German-Moselle-Frankish dialect which should be regarded as a distinct language related to German. French is spoken by 13 100 as a mother-language and German has 9 200 mother-language speakers.

Company Types

The following company types may be found in Luxembourgeois addresses:

Affaire Personnelle
ASBL (Association sans But Lucratif) (Indicates a Charity)
Association de Fait
Association Momentanée
SA (Société Anonyme)
SC (Société Cooperative)
SCS (Société en Commandite)
SNC (Société en Nom Collectif)
Société Cooperatieve
Société en Commandité par Actions
Société en Commandité Simple
Société Etrangère
SPRL (Sociéte de Personnes a Responsibilité Limitée)
SPRL (Société Privée a Responsibilité Limitée)

Addresses

Street names can either be in French or Letzebuergesch. Increasingly, especially in the capital, street names are given in both languages.

The structure of the address is slightly different according to the language of the address inasmuch as in a French address, the thoroughfare type is prefixed to the thoroughfare name with spaces between the words, whereas addresses in Letzebuergesch have the thoroughfare type suffixed to the thoroughfare name without a space. Otherwise, addresses are structured thus:

Recipient name
number[ ]Thoroughfare
postal code[ ]TOWN NAME

or

Recipient name
number[,]Thoroughfare
postal code[ ]TOWN NAME

For example:

M. Jacques Muller
71 route de Longwy
4750 PETANGE

Thoroughfare types given in French should be written with the first letter in lower case.

Thoroughfare types

As Letzebuergesch itself has a number of dialects and therefore a number of different spellings for thoroughfare types depending on the region, a list of the thoroughfare types in Letzebuergesch cannot be given here.

Please refer to the chapters on France and Belgium for lists of commonly occurring thoroughfare types and abbreviations as found when addresses are written in French.

Postal codes

Postal codes in Luxembourg consist of a block of 4 numbers, beginning with a number between 1 and 9, and they are written on the last line of the address preceding the town name. Postal codes beginning with the following numbers are currently not used:

30,31,50,51,60,70,71,78,79,89

The first two digits indicate the delivery office.

Towns

The following list provides foreign-language equivalents for Letzebuergesch settlement names:

Letzebuergesch	*English*	*French*	*German*	*Italian*	*Spanish*	*Dutch*
Bäerdrëf		Berdorf	Berdorf			
Bauschelt		Boulaide	Bauschleiden			
Bech-Maacher		Bech-Kleinmacher	Bech-Kleinmacher			
Befort		Beaufort	Beaufort			

Béiwen-Atert		Boevange-sur-Attert	Boewingen			
Betebuerg		Bettembourg	Bettemburg			
Bettenduerf		Bettendorf	Bettendorf			
Branebuerg		Brandenbourg	Brandenburg			
Bungeréf		Bigonville	Bondorf			
Buurschent		Bourscheid	Bourscheid			
Déifferdéng		Differdange	Differdingen			
Diddeléng		Dudelange	Düdelingen			
Dikrech		Diekirch	Diekirch			
Dol		Dahl	Dahl			
Éislak		Ösling	Oesling			
Ëlwen		Troisvièrges	Ulflingen			
Énsber-Lëlz		Insenborn-Lultzhausen	Insenborn-Lultzhausen			
Esch-Sauer		Easch-sur-Sûre	Esch an der Sauer			
Esch-Uelzecht		Esch-sur-Alzette	Esch an der Alzette			
Ettelbréck		Ettelbruck	Ettelbrück			
Fiels		Larochette	Fels			
Gréiwenmaacher		Grevenmacher	Grevenmacher			
Heischent		Heiderscheid	Heiderscheid			
Hesper		Hespérange	Hesperingen			
Housen		Hosingen	Hosingen			
Iechternach		Echternach	Echternach			
Ierpeldéng		Erpeldange	Erpeldingen			
Jonglënster		Junglinster	Junglinster			
Kaunerëf		Kaundorf	Kaundorf			
Klierf		Clervaux	Clerf			
Léifreg		Liefrange	Liefringen			
Lëtzebuerg	Luxembourg	Luxembourg	Luxemburg	Lussemburgo	Luxemburgo	Luxemburg
Miersch		Mersch	Mersch			
Moellerdall		Mullerthal	Müllertal			
Monnerech		Mondercange	Monnerich			
Munnerëf		Mondorf-les-Bains	Bad Mondorf			
Munzel		Munshausen	Munshausen			
Nidderkäerjhéng		Bascharage	Niederkirchen			
Nouspelt		Nospelt	Nospelt			
Pärel		Perlé	Perlé			
Péiténg		Pétange	Petingen			
Réiden-Atert		Redange-sur-Attert	Redingen an der Attert			
Reisduerf		Reisdorf	Reisdorf			
Réimech		Remich	Remich			
Réiser		Roeser	Roeser			
Rëmëléng		Rumelange	Rümelingen			
Schëffléng		Schifflange	Schifflingen			
Sëll		Saeul	Saeul			
Simmer		Septfontaines	Simmern			
Stengefort		Steinfort	Steinfort			
Suessem		Sanem	Sassenheim			
Usechdrëf		Arsdorf	Arsdorf			
Useldéng		Useldange	Useldingen			
Veianan / Veinen		Vianden	Vianden			
Walfer		Walferdange	Walferdingen			

Wellesteen		Wellenstein	Wellenstein			
Wëlwerwolz		Wilwerwiltz	Wilwerwiltz			
Wëntger		Wincrange	Wintger			
Wolz		Wiltz	Wiltz			
Wuermeldéng		Wormelange	Wormeldingen			

Administrative districts

Luxembourg has 3 districts and 12 cantons:

District	*Canton*
Diekirch	Clervaux Diekirch Redange Vianden Wiltz
Grevenmacher	Etternach Grevenmacher Remich
Luxembourg	Capellen Esch-sur-Alzette Luxembourg Mersch

Telephone numbers

Luxembourg has no area codes.

Macedonia, Former Yugoslav Republic of
Makedonija

Official name: Former Yugoslav Republic of Macedonia, Republika Makedonija
Area: 25 713 sq. km (9 925 sq. miles)
Population: 2 033 964
Capital: Skopje
Currency: Denar (MKD)
International telephone access code: 389

Languages

The official language, Macedonian, is spoken by 1 386 000 people. There are 242 250 speakers of Albanian. Also spoken are Balkan Gagauz Turkish, Adyghe, Macedo Romanian, Balkan Romani, Serbo-Croat and Turkish.

Address Formats

Address formats follow those used in other parts of the former Yugoslavia:

Name
thoroughfare type[ ]Thoroughfare name [ ]number
postal code[ ]SETTLEMENT{[ ]sorting code}

For example:

Peter Kostovski
ul. Kosle br.15
91000 SKOPJE 2

Addresses in Skopje can have a numeric sorting code (between 1 and 36) following the city name.

Postal codes

The postal code consists of a block of 5 digits. The codes used are the same as were used when the country was part of Yugoslavia. All codes begin with '9'.

Towns

The large Albanian-speaking minority in the west of the country have their own names for some settlements:

Macedonian	*Albanian*
Bitola	Manastir
Debar	Dibër
Kicevo	Kërçova

Ohrid	Ohër
Skopje	Shkup
Tetovo	Tetova

Madagascar
Madagasikara

Official name: Democratic Republic of Madagascar, Repoblika Demokratika Malagasy
Area: 592 800 sq. km (228 821 sq. miles)
Population: 12 185 000
Capital: Antananarivo
Currency: 1 Madagascar Franc (FMG,MgFr) = 100 centimes
International telephone access code: 261

Languages

Six languages are spoken in Madagascar. The national language, Malagasy, is spoken by 10 152 000 people. Comorian is spoken by 25 000; French by 18 000; Antankarana Malagasy by 88 000; Southern Malagasy by 2 606 000 and Tsimihety Malagasy by 1 016 000.

Example address format

M. Rakoto
Lot IV, 60 ter
Ankorondrano - Est
202 ANTSIRANANA

Addresses not written in a native language will be written in French.

Postal codes

The postal code consists of a block of 3 digits. The first digit indicates the province, the final two the *commune* (municipality).

Malawi
Malaêi

Official name: Republic of Malawi
Area: 118 484 sq. km (45 735 sq. miles)
Population: 9 438 000
Capital: Lilongwe
Currency: 1 Kwacha (MK) = 100 tambala
International telephone access code: 265

Languages

Malawi counts 15 languages. The official languages are English and Nyanja (3 200 000 speakers). Also spoken are Afrikaans; Kachchi; Kokola (74 466 speakers); Lambya (41 000 speakers); Lomwe (1 550 000 speakers); Mpoto (40 000 speakers); Ngoni (758 000 speakers); Nkakyusa-Ngonde (300 000 speakers); Malawi Sena (255 000 speakers); Tonga (662 000 speakers); Yao (1 003 000 speakers) and Zulu (37 480 speakers).

Example address format

Mr. W.M. Lundu
P.O. Box 537
BLANTYRE

Addresses will usually be a postbox or private bag number and will be written in English.

Postal codes

Malawi has no postal code system.

Malaysia

Official name: Federation of Malaysia, Persekutuan Tanah Malaysia
Area: 329 749 sq. km (127 283 sq. miles)
Population: 18 630 000
Capital: Kuala Lumpur
Currency: 1 Malaysian Dollar/Ringgit (M$) = 100 cents
International telephone access code: 60

Languages

38 languages are spoken on Peninsula Malaysia, a further 54 are spoken in Sabah and 45 in Sarawak. The official language, Bahasa or Malay, is spoken by about 47% of the population. There are large numbers of Chinese-, English- and Tamil-speakers.

Example address format

Mr. Ahmad b. Ghazili
32 Jalan Tempinis
Bangsar
59100 KUALA LUMPUR

Addresses written in a non-native language will usually be written in English.

Postal codes

The postal code consists of a block of 5 digits. The first two digits specify the main delivery office, the last three the delivery area.

Maldives
Dhivehi Jumhuriya

Official name: Republic of Maldives, Dhivehi Jumhuriya
Area: 300 sq. km (116 sq. miles)
Population: 226 000
Capital: Malé
Currency: 1 Rufiyaa (Mrf, Rf) = 100 laaris
International telephone access code: 960

Languages

The national language is Maldivian. Small numbers speak Sinhalese, Arabic and Indian languages.

Example address format

Managing Director
Maldives Post Limited
B-194 Chandhari Magu
MALE 20-03

Postal codes

The postal code consists of 4 digits in the format:

99[-]99

It is written following the settlement name.

Mali

Official name: Republic of Mali, République du Mali
Area: 1 240 192 sq. km (478 714 sq. miles)
Population: 8 338 000
Capital: Bamako
Currency: 1 CFA Franc (CFAFr) = 100 centimes
International telephone access code: 223

Languages

Mali counts 32 languages. The official language is French. There are 2 700 000 speakers of Bambara; 462 000 speakers of Dogon; 911 200 speakers of Fulfulde; 668 000 speakers of Malinke; 600 000 speakers of Songai and 700 000 speakers of Soninke.

Example address format

For the city of Bamako:

M. Kalilou Sissoko
rue Magnabougou 406 porte 39
BAMAKO

For other settlements:

M. Seydou Diarra
Commerçant quartier no. 1
N'GOUMA

Addresses will usually be found written in French.

Postal codes

Mali has no postal code system.

Malta

Official name: Republic of Malta, Repubblika Ta'Malta
Area: 316 sq. km (122 sq. miles)
Population: 360 000
Capital: Valetta
Currency: Maltese pound/lira matija (LM) = 100 cents
International telephone access code: 356

Languages

Malta has two official languages: Maltese, spoken by 96 per cent of the population and English, spoken by 2 per cent. Italian is spoken by 2 per cent of the population.

Addresses

Addresses are written using the following structure:

number[,]Thoroughfare
SETTLEMENT[ ]POSTAL CODE
{Island name}

Street names are usually written in Maltese, but some may be found translated into English. The name of the island is optional when the address is on the island of Malta, but is usually stated when the address is on Gozo (Għawdex) or Comina.

Postal codes

The postal code consists of three capital letters, indicating the delivery office, followed by two numbers on the island of Malta, and three numbers on the island of Gozo indicating the postperson's beat. The letters and numbers have a space between them, as for example:

VCT[ ]101

It is added after, and on the same line as, the settlement name. Government departments and ministries have the postal code CMR 0Z.

Towns

Valetta s know as *La Valette* in French. The following list gives a list of Maltese town names with their English equivalents:

Maltese	*English*
Birgu	Vittoriosa
Bormla	Cospicua
Għajn Sielem	Kemmuna
Rabat	Victoria
Raħal Ġdid	Paolo
San Pawl Il-Baħar	St Paul's Bay
Wied Il-Għajn	Marsascala

Marshall Islands

Area: 180 sq. km (70 sq. miles)
Population: 50 000
Capital: Dalap-Uliga-Darrit
Currency: 1 US Dollar ($, US$) = 100 cents
International telephone access code: 692

Languages

Most of the population speak Marshallese, the official language, in one of two dialects.

Address Format etc.

Recently independent of the United States (1990), it still forms part of the United States' postal system. Its state code is MH and its postal codes fall in the range 96960-70.

The name of the island or reef may be included in the address.

Please refer to the chapter on the United States of America for further information.

Martinique

Martinique is a *département* of France. It forms part of the French mail system.

Area: 1 079 sq. km (416 sq. miles)
Population: 338 000
Capital: Fort-de-France
Currency: 1 French Franc (Ffr) = 100 centimes
International telephone access code: 596

Languages

The official language is French, though 96% of the population speak Lesser Antillean Creole French.

Address formats

Please refer to the chapter on France for address information.

Postal codes

All Martinique postal codes commence with the digits 972.

Mauritania
Mūritāniyā (Arabic), Mauritanie (French)

Official name: Islamic Republic of Mauritania, République Islamique de Mauritanie
Area: 1 029 920 sq. km (397 549 sq. miles)
Population: 2 100 000
Capital: Nouakchott
Currency: 1 Ouguiyja (U, UM) = 5 khoums
International telephone access code: 222

Languages

Mauritania has 8 languages. Hassaniya Arabic (1 800 000 speakers) is the official language. There are 150 000 speakers of Fulfulde.

Example address format

M. Hamed Ould M'Hmed
BP 35
NOUAKCHOTT

Delivery is to postboxes only. This is usually written in French as *BP*, or *Boite Postale.*

Postal codes

Mauritania has no postal code system.

Mayotte

Mayotte is a *départment* of France. It forms part of the French mail system. It is the fourth island of the Comoros archipelago.

Area: 374 sq. km (144 sq. miles)
Population: 98 000
Capital: Dzaoudzi
Currency: 1 French Franc (Ffr) = 100 centimes
International telephone access code: 269

Languages

Most people (about 95%) speak Comorron. About 40% also speak Malagasy. There are also 2 744 speakers of Swahili and about 2 450 speakers of French, the official language.

Address formats

Please refer to the chapter on France for address information.

Postal codes

All Mayotte postal codes commence with the digits 976, or 985 for *Cédex* addresses.

Mexico
México

Official name: United Mexican States, Estados Unidos México
Area: 1 978 800 sq. km (763 817 sq. miles)
Population: 84 440 000
Capital: Mexico City
Currency: 1 Mexican Peso (Mex$) = 100 centavos
International telephone access code: 52

Languages

The official language, Spanish, is spoken as a first language by about 88% of the population. The remaining 12% speak one of 288 other, mainly Indian, languages. A significant proportion of these people do not speak Spanish. The languages with the largest numbers of speakers are Chol (130 000); Maya (700 000); Mazahua (350 000); Nahuatl (in 27 different forms 1 376 898); Otomí (in 9 different forms 220 000); Purépecha (120 000); Totonaca (in 8 different forms 260 000); Tzeltal (in 2 different forms 300 000); Tzotzil (in 6 different forms 265 000); Zapoteco (in 57 different forms 494 000).

Address Format

Addresses are written in the format:

Name
{thoroughfare type[ ]}Thoroughfare name[ ]number{[,]floor etc. indicators}
[Col.] Section indicator
postal code[ ]SETTLEMENT[,]STATE ABBREVIATION

For example:

Sra Otilia Ramos Perez
Urión 30
Col. Atlatilco
02860 MEXICO, D.F.

The Spanish word for street, *calle*, is usually not written in the street address line. The abbreviation *Col.* is short for *Colonia* and often forms a vital part of addressing.

The state code is written after the settlement name. The abbreviations used are:

State	*Abbreviation*
Aguascalientes	AGS
Baja California	BC
Baja California Sur	BCS

Campeche	CAM
Coahuila de Zaragoza	COAH
Colima	COL
Chiapas	CHIS
Chihuahua	CHIH
Distrito Federal	DF
Durango	DGO
Guanajuato	GTO
Guerrero	GRO
Hidalgo	HGO
Jalisco	JAL
México	MEX
Michoacán de Ocampo	MICH
Morelos	MOR
Nayarit	NAY
Nuevo León	NL
Oaxaca	OAX
Puebla	PUE
Querétaro Arteaga	QRO
Quintana Roo	QROO
San Luís Potosí	SLP
Sinalóa	SIN
Sonora	SON
Tabasco	TAB
Tamaulipas	TAMPS
Tlaxcala	TLAX
Veracruz	VER
Yucatán	YUC
Zacatecas	ZAC

Postal codes

Mexican postal codes (*Codigo Postal* or *CP*) consist of a block of 5 digits. Each digit is associated to a geographical area of the country. The first two digits refer to the federal entity, or, in the case of the Distrito Federal (Mexico City), to a neighbourhood. The third digit indicates an important town or city, a municipality or one of the ten areas into which the Distrito Federal is divided. The fourth digit indicates a municipality or suburb or estate within a town. The final digit indicates a group of blocks or the specific street address of a large-user.

Towns

Mexico is known as *Mexiko* in German.

Administrative areas

The abbreviations of Mexico's 31 states and 1 district (*Distrito Federal*) are used in addresses. Please see the section on address format for further information.

Micronesia, Federated States of

A federation of four states (Yap, Chuuk (Truk), Pohnpei (Ponape) and Kosrae (Kusaie)) in the Western Pacific. It became independent of the United States in 1991 but remains part of its postal system.

Area: 700 sq. km (270 sq. miles)
Population: 114 000
Capital: Palikir
Currency: 1 US Dollar ($, US$) = 100 cents
International telephone access code: 691

Languages

The national languages are Chuuk (38 341 speakers); English (3 540 first-language speakers); Kosraean (6 900 speakers); Ponapean (27 700 speakers) and Yapese (6 592 speakers). A further 11 languages are spoken.

Address Format etc.

Recently independent of the United States (1991), it still forms part of the United States' postal system. Its state code is FM and its postal codes fall in the range 96941-4.

The name of the island or reef may be included in the address.

Moldova

The area to the north and east of the Dnestr River is controlled by rebel Russian and Gargauz minorities. Mail deliveries may consequently be affected.

Official name: Republic of Moldova, Republika Moldovenească
Area: 33 700 sq. km (13 800 sq. miles)
Population: 4 341 000
Capital: Chisinau (Kishinev)
Currency: Leu (MDL) (plural Lei)
International telephone access code: 373

Languages

The official language, Romanian, is spoken by some 59% of the population. There are some 20 000 Belorussian-speakers; 361 000 Bulgarian-speakers; 1 859 Crimean Turkish-speakers; 173 000 Gargauz-speakers; 7 000 German-speakers; 562 000 Russian-speakers; 12 000 Balkan Romani-speakers and 600 000 Ukrainian-speakers.

Example address format

Ion POPESCU
Str. Codru 4, Ap. 8
2019 CHISINAU

Postal code

Postal codes consist of a block of 4 digits. The first two digits are the routing area and code, the final two the delivery office and code.

Monaco

Monaco is a tiny but completely independent country entirely surrounded on its landward borders by France. For most rules and formats relating to this principality, please refer to the chapter on France.

Official name: Principality of Monaco
Area: 1.95 sq. km (0.75 sq. miles)
Population: 29 712
Capital: Monaco-Ville
Currency: 1 French franc (Fr) = 100 centimes
International telephone access code: 377

Languages

The official language is French (17 400 speakers). Other languages spoken include Italian, Monégasque (a French dialect, a mixture of Provençals and Ligurian) (5 100 speakers), Provençals (4 500 speakers) and English.

Company names, company types, contact names, addresses, postbox

The same rules and formats are used as in France. Please refer to the chapter on France.

Postal codes

Monaco forms part of the French postal system, and its addresses will usually be found mixed up with French addresses in databases. They can be identified by their postal codes, all of which begin with the number 980. The codes used are as follows:

All street addresses		98000
Postbox addresses in:	Condamine	98011-98012
	Fontvieille	98013-98014
	Monaco Ville	98015
	Monte Carlo	98001-98007
Public Services		98020
Business Reply addresses		98029
Special courier		98030
Radio Monte Carlo		98080
Tele Monte Carlo		98090

Mongolia
Mongol Ard Uls

Official name: State of Mongolia
Area: 1 566 500 sq. km (604 800 sq. miles)
Population: 2 156 300
Capital: Ulan Bator
Currency: 1 Tugrik (Tug) = 100 möngö
International telephone access code: 976

Languages

12 languages are spoken in Mongolia. The national language is Mongolian (Khlakha), spoken by about 90% of the population. There are 64 000 speakers of Buriat; 35 000 Mandarin-speakers; 205 000 Kalmyk-Oirat-speakers; 120 000 Kazakh-speakers and 27 000 Tuvin-speakers.

Example address formats

Ministry of Infrastructure and Development
ULAANBAATAR 210646

Mongol Post Company
P.O. Box 1106
ULAANBAATAR 210613

Postal codes

Postal codes consist of a block of 6 digits. The first two indicate the town or provincial centre, the middle two the district and the final two the post office.

Morocco
Al-Magrib

Morocco occupies the territory of Western Sahara, which has rebels fighting for independence (there is currently a cease-fire). Mail destined for Western Sahara will be addressed via the Moroccan postal system.

Official name: Kingdom of Morocco, al-Mamlaka al-Maghrebia
Area: 409 200 sq. km (157 951 sq. miles)
Population: 26 240 000
Capital: Rabat
Currency: 1 Moroccan Dirham (DH) = 100 Moroccan francs
International telephone access code: 212

Languages

Morocco has 11 languages. The official language is Standard Arabic. There are 40 000 speakers of Hassaniya Arabic; 18 000 of Judeo-Moroccan Arabic, 18 800 000 of Moroccan Spoken Arabic; 50 000 of Ghomara; 20 000 of Spanish; 2 300 000 of Tachelhit; 1 900 000 of Central Atlas Tamazight and 1 500 000 of Tarifit.

Example address format

M. Ali Amam
23, rue du Sebou
93150 MARTIL

Addresses written in a non-native language will usually be found written in French. Some will be written in Spanish.

Postal codes

Moroccan postal codes consist of a block of 5 digits.

Mozambique
Moçambique

Official name: Republic of Mozambique, República de Moçambique
Area: 799 380 sq. km (308 641 sq. miles)
Population: 16 142 000
Capital: Maputo
Currency: 1 Metical (Mt, MZM) = 100 centavos
International telephone access code: 258

Languages

33 languages are spoken in Mozambique. The official language is Portuguese. There are 760 000 speakers of Chopi; 664 279 speakers of Chwabo; 1 300 000 speakers of Lomwe; 350 000 speakers of Makhuwa-Maca; 2 500 000 speakers of Makhuwa-Makhuwana; 1 500 000 speakers of Makhuwa-Ketto; 900 000 speakers of Makhuwa-Shirama; 360 000 speakers of Makonde; 100 000 speakers of Manyika; 402 861 speakers of Marendje; 100 000 speakers of Mwani; 109 000 speakers of Ndau; 141 000 speakers of Nsenga; 423 000 speakers of Nyanja; 262 455 speakers of Nyungwe; 423 797 speakers of Ronga; 1 086 040 speakers of Sena; 759 923 speakers of Shona; 223 971 speakers of Tonga; 1 500 000 speakers of Tswa and 194 107 speakers of Yai.

Example address format

Sr. E. Magagula
Avenida Salvador Allende, 889
00300 MAPUTO

Addresses will often be written in the ex-colonial language, Portuguese. They follow the Portuguese structure - thoroughfare types are written first and with a capital first letter, the house number is at the end of the street address string often followed by an indication of floor, stairwell etc. For a full description of thoroughfare types and other address components, please refer to the chapter on Portugal.

Postal codes

The postal code (*Codigo Postal*, or *CP*) consists of a block of 5 digits.

Towns

Maputo may still be found written as the Portuguese *Lourenco Marques*.

Namibia

Official name: Republic of Namibia
Area: 824 292 sq. km (318 261 sq. miles)
Population: 1 520 000
Capital: Windhoek
Currency: Namibian Dollar (N$)
International telephone access code: 264

Languages

28 languages are spoken in Namibia. The official language is English (100 000 speakers). There are 146 000 Afrikaans-speakers; 141 000 Herero-speakers; 30 000 Kwambi-speakers and 90 000 Nama-speakers.

Example address format

The General Manager
NamPost
PO Box 287
WINDHOEK

Addresses written in a non-native language are likely to be written in English. Deliveries are to postboxes only.

Postal codes

There is no postal code system in Namibia.

Towns

The following list gives German equivalents of Namibian town names:

Local Name	*German*
Kanus	Kalkfontein
Walvisbaai	Walfisch-Bai
Windhoek	Windhuk

Nauru
Naeoro

Official name: Republic of Nauru, Naeoro
Area: 21.3 sq. km (8.2 sq. miles)
Population: 9 333
Capital: There is no official capital.
Currency: 1 Australian Dollar (A$) = 100 cents
International telephone access code: 674

Languages

The official language, Nauruan, is spoken by 6 000 people. English is widely spoken as a second language.

Example address format

Mr. John James
Boe District
P.O. Box 153

Addresses written in a non-native language will be written in English. Nauru is split into districts, which form part of the address. The districts are:

Aiwo
Anabar
Anabare
Anetan
Boe
Buada
Denig
Ewa
Ijuw
Meneng
Nibok
Yaren

Postal codes

Nauru has no postal code system.

Nepal
Nepāl

Official name: Kingdom of Nepal, Sri Nepala Sarkar
Area: 145 391 sq. km (56 121 sq. miles)
Population: 19 800 000
Capital: Kathmandu
Currency: 1 Nepalese Rupee (Nrp, NRs) = 100 paise/pice
International telephone access code: 977

Languages

Nepal counts 124 languages. The official language is Nepalese, with 9 900 000 speakers. The other main languages are Awadhi (540 000 speakers); Bhojpuri (1 370 000 speakers); Limbu (254 088 speakers); Eastern Magar (288 383 speakers); Western Magar (210 000 speakers); Maithili (2 260 000 speakers); Newari (700 000 speakers); Eastern Tamang (600 000 speakers); Northwestern Tamang (200 000 speakers); South-western Tamang (100 000 speakers); Dang Tharu (228 000 speakers) and Rana Thakur Tharu (194 000 speakers).

Example address format

Mr. Ram Karki
Chapakot VDC-6
Phulbari
SYANGJA 33807

Postal codes

Postal codes consist of a block of 5 digits. The first indicates the region, the next two the district and the final two the post office.

THE NETHERLANDS: Postal regions and language areas

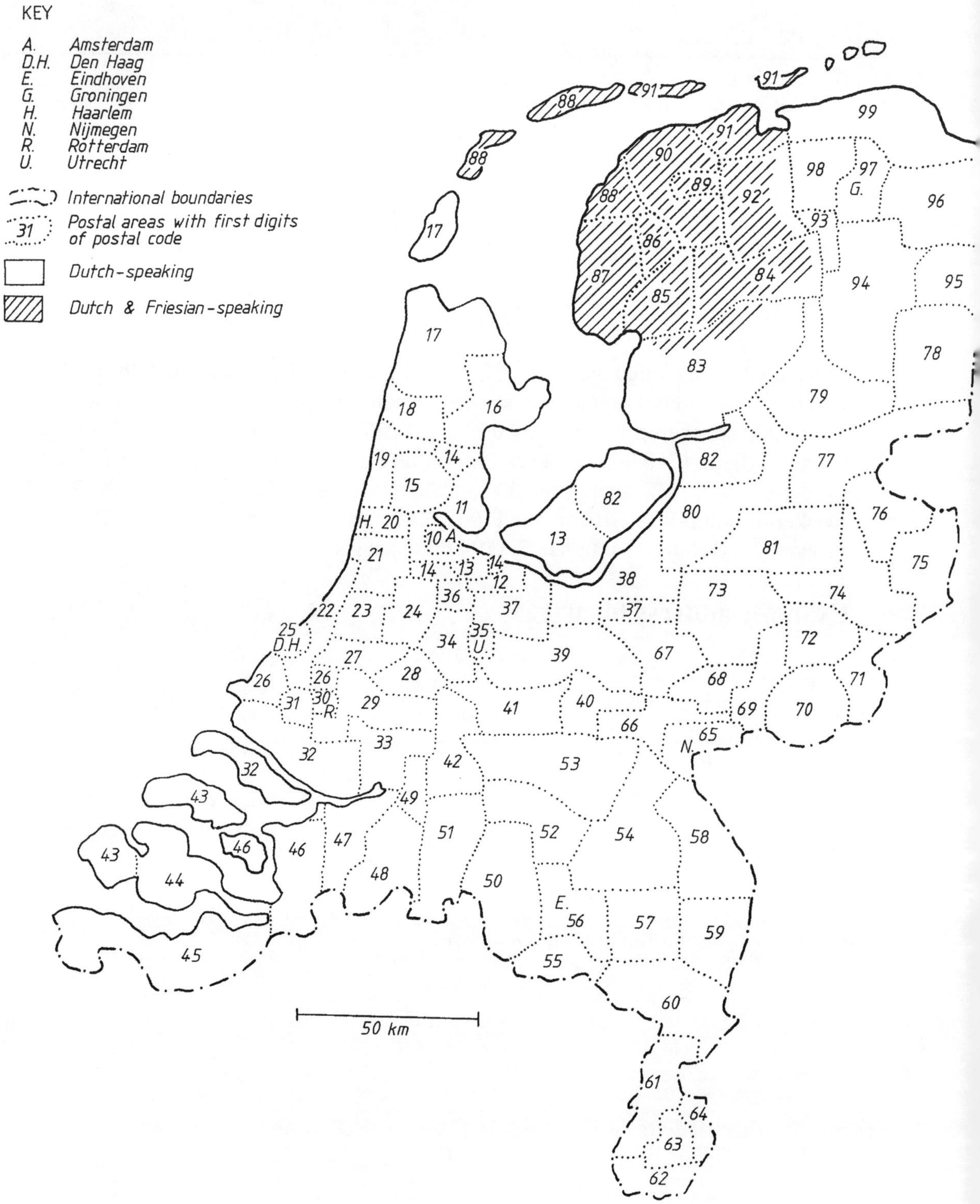

The Netherlands
Nederland

Holland comprises two provinces in the west of the country and no more. You should therefore refrain from addressing mail to 'Holland' and use the correct term - 'The Netherlands'.

Official Name: Kingdom of the Netherlands, Koninkrijk der Nederlanden
Area: 33,938 sq. km (13,104 sq. miles)
Population: 15 312 000
Capital: Amsterdam
Currency: 1 Guilder = 100 cents
International telephone access code: 31

Languages

Dutch, spoken by 88 per cent of the population as a mother language, is the official language. Friesian, spoken in Friesland, a province in the northern part of the country, is spoken by 5 per cent of the population. Most speakers of Friesian are bilingual in Dutch. Low Saxon, a German dialect, is spoken in the north and central areas along the German border. Most of these speakers are bilingual in Dutch.

Company names

It is more correct, where the *nature* of a company is mentioned in its name, that this *precedes* the name of the company, thus:

Bakkerij Janssens

You will often, however, find these activity indications *after* the company name, thus:

Janssens, Bakkerij
Janssens (Bakkerij)

Company types

The following company types may be found in Dutch company names:

Buitenlands Filiaal
BV (Besloten Vennootschap met beperkte aansprakelijkheid)
Coöperatie
CV (Commanditaire Vennootschap)
Eenmanszaak (one-person company)
Mij (Maatschappij)
NV (Naamloze Vennootschap)
Stichting
Vereniging
VOF (Vennootschap Onder Firma)

Contact names

Dutch personal names often contain prepositions, especially 'van de' and 'van der' which mean, literally, 'of the'. As a rule, these parts of the persons name are written in lower case, thus:

Hans van de Duinen

Note, however, that when used without a first name, the first letter of the first preposition is written with an upper case first letter as follows:

Dhr Van de Duinen

Most Dutch people have two names - their official name and their day-to-day name. Thus a person with the official name J.C.M.P. (Johannes Cornelis Maria Pieter) van Agt may be known as Hans or Cees, for example. On mailings, one should avoid using either the day-to-day name or the official name - the abbreviation of the official name should be used. It is virtually impossible to match the official and day-to-day names of individuals on the basis of name only. In Dutch databases, therefore, two fields are best reserved for the first name - one containing the initials of the official first name, the other containing the day-to-day first name for recognition purposes.

The salutation which would be used on an address label is inappropriate for use within a letter.

Married Dutch women may take their husband's name but retain their own as a second surname in this way:

Marijke van den Broek marries Jan Nijpels

and becomes

Marijke Nijpels-van den Broek

Other married women retain their maiden names, though any children take the father's surname.

For the Attention of

For written communications to people within companies, the abbreviation T.a.v., short for *Ter Attentie van* or *Ten aanzien van* and meaning 'For the attention of' often precedes the person's name in this way:

Bakkerij Janssens
T.a.v. Dhr. A. Janssens

Addresses

Addresses are written in the format:

Name
Thoroughfare Name thoroughfare type[ ]number
POSTAL CODE[ ]SETTLEMENT

For example

Jan Janssen
Reguliersstraat 17
2379 LA GRONINGEN

There should be two spaces between the postal code and the settlement name.

There are three official formats for writing Dutch addresses. The first, the 'official' format, is as follows:

- Street address with maximum 43 characters in mixed case
- The town with maximum 24 characters in upper case
- The IJ written as IJ (see section on Dutch in the chapter on Diacritical Marks)

For example:

Burgemeester de Cock van Opijnenstraat 1
4001 VL TIEL

The second format is used by the Ministry of Internal Affairs for its address databases:

- Street address with maximum 24 characters in mixed case
- The town with maximum 24 characters in upper case
- the IJ written as IJ

For example:

Burg d Cock v Opijnenstr 1
4001 VL TIEL

The third format is used by the post office:

- Street address with maximum 17 letters in upper case
- The town with maximum 18 letters in upper case
- The IJ written as Y

For example:

DE C V OPYNENSTR 1
4001 VL TIEL

In terms of database management, it is preferable to use a mixture of all three systems, thus:

- Street address, complete, in mixed case
- Town name, complete, in upper case
- The IJ as IJ

For example:

> Burgemeester de Cock van Opijnenstraat 1
> 4001 VL TIEL

In some databases, you may find that the prepositions, titles, initials and articles are put behind the rest of the thoroughfare type, thus:

> Koningin Julianastraat becomes Julianastr., kon.;

and

> Meester P. Troelstralaan becomes Troelstraln., mr. p.

but this system should *not* be used when addressing envelopes.

Some streets in The Netherlands are themselves numbered. Thus the figures le, 2e etc. in front of the street name indicate the number of the *thoroughfare,* not of the habitation. These mean 1st, 2nd etc.

If you can choose between a street address and a postbox number for mailings, always use the postbox number with its postal code.

If you wish to add codes or messages to the label, these should always be placed above and to the left of the address.

Houseboats without a house number should have the house number replaced with the letters *AB (aan boord* = on board) and the name of the boat.

Caravans without a house number should have the number replaced by the letters *WW* (*woonwagen* = caravan).

The PTT (the Dutch Post Office) prefers addresses to have only 3 lines:

1. The name of the person or company.
2. The street name and house number; or the word 'Postbus' with a postbox number.
3. The postal code and the town.

For example:

> Dhr. J. van Dieten
> Morsstraat 111
> 2312 BK LEIDEN

or

Dhr. J. van Dieten
Postbus 12
2310 AA LEIDEN

Street addresses should be written:

Thoroughfare[ ]number.

The last line should always consist of the postal code followed by the town name.

If an address has a box number ('bus') this should be added after the address so:

Thoroughfare[ ]number[bus]number

The thoroughfare type is suffixed to the thoroughfare name without a space. For example:

Haarlemmerdijk 23
Boslaan 98
Groenweg 2

The thoroughfare name may also consist of different components separated with a space thus:

Eerste Anjeliers Dwaasstraat

This is usually the case when the street name begins with an adjective such as 'first', 'long' etc.

The abbreviation *t/m* between numbers in an address is an abbreviation for *tot en met* meaning 'up to and including'.

Thoroughfare types

Below is a list of the most commonly occurring thoroughfare types, with the abbreviated form(s) which you are most likely to find in address databases:

Thoroughfare	*Abbreviation*
Baan	
Berg	
Boulevard	Bd, Bld, Boulev
Dijk	Dk
Donk	
Dwarsstraat	Dwstr
Dwarsweg	Dwwg
Gracht	Gr

Kade	Kd
Kanaal	Kan
Laan, Leane, Loane	Ln
Markt	
Park	Pk
Plantsoen	Plnts
Plein	Pln
Singel	Sngl
Straat, Strjitte	Str
Straatweg	Strwg
Wal	
Weg	Wg

Other nouns, adjectives and prepositions commonly found in address databases:

Dutch

Neuter	*Abbrev.*	*Gendered and Plural (where different from neuter form)*	*Abbrev.*	*Translation*
het (sometimes 't)		de		the
een				a, an
en				and
tot				till, until, up to
voor				for
van				of, from
op, naar				to, towards
bij				near, by
aan				on (sea, for example), at
aan de	a/d			on (a river)
op				on
in				in
tegenover				opposite
naast				next to
achter				behind
vóór				in front of
tussen				between
over				over
onder				under
met				with
nieuw	nw.	nieuwe	nwe.	new
oud		oude		old
kort	k.	korte	kte.	short
lang	1.	lange	lge.	long

hoog	hg.	hoge	hg.	high
laag	lg.	lage	lg.	low
groot	g./gt.	grote	g./gte.	large
klein	k./kl.	kleine	k./kle.	small
		gedempte	ged.	filled-in (of a canal)
		heilige	h.	holy
		kromme	kr.	crooked, curved
		verlengde	verl.	extended
noord	n.			north
		noordzijde	nz.	north side
oost	o.			east
		oostzijde	oz.	east side
zuid	z.			south
		zuidzijde	zz.	south side
west	w.			west
		westzijde	wz.	west side
kasteel	kast.			castle
sint	st.			saint
Industriepark				industrial estate

Friesian

Neuter	*Abbrev.*	*Gendered and Plural (where different from neuter form)*	*Abbrev.*	*Translation*
it (sometimes 't)		de (sometimes 'e)		the
in				a, an
en				and
oant, oan, ta				till, until, up to
foar				for
fan				of, from
nei				to, towards
by				near, by, close to
op				on
yn				in, into
foaroer				opposite
nêst, njonken				next to
efter				behind
foar				in front of
tusken				between
oer				over
ûnder				under
boppe				above
mei				with
nij		nije		new
âld		âlde		old

koart	kt.	koarte	kte.	short
lang	l.	lange	lge.	long
heeg	hg.	hege	hg.	high
leeg	lg.	lege	lg.	low
great	g./gt.	greate	g./gte.	large
lyts		lytse		small
noard	n.			north
east	e.			east
súd	s.			south
west	w.			west
sint	st.			saint

Addresses will also often contain the names of people with their titles or salutations. These titles are, and can be abbreviated, as follows:

Title	*Abbreviation*	*Translation*
Aalmoezenier	Aalm	Chaplin
Admiraal	Adm	Admiral
Baron	Bar	Baron
Baronesse	Bsse	Baroness
Bisschop	Biss	Bishop
Burgemeester	Burg	Mayor
Commissaris	Comm	Commissioner
Deken	Dkn	Deacon
doctorandus	drs	academic grade, masters degree, no translation
Dokter, Doctor	Dr	Doctor
Dominee	Ds	Minister, Vicar, Padre
Douairière	Dre	Dowager
Gebroeders	Gebr	Brothers
Generaal	Gen	General
Graaf	Gr	Earl
Gravin	Gr	Duchess
Hertog	Htg	Duke
Ingenieur	Ir	Engineer
Jonkheer	Jhr	Esquire
Kanunnik	Kan	Canon
Kapelaan	Kap	Curate, Chaplain
Kapitein	Kapt	Captain
Kardinaal	Kard	Cardinal
Keizer	Kzr	Emperor
Kolonel	Kol	Colonel
Koning	Kon	King
Koningin	Kon	Queen
Luitenant-Generaal	Lt Gen	Lieutenant-General
Majoor	Maj	Major
meester	mr	Mister (academic grade)

Minister	Min	Minister (political)
Monseigneur	Mgr	Monseigneur
Notaris	Not	Notary
Pastoor	Past	Pastor
Pater	Ptr	Father (religious)
Paters	Ptrs	Fathers (religious)
President	Pres	President
Prins	Pr	Prince
Princes	Pr	Princess
Professor	Prof	Professor
Rector	Rect	Rector
Ridder	Rdr	Knight
Secretaris	Secr	Secretary
Sinjeur	Sinj	Cleric
Sint	St	Saint
Wethouder	Weth	Alderman
Zuster	Zr	Sister (religious)
Zusters	Zrs	Sisters (religious)

Thoroughfares in Friesland

In Friesland, in the north of The Netherlands, Friesian is spoken. It is uncommon to come across a street name in Friesian in address databases, although Friesian-speakers themselves use them. Thoroughfares are only given a single name (although they are easily translated by users), in Dutch or in Friesian, and this is the one to be used by preference.

Postbox

This is written *Postbus*, abbreviated to *PB*.

Postboxes have their own postal codes. The PTT prefers the use of the postbox number to the street address. Do not use both the street address and the postbox address. If you do this, the PTT will attempt to deliver the package only to the postbox number. If the postal code for this postbox is incorrect (i.e. it refers to the street address), then the package will be returned as undeliverable.

Dutch companies will often provide both a street address and a postbox address with only one postal code in this way:

> Bakker Het Dagelijkse Brood
> Hoofdstraat 12
> Postbus 187
> 6872 AG POSTSTAD

In these cases, the postal code belongs always to the postbox number.

Postal codes

There are more than 575 000 postal codes in The Netherlands, and around 30 000 are changed each year as new streets are created. Postal codes have 4 digits and two letters, the digits starting with a number between 1 and 9. The layout is as follows:

9999[ ]AA

The postal code is written before, and on the same line as, the town name.

The digits indicate the town or district, the letters a group of some 25 habitations, offices, factories or postboxes. There is no correlation between codes and administrative districts.

The letters F, I, O, Q, U and Y never appear in postal codes.

There should be no punctuation anywhere within the postal code, and there should be nothing written underneath the postal code.

The PTT produces software and look-up tables to aid users in keeping their databases up to date.

Towns

St., the abbreviation for *Sint* (Saint), can in all cases be used in town names except for the settlement of *Sintjohannesga.*

Town names consisting of more than one word are not usually hyphenated.

Town names can begin with an apostrophe, followed by an 's' or a 't'. Some of these names have alternative spellings which are perfectly acceptable to use (though the former spellings are the official spellings), i.e:

's-Hertogenbosch = Den Bosch
's-Gravenhage = Den Haag

Town names sometimes include the link *aan* or *aan de*, meaning ‘on’ or 'on the'. *Aan de* is often abbreviated to *a/d.*

The following list gives foreign language equivalents of Dutch town names:

Dutch	*English*	*French*	*German*	*Spanish*	*Italian*
Arnhem			Arnheim		
Den Helder		Le Helder			
Groningen		Groningue			
Hoek van Holland	The Hook of Holland				
Leiden		Leyde			
Nijmegen		Nimègue	Nimwegen		
's-Hertogenbosch /		Bois-le-Duc	Herzogenbusch		

Den Bosch					
's-Gravenhage / Den Haag	The Hague	La Haye		La Haya	L'Aia
Utrecht			Ütrecht		
Vlissingen	Flushing	Fléssingue		Flesingue	Flessinga

Town names in Friesland

In Friesland, in the north of The Netherlands, Friesian is spoken. Where a municipality *(gemeente)* recognizes both a Friesian and a Dutch name for the municipality, the PTT prefers that the Dutch name is used. Where the municipality uses a unilingual Friesian name, the PTT prefers that this name is used. It is preferable as far as the recipient is concerned that the town name corresponding to his/her preferred language is used.

The following list is of settlements in Friesland which have both Dutch and Friesian names:

Dutch	*Friesian*
Aalsum	Ealsum
Abbega	Abbegea
Aegum	Eagum
Akmarijp	Eagmaryp
Anjum	Eanjum
Appelscha	Appelskea
Augsbuurt	Lytsewâld
Augustinusga	Stynsgea
Baaiduinen	Baaidunen
Baijum	Baaium
Bakhuizen	Bakhuzen
Bakkeveen	Bakkefean
Bantega	Bantegea
Beers	Bears
Beetgum	Bitgum
Beetgumermolen	Bitgummole
Beetsterzwaag	Beetstersweach
Bergum	Burgum
Berlikum	Berltsum
Birdaard	Burdaard
Blauwhuis	Blauhús
Blesdijke	Blesdike
Blija	Blije
Boelenslaan	Boelensloane
Bolsward	Boalsert
Boornbergum	Boarnburgum
Boornzwaag	Boarnsweach
Bornwird	Boarnwert
Bozum	Boazum
Britswerd	Britswert

Broeksterwoude	Broeksterwâld
Buitenpost	Bûtenpost
Burgwerd	Burchwert
Burum	Boerum
Cornjum	Koarnjum
Cornwerd	Koarnwert
Damwoude	Damwâld
Dedgum	Dedzjum
Deersum	Dearsum
Delfstrahuizen	Dolsterhuzen
De Veenhoop	De Feanhoop
De Wilgen	De Wylgen
Dijken	Diken
Dongjum	Doanjum
Doniaga	Dunegea
Drachtster Compagnie	Drachtster Kompenije
Driesum	Driezum
Drogeham	Droegeham
Dronrijp	Dronryp
Echten	Ychten
Echtenerbrug	Ychtenbrêge
Edens	Iens
Ee	Ie
Eernewoude	Earnewâld
Eesterga	Jistergea
Eestrum	Jistrum
Elahuizen	Ealahuzen
Elsloo	Elslo
Engelum	Ingelum
Engwierrum	Ingwierrum
Exmorra	Eksmoarre
Ferwerd	Ferwert
Ferwoude	Ferwâlde
Finksum	Feinsum
Firdgum	Furdgum
Fochteloo	Fochtel
Follega	Follegea
Folsgare	Folsgeare
Formerum	Formearum
Franeker	Frjentsjer
Frieschepalen	Fryske Peallen
Gaastmeer	Gaastmar
Garijp	Garyp
Gauw	Gau
Genum	Ginnum
Gerkesklooster	Gerkeskleaster
Gersloot	Gersleat

Giekerk	Gytsjerk
Goënga	Goaiïngea
Goëngahuizen	Goaiïngahuzen
Goëngarijp	Goaiïngaryp
Gorredijk	Gordyk
Grouw	Grou
Hantumeruitburen	Hantumerútbuorren
Hanturnhuizen	Hantumhuzen
Hardegarijp	Hurdegaryp
Harlingen	Harns
Hartwerd	Hartwert
Haskerdijken	Haskerdiken
Haskerhome	Haskerhoarne
Haulerwijk	Haulerwyk
Heeg	Heech
Heerenveen	It Hearrenfean
Hemelum	Himmelum
Hempens	Himpens
Hemrik	Himrik
Hennaard	Hinnaard
Herbaijum	Hjerbeam
Hiaure	Lyste Jouwer
Hijlaard	Hilaard
Hindeloopen	Hylpen
Hitzum	Hitsum
Hogebeintum	Hegebeintum
Holwerd	Holwert
Hoom	Hoarne
Hoornsterzwaag	Hoarnstersweach
Huins	Húns
Idskenhuizen	Jiskenhuzen
Idzega	Idzegea
Idzegahuizum	Skuzum
IJlst	Drylts
IJsbrechtum	Ysbrechtum
Indijk	Yndyk
Irnsum	Jirnsum
Janum	Jannum
Jorwerd	Jorwert
Joure	Jouwer
Jubbega	Jobbegea
Jutrijp	Jutryp
Katlijk	Ketlik
Kimswerd	Kimswert
Kinnum	Kinum
Koefurderrige	Kûfurderrige
Kolderwolde	Kolderwâlde

Kollumerzwaag	Kollumersweach
Kootstertille	Koatstertille
Kornwerderzand	Koarnwertersân
Kortehemmen	Koartehimmen
Kubaard	Kûbaard
Langedijke	Langedike
Langezwaag	Langsweagen
Langweer	Langwar
Leeuwarden	Ljouwert
Legemeer	Legemar
Lioessens	Ljussens
Lions	Leons
Lippenhuizen	Lippenhuzen
Loënga	Loaiïngea
Longerhouw	Longerhou
Luinjeberd	Lûnbert
Lutkewierum	Lytsewierrum
Luxwoude	Lúkswâld
Makkinga	Makkingea
Marssum	Marsum
Menaldum	Menaam
Metslawier	Mitselwier
Midlum	Mullum
Midsland	Midslân
Minnertsga	Minnertsgea
Mirns	Murns
Molenend	Mûnein
Molkwerum	Molkwar
Morra	Moarre
Munnikeburen	Munnekebuorren
Munnikezijl	Muntsjesyl
Niawier	Nijewier
Nieuwehorne	Nijhoarne
Nieuweschoot	Nijskoat
Nijeberkoop	Nijeberkeap
Nijega	Nyegea
Nijeholtpade	Nijeholtpea
Nijeholtwolde	Nijeholtwâlde
Nijelamer	Nijelemmer
Nijemirdum	Nijemardum
Nijetrine	Nijetrine
Nijhuizum	Nijhuzum
Nijland	Nijlân
Noordbergum	Noardburgum
Noordwolde	Noardwâlde
Oenkerk	Oentsjerk
Offingawier	Offenwier

Oldeberkoop	Aldeberkeap
Oldeboorn	Aldeboarn
Oldeholtpade	Aldeholtpea
Oldeholtwolde	Aldeholtwâlde
Oldelamer	Aldlemmer
Oldeouwer	Alde Ouwer
Oldetrijne	Aldetrine
Oosterbierum	Easterbierrum
Oosterend	Easterein (in the municipality of Littenseradiel)
Oosterend	Aasterein (on the island of Terschelling)
Oosterlittens	Easterlittens
Oostermeer	Eastermar
Oosternijkerk	Easternijtsjerk
Oosterwierum	Easterwierrum
Oosterwolde	Easterwâlde
Oosterzee	Eastersee
Oosthem	Easthim
Oostrum	Eastrum
Oost-Vlieland	East-Flylân
Opeinde	Pein
Oppenhuizen	Toppenhuzen
Oranjewoud	Oranjewâld
Oude Bildtzijl	Aldebiltsyl
Oudega	Aldegea (applies to all three settlements with this name in Friesland)
Oudehaske	Aldehaske
Oudehorne	Aldhoarne
Oude Leije	Aldeleie
Oudemirdum	Aldemardum
Oudeschoot	Aldskoat
Oudkerk	Aldtsjerk
Oudwoude	Aldwâld
Ouwsterhaule	Ousterhaule
Ouwster-Nijega	Ousternijegea
Paesens	Peazens
Parrega	Parregea
Peperga	Pepergea
Pietersbierum	Pitersbierrum
Pingjum	Penjum
Poppingawier	Poppenwier
Rauwerd	Raard
Ravenswoud	Ravenswâld
Ried	Rie
Rijperkerk	Ryptsjerk
Rijs	Riis

Rinsumageest	Rinsumageast
Rohel	Reahel
Roodhuis	Reahûs
Roodkerk	Readtsjerk
Roordahuizum	Roardhuzum
Rottevalle	Rottefalle
Ruigahuizen	Rûgehuzen
Sandfirden	Sânfurd
Schalsum	Skalsum
Scharnegoutum	Skearnegoutum
Scharsterbrug	Skarsterbrêge
Scherpenzeel	Skerpenseel
Schettens	Skettens
Schiermonnikoog	Skiermûntseach
Schingen	Skingen
Schraard	Skraard
Seerijp	Stryp
Sexbierum	Seisbierrum
Siegerswoude	Sigerswâld
Sijbrandaburen	Sibrandabuorren
Sijbrandahuis	Sibrandahûs
St. Annaparochie	St. Anne
St. Jacobiparochie	St. Jabik
Sintjohannesga	St. Jansgea
St. Nicolaasga	St. Nyk
Sloten	Sleat
Smallebrugge	Smelbrêge
Smalle Ee	Smelle Ie
Snakkerburen	Snakkerbuorren
Sneek	Snits
Snikzwaag	Sniksweach
Sonnega	Sonnegea
Spanga	Spangea
Stavoren	Starum
Stroobos	Strobos
Suameer	Sumar
Suawoude	Suwâld
Surhuisterveen	Surhústerfean
Surhuizum	Surhuzum
Teerns	Tearns
Terband	Terbant
Terhorne	Terherne
Ter Idzard	Teridzert
Terzool	Tersoal
Tietjerk	Tytsjerk
Tijnje	Tynje
Tirns	Turns

Tjalhuizum	Tsjalhuzum
Tjalleberd	Tsjalbert
Tjerkgaast	Tsjerkgaast
Tjerkwerd	Tsjerkwert
Twijzel	Twizel
Twijzelerheide	Twizelerheide
Tzum	Tsjom
Tzummarum	Tsjummearum
Uitwellingerga	Twellingea
Ureterp	Oerterp
Valom	Falom
Veenklooster	Feankleaster
Veenwouden	Feanwâlden
Vegelinsoord	Vegelinsoard
Vinkega	Finkegea
Vrouwenparochie	Froubuorren
Waaxens	Waaksens (both settlements with this name in Friesland)
Wanswerd	Wânswert
Warfstermolen	Warfstermûne
Warga	Wergea
Wartena	Warten
Waskemeer	Waskemar
Welsrijp	Wjelsryp
Westergeest	Westergeast
Westhem	Westhim
West-Terschelling	West-Skylge
Wieuwerd	Wiuwert
Wijckel	Wikel
Wijnaldum	Winaam
Wijnjewoude	Wynjewâld
Wijns	Wyns
Wirdum	Wurdum
Witmarsum	Wytmarsum
Wolvega	Wolvegea
Wons	Wûns
Workum	Warkum
Woudsend	Wâldsein
Wouterswoude	Wâlterswâld
Ypecolsga	Ypelkolsgea
Zurich	Surch
Zwaagwesteinde	Westerein
Zwagerbosch	Sweagerbosk
Zweins	Sweins

In all other cases, the settlement has a unilingual name.

Administrative districts

The Netherlands is split into 12 provinces:

Drenthe (Dr.)
Flevoland (Fl.)
Friesland (Fr.)
Gelderland (Gld.)
Groningen (Gr.)
Limburg (Lim.)
Noord Brabant (N.Br.)
Noord Holland (N.H.)
Overijssel (Ov.)
Utrecht (Utr.)
Zeeland (Zld.)
Zuid Holland (Z.H.)

These are not used in addresses unless no postal code is used and a town of the same name exists in more than one province.

These provinces are further split into *gemeentes,* municipalities which contain one or more settlements.

New Caledonia
Nouvelle-Calédonie

New Caledonia is an overseas territory of France. It forms part of the French mail system.

Area: 18 575 sq. km (7 170 sq. miles)
Population: 178 000
Capital: Nouméa
Currency: 1 French Franc (Ffr) = 100 centimes
International telephone access code: 687

Languages

The official language is French (53 400 first-language speakers). 37 other languages are spoken, many by small numbers. The mains ones of these are: Ajië (5 000 speakers); Bislama (1 200 speakers); Cemuhî (2 500 speakers); Dehu (15 000 speakers); Dumbea (1 400 speakers); East Futuna (3 000 speakers); Fwâi (1 000 speakers); Iaai (2 200 speakers on Ouvéa Island); New Caledonian Javanese (6 750 speakers); Nengone (6 050 speakers on Mare Island); Numee (1 800 speakers); Nyâlayu (1 400 speakers); Paicî (5 500 speakers); West Uvean (1 870 speakers on Ouvea Atoll); Wallisian (9 000 speakers); Xârâcùù (3 500 speakers) and Yuaga (2 000 speakers).

Address formats

Please refer to the chapter on France for address information.

Postal codes

All New Caledonia postal codes commence with the digits 988.

New Zealand
Aotearoa (Maori)

Official name: New Zealand, Aotearoa
Area: 268 812 sq. km (103 761 sq. miles)
Population: 3 434 950
Capital: Wellington
Currency: 1 New Zealand Dollar ($NZ) = 100 cents
International telephone access code: 64

Languages

The official languages are English (3 213 000 speakers) and Maori (50-70 000 speakers).

Address format

Addresses are formatted as follows:

NAME
NUMBER{[-]APARTMENT NUMBER}[ ]THOROUGHFARE NAME[ ]THOROUGHFARE TYPE
SUBURB
SETTLEMENT[ ]POSTAL CODE

For example:

MR N SMITH
2-76 AUCKLAND AVENUE
MIRAMAR
WELLINGTON 1003

The house number may be followed by an apartment number separated from the house number by a hyphen. Addresses may also be to PO Boxes (written

P[ ]O[ ]Box

to ease OCR recognition), Private Bags or Rural Deliveries. Ensure that only one type of address is used.

Though the New Zealand postal authorities prefer the address to be in upper case, an address always looks better, as far as the user is concerned, in mixed case.

Postal codes

Postal codes consist of a block of 4 digits. The first two digits indicate the circulating district, the last two the mode of delivery.

Towns

The following list provides Maori equivalent names for New Zealand town names:

English	*Maori*
Auckland	Tamaki-Makaurau
Christchurch	Otautahi
Dunedin	Otepoti
Hamilton	kirikiriroa
Invercargill	Murihiku
Napier	Ahuriri
Nelson	Whakatu
New Plymouth	Ngamotu
Palmerston North	Te Papaioea
Wellington	Te Whanganui-a-Tara

Nicaragua

Official name: Republic of Nicaragua, República de Nicaragua
Area: 148 000 sq. km (57 128 sq. miles)
Population: 4 130 000
Capital: Managua
Currency: 1 New Córdoba (C$) = 100 centavos
International telephone access code: 505

Languages

The official language is Spanish, spoken by most of the population. There are also 1 500 speakers of Garífuna; 154 400 of Mískito (around Puerto Cabezas and along the northern Caribbean coast); 24 speakers of Rama; 6 700 speakers of Sumo and 30 000 speakers of Western Caribbean Creole English, around Bluefields and along the southern Caribbean coast).

Example address format

Sr. Francisco Ramirez
42 Ave. S.E. 346
MANAGUA 3416-007

Postal codes

The postal codes consist of a block of 4 digits, or for Managua 7 digits in the format:

9999[-]999

The first digit indicates the postal region, the second the district and the final two the postal area. For Managua, the three digits after the hyphen indicate a block of houses.

Niger

Official name: Republic of Niger, République du Niger
Area: 1 267 000 sq. km (489 191 sq. miles)
Population: 8 154 000
Capital: Niamey
Currency: 1 CFA Franc (CFAFr) = 100 cents
International telephone access code: 227

Languages

Niger counts 21 languages. The official language is French. The most widely-spoken languages are: Arabic (in 3 forms, 277 000 speakers); Sokoto Fulfulde (709 500 speakers); Hausa (3 600 000 speakers); Manga Kanuri (350 000 speakers); Songai (390 000 speakers); Air Tamajeq (250 000 speakers), Tahoua Tamajeq (350 000 speakers) and Zarma (1 495 000 speakers).

Example address format

M. Mamane Madjidadi
B.P. 30
DOSSO

Any address written in a non-native language will be written in French. Deliveries are made only to post boxes (*Boite Postale*, or *BP*).

Postal codes

Niger has no postal code system.

Nigeria

Official name: Federal Republic of Nigeria
Area: 923 768 sq. km (356 574 sq. miles)
Population: 88 500 000
Capital: Abuja
Currency: 1 Naira (N) = 100 kobo
International telephone access code: 234

Language

The national language is English. 477 other languages are spoken, with a complex geographical spread. The most widely spoken are: Anaang (1 000 000 speakers); Ebira (1 000 000 speakers); Edo (1 000 000 speakers); Fulfulde (7 611 000 speakers); Hausa (an official language in the North) (18 525 000 speakers); Igbo (an official language in the Southeast) (17 000 000 speakers); Yerwa Kanuri (3 000 000 speakers); Tiv (2 212 000 speakers) and Yoruba (18 850 000 speakers).

Example address format

Mr. J.C.E. Okpala
P.M.B. 12537
Lafiaji Building
LAGOS

Addresses written in a non-native language will usually be written in English.

Postal codes

Nigeria has no postal code system.

Northern Mariana Islands

Northern Mariana Islands is a commonwealth territory of the United States. It forms part of the United States' postal system.

Official name: Northern Mariana Islands
Area: 471 sq. km (182 sq. miles)
Population: 43 345
Capital: Saipan
Currency: 1 United States Dollar (US$) = 100 cents
International telephone access code: 1

Languages

The national language is English. There are 3 000 speakers of Carolinian and 14 205 speakers of Chamorro. Tanapag is also spoken.

Address Information

Northern Mariana Islands forms part of the United States' postal system. Its state code is MP and its postal codes fall in the range 96950-2.

Please refer to the chapter on the United States of America for further information.

Telephone numbers

The area code for all telephone numbers in Northern Mariana Islands is 670.

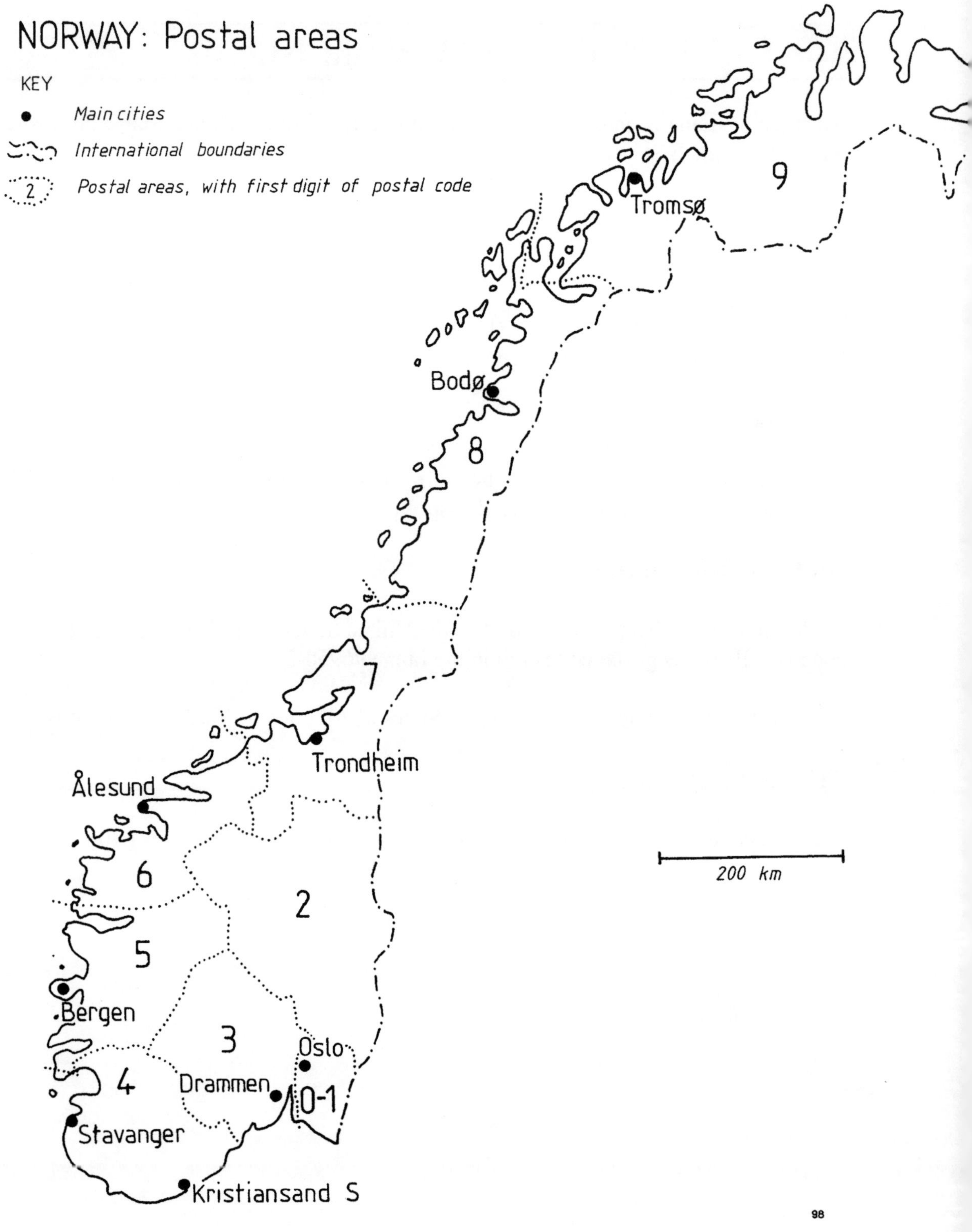
NORWAY: Postal areas
KEY
Main cities
International boundaries
2 Postal areas, with first digit of postal code
9
Tromsø
Bodø
8
7
Trondheim
Ålesund
6
2
5
Bergen
3
Oslo
4
Drammen
0-1
Stavanger
Kristiansand S
200 km
98

Norway
Norge

Official name: Kingdom of Norway, Kongeriket Norge
Area: 323 877 sq. km (125 050 sq. miles)
Population: 4 259 000
Capital: Oslo
Currency: 1 Norwegian krone (NKr)= 100 øre
International telephone access code: 47

Languages

Norwegian, the official language, has two forms: Bokmål or Riksmål and Nynorsk or Landsmål. All children in Norway learn both forms at school. The former is that spoken in Oslo and most other urban areas. The two forms together are spoken by 99 per cent of the population. Saami (in 5 different forms) is spoken by the 22 500 Saami living in the far north of the country. There are small numbers of Romani-speakers.

Company types

The following company types may be found in Norwegian address databases:

AL (Andelslag - co-operative society)
ANS
AS (Aksjeselaskap - limited liability)
Gruppen

Addresses

Addresses are written in this format:

Recipient name
Thoroughfare[ ]number
postal code[ ]SETTLEMENT{[ ]Sorting code}

For example:

Hans Hansen
Svingen 22
0107 OSLO 1

There should be two spaces between the postal code and the settlement name.

The thoroughfare type is suffixed to the street name without a space. As with other Scandinavian languages, the definite article does not appear as a separate word but as *-en* or *-et* at the end of a word (see language rules below). Thus 'way' is *vei,* 'the way' is *veien.*

Thoroughfare types

The most commonly occurring thoroughfare types, with their abbreviations, are listed below:

Thoroughfare Type	*Abbrev.*
Allè	
Allèen	
Bakken	
Bukt	
Byen	
Dalen	
Flate	
Gata (dialect)	G, Gt
Gate(n)	G, Gt
Lia	
Park	
Plassen	Pl
Stortorget	
Stredet	
Svingen	
Target	
Vegen (dialect)	V.
Vei(en)	V.

Other common nouns, adjectives and prepositions commonly found in address databases

NB: This list is for Bokmål. The ending of the adjectives changes according to the gender of the noun to which it refers and whether it is singular or plural. The plural in Norwegian is made by adding *-(e)r* to the end of a word, or *-(e)ne* when the word is preceded by the definite article.

Bokmål	*English*
den, det	the (but only when followed by an adjective preceding a noun. Otherwise *-en* (gendered) or *-et* (neuter) is added to the end of the noun. So, for example, *vei* = road, *den store vei* = the big road, but ...*veien*)
en, et	a, an
og	and
til, inntil	till, until, up to
for, til	for
fra	of
av, fra	from
til	to, towards
ved, nær	near, by
på	on

i	in
overfor	opposite
ved siden av, nærmest, nest	next to
bak, bakerst	behind
foran	in front of
mellom, imellom	between
over	over
under	under
med	with
ny	new
gammel	old
kort	short
lang	long
stor	big
liten, lita, lite, lille, små (plural)	small
nord	north
øst	east
syd	south
vest	west
Industriebygget	Industrial estate

(NB: When used with nouns, the words for north, south, east and west are prefixed without a space to the noun to which they refer. For example, Sydgate = South Street).

Postbox

This is written as *Postboks*, abbreviated to *PB* or *POB*

Postal codes

Norwegian postal codes consist of a block of 4 digits, beginning with a number from 0 to 9. The postal code is placed on the last line of the address and precedes the town name. In the larger cities, a number indicating the sorting office may be written after the town name, for example:

0501 OSLO 5

Administrative districts

Norway has 19 counties *(Fylker),* which do not appear in addresses. They are listed below:

Akerhus
Aust-Agder
Buskerud
Finnmark
Hedmark
Hordaland
More og Romsdal
Nord-Trøndelag
Nordland
Oppland
Oslo
Østfold
Rogaland
Sogn og Fjordane
Sør-Trøndelag
Telemark
Troms
Vest-Agder
Vestfold

Oman
'Umān

Official name: Sultanate of Oman, Saltanat 'Umān
Area: 300 000 sq. km (115 800 sq. miles)
Population: 1 640 000
Capital: Musqaţ (Muscat)
Currency: 1 Rial Omani (RO) = 1 000 baizas
International telephone access code: 968

Language

The national language is standard Arabic. There are 70 000 speakers of Dhofari Spoken Arabic; 441 000 of Gulf Spoken Arabic; 720 000 of Omani Spoken Arabic; 130 300 of Southern Balochi; 1 000 of Bathari; 25 000 of Western Farsi; 700 of Harsusi; several hundreds of Hobyot; 25 000 of Jibbali; 3 000 of Kumzari (on the Musandram Peninsula only); 5 000 of Luwati and 15 000 of Mehri.

Example address format

Contact name
P.O. Box 615
MUSQAŢ
111

Postal codes

The postal code consists of a block of 3 digits written on the last line of the address. The first digit (between 1 and 8) indicates the governorate or region, the last two the post office. The first digit of the postal code for each governorate or region is:

Governorates:

Dhufar	2
Musandam	8
Musqaţ	1

Regions:

Al-Batinah	3
Al-Dhahira	5
Al-Sharqiyah	4
Al-Wosta	7
The Interior	6

Towns

Musqaţ is known as *Muscat* in English and *Mascate* in French.

Pakistan
Pākistān

Official name: Islamic Republic of Pakistan, Islam-i Jamhuriya-e Pākistān
Area: 803 943 sq. km (310 322 sq. miles)
Population: 117 430 130
Capital: Islamabad
Currency: 1 Pakistan Rupee (PRs, Rp) 100 paisa
International telephone access code: 92

Languages

Pakistan has 66 languages. The official languages are Urdu (10 719 000 mother-tongue speakers) and English (mainly second-language speakers). The other main languages are: Eastern Balochi (1 730 000 speakers) (written in Urdu script); Southern Balochi (2 350 000 speakers) (written in Urdu script); Western Balochi (1 000 000 speakers) (written in Urdu script); Brahui (1 500 000 speakers) (written in Nastaliq script); Eastern Farsi (1 000 000 speakers); Gujarati (44 000 000 speakers); Northern Hindko (1 875 000 speakers); Western Panjabi (30-45 000 000 speakers) (written using Perso-Arabic script); Eastern Pashto (9 585 000 speakers) (written using Perso-Arabic script); Southern Pashto (1 000 000 speakers) (written using Perso-Arabic script); Saraiki (15 000 000 speakers) and Sindhi (16 992 000 speakers) (written in Arabic and Gurumukhi scripts).

Example address format

Mr Nusratullah Khan
House No 17-B
Street No. 30
Sector F-7/1
ISLAMABAD-44000

Addresses written in a non-native language will be written in English.

Postal code

Pakistani postal codes consist of a block of 5 digits. The first two indicate the routing district, the last three the post office.

Palau
Belau

Palau is an archipelago of some 350 Pacific islands of which 8 are inhabited.

Official name: Republic of Belau
Area: 494 sq. km (191 sq. miles)
Population: 15 122
Capital: Koror
Currency: United States Dollar (USD, US$)
International telephone access code: 680

Languages

The national languages are English and Palauan, the most widely spoken language. There are some 600 speakers of Sonsorol, and 22 of Tobian on Tobi Island.

Recently independent of the United States, it still forms part of the United States' postal system. Its state code is PW and its postal code is 96940.

The name of the island may be included in the address.

Please refer to the chapter on the United States of America for further information.

Panama
Panamá

Official name: Republic of Panama, República de Panamá
Area: 77 082 sq. km (29 753 sq. miles)
Population: 2 515 000
Capital: Panamá (Panama City)
Currency: 1 Balboa (B, Ba) = 100 cents
International telephone access code: 507

Languages

Panama has 13 languages. The national language is Spanish, with 2 100 000 speakers. Other widely spoken languages are: Guaymí (128 000 speakers) and Western Caribbean Creole English (1-300 000 speakers).

Address format example

Sr. Francisco Gonzalez
El Cacao
TONOSÍ
PROVINCIA DE LOS SANTOS

A 1-2 digit sorting code may be found following the city name for addresses in Panama City.

The province name may be found in the address as above. The provinces are:

Bocas del Toro
Chiriqui
Coclé
Colón
Darién
Herrera
Los Santos
Panamá
San Blas
Veraguas

Postal codes

Panama has no postal code system.

Paraguay

Official name: Republic of Paraguay, República del Paraguay
Area: 406 750 sq. km (157 000 sq. miles)
Population: 4 520 000
Capital: Asunción
Currency: 1 Guarani (G) = 100 céntimos
International telephone access code: 595

Languages

Paraguay has 21 languages. The official language, Spanish, is spoken by no more than 110 000 people. The most widespread language is Paraguayan Guaraní, with 4 648 000 speakers. There are also some 38 000 German-speakers in Paraguay.

Example address format

Sr. Juan Carlos Monzon
Alberdi 130
ASUNCIÓN

If the address is written in Spanish and the thoroughfare type is *calle* (Street), then this is not written in the address. The thoroughfare type is written commencing with a lower-case letter. For a full list of thoroughfare types, please refer to the chapter on Spain.

Postal codes

Paraguay has no postal code system.

Town names

Though Spanish is the official language, Guaraní is the widest spoken, and many settlements have names in both languages:

Spanish	*Guaraní*
Acahay	Akã'ai
Amambay	Amambái
Asunción	Paraguay
Caacupé	Ka'akupe
Caaguazu	Ka'aguasu
Caazapá	Ka'asapa
Cambyretá	Kambyretã
Capiatá	Kapiatã

Curupaytí	Kurupa'yty
Encarcación	Itapúa
Ibicui	Yvyku'i
Iguazú	Yguasu
Itacurubí	Itakuruvi
Itaipú	Itaipu
Ivytymí	Yvytymi
Izozog	Ysoso
Mbaracayú	Mbarakaju
Minas-cué	Minas kue
Ñeembucú	Ñe'ẽmbuku
Piribebuy	Pirivevúi
Quyindy	Ky'ỹindy
Sapucai	Sapukái
Tuyutí	Tujutĩ
Yaciretá	Jasyretã
Ycuamandiyú	Ykuamandyju
Ypacaraí	Ypakarao
Yvyyaú	Yvy ja'u

Peru
Perú

Official name: Republic of Peru, República del Perú
Area: 1 285 640 sq. km (495 871 sq. miles)
Population: 22 454 000
Capital: Lima
Currency: 1 New Sol = 100 centavos
International telephone access code: 51

Languages

The official languages are Spanish (20 000 000 speakers) and Quechua (3 821 000 speakers in 33 different forms). 61 other, mainly Indian, languages are spoken, and bilingualism is limited. The main one is Central Aymara (350 320 speakers around Lake Titicaca).

Example address format

Sra. Esperanza Alcala V.
calle La Merced 125
AREQUIPA

If the address is written in Spanish and the thoroughfare type is *calle* (Street), then this may not be written in the address. The thoroughfare type is written commencing with a lower-case letter. For a full list of thoroughfare types, please refer to the chapter on Spain.

Address for the cities of Lima and Callao may have a one- or two-digit sorting code written to the right of the city name.

Postal codes

Peru has no postal code system.

The Philippines
Pilipinas

Official name: Republic of the Philippines, Republika ñg Pilipinas
Area: 299 679 sq. km (115 676 sq. miles)
Population: 63 609 000
Capital: Manila
Currency: 1 Philippine Peso (PP) = 100 centavos
International telephone access code: 63

Languages

168 languages are spoken in the Philippines, with a complex geographical distribution. The official languages are Tagalog (Filipino, 14 850 000 speakers) and English (15 371 speakers, with 52% of the population claiming it as a second language). The most widespread other languages are: Aklanon (350 000 speakers); Albay Bicolano (480 000 speakers); Central Bicolano (2 500 000 speakers); Iriga Bicolano (180 000 speakers); Binukid (100 000 speakers); Koronadal Blaan (100 000 speakers); Sarangani Blaan (200 000 speakers); Capiznon (445 716 speakers); Cebuano (15 230 000 speakers); Chavacano (280 000 speakers); Min Nan Chinese (500 000 speakers); Davawenyo (124 486 speakers); Hiligaynon (6 000 000 speakers); Ibanag (500 000 speakers); Ilocano (8 000 000 speakers); Itawit (105 556 speakers); Kankanaey (150 000 speakers); Kinaray-A (350 000 speakers); Magindanaon (1 000 000 speakers); Maranao (602 613 speakers); Masbatenyo (332 828 speakers); Pampangan (2 000 000 speakers); Pangasinan (2 000 000 speakers); Romblomanon (200 000 speakers); Central Sama (100 000 speakers); Waray Sorsogon (185 000 speakers); Tausug (330 000 speakers) and Waray-Waray (3 000 000 speakers).

Address format

Addresses are written in different formats according to the destination within the Philippines. For mail destined for Manila, the format is:

Postbox address:

Contact name
[P.O. Box]number[,]Name of post office
postal code[ ]{District name[,]}[MANILA]

For example:

Mr. Juan dela Cruz
P.O. Box 1021, Manila Central Post Office
1050 MANILA

Street address:

Contact name
number[ ]Thoroughfare name[,]District name
postal code[MANILA]

For example:

Mr. Juan dela Cruz
979 Kundiman Street, Sampaloc
1009 MANILA

For mail destined to areas within Metropolitan Manila other than Manila itself:

Postbox address:

Contact name
[P.O. Box]number[,]Name of post office
postal code[ ]{District name[,]}[METRO MANILA]

For example:

Mr. Juan dela Cruz
P.O. Box 1021, Araneta Center Post Office
1036 Quezon City, METRO MANILA

Street address:

Contact name
number[ ]Thoroughfare name{[,]Subdivision and/or village}
{Barangay Name, City/Municipality}
postal code[METRO MANILA]

For example:

Mr. Juan dela Cruz
979 Maria Street, Carmona, Makati
2010 METRO MANILA

For mail destined to other parts of the Philippines:

Name
number[ ]Thoroughfare name{[,]District name and/or village}
{Barangay Name, City/Municipality}
postal code[ ]PROVINCE

For example:

Mr. Juan dela Cruz
979 Maria Street, Sofia Subdivision
1270 PAMPANGA

Addresses are usually written in English, although there is some transliteration of street names into Tagalog. Officially English should be used.

The most common thoroughfare types found are Avenue, Street and Alley.

Postal codes

Postal codes consist of a block of 4 digits. The last two digits are '00' for areas where central post offices are located. Codes beginning '0' are large-user postal codes.

Administrative units

Barangay is the unit of administration in the Philippines. They may be as small as a village. A postal code may cover a single barangay, part of one or more than one. They may appear in addresses above the line containing the postal code.

Poland
Polska

Official name: Republic of Poland, Polska Rzeczpospolita
Area: 312 683 sq. km (120 727 sq. miles)
Population: 38 423 000
Capital: Warszawa (Warsaw)
Currency: 1 Złoty (ZI)= 100 groszy
International telephone access code: 48

Languages

The official language, Polish, is spoken by 98% of the population. Ukrainian is spoken by about 1 500 000 people; German by 1 400 000 people; Belorussian by 230 000; Kashubian by 200 000 and Romani (in four forms) by about 30 000 people.

Company Types

The following company types may be found in Polish addresses:

PHUP
PPH
PPHU
S.A.
s.c.
Spolka z o.o. (or Sp. z o.o.) (limited company)

Contact Names

Children usually take the surnames of their fathers. It is becoming popular to take two surnames (one from each parent). For example, *Plichta-Bakowski*, *Plichta* from the father and *Bakowski* from the mother. Female spouses often have double surnames, the first part her maiden name, the second the surname of her husband. Rarely, women do not take their husbands surname, or children take the mother's surname.

Addresses

Addresses are written in this format:

Salutation
Recipient name
thoroughfare type[ ]Thoroughfare name[ ]number
postal code[ ]SETTLEMENT

for example:

Sz. P.
Jan Kalinkowski
ul.Cicha 5
62-806 KALISZ

Sorting codes (a number after the settlement name) are sometimes found in addresses but they are not required.

Thoroughfare types are written beginning with a lower-case letter.

The house number may be followed by an 'm' or '/' to indicate a flat number. In the following examples of layout, the house number is 12, the flat number 3:

ul. Mala nr 12 m. 3
ul. Mala 12/3
ul. Mala 12 m. 3
ul. Mala nr 12/3

Additional numbers or characters may indicate different entrances to the building. For example:

ul. Mala 12/4/223
ul. Mala 12A/3

In all cases the house number layout is familiar to Poles and the Polish Post Office and should not be altered.

Some villages have no street names - each house has its own number, which follows the village name like this:

Mscijewo 11

Thoroughfare types

Common thoroughfare types with their abbreviations are:

Thoroughfare type	*Abbreviation*	*Translation*
plac	pl.	Square
aleja	al.	Avenue
ulica	ul.	Street

Other nouns, adjectives and prepositions commonly found in address databases

NB: (m) = masculine; (f) = feminine; (n) = neuter

Polish	*English*
wschod	East
wschodni (m), wschodnia (f), wschodnie (n)	Eastern

zachod	West
zachodni (m), zachodnia (f), zachodnie (n)	Western
poludnie	South
poludniowy (m), poludniowa (f), poludniowe (n)	Southern
polnoc	North
polnocny (m), polnocny (f), polnocne (n)	Northern
maly (m), mala (f), male (n)	Little
wielki (m), wielka (f), wielkie (n)	Great
nowy (m), nowa (f), nowe (n)	New
stary (m), stara (f), stare (n)	Old
krotki (m), krotka (f), krotkie (n)	Short
dlugi (m), dluga (f), dlugie (n)	Long
swiety (m), swieta (f) (both abbreviated to sw.)	Saint

Postbox

The Polish word for Postbox is *skrytka pocztowa*, abbreviated to *skr. poczt.* "POBox" and "PO" are also used.

Postal codes

Polish postal codes have 5 digits and are written in this format:

99[-]999

Each postal code defines a postal area which may cover a district, a small town, a street or part of a street. Poles often use postal code incorrectly - for example, many will use the code 64-920 for every address in the town of Piła, whereas the town has three postal code areas. When no postal code is used, a region name is required in the address.

The first digit indicates the district as follows:

District	*First digit of postal code*
Warszawa	0
Olsztyn	1
Lublin	2
Kraków	3
Katowice	4
Wroclaw	5
Poznan	6
Szczecin	7
Gdansk	8
Lódz	9

Towns

Polish borders have changed greatly throughout history; many settlements have corresponding names in German and Russian in particular. The following list gives the foreign language equivalents of the main Polish town names:

Polish	*English*	*French*	*German*	*Spanish*	*Italian*
Bydgoszcz			Bromberg		
Bytom			Beuthen		
Częstochova			Tschenstochau		
Elbląg			Elbing		
Gdańsk	Danzig		Danzig		Danzica
Gdynia			Gdingen		
Gliwice			Gleiwitz		
Glogów			Glogau		
Gniezno			Gnesen		
Gorzów Wielkopolski			Landsberg		
Grudzią			Graudenz		
Kalisz			Kalisch		
Katowice			Kattowitz		
Kłodzko			Glatz		
Kołobrzeg			Kolberg		
Kostrzyn			Küstrin		
Koszalin			Koslin		
Kraków	Crakow	Cracovie	Krakau		Cracovia
Kwidzyn			Marienwerder		
Legnica			Liegnitz		
Łomza			Lomscha		
Malbork			Marienburg		
Nysa			Neiße		
Olsztyn			Allenstein		
Oświęucim	Auschwitz				
Piła			Sneidemuhl		
Poznań			Posen		
Słupsk			Stolp		
Sosnowiec			Sosnowitz		
Stebark			Tannenberg		
Swinoujście			Swinemünde		
Szczecin	Stettin		Stettin		Stettino
Szczecinek			Neustettin		
Toruń			Thorn		
Warszawa	Warsaw	Varsovie	Warschau	Varsovia	
Wrocław	Breslau		Breslau		

All accented town names are usually written without accents in English.

Administrative districts

Poland has 49 provinces *(Voivodships)*. They are not used in addresses. They are listed below:

Biała Podlaska
Białystok
Bielsko-Biała
Bydgoszcz
Chełm
Ciechanów
Częstochowa
Elbląg
Gdańsk
Gorzów Wielkopolski
Jelenia Góra
Kalisz
Katowice
Kielce
Konin
Koszalin
Kraków
Krosno
Legnica
Leszno
Lódź
Lomża
Lublin
Nowy Sącz
Olsztyn
Opole
Ostrolęka
Piotrków Trrybunalski
Piła
Płock
Poznań
Przemyśl
Radom
Rzeszów
Siedlce
Sieradz
Skierniewice
Słupsk
Suwałki
Szczecin
Tarnobrzeg
Tarnów
Toruń
Wałbrzych
Warszawa
Włocławek

Wrocław
Zamość
Zielona Góra

PORTUGAL: Postal areas

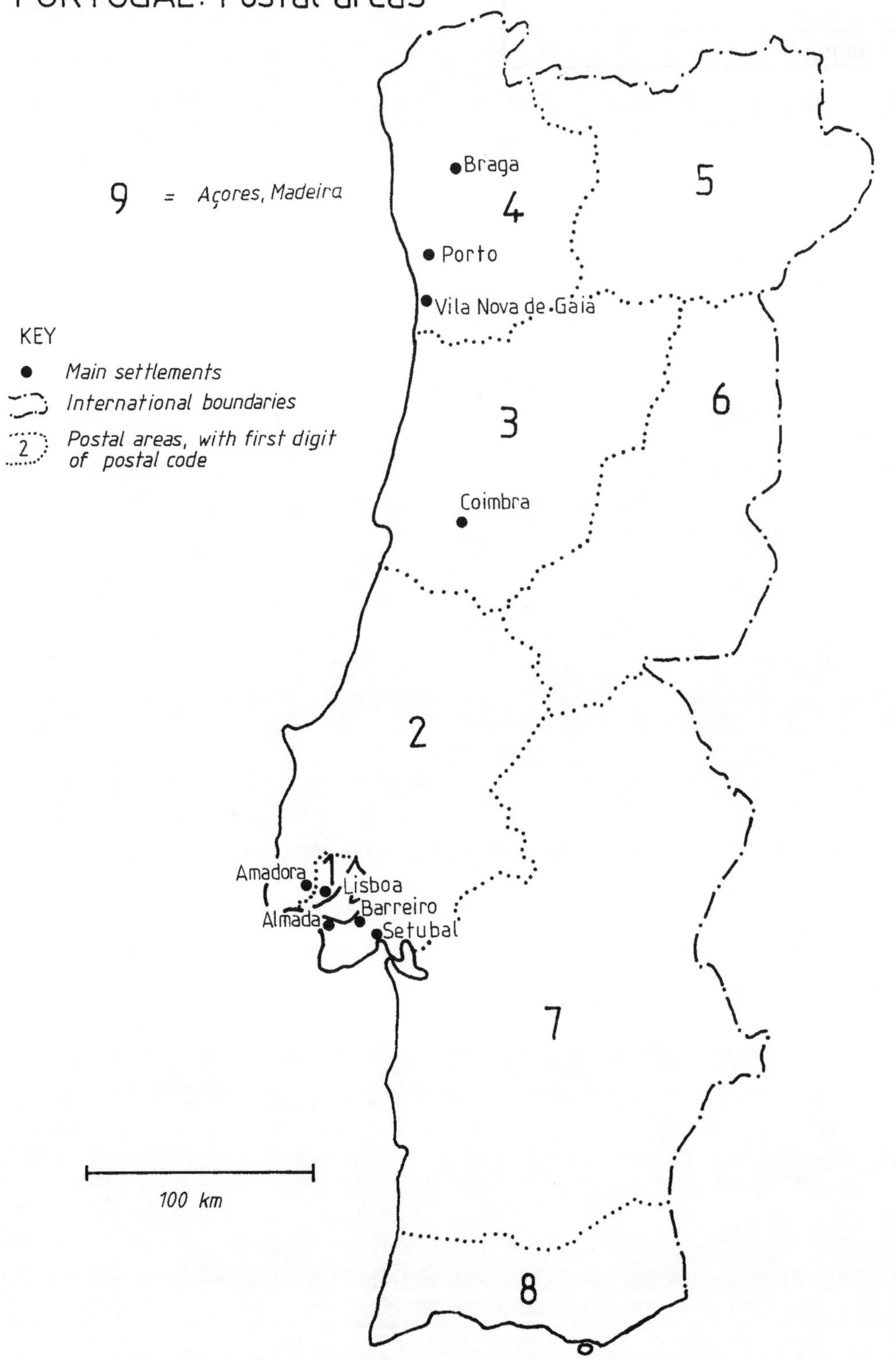

Portugal

Official name: Republic of Portugal, República Portuguesa
Area: 92 389 sq. km (35 672 sq. miles)
Population: 9 831 967
Capital: Lisboa (Lisbon)
Currency: 1 Portuguese Escudo (Esc) = 100 centavos
International telephone access code: 351

Languages

Portuguese is spoken by the most of the population. There are 5 000 Caló-speakers; 15 000 Galician-speakers in Tras Os Montes; 10 000 speakers of Mirandesa, also in Tras Os Montes; and 500 Vlach Romani-speakers.

For the attention of

This is written *Ã atenção do Exmo. Senhor ...* for men and *Ã atenção do Exma. Senhora ...* for women in Portuguese.

Company types

C.ª in a company name means *Companhia* (Company). Other company types found in Portuguese address are:

> Associaçao
> CRL (Cooperative de responsabilidade limitada)
> Empresa Publicas
> Lda (Sociedade por quotas)
> SA (Sociedade Anõnima)

Contact names

The Portuguese each have four names: two first names and two surnames, which will differ within the same family. The first surname comes from the mother, the second from the father. When addressing women, the first name should be used after the salutation. When addressing men, a first name or a surname may be used after the salutation. First names are more important in Portugal than in many other countries. The whole name should be written in addresses.

Addresses

Addresses consist of three or four lines, comprising the following:

1. The recipient's name
2. The street name and number
3. The region (not obligatory)
4. The postal code and town.

Addresses are written in this format:

Recipient name
Thoroughfare type[ ]Thoroughfare name[ ]number
{Region}
postal code[ ]TOWN NAME{[CODEX]}

For example:

Senhor Carlos Manuel Pereira
Rua Conde Redondo 80
1192 LISBOA CODEX

Addresses may be found where the house number is preceded by a comma, like this:

Rua Conde Redondo, 80

As in Spain, the house number is often followed by a series of letters and punctuation to indicate floor numbers, stairway numbers and so on. The name and address of the sender should not be written on the back but on the top left-hand corner of the front of the envelope.

Building Indicators

Portuguese	*English*
andar	floor
apartado	apartment
edificio	building
sala	suite

Thoroughfare types

Thoroughfare types are written before and separately from the thoroughfare name. Here is a list of the most commonly occurring thoroughfare types with their common abbreviations:

Thoroughfare Type	*Abbrev.*
Alameda	
Arco	
Avenida	Av., Avda., Ave.
Azinhaga	

Bai	
Bairro	Ba.
Baluarte	
Beco	
Cais	
Calçada	Cc.
Calçadinha	
Caminho	Cam.
Campo	
Carreiro	
Casal	
Charneca	
Circular	
Entrada	
Escadas	
Escadinhas	
Escultor	
Esplanada	
Estação	
Estrada	Est.
Forte	
Fraião	
Impasse	
Jardim	
Ladeira	
Largo	L., Lgo.
Larguinho	Larg.
Local	
Lomar	
Lugar	
Mercado	
Monte	
Nogueiró	
Parque	
Passeio	
Pátio	
Praça	Pr.
Praceta	
Praia	
Quarto, Quarta	Qt., Qto., Qta.
Quinta	Qu.
Rampa	
Rodovia	
Rotunda	
Rua	R.
Rua Particular	
Ruas	

São, Santa, Santo	S.
Sítio	
Tenões	
Terreiro	
Transversal	
Travessa	
Túnel	
Urbanização	
Vale	
Vereda	
Via	
Viaduto	
Viela	
Vila	
Vivenda	
Volta	

The exact form of the thoroughfare type and any prepositions within the address will be determined by grammar. For example, you will find the following:

Rua de	masculine singular before a proper noun
Rua do	masculine singular before any other noun
Rua da	feminine singular
Rua dos	masculine plural
Rua das	feminine plural

Other address indications

Portuguese addresses often contain indications of floor or staircase number and so on, which are needed for the correct delivery of a package. The following words give these indications:

andar	floor
direito (dto.)	right
esquerdo (esq.)	left
rés-do-chão (r/c)	ground floor

The words 'first', 'second' and so on are written as a number followed by a superscript 'o' (^{o}), for example:

1°, 2° etc.

Other nouns, adjectives and prepositions commonly found in address databases:

NB: The form of each word can change according to whether the following word is masculine or feminine, singular or plural, or the definite article. Where more than one form is given, they are in the order masculine singular, feminine singular, masculine plural and feminine plural.

Portuguese Word	*Translation*
o, a, os ,as	the
um, uma	a, an
e	and
até	till, until, up to
para	for
de	of, from
do, da, dos, das	of the, from the
a	to, towards
ao, á, aos, ás	to the, towards the
perto	near, by
em	on, in
no, na, nos, nas	on the, in the
defronte de	opposite (proper noun)
defronte do, da, dos, das	opposite (other noun)
junta a	next to (proper noun)
junta ao, á, aos, ás	next to (other noun)
atrás de	behind (proper noun)
atrás do, da, dos, das	behind (other noun)
em frente de	in front of (proper noun)
em frente do, da, dos, das	in front of (other noun)
entre	between
sobre	over
debaixo de	under (proper noun)
debaixo do, da, dos, das	under (other noun)
com	with
nova, nova, novos, novas	new
velho, velha, velhos, velhas	old
curio, curta, curtos, curtas	short
longo, longa, longos, longas	long
grande, grandes	large
pequeno, pequena, pequenos, pequenas	small
norte, do norte, setentrional	north, northern
leste, este, do leste, do este, oriental	east, eastern
sul, do sul, meridional	south, southern
oeste, do oeste, ocidental	west, westerm
São (male saint), Santa (female saint)	Saint

Postbox

This is written as *Case Postale* in Portugal.

Postal codes

Postal codes consist of a block of 4 digits, starting with a number between 1 and 9, and are always followed on the last line of the address by the town name in upper case. Large users are indicated by the word *CODEX* after the name of the town.

Towns

Lisboa is *Lisbon* in English, *Lissabon* in German and Dutch, *Lisbonne* in French, *Lisboa* in Spanish and *Lisbona* in Italian.

Porto is *Oporto* in English, French, Spanish and Dutch.

Administrative districts

Portugal has 11 provinces, 18 districts and the two autonomous island groups of Ilhas dos Açores (Azores) and Ilha de Madeira:

Provinces

Algarve
Alto-Alentejo
Baixo-Alentejo
Beira-Alta
Beira-Baixa
Beira-Litoral
Douro-Litoral
Estremadura
Minho
Ribatejo
Trás-os-Montes e Alto-Douro

Districts

Aveiro
Beja
Braga
Bragança
Castelo Branco
Coimbra
Évora
Faro
Guarda

Leiria
Lisboa
Porto
Portalegre
Santarém
Setúbal
Viana do Castelo
Vila Real
Viseu

Puerto Rico, The Commonwealth Of

Puerto Rico is a self-governing territory of the United States. It forms part of the United States' postal system.

Official name: The Commonwealth of Puerto Rico
Area: 8 897 sq. km (3 434 sq. miles)
Population: 3 522 037
Capital: San Juan
Currency: 1 United States Dollar (US$) = 100 cents
International telephone access code: 1

Languages

The national languages are English, with 82 000 mother-language speakers and Spanish, with 2 690 000 speakers. There are also a very small number of Dutch Creole-speakers.

Address Formats

In Puerto Rico, addresses are mainly written in Spanish. When this is the case, the most important part of the address is the Urbanization District (*Urb*). These may be known as *extensiones, jardines, mansiones, parques, repartos* or *villas*. If these names are present, the word *Urb* is then obsolete. For example:

SR JUAN CARLOS
URB LOS AMIGOS
23 CALLE JUANITA
SAN JUAN PR 00602-1211

Please refer to the chapter on the United States of America for further information on address components and layout.

Postal codes

All Puerto Rico postal codes fall in the ranges 00601-00799 and 00901-00999.

Administrative districts

The state code, as written in addresses, is *PR.*

Telephone numbers

All telephone numbers in Puerto Rico have the area code 787.

Qatar

Official name: State of Qatar, Dawlat al-Qatar
Area: 11 437 sq. km (4 415 sq. miles)
Population: 520 000
Capital: Ad Dawḩah (Doha)
Currency: 1 Qatar Riyal (QR) = 100 dirhams
International telephone access code: 974

Languages

The national language is standard Arabic. About 103 600 people speak Gulf Spoken Arabic. There are also 73 000 Western Farsi-speakers in Qatar.

Example address format

Abdullah Al Muraikhi
Po. Box 213
QATAR

Postal codes

There is no postal code system in Qatar.

Towns

Ad Dawḩah is known as *Doha* in English.

Réunion

Réunion, an island off the coast of Madagascar, is a *département* of France. It forms part of the French mail system.

Area: 2 512 sq. km (970 sq. miles)
Population: 641 000
Capital: St Denis
Currency: 1 French Franc (Ffr) = 100 centimes
International telephone access code: 262

Languages

The official language is French, though 87% of the population speak Réunion Creole French. There are some 120 000 speakers of Tamil.

Address formats

Please refer to the chapter on France for address information.

Postal codes

All Réunion postal codes commence with the digits 974.

Romania
Romănia

Official name: Republic of Romania
Area: 237 500 sq. km (91 699 sq. miles)
Population: 23 397 000
Capital: Bucureşti (Bucharest)
Currency: 1 leu (plural lei) = 100 bani
International telephone access code: 40

Languages

The official language, Romanian, is spoken by 87% of the population. Other languages spoken are Hungarian (9%), German (2%) and Romani (1%). Also spoken are Bulgarian (10 439 speakers); Crimean Turkish (25 000 speakers); Gagauz; Greek; Polish (10 000 speakers); Serbo-Croatian (80 000 speakers) and Turkish (150 000 speakers).

Language use, especially amongst the large Hungarian minority, is a sensitive issue in Romania.

Addresses

Addresses are written in the following format:

> Recipient name
> Thoroughfare[ ]number
> postal code[ ]CITY NAME

For example

> Gheorghe Petraru
> Bd olescu 38
> 0500000 BUCUREŞTI

The house number is sometimes found in front of the thoroughfare string.

Postal code

Postal codes consist of a block of 7 digits. The first digit indicates the postal region. If the last 6 digits are '0', the postal code is for the capital of the postal region. If the last 4 digits only are '0', the postal code is for the capital of the administrative department and/or for the zonal post office. If the last 2 digits only are '0', the postal code is for a post office. If the second or fourth digit is '9', the postal code is for a routing office. The whole postal code refers to a locality.

Towns

The following table provides other-language alternatives for Romanian settlement names. Note that Hungarian is widely spoken in the Transylvanian region of Hungary but that its use causes friction between Romanian- and Hungarian-speakers:

Romanian	*Hungarian*	*German*	*English*	*French*	*Italian*	*Spanish*
Aiud	Nagyened	Strassburg				
Alba Iulia	Gyulafehérvár	Weissenburg				
Aleşd	Élesd					
Baia Mare	Nagybánya	Frauenbach				
Bistriţa	Beszterce	Bistritz				
Braşov	Brassó	Kronstadt				
Bucureşti		Bukarest	Bucharest	Bucarest	Bucarest	Bucarest
Călan	Pusztakalán	Kalan				
Caransebeş	Karánsebes	Karansebesch				
Carei	Nagykároly	Karol				
Chişineu-Criş	Kisjenő					
Cîmpia Turzii	Aranyosgyéres	Jerischmarkt				
Cîmpulung Moldovenesc	Hosszúmező					
Cisnădie	Nagydisznód	Heltau				
Cluj	Kolozsvár	Klausenburg				
Codlea	Feketehalom	Zeiden				
Copşa Mică	Kiskapus					
Covasna	Kovászna	Kowasna				
Cristuru Secuiesc	Székelykeresztúr	Kreutz				
Curtici	Kürtös	Kurtitsch				
Dej	Dés	Desch				
Deta	Detta					
Deva	Déva	Diemrich				
Făgăraş	Fogaras	Fogarasch				
Galaţi		Galatz				
Hunedoara	Vajdahunyad	Eisenmarkt				
Ineu	Borosjenő					
Întosura Buzălui	Bodzafordeló	Bozau				
Jimbolia	Zsombolya	Hatzfeld				
Luduş	Marosludas	Ludasch				
Lugoj	Lugos	Lugosch				
Lupeni	Lupény	Schylwolfsbach				
Marghita	Margitta					

Mediaş	Medgyes	Mediasch				
Miercurea Ciuc	Csíkszereda	Szeklerburg				
Năsăud	Maszód	Nussdorf				
Negreşti-Oaş	Avasfelsőfalu					
Ocna Mureş	Marosújvár	Miereschall				
Odorheiu Secuiesc	Székelyudvarhely	Hofmarkt				
Oradea	Nagyvárad	Großwardein				
Orăştie	Szászváros	Broos				
Oraviţa	Oravicabánya	Orawitza				
Petrila	Petrilla					
Petroşani	Petroszény	Petroscheni				
Piatra-Neamţ	Karácsónkő					
Pîncota	Pankota	Pankota				
Rădăuţi	Rádóc	Radautz				
Reghin	Szaszrégen	Sächsisch Reen				
Reşiţa	Resicabánya	Reschitza				
Rupea	Kőhalom	Reps				
Săcele	Négyfalu	Vierdörfer				
Salonta	Nagyszalonta					
Satu Mare	Szatmárnémeti	Sathmar				
Sebeş	Szászsebes	Mülbach				
Sfîntu Gheorghe	Sepsiszentgyörgy	Sankt Georgen				
Sibiu	Nagyszeben	Hermannstadt				
Sighetul Marmaţiei	Máramarossziget	Sighet				
Sighişpoara	Segesvár	Schässburg				
Simeria	Piski	Pischki				
Sînnicolau Mare	Nagyszentmiklós	Groß-santnikolaus				
Timişoara	Temesvár	Temeschburg / Temeschwar				
Tîrgu Mureş	Marosvásárhely	Neustadt				
Tîrgu Secuiesc	Kézdivásárhely	Szekler Neumarkt				
Topliţa	Maroshéviz	Töplitz				
Turda	Torda	Thorenburg				
Vulcan	Zsilyvajdejvulkán	Wulkan				
Zărnesti	Zernest	Zernescht				
Zalău	Zilah	Waltenberg				

Administrative districts

Romania has 41 counties *(Judet)*. They are not used in addresses. They are listed below:

Alba
Arad
Argeş
Bacău
Bihor
Bistrita-Năsăud
Botoşani
Brăila
Braşov
Bucureşti
Buzău
Călăraşi
Caraş-Severin
Cluj
Constanţa
Covasna
Dîmboviţa
Dolj
Galaţi
Giurgui
Gorj
Harghita
Hunedoara
Ialomiţa
Iaşi
Maramureş
Mehedinţi
Mureş
Neamţ
Olt
Prahova
Sălaj
Satu Mare
Sibiu
Suceava
Teleorman
Timiş
Tulcea
Vaslui
Vîlcea
Vrancea

Russia
Rossiyskaya

Official name: Russian Federation, Rossiyskaya Federatsiya
Area: 17 075 400 sq. km (6 591 100 sq. miles)
Population: 148 800 000
Capital: Moscow
Currency: 1 Rouble (R) = 100 kopec
International telephone access code: 7

Languages

96 languages are spoken in Russia. Nationalist feelings run high and language use is important - care must be taken in choosing the language in which to mail to individuals within Russia.

The national language is Russian (about 140 000 000 speakers). Other widespread languages are: Bashkir (in Bashkir ASSR, 948 720 speakers); Chechen (in Chechenia, 944 600 speakers); Chuvash (in Chuvashia, 1 774 000 speakers) and Tatar (in Tatarstan, 5 715 000 speakers).

Example address format

103009 MOSCOU K-9
prospekt Tverskaya 9, appart. 187
Ivanova I.S.

Note that the order of address lines in Russia is the opposite to that used in Western Europe - the postal code and town comes first, then the street address, then the name of the person or company. The name of the country comes above the top line, but as the Russian postal authorities prefer that the postal code is the first item in the address, the country name is probably best written below the other address lines.

Postal codes

Postal codes consist of a block of 6 digits. The code used is that in use since before the break-up of the Soviet Union. The first three digits indicate the region or large town, the last three the post office.

Towns

The following list gives foreign language equivalents of Russian town names:

Russian	*English*	*French*	*German*
Gatchina			Gattschina
Kronshtadt			Kronstadt
Lomonosov			Oranienbaum
Moskva	Moscow	Moscou	Moskau

Pskov			Pleskau
Pushkin			Puschkin

Rwanda

Clashes between government forces and Hutu rebels continues, especially in the north of the country. Mail services to these areas may consequently be affected.

Official name: Republic of Rwanda, Republika y'u Rwanda
Area: 26 338 sq. km (10 166 sq. miles)
Population: 7 902 000
Capital: Kigali
Currency: 1 Rwanda Franc (RF) = 100 centimes
International telephone access code: 250

Languages

The official languages are French and Kinyarwanda (spoken by 98.3% of the population). There are a small number of Hima-speakers.

Example address format

M. Pierre Simon
B.P. 3425
KIGALI

Any address written in a non-native language will be written in French. Deliveries are made only to post office boxes (*Boite Postale*, or *BP*).

Postbox

This is written as *Boite Postale*, or *BP*.

Postal codes

Rwanda has no postal code system.

Saint Kitts and Nevis

Comprises the islands St Kitts (St Christopher), Nevis and Sombrero. The legislators of Nevis have voted to secede from the federation. If, as is likely, the voters back this secession, the federation shall split into two independent states.

Official name: Federation of St Kitts and Nevis
Area: 269 sq. km (104 sq. miles)
Population: 43 100
Capital: Bassterre
Currency: 1 East Caribbean Dollar (EC$) = 100 cents
International telephone access code: 1

Languages

The national language is English, though most people speak Lesser Antillean Creole English.

Example address format

Mrs Angela Caines
Greenlands
BASSTERRE, ST. KITTS

The name of the island may appear in the address after the town name. The island names are:

St Kitts (St Christopher)
Nevis
Sombrero

Postal code

St Kitts and Nevis has no postal code system.

Telephone numbers

All telephone numbers in St. Kitts and Nevis have the area code 869.

Saint Lucia

Official name: Saint Lucia
Area: 616 sq. km (238 sq. miles)
Population: 136 041
Capital: Castries
Currency: 1 East Caribbean Dollar (EC$) = 100 cents
International telephone access code: 1

Languages

The national language is English, though 80% of the population people speak Lesser Antillean Creole French.

Example address format

Postmaster General
General Post Office
Bridge Street
CASTRIES

Postal code

St Lucia has no postal code system.

Telephone numbers

All telephone numbers in St Lucia have the area code 758.

Saint Pierre and Miquelon
Saint-Pierre-et-Miquelon

The islands of Saint Pierre and Miquelon, off the southwest coast of Newfoundland, Canada, form a *département* of France.

Area: 240 sq. km (93 sq. miles)
Population: 6 400
Capital: St Pierre
Currency: 1 French Franc (Ffr) = 100 centimes
International telephone access code: 508

Languages

The official language is French, spoken by 97.6% of the population. The remainder speak English.

Address formats

Please refer to the chapter on France for address information.

Postal codes

All St Pierre and Miquelon postal codes commence with the digits 975.

Saint Vincent and the Grenadines

Official name: Saint Vincent and the Grenadines
Area: 390 sq. km (150 sq. miles)
Population: 114 000
Capital: Kingstown
Currency: 1 East Caribbean Dollar (EC$) = 100 cents
International telephone access code: 1

Languages

The national language is English, though most people speak Lesser Antillean Creole English.

Example address format

Mr John Public
New Montrose
KINGSTOWN

Postal code

St Vincent and the Grenadines has no postal code system.

Telephone numbers

All telephone numbers in St Vincent and the Grenadines have the area code 809.

San Marino

San Marino is a tiny but completely independent state encircled by Italy. For most rules and formats relating to this republic, please refer to the chapter on Italy.

Official Name: Most Serene Republic of San Marino, Serenissima Repubblica di San Marino
Area: 60.5 sq. km. (23.4 sq. miles)
Population: 23 600
Capital: San Marino
Currency: 1 Italian lira (L, Lit)/1 San Marino Lira = 100 centesimi (San Marino forms
part of the Italian economic area.)
International telephone access code: 378

Languages

Italian is the national language. Most of the population speak the Emiliano-Romagnolo dialect.

Company names, contact names, addresses, postbox

The same rules and formats are used as in Italy. Please refer to the chapter on Italy.

Postal codes

San Marino forms part of the Italian postal system. Its addresses will usually be found in Italian address databases. They can be identified by their postal code, 47031, and, where written, their region, which is *SM* for San Marino.

Towns

San Marino is known as *St. Marin* in French.

Administrative districts

San Marino is sub-divided into 9 Castles, each corresponding to a village.

São Tomé and Príncipe
São Tomé e Príncipe

Official name: Democratic Republic of São Tomé and Príncipe, República Democrática de São Tomé e Príncipe
Area: 1 001 sq. km (387 sq. miles)
Population: 124 000
Capital: São Tomé
Currency: 1 Dobra (Db) = 100 centimos
International telephone access code: 239

Languages

The national language is Portuguese, with some 2 580 speakers. There are 103 200 speakers of Gulf of Guinea Crioulo, and 12 000 of Fang.

Example address format

Sra. Eugenia Fernandes
Av. Marginal 12 de Julho
RIBEIRA AFONSO

Any address written in a non-native language will be written in Portuguese. The rules for Portuguese addresses will be followed - thoroughfare type first with an upper case first letter followed by thoroughfare name then number. For more information on thoroughfare types and other address components, please refer to the chapter on Portugal.

Postal codes

São Tomé and Príncipe has no postal code system.

Saudi Arabia
Al-'Arabīyah as-Sa'ūdīyah (Arabic)

Official name: Kingdom of Saudi Arabia, al-Mamlaka-al 'Arabīyah as-Sa'ūdīyah
Area: 2 331 000 sq. km (899 766 sq. miles)
Population: 15 267 000
Capital: Ar-Riyād (Riyadh)
Currency: 1 Saudi Arabian Riyal (SAR, SRIs) = 100 halalah
International telephone access code: 966

Languages

The national language is standard Arabic. There are 200 000 speakers of Gulf Spoken Arabic; 6 000 000 of Hijazi Spoken Arabic and 8 000 000 of Najdi Spoken Arabic.

Example address format

General Director of Post
RIYADH 11142

The postal code is written to the left of the city if the address is written in Arabic script, to the right if written in Latin script.

Postal codes

Postal codes consist of a block of 5 digits.

Towns

The following list gives foreign language equivalents of Saudi town names:

Arabic	*English*	*French*
Al Madinah	Medina	Médine
Ar Riyād	Riyadh	Riyadh
Aẓ Ẓahrān	Dhahran	Dhahran
Makkah	Mecca	La Mecque

Senegal
Sénégal (French)

Official name: Republic of Senegal, République du Sénégal
Area: 196 790 sq. km (75 729 sq. miles)
Population: 7 952 000
Capital: Dakar
Currency: 1 CFA Franc (CFAFr) = 100 centimes
International telephone access code: 221

Languages

The official language is French. Seven national languages are recognized: Pulaar Fulfulde (1 946 000 speakers); Jola-Fogny (210 000 speakers); Malinka (258 500 speakers); Mandinka (445 500 speakers); Serere-Sine (848 000 speakers); Soninke (150 000 speakers) and Wolof (2 620 000 speakers). 31 other languages are spoken. The most widely spoken of these are: Balanta (78 000 speakers); Upper Guinea Crioulo (a Portuguese Creole, 55 000 speakers) and Fuuta Jalon (100 000 speakers).

Example address format

M. Arona Diop
7, rue Mousse Diop
DAKAR PEYTAVIN
DAKAR

Addresses in a non-native language will usually be found written in French. Please refer to the chapter on France for address component information.

Postal codes

Senegal has no postal code system.

Seychelles

Official name: Republic of Seychelles
Area: 453 sq. km (175 sq. miles)
Population: 68 700
Capital: Victoria
Currency: 1 Seychelles Rupee (SR) = 100 cents
International telephone access code: 248

Languages

The official language is Seselwa (Seychelles Creole French), spoken by 95.7% of the population. There are 1 601 English-speakers and 977 French-speakers.

Example address format

M. N. Charles
Gopolia
Plaisance
MAHE

or

M. N. Charles
PO Box 60
Plaisance
MAHE

Any address written in a non-native language may be written in French or English. Most mail is delivered to private boxes.

The name of the island is included in the address. There are 92 islands - the main ones are:

La Digue
Mahe
Praslin

Postal codes

Seychelles has no postal code system.

Sierra Leone

At the time of going to press, Sierra Leone was embroiled in civil war. Mail deliveries may consequently be affected.

Official name: Republic of Sierra Leone
Area: 71 740 sq. km (27 692 sq. miles)
Population: 4 274 000
Capital: Freetown
Currency: 1 Leone (Le) = 100 cents
International telephone access code: 232

Languages

The official language is English. 22 other languages are spoken. The most widespread of these are: Fuuta Jalon (178 400 speakers); Kisi (125 000 speakers); Kono (190 000 speakers); Krio (472 600 speakers - 95% of the remainder of the population speak Krio as a second language and it is the lingua franca of the country); Kuranko (250 000 speakers); Limba (340 000 speakers); Loko (115 000 speakers); Mende (1 460 000 speakers); Sherbro (135 000 speakers); Susu (120 000 speakers) and Themne (1 200 000 speakers).

Example address format

Mr John Kamara
7A Ross Road Cline
FREETOWN

Any address written in a non-native language will be written in English.

Postal codes

Sierra Leone has no postal code system.

Singapore

Official name: Republic of Singapore
Area: 618 sq. km (238 sq. miles)
Population: 2 792 000
Capital: Singapore City
Currency: 1 Singapore Dollar/Ringgit (S$) = 100 cents
International telephone access code: 65

Languages

The four official languages are English (227 000 speakers); Malay (396 000 speakers); Mandarin Chinese (201 000 speakers) and Tamil (90 000 speakers). 22 other languages are spoken. The main ones area Hakka Chinese (69 000 speakers); Min Nan Chinese (the most widely understood language in Singapore, with 1 170 000 speakers) and Yue Chinese (314 000 speakers).

Address Format

Addresses are formatted as follows:

> Name
> number[ ]Thoroughfare name[ ]Thoroughfare type
> Settlement[ ]postal code

For example

> Singapore Post Tanglin Branch
> 56 Tanglin Road
> Singapore 247964

For Housing and Development Board (HDB) residential blocks, the block number is included in the address and in the postal code:

> Blk *335* Smith Street
> Singapore 050*335*

Blocks in the same sector with the same number are differentiated by the third digit of the code:

> Blk *110* Simei Street
> Singapore 52**0***110*

> Blk *110* Tampines Street
> Singapore 52**1***110*

For postbox addresses, the name of the post office containing the box should be included before the postbox number, as in this example:

Tanglin Central PO Box 99
Singapore 247987

Postal codes

Postal codes of the new system, introduced on 1st September 1995, consist of a block of 6 digits. This allows Singapore Post to assign a single code to every building in Singapore and to allow mail sorting on the basis of sequence of delivery.

The first two digits are the sector code, the last four the delivery point (i.e. building).

Postal codes are assigned on the basis of the alphabetical order of the street name per sector. Thus streets with names beginning with 'A' are coded first, then 'B' and so on.

For Housing and Development Board (HDB) residential blocks, the block number is included in the postal code:

Towns

Singapore is known as *Singapur* in German and *Singapour* in French.

Slovakia
Slovenska

Official name: Republic of Slovakia, Slovenska Republiká
Area: 49 035 sq. km (18 927 sq. miles)
Population: 5 274 335
Capital: Bratislava
Currency: 1 Slovak Crown = 100 halers
International telephone access code: 421

Languages

The official language is Slovakian with 4 865 450 speakers. Speakers of Slovakia's 7 other languages are given scarce legal recognition. There are 597 400 Hungarian speakers in the south along the border with Hungary; 50 000 Polish-speakers; 100 000 Romani-speakers (in two forms); 100 000 Rusyn (Ruthenian) speakers in the northeast in the Preshov region and 100 000 Ukrainian-speakers. Serbo-Croatian is also spoken in three villages near Bratislava.

Contact names

Children and female spouses usually take the name of the father/husband. Females take a feminized version of the name ending in *-ova*. For example, Miro Foltan is the son of Jozef Foltan and Anna Fontanova. Some women add their maiden name as a first surname followed by their husband's name like this: Ann Petrova Foltanova. The abbreviation *rod.*, short for *rodena* meaning "né" may be found in some names.

In some (very few) modern families, the wife may retain her maiden name, and the children may take her surname. In some cases the husband may take the wife's maiden name as his new surname.

Company Types

Words indicating company type usually follow company names, but there are some exceptions, for example:

Chemicke zavodny J. Dimitrova

Company names are often followed by the name of the town where they are based, for example:

Slovnaft Bratislava

The following company types may be found in Slovak databases:

a.s
spol.

s.r.o. or s r.o.
v.o.s.

Address format

Addresses are formatted as follows:

Salutation
Name
thoroughfare type[ ]Thoroughfare name[ ]number
postal code[ ]SETTLEMENT{[ ]sorting code}

For example:

Pan
Jozef Foltan
cesta Bratislava 97
817 99 TRENČIN 1

A sorting code (following the city name) may be used for larger cities.

Thoroughfare Types

Slovak	*Abbrev.*	*English*
alej		Alley
brana		Gardens
centrum	centr.	Centre
cesta		Drive, Drove, Road, Route, Track, Way
chodnick		Lane, Path, Track
dvor		Court, Yard
haj		Grove
hradska		Highway
kopec		Hill
korzo		Parade
nadvorie		Court, Yard
namestie	nam.	Place, Square
park		Park
pole		Field
priesmyk	p.	Gardens
promenada		Parade
molo		Quay
rad		Road
sidlisko		Estate
stredisko	stred.	Centre
terasa		Terrace
trat		Route
trh		Market

trieda	tr.	Avenue, Road
ulica	ul.	Street, Way
ulicka		Lane
vrch		Hill

Thoroughfare types are written commencing with a lower-case letter.

Other nouns, adjectives and prepositions commonly found in address databases

NB: (m) = masculine, (f) = feminine, (n) = neuter, (pl) = plural
Prepositions begin with a lower case letter. Prepositions do not have gendered forms.

Slovakian	*English*
a	and
do	till, until
(po)nad	up to
pre	for
zod	from
do, ku	to
k, ku, na	towards
blizky, vedla	near
okolo, vedla, cez, po, pri, k, ku	by
na, popri, o	on
v, u, na	at
v, vo	in
oproti, naproti	opposite
vedla	next to
za	behind
pred	in front of
medzi	between
cez, (po)nad	over
pod	under
za, (po)nade, mimo, viac nez	beyond
smerom	facing
pod	beneath
s, so	with
novy (m), novya (f), nove (n)	new
stary (m), stara (f), stare (n)	old
kratky (m), kratka (f), kratke (n)	short
dlhy (m), dlha (f), dlhe (n)	long
maly (m), mala (f), male (n)	little
velky (m), velka (f), velke (n)	great
vychod	east
vychody (m), vychoda (f), vychode (n)	eastern
zapad	west
zapady (m), zapada (f), zapade (n)	western

juh	south
juzny (m), juzna (f), juzne (n)	southern
sever	north
severny (m), severna (f), severne (n)	northern
Svaty (m), Svata (f) (both abbreviated to Sv.). This may become Svatej in a house name.	Saint

Postal codes

Postal codes (*Postovni Smerovaci Cisla v SR*, or *PSC*) have five digits and are written in the format:

999[ ]99

The postal codes used are still those used before the breakup of Czechoslovakia on 1st January 1993. Slovakian postal codes commence with the numbers 0, 8 or 9.

Postbox

Postbox is written *postova schranka.* "P.O. Box" and "box" are also often seen.

Towns

A law has been passed stating that a town containing more than 20% non-Slovakian speakers (for example Hungarian-speakers near to the border with Hungary) is allowed to have a second name, but this name is to be used only locally by Hungarian-speakers and <u>not</u> in any official form or mass media. This is a hot issue and causes friction between Hungarian- and Slovakian-speakers.

Settlements with both Hungarian and Slovakian names are:

Slovakian	*Hungarian*
Banská Bystrica	Besztercebánya
Bratislava	Pozsony
Dunajská Streda	Dunaszerdahely
Fil'akovo	Fülek
Humenné	Homonna
Jarovce	Horvátjárfalu
Košice	Kassa
Levice	Léva
Lučenec	Losonc
Martin	Zsitvaszentmárton
Mihalovce	Nagymihály
Nitra	Nyitra
Nová Zámky	Érsekújvár
Poprad	Poprád
Prešov	Epérjes

Rimavská Sobota	Rimaszombat
Rožňava	Rozsnyó
Samorin	Somorja
Spišská Nová Ves	Igló
Štúrovo	Párkány
Topol'cany	Nagytapolcsány
Trenčín	Trencsén
Trnava	Nagyszombat
Žilina	Zsolna
Zvolen	Zólyom

The three villages where Croat is still spoken are Čunovo, Jarovce (Hrvatski Jandrof in Croat) and Rusovce (Rosvar in Croat).

In the Rusyn-speaking area, some settlements have both Slovakian and Rusyn names:

Slovakian	*Rusyn*
Beloveza	Biloveza
Benatina	Benjatyna
Bodruzal'	Bodruzal
Bogliarka	Boglarka
Cernina	Cernyny
Davidov	Davydiv
Dedacov	Didaciv
Duplin	Duplyn
Fricka	Frycka
Helcmanovce	Hel'cmanovci
Jakubany	Jakubjany
Jarabina	Orjabyna
Kamienka	Kamjunka
Osturna	Osturnja

The following list gives German equivalents of Slovakian settlement names:

Slovakian	*German*
Bratislava	Preßburg
Břeclav	Lundenburg
Devin	Theben
Hevlin	Höflein
Hodonin	Göding
Hrádek	Erdberg
Hrušovany	Grusbach
Komárno	Komorn
Košice	Kaschau
Lechovice	Lechwitz
Litobratřice	Leipertitz
Mikjulov	Nikolsburg

Nitra	Neutra
Olbramkostel	Wolframkirchen
Pretržalka	Engerau
Prosiměřice	Proßmeritz
Rancířov	Ranzern
Šafov	Schaffa
Sedlec	Voitelsbrunn
Tasovice	Taßwitz
Trenčin	Trentschin
Únanov	Winau
Velké Laváre	Großschützen
Vranov	Frain
Vratěnin	Erattgarten
Žilina	Sillein
Znojmo	Znaim

Administrative Regions

Slovakia consists of the following regions, which are not used in addresses:

Středoslovenský
Východoslovenský
Západoslovensky

Slovenia
Slovenija

Official name: Republic of Slovenia, Republika Slovenija
Area: 20 251 sq. km (7 817 sq. miles)
Population: 1 974 000
Capital: Ljubljana
Currency: 1 Slovene Tolar = 100 paras
International telephone access code: 386

Languages

The official language is Slovenian. Italian (along the coastal strip - 3 000 speakers) and Hungarian (in the northeast along the border with Hungary - 10 500 speakers) are accorded official recognition and in these areas both town names and street names may be written in either language. There are a small number of Friulian- and German-speakers.

Address Format

Addresses may be written in Slovenian, in Italian (along the coastal strip) or in Hungarian (along the Hungarian border). The format is:

Contact name
thoroughfare name [ ]number
postal code[ ]SETTLEMENT

For example:

Ben Kovac
Cankarjeva 18
1000 LJUBLJANA

In small villages, thoroughfares are not named and each house in the village will have a unique number. In these cases, the thoroughfare name will be replaced with the village name.

Postbox

This is written as *postni predal* in Slovenian, abbreviated to *PP*.

Postal codes

Postal codes are formed of a block of 4 digits. These four digits are the unchanged last four digits of the code when Slovenia was part of Yugoslavia (i.e. without the preceding '6').

Towns

Those town names shown preceded by an asterisk are in those areas where Italian or Hungarian have recognition as minority languages. In these cases, the town name used in the address may be adjusted to equal the language of the recipient.

Slovenian	*Italian*	*Hungarian*	*German*
* Ankaran	Ancarano		
* Banuta		Bánuta	
* Berkovci		Berkeháza	
Bertoki	Bertocchi		
Celje			Cilli
* Čentiba		Csente	
* Čikečkavas		Csekefa	
* Dobrava	Dobrava		
* Dobrovnik		Dobronak	
* Dolga vas		Hosszüfalu	
* Dolina		Vőlgyifalu	
* Dolnji Lakoš		Alsólakos	
* Domanjševci		Domonkosfa / Domankosfa	
* Dragonja	Dragogna		
Dravograd			Unterdrauberg
* Genterovci		Gőntérháza	
* Gor. Lakoš		Felsőlakos	
* Hodoš		Hódos	
Hrvatini	Crevatini		
* Izola	Isola		
Jesenice			Aßling
* Kamovci		Kámaháza	
Kočevje			Gottschee
Kobarid	Caporetto		
* Koper	Capodistria		
Kranj			Krainburg
* Krplivnik		Kapornak	
Krško			Gurkfeld
Lendava		Lendva	
* Lendavske gorice		Lendvahegy	
Ljubljana	Lubiana		Laibach

* Lucija	Lucia		
Maribor			Marburg
* Mostje		Hidvég	
* Motvarjevci		Szentlászló	
* Paracag	Parezzago		
* Petišovci		Petesháza	
* Piran	Pirano		
* Portoroz	Portorose		
Postojna	Postumia		Adelsberg
* Prosemjakovci		Pártosfalva	
Radlje ob Dravi			Mahrenburg
* Radmožanci		Radamos	
* Secca	Sezza		
* Sečovlje	Sicciole		
* Škocjan	San Canziano		
* Središče		Szerdahely	
* Strunjan	Strugnano		
*Tolmin	Tolmino		
* Žitkovci		Zsitkóc	

Solomon Islands

Official name: Solomon Islands
Area: 27 556 sq. km (10 637 sq. miles)
Population: 329 000
Capital: Honiara
Currency: 1 Solomon Islands Dollar (SI$) = 100 cents
International telephone access code: 677

Languages

The official language is English. 65 other languages are spoken. The most widely spoken of these are 'Are'are (10 800 speakers); Kwaio (10 600 speakers); Kwara'ae (21 000 speakers); Lau (10 300 speakers) and To'abaita (18 400 speakers).

Example address format

Ms R. Pana
P.O. Box G25
HONIARA
GUADALCANAL

Deliveries are made to postboxes. Postboxes may be a combination of letters and numbers. The name of the island is written on the last line of the address.

Postal codes

Solomon Islands has no postal code system.

South Africa
Suid-Afrika (Afrikaans)

Official name: Republic of South Africa, Republiek van Suid-Afrika (Afrikaans)
Area: 1 233 404 sq. km (476 094 sq. miles)
Population: 32 000 000
Capital: Pretoria
Currency: 1 Rand (R) = 100 cents
International telephone access code: 27

Languages

South Africa has 11 national languages. These are: Afrikaans (6 200 000 speakers); English (3 500 000 speakers); Ndebele (588 000 speakers); Northern Sotho (3 840 000 speakers); Southern Sotho (2 704 000 speakers); Swati (1 019 000 speakers); Tsonga (1 646 000 speakers); Tswana (2 822 000 speakers); Venda (666 000 speakers); Xhosa (6 858 000 speakers) and Zulu (8 778 000 speakers). There are 15 other languages spoken.

Address Format

Addresses are written in the following format:

> Contact name
> number[ ]Thoroughfare
> Settlement
> postal code

For example:

> Mr. K. Rhind
> 67 Wells Road
> Springs
> 1559

Alternatively, the postal code is often found written before the town name in this format:

> Contact name
> number[ ]Thoroughfare
> postal code[ ]Settlement

For example:

> Mr. K. Rhind
> 67 Wells Road
> 1559 Springs

Although the state/province may often be found in addresses, these should not be printed. The South African Post Office request that no punctuation at all be included in the address. The postal code should be on the last line, even if posted from abroad - in that case the country name goes on the line preceding the postal code or, in the first format above, on the same line but following the postal code as follows:

Republic of South Africa
1559

or

1559 Republic of South Africa

The settlement name is that where the delivering post office is situated, not necessarily the same as the location where the person actually lives/works.

Thoroughfare types

Afrikaans	*English*
Doodloopstraat	Cul-de-sac
Heuwel	Hill
Laan	Lane
Mark	Market
Plein	Square
Rylaan	Drive
Steeg	Alley
Straat	Street
Wandelweg	Promenade
Weg	Way

Postbox

This is written *PO Box* in English and *Posbus* in Afrikaans.

Postal codes

Postal codes consist of a block of 4 digits and refer to a post office.

Town Names

Note that the casing patterns in certain South African languages are different to those to which non-speakers are used, even in upper case. For example:

eLIKWATINI
Ga-THLOSE
kwaNALA

Many town names have three versions - English, Afrikaans and local South African language. Direction indicators (East, Eastern etc.) written in Afrikaans (*Oos*, *Wes*,

Noord, *Suid*, *Ooster*, *Wester*, *Noorder* and *Suider*) always have a hyphen between them and the rest of the town name. For example "Lingelethu-Wes". The English equivalents never have a hyphen: "Lingelethu West".

The following list gives equivalents for settlement names in Zulu/Xhosa:

English	*Zulu/Xhosa*
Durban	Thekwini
Johannesburg	Goli
Pretoria	Pitoli
Cape Town	Kapa
Pietermaritzburg	Mgungundlovu
Port Elizabeth	Bhayi

Cape Town is known as *Kapstadt* in German, *Le Cap* in French and *Kaapstad* in Afrikaans and Dutch.

Administrative areas

These should never be added to addresses. During the apartheid regime, the provinces were:

Cape Province/Kaapprovinsie
Natal
Orange Free State/Oranje-Vrijstaat
Transvaal

They are now:

Eastern Cape
Free State
Gauteng
Kwazulu/Natal
Mpumalanga
North West Province
Northern Cape
Northern Province
Western Cape

South Korea
Taehan Min'guk

Official name: Republic of Korea, Taehan Min'guk
Area: 98 913 sq. km (38 180 sq. miles)
Population: 43 663 000
Capital: Seoul
Currency: 1 Won (W) = 100 chon
International telephone access code: 82

Languages

Most of the population speak the national language, Korean. There are some 24 000 speakers of Chinese.

Example address format

Ministry of Information and Communication
116 Shinmullo 1-ga
Chongno-gu
SEOUL 110-700

Postal codes

These consist of 6 digits in the format:

999[-]999

The first three digits indicate the province or large town, the zone and a small town, district or country. The final three digits indicate the delivery area, postbox or large building.

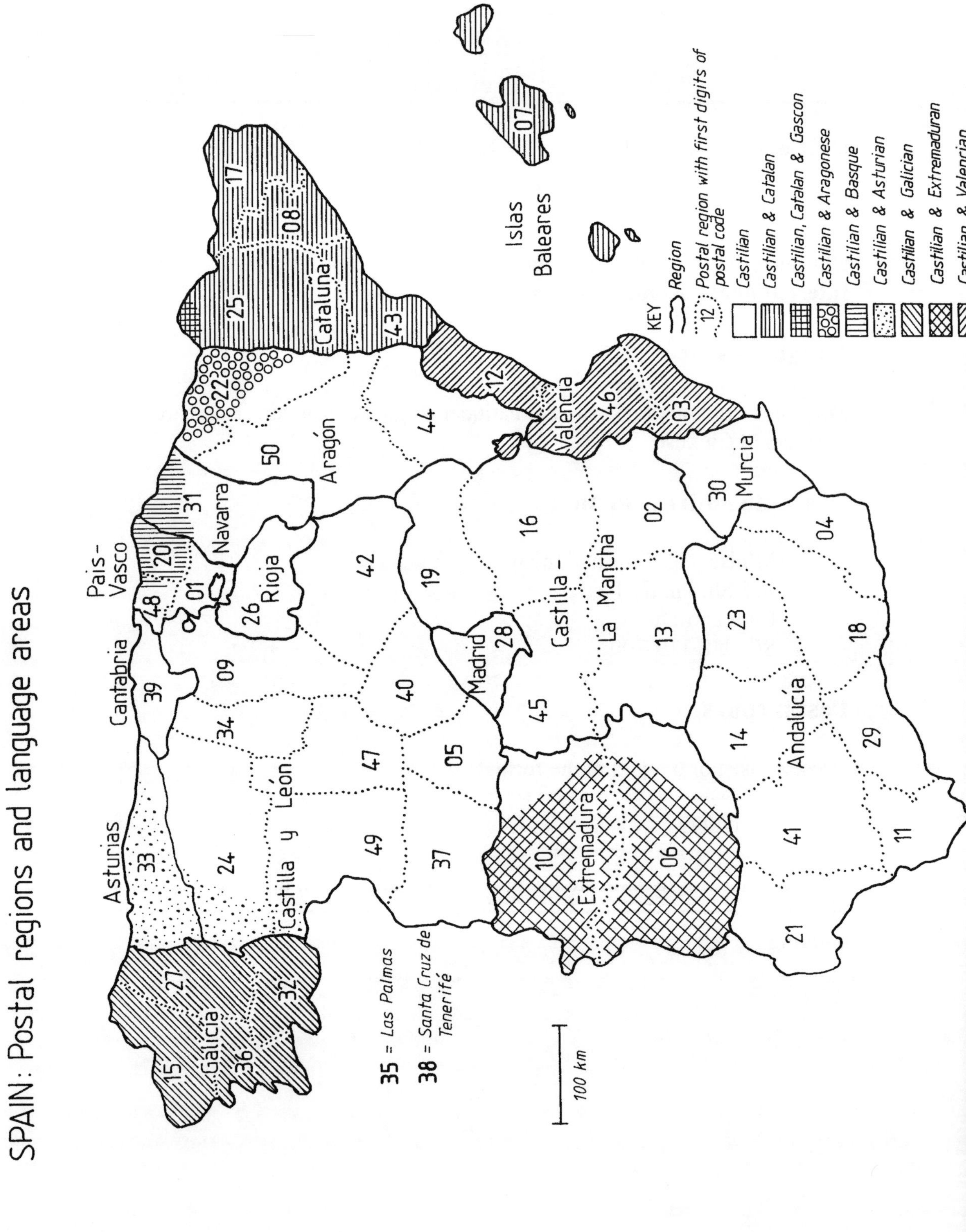
SPAIN: Postal regions and language areas
Galicia
Asturias
Cantabria
País-Vasco
Navarra
Rioja
Aragón
Cataluña
Castilla y León
Madrid
Castilla - La Mancha
Extremadura
Valencia
Murcia
Andalucía
Islas Baleares
35 = Las Palmas
38 = Santa Cruz de Tenerifé
100 km
KEY
Region
Postal region with first digits of postal code
Castilian
Castilian & Catalan
Castilian, Catalan & Gascon
Castilian & Aragonese
Castilian & Basque
Castilian & Asturian
Castilian & Galician
Castilian & Extremaduran
Castilian & Valencian

Spain
España

Official name: Kingdom of Spain, Reino de España
Area: 504 782 sq. km (194 897 sq. miles)
Population: 38 425 679
Capital: Madrid
Currency: 1 Spanish peseta = 100 centimos
International telephone access code: 34

Languages

Castellano (Castilian Spanish) is the official language for the whole of Spain, but several of Spain's autonomous regions have their own languages which are legally treated on a par with Castellano. Castellano is spoken by 70 per cent of the Spanish population. Català (Catalan) is spoken by 21 per cent of the population, and has official status in the regions of Catalonia, Valencia (where it differs very slightly from Catalan and is called Valencian) and the Balearic Islands. Galego (Galician) is spoken by 7 per cent of the population, and is recognized in Galicia. Euskera (Basque) is spoken by 1 per cent of the population, and is recognized in the Basque region and Navarre. There are also some 11 000 speakers of Aragonese; 100 000 speakers of Asturian; 40 000 spcakcrs of Caló; 200 000 speakers of Extremaduran; 10 500 speakers of Fala; 3 814 speakers of Gascon and about 750 speakers of Vlach Romani.

In Navarre, the official language is Castilian, but Basque is spoken and has legal protection. The province defines Basque as being the main language in the following municipalities:

Abaurrea
Alta
Abaurrea Baja
Alsasua
Anue
Araitz
Arantza
Arano
Arakil
Arbizu
Areso
Aria
Aribe
Arruazu
Bakáiku
Basaburua Mayor
Baztan
Bertizarana
Betelu
Burguete

Donamaría
Etxalar
Etxarri-Aranatz
Elgorriaga
Erasun
Ergoien
Erro
Esteribar
Ezkurra
Garaioa
Garralda
Goizueta
Huarte-Arakil
Igantzi
Imotz
Inañeta
Ituren
Iturmendi
Labaien
Lakuntza
Lantz
Larraun
Leitza
Lesaka
Oitz
Olazagutia
Orbaitzeta
Orbara
Roncesvalles
Saldias
Santesteban
Sunbilla
Ultzama
Urdax
Urdiain
Urrotz
Valcarlos
Vera de Bidasoa
Villanueva
Ziordia
Zubieta y Zugarramurdi

Both Castilian and Basque are spoken in the following municipalities:

Abárzuza
Ansoain
Aoiz
Arce
Atez
Barañain

Burgui
Burlada
Ciriza
Cizur
Echarri
Echauri
Egüés
Escároz
Esparza
Estella
Ezcabarte
Garde
Goñi
Güesa
Guesálaz
Huarte
Isaba
Iza
Izalzu
Jaurrieta
Juslapeña
Lezaun
Lizoain
Ochagavía
Odieta
Oláibar
Olza
Ollo
Oronz
Oroz Betelu
Pamplona
Puente la Reina
Roncal
Salinas de Oro
Sarriés
Urzainqui
Uztárroz
Vidángoz
Vidaurreta
Villava
Yerri y Zabalza

All other municipalities have Castilian as their main language.

Note that the above lists give the municipality names in Castilian. For the equivalent Basque names, please refer to the Towns section.

There are no clear-cut geographical boundaries between the speakers of the different dialects and languages spoken in Spain.

Company types

The following company types will be found in company names:

Comerciante Individual
Cooperativa (Co-operative)
Fundacion (Foundation)
SA (Sociedad Anónima)
SAE (Sociedad anonima Española)
SAL (Sociedad anonima laboral)
SCL (Sociedad Cooperative Limitada)
SL (Sociedad Limitada - Limited company)
Sociedad Civil (non-profit entity)
Sociedad Colectiva (General Partnership)
Sociedad Comanditaria (General and Limited partnership)
Sociedad de Cartera (Portfolio company)

Contact names

Spanish people have two surnames, and members of the same family do not necessarily have the same surnames. A person's first surname is their father's first surname, their second surname is their mother's first surname. For example:

José Jimenez Perez marries Margarita Diaz Jimenez

their children, Manuel and Isabel, will be known as:

Manuel Jimenez Diaz and Isabel Jimenez Diaz

A woman keeps her maiden name after marriage. The first surname is considered the most important, but the full set of names will appear on official documents.

For the Attention of

This is written *A la Atención del,* or *para a (p.a.)* in Spanish.

Addresses

Addresses are written in the following format:

Contact name
{thoroughfare type[]}Thoroughfare name[,]house number{[-]floor/flat/staircase number etc.}
postal code[ ]TOWN[(]Province[)]

For example:

Sra Ana Jimenez
calle Alcalá, 142 - 2° D
03201 ELCHE (Alicante)

Calle, the Spanish word for street, is by far the most commonly occurring thoroughfare type and for this reason is rarely written. You would be more likely to find the example address given above written as:

Alcalá, 142 - 2° D

The floor/flat/staircase number can be followed by a superscripted 'o' (a masculine word) or 'a' (a feminine word).

The 'D' in this example means *derecha,* right. An 'I', *izquierda,* would indicate left. The words for right and left in Catalan are *dreta* and *esquerra* respectively, *dereita* and *esquerda* in Galician and *zuzen* and *ezkerkada* in Basque.

The thoroughfare type, when included, is written before, and separately from, the thoroughfare name. It should be written with the first letter in lower case.

Spanish addresses may contain the kilometre number of a house or company on long or intercity routes.

The return address of the sender can be written either on the back of the envelope or in the top left-hand corner of the front of the envelope.

Thoroughfare types

Below is a list of the most commonly occurring thoroughfare types, with the abbreviated form(s) which you are most likely to find in address databases:

Castilian	*Abbreviation*	*Catalan*	*Galician*	*Basque*
avenida	av.	avinguda	avenida, ample, alameda, chea	bidezabal, bidehandi, bidenausi
bajada		baixada	baixada	
calle	c/	carrer	rúa	bide, autobide, zidor, bide
callejón	cj.		ruela, viela	kaletarte, karrika, zeharkale
callejuela			ruela, viela	
camino	cm.	camí	camiño	
carretera	ctra., cr., cte	carretera	estrada	autobidezebal, autopista
cuesta		pujada	costa, encosta	
glorieta	g.		glorieta	
paseo	p.o, p.°	passeig	paseo	
plaza	p.	plaça	praza	plaza, enparantza
plazuela		placeta	praciña	
rambla	rbla.	rambla	rambla	
ronda	rd.	ronda	ronda	
rotonda			rotunda	
rúa			rúa	kale, karrika

sendero		drecera	sendeiro	basabide,bidexka, bidetxo, bidezidor, Zaldibide, bideska
subida		pujada	subida, costa, suba	
travesía		travessera	travesía	bidegurutze, bidebieta, karrikagurutze, gurutzagune
vía		via	vía	pasabide, pasagune, iraganleku, pasaleku, pasatoki, pasarte

Other nouns, adjectives and prepositions commonly found in address databases

Castilian

NB: Prepositions retain a lower case first letter when used in a mixed-case field. The following abbreviations are used: (m) = masculine; (f) = feminine; (s) = singular; (pl) = plural.

Castilian	*English*
el (m s) / la (f s) / los (m pl) / las (f pl)	the
un (m) / una (f)	a, an
y (before a word beginning with i- or hi-, this becomes 'e')	and
hasta	till, up to, until
para	for
de	of
a	to, towards
en	in
cerca de	near
junta a	near, next to
enfrente de	opposite
detrás de	behind
entre	between
debajo de	under
al lado de	next to
encima de	on (top of)
con	with
nuevo (m)/nueva (f)	new
viejo (m)/vieja (f)	old
corto (m)/corta (f)	short
largo (m)/larga (0	long
gran (before the noun to which it refers), grande (after the noun to which it refers)	large

pequeño (m)/perqueña (f)	small
norte	north
este	east
oeste	west
sur	south
San (m) / Santa (f)	Saint

Adjectives referring to plural nouns add an 's' on the end.

Catalan

Catalan	*English*
al(m s)/la (f s)/els (m pl)/les (f pl)	the
un (m)/una (f)	a, an
i (before a word beginning with i- or hi-, this becomes 'e')	and
fins	till, up to, until
per	for
de	of
a	to, towards
en/a/amb/en	in
prop de	near
al constat de	near, next to
davant de	opposite
darrera de	behind
entre	between
sota	under
al costat de	next to
sobre/damunt	on (top of)
amb	with
nou (m)/nova (f)	new
vell (m)/vella (f)	old
curt (m)/curta (f)	short
llarg (m)/llarga (f)	long
gran	large
petit (m)/petita (f)	small
nort	north
est	east
oest	west
sud	south
Sant (m)/Santa (f)	Saint

Galician

Galician	*English*
o, lo, a, la, os, los, as, las	the
un, unha	a, an

y, e	and
ata	till, up to, until
para	for
de, del, dela, deles, delas	of
en, nel, nela, neles, nelas	in
a	to, towards
cerca de	near
xunto a	near, next to
defronte de, enfronte de	opposite
detrás de	behind
entre	between
debaixo de, so	under
al lado de	next to
encima de, enriba de	on (top of)
con	with
nove, novo	new
vello, vella	old
curto, curta	short
largo, large, longo, longa	long
gran	large
pequeno	small
norte	north
este, leste	east
oeste	west
sur	south
San, Santa	Saint

Basque

Basque is a tremendously complex language with a large number of declensions which make recognition of certain words for a non-speaker very difficult. The definite article, for example, is suffixed to another word and can take one of four forms (*-a*, -*ak*, *-ek* and *-ok*) depending on whether the word is singular, plural, transitive or denoting a group. Many prepositions and adjectives form prefixes or suffixes to other words, and change their form according to their context. As their form and case are dependent on their context, no list of prepositions or adjectives is given here.

Postbox

This is written as *Apartado* (abbreviated to *Apto.*) in Castilian and Galician, *Apartat* or *Apartat de Correus* in Catalan.

Postal codes

Postal codes in Spain consist of a block of 5 digits which should be placed before the town name on the last line of the address.

The first two digits of the postal code, ranging from 01 to 50, indicate the province. The third digit indicates a place within the province. If this digit is 0, the address is in the capital of the province, if it is 1 it is in the vicinity of the capital, and so on. The higher this number, the further the address is from the region's capital. The last two digits are split into three ranges of numbers to indicate:

- Postboxes
- Delivery addresses
- Large users

More than one municipality can share the same postal code, whilst in larger cities the postal codes refer to groups of streets.

Certain codes are fixed:

nn080: for private postboxes
nn071: for official (governmental) postal address/postboxes
nn070: for Post Office boxes

Towns

The following two lists give alternative town names, the first for indigenous languages, the second for other languages. The first list gives only the alternatives for the larger settlements - many smaller settlements will also have two names. It is important to try to use the version corresponding to the language of the respondent rather than just the Castilian version.

Castilian	*Catalan/Valencian*	*Basque*	*Galician*	*Asturian*	*Aragonese*
Abárzuza		Abartzuza			
Abaurrea Alta		Abaurregaina			
Abaurreat Bzaja		Abaurrepea			
Adsubia	L'Atzúvia				
Aézcoa		Aezkoa			
Ainsa					L'Ainsa
Alás-Cerc	Alàs-Serc				
Alayor	Alaior				
Albañá	Albanyà				
Alberique	Alberic				
Albiñana	l'Albinyana				
Albocácer	Albocàsser				
Alcácer	Alcàsser				
Alcalá de Chivert	Alcalà de Xivert				
Alcampel	el Campell				
Alcira	Alzira				
Alcoy	Alcoi				
Alcudia de Carlet	l'Alcúdia				
Aldaya	Aldaia				
Alfar	el Far de l'Empordà				
Alfaz del Pí	l'Alfàs				
Alfondeguilla	Fondeguilla				
Alicante	Alacant				
Almazora	Almassora				

Almusafes	Almussafes				
Alquería de Aznar	Alqueria d'Asnar / el Ràfol Blanc				
Alquezar					Alquezra
Alsasua		Altsasu			
Altorricón	el Torricó				
Ametlla de Mar	l'Ametlla de Mar				
Amorebieta		Zornotza			
Ampurdan	Empordà				
Ampurias	Empúries				
Andoáin		Andoain			
Andraitx	Andratx				
Ansoain		Antsoain			
Aoiz		Agoitz			
Arce		Artzibar			
Arén	Areny de Noguera				
Arens de Lledó	Arenys de Lledó				
Argentera	l'Argentera				
Artá	Artà				
Aytona	Aitona				
Azanuy	Açaniu				
Azcoitia		Azkoitia			
Azlor					Aflor
Baldellou	Valldellou				
Bagur	Begur				
Bakáiku		Bakaiku			
Bañalbufar	Banyalbufar				
Bañeres	Banyeres del Penedès				
Bañolas	Banyoles				
Baracaldo		Barakaldo			
Barbastro					Balbastro
Barañáin		Barañain			
Barranca		Sakana			
Basaburua Mayor		Basaburua			
Baztán		Baztan			
Beasáin		Beasain			
Bell-lloc	Bell-lloc d'Urgell				
Bellver de Cerdaña	Bellver de Cerdanya				
Benabarre	Benavarri				Benabarri
Benasque	Benasc				Benás
Benavent de Lérida	Benavent de Segrià				
Benicasim	Benicàssim				
Benisa	Benissa				
Benisalem	Benissalem				
Benisanó	Benissanó				
Benitachell	El Poplenou de Benitatxell				
Benlloc	Bell-lloc del Pla / Bell-lloc del Pla de Benifaixons				
Beranúy	Beranui				
Bétera	Bètera				
Bilbao		Bilbo			
Bisaurri					Bisagorri

Bisbal del Panadés	la Bisbal del Penedès				
Bolea					Boleya
Borjas Blancas	Les Borges Blanques				
Buerba					Buarba
Burguete		Auritz			
Burgui		Burgi			
Burjasot	Burjassot				
Burlada		Burlata			
Burriana	Borriana				
Cadaqués	Cadaquès				
Calaceite	Calaceit				
Caladrones	Calladrons				
Calasanz	Calasanç				
Caldas de Estrach	Caldes d'Estrac				
Caldas de Montbuy	Caldes de Montbui				
Callosa de Ensarriá	Callosa d'en Sarrià				
Calpe	Calp				
Calviá	Calvià				
Camprodón	Camprodon				
Canfranc Estación					Canfran Estazion
Cangas de Onís				Cangues d'Onís	
Carcagente	Carcaixent				
Caso				Casu	
Castejón de Sos	Castilló de Sos				Castilló de Sos
Castellar de Nuch	Castellar de N'Hug				
Castellfor	Castellfort				
Castelló de Ampurias	Castelló d'Empúries				
Castellon	Castelló				
Castellón de la Plana	Castelló de la Plana				
Castillo de Aro	Castell d'Aro				
Castillonroy	Castellonroi				
Cerdá	Cerdà				
Cerdañola	Cerdanyola				
Ceresa					Zeresa
Cerler					Sarllé
Cerollera	la Sorollera				
Chilches	Xilxes				
Ciriza		Ziriza			
Ciscar	Siscar				
Ciudadela	Ciutadella				
Cizur		Zizur			
Colomés	Colomers				
Cornellá	Cornellà de Llobregat				
Cretas	Cretes				
Crevillente	Crevillent				
Cudillero				Cuideiru	
Daimuz	Daimús / Demús				
Denia	Dénia				

Donamaría		Donamaria			
Duranguesado		Durangaldea			
Echarri		Etxarri			
Echauri		Etxauri			
Egüés		Eguesibar			
Eíbar		Eibar			
El Grado					Lo Grau
El Humo de Muro					Lumo Muro
Elche	Elx				
Encartaciones		Enkarterriak			
Erasun		Eratsun			
Eriste					Grist
Erro		Erroibar			
Escabarte		Ezkabarte			
Esparza		Espartza			
Esplugas de Llobregat	Esplugues de Llobregat				
Esporlas	Esporles				
Estella		Lizarra			
Estellenchs	Estellencs				
Estopiñán	Estopanyà				
Ezcároz		Ezkaroze			
Fabara	Favara de Matarranya				
Facheca	Fageca				
Favareta	Favera de la Ribera				
Fayón	Faió				
Ferrerías	Ferreries				
Figueras	Figueres				
Floresta	la Floresta				
Fontcuberta	Fontcoberta				
Fontenares	l'Alforí / Fontanars dels Alforins				
Formigales					Fornigals
Fórnoles	Fórnols del Tossal				
Franquesas del Vallés	les Franqueses del Vallès				
Fuente Encarroz	Font d'En Carròs				
Fuenterrabía		Hondarribia			
Fuentespalda	Fondespatla				
Gabasa	Gavasa				
Galdácano		Galdakao			
Gandía	Gandia				
Gavá	Gavà				
Gavin					Gabin
Gayá	Gaià				
Gerona	Girona				
Gijón				Xixón	
Gistaín					Chistén
Goñi		Goñerri			
Goyerri		Goierri			
Grado				Grao	
Granadella	la Granadella				
Guecho		Getxo			
Guernica		Gernika			
Güesa		Gorza			
Guesálaz		Gesalatz			

Guetaria		Getaria			
Hecho					Echo
Hoya de Huesca					Plana de Uesca
Hoz de Jaca					Oz de Chaca
Huarte		Uharte			
Huarte-Arakil		Uharte-Arakil			
Huesca					Uesca
Ibiza	Eivissa				
Illano				Eilao	
Irún		Irun			
Isaba		Izaba			
Iza		Itza			
Izalzu		Itzaltzu			
Jaca					Chaca
Jacetania					Chazctania
Janovas					Xanobas
Jasa					Chasa
Jativa	Xàtiva				
Jaurrieta		Eaurta			
Javea	Xàbia				
Javierre					Ixabierre
Javierregay					Xabierregai
Jijona	Xixona				
Juslapeña		Xulapain			
La Ametlla	l'Ametlla del Vallès				
La Bajol	La Vajol				
La Cañada de Verich	la Canyada de Beric				
La Cenia	la Sénia				
La Codoñera	la Codonyera				
La Coruña			A Coruña		
La Fueva					A Fueba
La Junquera	La Jonquera				
La Nucía	la Nucia				
La Olla de Altea	l'Olla d'Altea				
La Pobla	Sa Pobla				
Lafortunada					L'Enfortunada
Laguardia		Biasteri			
Laguarres	Llaguerres				
Langreo				Llangréu	
Las Arenas		Areeta			
Las Regueras				Les Regueres	
Lascuarre	Lasquarri				Llascuarri
Laspaúles	les Paüls				
Laspuna					L'Espuna
Laviana				Llaviana	
Legazpia		Legazpi			
Leiza		Leitza			
Lena				Llena	
Lequeitio		Lekeitio			
Lérida	Lleida				
Liguerre de Cinca					Liguerre d'a Zinca
Liri					Llire
Liria	Llíria				

Llanada Alavesa		Arabako Lautada			
Llodio		Laudio			
Loarre					Lobarre
Los Molinos					Os Molins
Luarca				Lluarca	
Mahón	Maó				
Marquina		Markina			
Menquinenza	Mequinensa				
Mieres del Camino				Mieres del Camín	
Mogente	Moixent				
Molins de Rey	Molins de Rei				
Mollerusa	Mollerussa				
Mondragón		Arrasate			
Montanúy	Montanui				
Monte Perdido					O Mon Perdito
Mundaca		Mundaka			
Murillo de Gallego					Morillo de Galligo
Nanclares de Oca		Langraiz			
Naval					Nabal
Nocito					Nozito
Nonaspe	Nonasp				
Ochagavía		Otsagi			
Oláibar		Olaibar			
Olazagutia		Olazti			
Olite		Erriberri			
Olivan					Oliban
Ollo		Ollaran			
Olvena					Olbena
Olza		Oltza			
Ondárroa		Ondarroa			
Onteniente	Ontinyent				
Orduña		Urduña			
Orense			Ourense		
Oronz		Orontze			
Oros Bajo					Oris Baxo
Oroz Betelu		Orotz-Betelu			
Oviedo				Uviéu	
Pajares				Payares	
Palma de Mallorca	Palma				
Pamplona		Iruñea			
Panillo					Paniello
Panticosa					Pandicosa
Pasajes		Pasaia			
Pesoz				Pezós	
Plató de Posets					Forau de Llardana
Playa de Aro	Platja d'Aro				
Plencia		Plentzia			
Pollensa	Pollença				
Pons	Ponts				
Posets					Llardana
Puente de Montañana	el Pont de Montanyana				Lo Pont de Montanyana

Puente la Reina		Gares			Puen d'a Reina
Puerto de Soller	Port de Sóller				
Puigcerdá	Puigcerdà				
Purroy de la Solana	Purroi				
Rentería		Errenteria / Orereta			
Ribadesella				Ribesella	
Ribagorza					Ribargorza
Ribera		Erribera			
Rioja Alavesa		Arabako Errioxa			
Roncal		Erronkari			
Roncesvalles		Orreaga			
Rosas	Roses				
Sabiñánigo					Samianigo
Sagunta	Sagunt				
Sahun					Saunc
Salazar		Zaraitzu			
Salinas de Oro		Jaitz			
Sallent de Gallego					Sallen de Galligo
Salvatierra		Agurain			
San Antonio Abad	Sant Antoni de Frutera				
San Carlos de la Rapita	Sant Carles de la Ràpita				
San Feliu	Sant Feliu				
San Francisco Javier	Sant Francesc de Formentera				
San Jorge	St Jordi del Maestrat				
San Juan de Plan					San Chuan de Plan
San Martín de Oscos				Samartín d'Ozcos	
San Martín del Rey Aurelio				Samartín del Rei Aurelio	
San Mateo	Sant Mateu				
San Rafael del Rio	St Rafael de Maestrat				
San Sadurni de Noya	Sant Sadurní d'Anoia				
San Sebastián		Donostia			
San Tirso de Abres				Santirso d'Abres	
Sangüesa		Zangoza			
Santa Cilia de Jaca					Santa Zilia de Chaca
Santa Cruz de la Serós					Santa Cruz d'as Serors
Santa Eulalia de Gallego					Santolaria de Galligo
Santa Eulalia de Oscos				Santalla d'Ozcos	
Santa Eulalia del Rio	Sant Eularia del Riu				

Santañy	Santanyi				
Santesteban		Doneztebe			
Santurce		Santurtzi			
Saravillo					Sarabillo
Sariego				Sariegu	
Sarriés		Sarze			
Sarvise					Sarbise
Seo de Urgell	La Seu d'Urgell				
Serrablo					Sarrablo
Serveto					Serbeto
Siétamo					Sietemo
Siresa					Siresa
Sobrarbe					Sobrarbe
Sobrescobio				Sobresobiu	
Somontano					Semontano
Sopelana		Sopela			
Soto del Barco				Sotu'l Barcu	
Tamarite de Litera	Tamarit de Llitera				
Tarrasa	Terrassa				
Teverga				Teberga	
Tolva	Tolba				
Torrente de Cinca	Torrent de Cinca				
Treviño		Trebiño			
Tudela		Tutera			
Urdax		Urdazubi			
Urzainqui		Urzainki			
Uztárroz		Uztarroze			
Valcarlos		Luzaide			
Valdemosa	Valdemossa				
Valderrobres	Vall-de-roures				
Valencia	València				
Vall de Uxo	La Vall d'Uixó				
Valle de Gistaín					Bal de Chistau
Valle de Hecho					Bal d'Echo
Valmaseda		Balmaseda			
Vegadeo				Veiga d'Eo	
Vera de Bidasoa		Bera			
Vergara		Bergara			
Vich	Vic				
Vidángoz		Bidankoze			
Vidaurreta		Bidaurreta			
Viella	Vielha				
Villafranca de Oria		Ordizia			
Villafranca del Penedes	Vilafranca del Penedès				
Villajoyosa	La Vila Joiosa				
Villanova					Bilanoba
Villanúa					Bellanuga
Villanueva		Hiriberri			
Villanueva de Oscos				Vilanova d'Ozcos	
Villanueva y Geltru	Vilanova I la Geltrú				
Villarreal	Vila-real				
Villava		Atarrabia			

Vinaroz	Vinaros				
Vio					Bio
Vitoria		Gasteiz			
Viu					Biu
Yerri y Zabalza		Deierri eta Zabaltza			
Zaidín	Saidi				
Zarauz		Zarautz			
Zubieta y Zugarramurdi		Zugarramurdi			
Zumárraga		Zumarraga			
Zumaya		Zumaia			

Castilian	*English*	*French*	*Italian*	*Dutch*
Barcelona		Barcelone	Barcellona	
Cádiz	Cadiz	Cadix	Cadice	
Cartagena		Carthagène		
Córdoba	Cordoba	Cordoue		
Granada		Grenade		
La Coruña / Corunna		La Corogne		
Málaga	Malaga			
Murcia		Murcie		
Pamplona		Pampelone		
Salamanca		Salamanque		
San Sebastián		Saint Sébastien		
Segovia		Ségovie		
Sevilla	Seville	Séville	Siviglia	
Toledo		Tolède		
Valencia		Valence		
Zaragoza	Saragossa	Saragosse		Sarragossa

Administrative districts

The name of the province in which an address is situated should be written in full between brackets after the name of the town.

Spain has 17 regions split into 50 provinces. The names of the provinces are usually the same as those of their capital cities. Exceptions have been specified in the table below.

Region	*Province*	*First 2 digits of postal code*
Andalucía	Almería	04
	Cádiz	11 (includes Ceuta)
	Córdoba	14
	Granada	18
	Huelva	21
	Jaén	23
	Málaga	29 (includes Melilla)
	Sevilla	41
Aragón	Huesca	22
	Teruel	44

	Zaragoza	50
Asturias	Oviedo	33
Canarias	Las Palmas	35
	Santa Cruz de Tenerifé	38
Cantabria	Santander	39
Castilla - La Mancha	Albacete	02
	Ciudad Real	13
	Cuenca	16
	Guadalajara	19
	Toledo	45
Castilla y León	Ávila	05
	Burgos	09
	León	24
	Palencia	34
	Salamanca	37
	Segovia	40
	Soria	42
	Valladolid	47
	Zamora	49
Cataluña (Catalonia)	Barcelona	08
	Gerona	17
	Lérida	25
	Tarragona	43
Comunidad Valenciana	Alicante	03
	Castellón	12
	Valencia	46
Extremadura	Badajoz	06
	Cáceres	10
Galicia	La Coruña	15
	Lugo	27
	Orense	32
	Pontevedra	36
Islas Baleares	Palma de Mallorca	07
La Rioja	La Rioja	26 (Capital: Logroño)
Madrid	Madrid	28
Murcia	Murcia	30
Navarra	Navarra	31 (Capital: Pamplona)
País Vasco	Álava	01 (Capital: Vitoria/Gastéiz)
	Guipúzcoa	20 (Capital: San Sebastián/Donostia)
	Vizcaya	48 (Capital: Bilbao/Bilbo)

Sri Lanka

Sri Lanka is embroiled in a civil war affecting particularly the northern and eastern areas of the country. Mail deliveries may consequently be affected.

Official name: Democratic Socialist Republic of Sri Lanka, Sri Lanka Prajathanthrika Samajavadi Janarajaya
Area: 65 610 sq. km (25 325 sq. miles)
Population: 17 464 000
Capital: Sri-Kayawardenapura
Currency: 1 Sri Lanka Rupee (SLR, SLRs) = 100 cents
International telephone access code: 94

Languages

The official languages are Sinhala (13 190 000 speakers) and Tamil (3 000 000 speakers). There are 5 other languages: English (97 000 speakers); Indo-Portuguese (2 250 speakers); Pali; Sri Lankan Creole Malay (50 000 speakers) and Veddah (300 speakers).

Example address format

Mr A.L. Perera
201 Shanthi Villa
Silkhouse Street
KANDY
20000

Addresses written in a non-native language will be written in English.

Postal code

Sri Lankan postal codes consist of a block of 5 digits. The first one indicates the province or the city of Colombo, the second the postal division and the rest the post office.

Towns

Colombo is known as *Kolombo* in German.

Sudan, The
As-Sūdān (Arabic)

There is a continuing civil war in Sudan affecting the east and south of the country. Mail deliveries will consequently be affected.

Official name: Republic of the Sudan, Jamhuryat as-Sūdān
Area: 2 505 870 sq. km (967 243 sq. miles)
Population: 29 900 000
Capital: Khartoum
Currency: 1 Sudanese Pound (Lsd, £S) 100 piastres
International telephone access code: 249

Languages

132 languages are spoken in Sudan. The geographical distribution of these languages is complex, especially in the south of the country. The official language is Standard Arabic. The most widespread languages are: Sudanese Spoken Arabic (15 000 000 speakers); Bedawi (951 000 speakers along the Red Sea Coast); Dinka (1 300 000 speakers in 5 forms) and Nuer (740 000 speakers).

Example address format

1111 KHARTOUM
P.O. Box 29
Abdul-Qadar Bakry Al-Shaïkh

Note that the order of address lines in The Sudan is the opposite to that used in Western Europe - the postal code and town comes first, then the mailing address, then the name of the person or company.

Postal codes

The postal code consists of a block of 4 digits - the first indicates the region, the second the postal zone, the third the exchange centre and the fourth the post office.

Towns

The following list gives foreign language equivalents of Sudanese town names:

Arabic	*English*	*French*	*German*
Bûr Sûdân	Port Sudan	Port Sudan	Port Sudan
El Khartûm	Khartoum	Khartoum	Khartum

Surinam
Suriname

Official name: Republic of Suriname, Republiek van Suriname
Area: 163 265 sq. km (63 020 sq. miles)
Population: 410 000
Capital: Paramaribo
Currency: 1 Suriname Guilder (Sgld, F) = 100 cents
International telephone access code: 597

Languages

There are 16 languages spoken in Surinam. The official language is Dutch. Other widespread languages are: Guyanese (50 000 speakers); Caribbean Hindi (150 000 speakers); Caribbean Javanese (60 000 speakers) and Sranan (120 000 speakers).

Example address format

Saskia Panka
Walapastraat 2
Bloemendal
PARAMARIBO

Any address written in a non-native language will be written in Dutch. For additional information on address components, please refer to the chapter on The Netherlands.

Postal codes

Surinam has no postal code system.

Swaziland

Official name: Kingdom of Swaziland
Area: 17 363 sq. km (6 702 sq. miles)
Population: 859 000
Capital: Mbabane
Currency: 1 Lilangeni (plural Emalangeni) (Li, E) = 100 lisente
International telephone access code: 268

Languages

The official languages are English and Swati (650 000 speakers). There are also 19 000 Tsonga-speakers and 76 000 Zulu-speakers.

Example address format

Mr Peter Makara
P.O. Box 125
MBABANE
H100

Deliveries are only to postboxes. Addresses written in a non-native language will be written in English.

Postal codes

The postal code consists of a letter (the first letter of the name of the region - an H, L, M or S) followed by three digits (indicating the post office). The names of the regions are:

Hhohho
Lubombo
Manzini
Shiselweni

SWEDEN: Postal areas

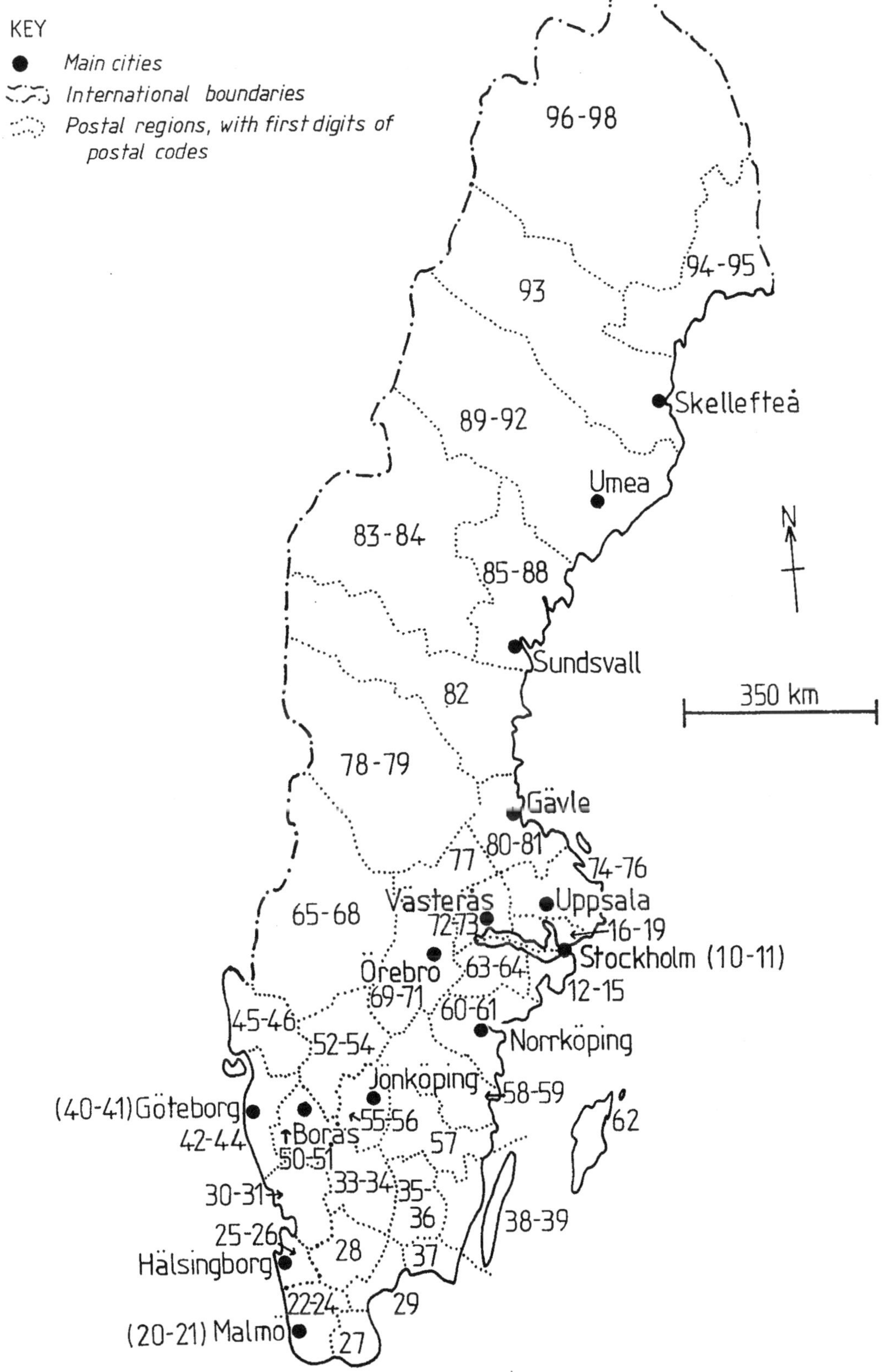

98

Sweden
Sverige

Official name: Kingdom of Sweden, Konungariket Sverige
Area: 440 945 sq. km (170 250 sq. miles)
Population: 8 644 119
Capital: Stockholm
Currency: 1 Swedish krona = 100 öre
International telephone access code: 46

Languages

The official language, Swedish, is spoken by 93 per cent of the population. Finnish is spoken by 3 per cent. There are some 3 000 Romani-speakers and 11 000 Saami-speakers (in 5 different forms) in the far north.

Company names

The company type *AB* (*Aktiebolag* - limited liability) will often be found in company databases.

Contact names

Generally in Sweden, you can indicate on your correspondence whether the contents are private or may be opened by others. Two formats are used. The following format indicates that your mail may be opened by others:

Company name
Department name
Contact name
Rest of address

The following format indicates that the mail is private and personal:

Contact name
Company name
Department name
Rest of address

Addresses

Addresses are written in the following format:

Recipient name
Thoroughfare[ ]number
postal code[ ]TOWN NAME

For example:

Fru Inger Lilja
Vasavagen 3
582 20 LINKOPING

There should be two spaces between the postal code and the settlement name.

Large companies have unique postal codes and their addresses contain no street address and therefore have only two lines. For example:

Super Gizmos AB
101 45 STOCKHOLM

Thoroughfare types are written after the thoroughfare name, without a space between them. As with other Scandinavian languages, the definite article does not appear as a separate word in Swedish but as a suffix (*-en*) at the end of a word.

The settlement name to be given in the address is that of the post-office distribution centre. Villages within an area served by a distribution centre in a larger settlement do not have to be separately mentioned on the address - the name of the larger centre with the postal code is sufficient. Isolated farmsteads, of which Sweden has many, are often addressed without a street address. The following form would be used:

Recipient name
Village[,]Farmstead name
postal code[ ]TOWN NAME

For example:

Jorgen Walgren
Hemsjöl, Långsmon
441 96 ALINGSÅS

Thoroughfare types

By far the most common thoroughfare types that will be encountered are *-gaten* and *-vägen*. A fuller list of thoroughfare types is:

alle
dallen
gate
gaten
grand
granden
lerig
liden
plan
promenader
race

stigen
strand
torg
vag
vägen

Nouns, adjectives and prepositions commonly found in address databases:

NB: In Swedish the form of an adjective depends on the gender of the noun to which it refers and whether it is singular or plural. The following abbreviations are used: (s) = singular, (pl) = plural.

Swedish	*English*
den (s), de (pl.)	the (but only when followed by an adjective preceding a noun. Otherwise the gender is indicated by adding a suffix to the noun)
en	a, an
och	and
till, intill	till, until, up to
för, framför, före, inför	for
av	of
från	from
till, åt	to, towards
via, i närheten	near, by
på	on
i, in	in
motliggande, på andra sidan	opposite
närmast	next to
bak, bakom	behind
framme, framför	in front of
mellan, emellan	between
över	over
under	under
med	with
ny, nya	new
gammal, gamla, gammalt	old
kort	short
lång	long
stor	big
liten (s), små (pl)	small
nord	north
ost	east
syd	south
väst	west

Postbox

This is written as *Box*.

Postal codes

Postal codes (*egna Postnummer*) consist of 5 digits, beginning with a number between 1 and 9, and written in the following structure:

999[ ]99

The first three digits are the outward sorting code, the last two the inward sorting code.

The first digits usually indicate the borough, the last indicate areas or streets within the borough. With larger cities, a whole range of postal codes exists and only the first digit is the same for the whole city. In medium-sized towns the first two digits are likely to be the same, whilst all three digits will be the same in more rural areas. Large companies and post-office boxes may have individual postal codes. Although the first three digits indicate an area, the name of the town given may differ. For example:

311 42 FALKENBERG
311 96 HEBERG

There are no postal codes in Sweden beginning with these numbers:

0, 32, 47, 48, 49, 99

Towns

Stockholm is known as *Stoccolma* in Italian and *Estocolmo* in Spanish. *Göteborg* is known as *Gothenburg* in English.

Administrative districts

Sweden has 24 counties *(Län)*. They are not used in addresses. They are listed below:

Alvsborgs Län
Blekinge Län
Gävleborgs Län
Göteborgs och Bohus Län
Gotlands Län
Hallands Län
Jämtlands Län
Jönköpings Län
Kalmar Län
Kopparbergs Län
Kristianstads Län
Kronobergs Län

Malmöhus Län
Norbottens Län
Örebro Län
Östergötlands Län
Skaraborgs Län
Södermanlands Län
Stockholms Län
Uppsala Län
Värmlands Län
Västerbottens Län
Västernorrlands Län
Västmanlands Län

SWITZERLAND: Postal regions and language areas

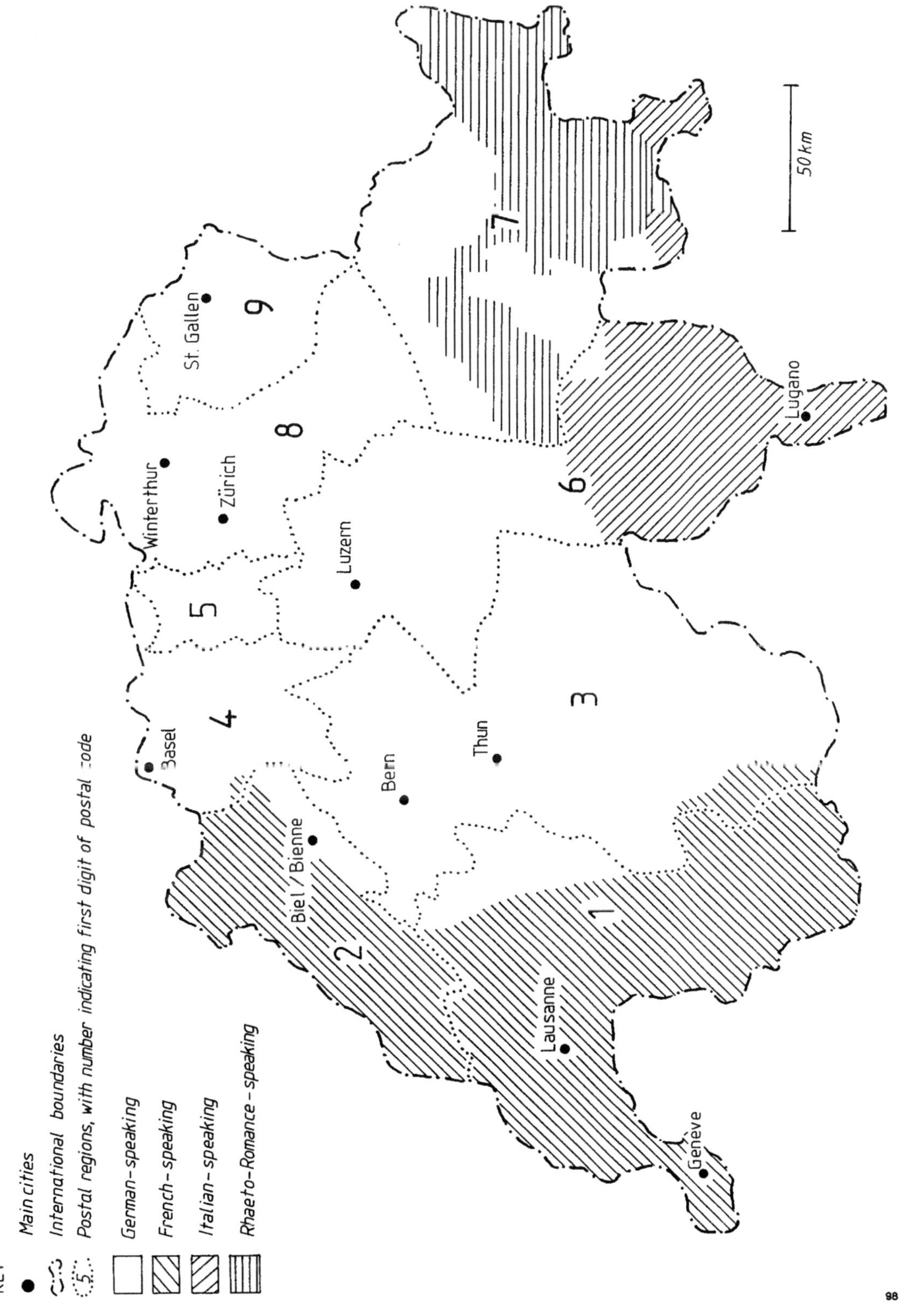

98

Switzerland
Schweiz/ La Suisse/Svizzera/Svizra

Official name: Swiss Federation, Schweizerische Eidgenossenschaft, Confédération Suisse, Confederazione Svizzera, Confederaziun Svizra.
Area: 41 293 sq. km (15 953 sq. miles)
Population: 6 750 693
Capital: Bern/Berne/Berna
Currency: 1 Swiss Franc/Franker = 100 centimes/Rappen
International telephone access code: 41

Languages

Switzerland has four official languages: German, French, Italian and Rhaeto-Romance. The percentage of people speaking each language as a mother tongue is as follows:

German	63.6%
French	19.2%
Italian	7.6%
Rhaeto-Romance	0.6%

The remaining 9 per cent speak other, non-indigenous, languages.

Swiss German differs from standard German and this needs to be taken into account in mailings.

Switzerland does not suffer the same kind of tension between members of different language groups as do many other multilingual European countries, and most Swiss speak more than one of the national languages. Although some kind of border can be drawn between the areas where the different languages are spoken, in many areas there is a great deal of mixing of peoples from the different language groups.

The smallest language group, Rhaeto-Romance, is only spoken in a few isolated Alpine valleys. Despite this, it exists in a number of different dialectical forms, and until recently there was no agreement of which form should be taken as a written standard. For this reason it is rare to come across Rhaeto-Romance in addresses or names.

Company names

In the German, French and Italian language areas, it is more correct, where the *nature* of a company is mentioned in its name, that this *precedes* the name of the company, thus:

Bäcker Schmidt
Boulangerie Dupont
Fornaio Andretti

You will often, however, find these activity indications *after* the company name, thus:

Schmidt, Bäcker
Schmidt (Bäcker)
Dupont, Boulangerie
Dupont (Boulangerie)
Andretti, Fornaio
Andretti (Fornaio)

Company types

The following company types will be found in company address databases:

German:	AG (Aktiengesellschaft)
	Einzelunternehmen
	Genossenschaft
	GmbH (Gesellschaft mit beschraenkter Haft)
	KG (Kommanitgesellschaft)
	OHG (Offene Handelsgesellschaft)
	Stiftung
French:	Affaire Personelle
	SA (Société anonyme)
	Sarl (Société à responsibilité limitée)
	Société en commandite simple
	Société en nom collectif
Italian:	SA

These abbreviations will also often be encountered in company names:

Gebr. = Gebrüder (brother, German)
Ste. = Société (company, French)
Cie. = Compagnie (company, French)

For the Attention of

In the German-speaking areas, the words *zu Händen,* abbreviated to *z.H.* or *z.Hd.* mean 'For the attention of'. In the French-speaking areas, this is written *A l'Attention du*. In the Italian-speaking areas it is written *A.C.A.* (*Alla Cortese Attenzione)* or simply as *Cortese*. One may also use *All' Attenzione d'* before a vowel, *All' Attenzione del* before a male name or *All' Attenzione della* before a female name.

Addresses

Structure

Addresses will be written in German, French, Italian or Rhaeto-Romance according to the language of the region. In bilingual regions, addresses may be written in either or both languages. In German-speaking areas, addresses are written in this format:

Salutation
Recipient name
Thoroughfare name thoroughfare type[ ]number
postal code[ ]TOWN NAME{[ ]sorting code}

For example:

Herrn Heinz Schmidt
Bahnhofstrasse 15
8000 ZÜRICH 2

In Italian-speaking areas, the address should be written in the following format:

Recipient name
thoroughfare type[ ]Thoroughfare name[ ]number
postal code[ ]TOWN NAME{[ ]sorting code}

For example:

Gaspare Andretti
Via Basilea 12
6500 BELLINZONA 1

In French-speaking areas, the address should be written in either of the following formats:

Recipient name
number[ ]thoroughfare type[ ]Thoroughfare name
postal code[ ]TOWN NAME{[ ]sorting code}

or

Recipient name
number[,]thoroughfare type[ ]Thoroughfare name
postal code[ ]TOWN NAME{[ ]sorting code}

For example:

Fernand Genoud
8 rue du Marché
1000 LAUSANNE 3

or

Fernand Genoud
8, rue du Marché
1000 LAUSANNE 3

In larger settlements, the settlement name may be followed by a 1- or 2-digit sorting code.

In German-speaking areas, the general rule is that the thoroughfare type part of the street address is suffixed to the rest of the address, thus:

Zentralstrasse
Zwingliplatz

However, there are two important exceptions. If the thoroughfare name refers to the real name of a place (e.g. a town name, a castle name, a forest name, etc.) or to a surname ending in *-er* then there is a space between the thoroughfare name and the thoroughfare type. The second exception is where complete personal names are used. In these cases, each component of the name and each thoroughfare type are separated with hyphens. Surnames *only* are *not* covered by this exception. Thus:

Züricher Strasse 2
William-Tell-Strasse 9
Durerstrasse
Calvinstrasse 7

In streets beginning with prepositions or some adjectives (*Am*, *An*, *Alter* etc.), the preposition is followed by a space, thus:

Alter Marktstrasse 3

In the French and Italian language regions, thoroughfare types should correctly begin with a lower case letter. Prepositions, articles etc. (e.g. *de*, *la* etc.) should also be written without a capital letter. In both the French- and the Italian-speaking regions, the thoroughfare type is written before and separately from the thoroughfare name, thus:

rue des Noirettes
route de Genève
via Ospedale
viale Cattaneo

Thoroughfare types

Below is a list of the most commonly occurring thoroughfare types, with the abbreviated form(s) which you are most likely to find in address databases:

German	*Abbreviations*
Allee	
Berg	
Boulevard	Bd.
Bruch	
Bühl	
Chaussee	Ch.
Damm	
Gasse	

Graben	
Hafen	
Hof	
Kamp	
Markt	
Platz	Pl.
Ring	
Strasse	Str.
Ufer	
Wall	
Weg	
Weide	

French	*Abbreviations*
allée	
avenue	ave.
boulevard	bd., bld.
canal	
centre	
champ	
chaussée	ch., chee., chée
chemin	
clos	
cour	
digue	
impasse	imp.
marché	
mont / montagne	mt.
parc	
place	pl.
quai	
quartier	qu.
route	rte.
Route National	RN
rue	r.
square	sq.
val/vallée	

Italian	*Abbreviations*
borgo	
contrada	c.da, c.^{da}
corso	c., cso., c.so, c.^{so}
frazione	fraz., fr.
largo	lgo.
lungofiume (*fiume* can be replaced with the name	

of a river)	
lungolago (*lago* can be replaced with the name of a lake)	
lungomare (*mare* can be replaced with the name of a sea)	
piazza	p., p.za, p.[za]
piazzale	p.le, p.[le]
strada	
traverse	
via	v.
viale	v.le, v.[le], vl.
vicolo	

Other nouns, adjectives and prepositions commonly found in address databases:

German

NB: German grammar rules governing articles, prepositions and adjectives are complex, and there is no need to explain them here. It is only necessary to be able to recognise them when and where they occur in addresses. For this reason a list without further explanation is provided. As a very general rule of thumb, the prepositions and adjectives listed may have one of the following endings added: nothing; *-e*; *-er*; *-em*; *-en* or *-es*.

German	*English*
der/die/das/den/dem/des	the
ein/eine/eines/einen/einem/einer	a, an
und	and
bis	till, until, up to
für	for
von	of, from
zu, nach	to, towards
bei, bei der/den/dem (beim)	near, at
an, an der/den/dem (am)	at, by, towards
auf, auf der/den/dem	on
in, in der/den/dem (im)	in
gegenüber	opposite, facing
nächst, neben, neben der/dem/den	next to
unter, hinter der/den/dem	behind
vor, vor der/den/dem	before, in front of
zwischen, zwischen der/den/dem	between, amongst
über, über der/den/dem	over, above, beyond
tinter, unter der/dem/den	under, beneath, below
mit	with

neu/neue	new
alt/alte	old
kurz/kurze/kurzen/kurzer/kurzem/kurzes (K.)	short
lang/lange/langen/langer/langem/langes (L./Lge.)	long
gross/grosse/grossen/grosser/grossem/grosses (G.)	large
klein/kleine/kleinen/kleiner/kleinem/kleines (K./Kl. /Kle.)	small
nord	north
ost	east
süd	south
west	west
Sankt (St.)	saint
Industrieterrein, Industriegebiet	industrial estate

French

NB: Except where specified, the plural form of adjectives is the correctly gendered singular form followed by an 's'. The following abbreviations are used: (m) = masculine form; (f) = feminine form; (pl) = plural form.

French	*English*
le (m)/la (f)/les (pl) (NB: le and la are written l' before a vowel or an unaspirated h)	the
un (m)/une (f)	a, an
et	and
à/au (m)/à la (f)/aux (pl)	till, until, up to, to
pour	for
de (before a proper noun)/du (m)/de la, de 1' (f)/des (pl)	of, from
à	at
près de	by, near to
sur	on (a river, the sea)
dans	in
cn facc dc	opposite
à côté de	next to
derrière	behind
devant	in front
entre	between
avec	with
sous	under
lès (occurs *only* in place names)	near
nouveau (m)/nouvelle (f)/nouveaux (m.pl.)/nouvelles (f.pl.) / nouvel (m, before a vowel or unaspirated h)	new
vieux (m, pl)/vieille (f)/vielles (f.pl.)/vieil (m, before a vowel or an unaspirated h)	old
court (m) (Ct.)/courte (f) (Cte.)	short
long (m) (Lg.)/longue (f) (Lgue.)	long
grand (m) (Gr./Grd.)/grande (f) (Gr./Grde.)	large
petit (m) (P./Pt.)/petite (f) (P./Pte.)	small

nord	north
est	east
sud	south
ouest	west
saint (m) (St.)/sainte (f) (Ste.)	saint
Parc Industriel, Zone d'Activités (Z.A.C.), Zone Industrielle (Z.I.), Zone Artisanale (Z.A.)	industrial estate

Italian

NB: The form which certain common words take in Italian depends on a number of factors such as the gender of the following word, whether the next word is the definite article, whether the first letter of the next word is a vowel or a consonant, and whether that consonant is a z, ps or an s+consonant. As this is rather complex, no explanation is given for each form but, where more than one form exists, each form is given.

Italian	*English*
il/i/l'/gli/lo/la/le	the
un/uno/una/un'	a, an
e	and
fino a, sino a	till, until
per	for
di	of
del/dei/dell'/ degli/dello/della/delle	of the
verve, a, in	to, towards
al, allo, alla, ai, agli, alle	towards the
presso, vicino a, accanto a	near, by, next to
su	on (sea, a river), over
sul, sulla, sullo, sulle, sella	on the
in	in
nel, nello, nella, a	in the
in faccia a, di fronte (a), dirimpetto (a)	opposite
dietro, dope, addietro, didietro	behind
davanti a, dinanzi a	in front of
fra, tra	between
sotto	under
sopra	over
con	with
nuovo, nuova, nuovi, nuove	new
vecchio, vecchie, vecchia, vecchi	old
corto, corta, carte, corti	short
lungo, lunge, lunghi, lunghe	long
grande, grandi	large
piccolo, piccola, piccoli, piccole	small
nord, del nord, settentrionale	north
est. dell'est, orientale	east
ovest, dell'ovest, occidentale,	west
sud, del sud, meridionale	south

Sann (masculine), Santa (feminine), Sant' (before a vowel), Santo (before a name beginning with a z, ps or s + consonant; e.g. Santo Stefano) (abbreviated to S., St., Sta.)	Saint
Zona Industriale	industrial estate

Postbox

This is written as *Postfach*, abbreviated to *PF*, in German; *Case Postale*, abbreviated to *CP*, in French; and *Casella Postale*, abbreviated to *CP* in Italian.

Postal codes

Postal codes consist of a block of 4 digits. The initial digit indicates the largest postal regions, and can be any number between 1 and 9. The second digit indicates the region within this area. The postal code areas do not correspond well to administrative boundaries. Most municipalities have their own number, although some numbers are shared and some numbers cover more than one municipality. In the latter cases, the municipality containing the distribution centre is used in the address, with the actual habitation address on the preceding line. The postal code is placed before and on the same line as the town name. Larger population centres have an additional digit after the town name to indicate the sorting district. The streets belonging to each postal district are listed in the telephone book of the area concerned.

Because physical access to the settlements of Büsingen in Germany and Campione d'Italia in Italy is easier through Switzerland, they have been ascribed the following postal codes by the Swiss Post Office:

8238 BÜSINGEN (German postal code 78266)
6911 CAMPIONE D'ITALIA (Italian postal code 22060)

Liechtenstein has been assigned the Swiss postal codes between 9485 and 9497.

As mentioned above, although most parts of Switzerland belong firmly to one or other language region, there are a number of areas where a language mix occurs. Rhaeto-Romance was, until recently, only a spoken language, so addresses in Rhaeto-Romance -speaking regions are usually written in German. This is a fluid situation and may change. Using the postal code, it is usually possible with a fair degree of accuracy to identify the language in which the address will be given, although, of course, the contents of the mailing should be done in the language of the recipient rather than the language of the area. The lists below show the postal codes belonging to each language area. Note that not all numbers in the sequence from 1000 to 9999 have been utilized; you can find out which postal codes do not exist by referring to the postal code lists published by the Swiss PTT.

French

1000-1589, 1602-1654, 1661-1699, 1701, 1720-1721, 1723-1728, 1730-1733, 1740-1782, 1785-1789, 1800-2074, 2087-2416, 2515-2525, 2534-2539, 2603-2746, 2748-2812, 2822-2826, 2828-2954, 3960-3968, 3971-3979.

German

1655-1657, 1711-1719, 1734-1738, 1792-1795, 1797, 2076, 2512-2514, 2540-2578, 2813-2814, 3000-3274, 3282-3284, 3286-3954, 3969-3970, 3981-6493, 7000-7563, 7710, 8000-8236, 8239-9479, 9500-9658

(Note that postal codes 9485-9497 belong to Liechtenstein and not Switzerland.).
(Note that 8238 Büsingen is in Germany, German postal code = 78266.)

Italian

6500-6910, 6912-6999, 7602-7610, 7741-7748

(Note that 6911 Campione d'Italia is in Italy, Italian postal code = 22060.)

Predominantly French with German

1595 (Faourg), 1700 (Fribourg, German minority very small), 1722 (Bourgillon), 1729 (Bonnefontaine), 1783 (Pensier), 1784 (Courtepin), 1791 (Courtaman), 1796 (Courgevaux), 2075 (Thielle-Wavre), 2747 (Corcelles BE only - Seehof, with the same postal code, is German speaking), 2827 (Mervelier)

Predominantly German with French

2532 (Magglingen/Macolin), 2533 (Evilard), 3280 (Murten), 3285 (Galmiz)

Bilingual German/French

2500-2505 (Biel/Bienne)

Towns

In the French-speaking areas, town names consisting of more than one word are hyphenated with the exception of towns beginning with the words *le* or *la*, where there is a space between this word and the next (other words in the same town name will be hyphenated).

As Switzerland has four official languages, most large towns have equivalent names in the other languages. The following lists give the correct town name in the local language and the equivalent names in the other official languages. As well as a list for each indigenous language, a list is provided of equivalent names in other European languages. Whatever the name of the town in the local language, the Swiss Post

Office will process equally efficiently mail with towns names spelt in one of the other official languages.

The lists of alternative town names include the postal codes and the canton abbreviation for each of the settlements concerned.

German-speaking areas

Canton/Postal code	*German*	*French*	*Italian*	*Rhaeto-Romance*
BS 4000-4091	Basel	Bâle	Basilea	
BE 3000-3030	Bern	Berne	Berna	Berna
VS 3900	Brig	Brigue		
GR 7000-7007	Chur	Coire	Coira	Cuira / Cuoira / Cuera
GR 7142	Cumbel			Cumbels
FR 3284	Fräschels	Frasses (Lac)		
BE 2076	Gals	Chules		
BE 3236	Gampelen	Champion		
FR 3215	Gempenach	Champagny		
FR 1735	Giffers	Chevrilles		
GL 8750	Glarus		Glarona	
SO 2540	Grenchen	Granges		
FR 3212	Gurmels	Cormondes		
FR 1655	Im Fang	La Villette		
FR 3210	Kerzers	Chiètres		
SO 4245	Kleinlützel	Petit-Lucelle		
LU 6000-6009	Luzern	Lucerne	Lucerna	
SA 3953	Leuk Stadt	Loèche-la-Ville		
SA 3954	Leukerbad	Loèche-les-Bains		
BE 2514	Ligerz	Gléresse		
BE 1797	Münchenwiler	Villars-les-Moines		
FR 3286	Muntelier	Montilier		
BE 3225	Müntschemier	Monsmier		
FR 3280	Murten	Morat		
VD 1595	Pfauen	Faoug		
BE 2542	Pieterlen	Perles		
FR 1716	Plaffeien	Planfayon		
VS 3942	Raron	Rarogne		
BE 3792	Saanen	Gessenay		
GR 7151	Schluein			Schleuis
FR 1711	Schwarzsee	Lac-Noir		
FR 1718	Rechthalten	Dirlaret		
VS 3970	Salgesch	Salquenen		
FR 1794	Salvenach	Salvagny		
SG 9000	Sankt Gallen	Saint-Gall	San Gallo	
FR 1717	Sankt Ursen	Saint-Ours		
SH 8200	Schaffhausen	Schaffhouse	Sciaffusa	

BE 2747	Seehof	Elay		
SO 4500	Solothurn	Soleure	Soletta	
VS 3952	Susten	La Souste		
FR 1712	Tafers	Tavel		
FR 3912	Termen	Thermen		
BE 3600	Thun	Thoune		
VS 3946	Turtmann	Tourtemagne		
BE 2513	Twann	Douanne		
FR 3214	Ulmiz	Ormay		
VS 3969	Varcn	Varonne		
VS 3930	Visp	Viège		
SP 4716	Welschenrohr	Rosières		
ZG 6300-6310	Zug	Zoug	Zugo	
ZH 8000-8099	Zürich	Zurich	Zurigo	

French-speaking areas

Canton/Postal code	*French*	*German*	*Italian*
FR 1722	Bourguillon	Bürglen	
FR 1792	Cordast	Grossguschelmuth	
FR 1796	Courgevaux	Gurwolf	
JU 2800	Delémont	Delsberg	
FR 1700-1701	Fribourg	Freiburg	Friburgo
BE 2535	Frinvillier	Friedliswart	
GE1200-1211 +1289	Genève	Genf	Ginevra
BE 2520	La Neuveville	Neuenstadt	
VD 1000-1007 +1010-1018	Lausanne		Losanna
JU 2807	Lucelle	Lützel	
BE 2740	Moutier	Münster	
BR 2534	Orvin	Ifflingen	
JU 2900	Porrentruy	Pruntrut	
BE 2515	Prêles	Prägelz	
BE 2732	Reconvilier	Rokwiler	
BE 2610	Saint-Imier	Sankt Immer	
VS 1950	Sion	Sitten	
BE 2710	Tavannes	Dachsfelden	
BE 2720	Tramelan	Tramlingen	
BE 2512	Tüscherz-Alfermée	Daucher	
BE 2537	Vauffelin	Füglisthal	

Italian-speaking areas

Canton/Postal code	*Italian*	*German*	*French*
TI 6500-6506	Bellinzona	Bellinzonae	Bellenz
TI 6951	Odogno	Lelgio	

Rhaeto-Romance-speaking areas

Canton/Postal code	*Rhaeto-Romance*	*Gernan*	*Italian*
GR 7153	Falera	Fellers	
GR 7130	Ilanz	Glion	
GR 7145	Degen	Igels	
GR 7265	Davos Wolfgang	Laret	
GR 6563	Mesocco	Misox	
GR 7537	Müstair	Münster	
GR 7522	La-Punt-Chamues-ch		Pont-Campovasto
GR 7550	Scuol	Schuls	
GR 7127	Sevgein	Seewis im Oberland	
GR 7174	S. Benedetg	St. Benedikt	San Benedetto
GR 7175	Sumvitg	Somvix	
GR 7166	Trun	Truns	
GR 7147	Vignogn	Vigens	

NB: 2500-2505 Biel/Bienne is a bilingual (French/German) town, and therefore is usually known by its French and German names together - hence Biel/Bienne. Its Italian equivalent is Bienna. There is another town called Biel, with the postal code 4105, known as Biel-Benken.

Other European Languages

Canton/Postal code	*Indigenous*	*English*	*Spanish*	*Dutch*
BS 4000-4091	Basel	Basle		Bazel
BE 3000-3030	Bern	Berne	Berna	
GE 1200-1211+ 1289	Genève	Geneva		
ZH 8000-8099	Zürich	Zurich		

Administrative districts

Switzerland is a federation of 23 cantons (of which 6 are demi-cantons). These, with their abbreviations and languages spoken are listed below:

NB: *= demi-canton
(G) = German; (F) = French; (I) = Italian; (R) = Rhaeto-Romance

(Demi-)Canton	*Abbreviation + language(s)*
Aargau	AG (G)
* Appenzell Innerrhoden	AI (G)
* Appenzell Ausserrhoden	AR (G)
* Basel Landschaft	BL (G)
* Basel Stadt	BS (G)
Bern/Berne	BE (G & F)
Fribourg	FR (F & G)
Genève	GE (F)
Glarus	GL (G)
Graubünden	GR (G & R & I)
Jura	JU (F)
Luzern	LU (G)
Neuchâtel	NE (F)
* Nidwalden	NW(G)
* Obwalden	OW(G)
Sankt Gallen	SG (G)
Schaffhausen	SH (G)
Solothurn	SO (G)
Schwyz	SZ (G)
Thurgau	TG (G)
Ticino	TI (I)
Uri	UR (G)
Vallais/Wallis	VS (F & G)
Vaud	VD (F)
Zug	ZG (G)
Zürich	ZH (G)

The canton abbreviations are often added to addresses after, and on the same line as, the town name, but they are not necessary provided that the postal code is used, and the Swiss PTT prefers that they are excluded from addresses.

Towns with the abbreviation FL (Fürstentum Liechtenstein) following their name are not in Switzerland but in the neighbouring country of Liechtenstein.

Syria
As-Sūrīyah (Arabic)

Official name: Syrian Arab Republic, al-jamhouriya al Arabia as-Sūrīyah
Area: 185 180 sq. km (71 479 sq. miles)
Population: 12 958 000
Capital: Dimashq (Damascus)
Currency: 1 Syrian Pound (LS, Syr £) = 100 piastres
International telephone access code: 963

Languages

The national language is Standard Arabic. 15 other languages are spoken. The most widespread of these are: Mespotamian Spoken Arabic (1 800 000 speakers in Eastern Syria); Najdi Spoken Arabic (500 000 speakers in the Syrian Desert); Northern Levantine Spoken Arabic (8 800 000 speakers); North Mesopotamian Spoken Arabic (300 000 speakers); Armenian (320 000 speakers) and Kurmanji (Kurdish) (938 000 speakers).

There is heavy prejudice against Kurdish-speakers - its teaching in schools is forbidden and its use heavily discouraged. It is therefore unlikely to be found in addresses.

Example address format

General Post Office
Av. Sa'as-Allah Al-Jabiry
DAMAS

Postal code

Syria has no postal code system.

Towns

The following list gives foreign language equivalents of Syrian town names:

Arabic	*English*	*French*	*German*
Al Lādhiqiyah	Latakia	Latakia	Latakia
Dimashq	Damascus	Damas	Damaskus
Ḩalab	Aleppo	Alep	Haleb
Ḩims	Homs	Homs	Homs

Tajikistan
Tojikiston

Official name: Republic of Tajikistan, Respublika i Tojikiston
Area: 143 100 sq. km (55 200 sq. miles)
Population: 4 969 000
Capital: Dushanbé
Currency: 1 Rouble (R) = 100 kopecks
International telephone access code: 7

Languages

The official language, Tajik, is spoken by some 53% of the population. There are some 237 000 Russian-speakers and 873 000 Northern Uzbek speakers. 9 other languages are spoken.

Example Address Format

Zourabekov Mourod Bakievitch
rue Khoutchandi 7
GM 735450 GARM

The postal code appears to be preceded by an abbreviation indicating the district. These are unique per region but not for the whole country. The abbreviations for each district are:

Under Republican Authority:

Chakhrina	SN
Djirgatal	DG
Faizabad	FZ
Garm	GM
Ghissar	GS
Kofarnikhon	KF
Komsomolabad	KM
Leninskii	LN
Nourek	NK
Rogoun	RG
Tadjikabad	TB
Tavildara	TD
Toursounzadé	TZ
Varzob	VZ

Dushanbé:

Dushanbé	DB

Gorno-Badakhchan:

Darvoz	DZ
Ichkamim	IK
Khorog	KG
Mourgab	MG
Rochtkala	RK
Rouman	RN
Vantch	VC

Khatlon:

Bokhtarskii	BH
Chaartouz	SZ
Dangera	DG
Djilihoul	JL
Gozimalik	GS
Kabodien	KD
Khovaling	HU
Kolkhozabad	KZ
Kouibychevsk	KH
Kouliab	KL
Koumsanghir	KS
Kourgan-Tioubé	KT
Moskovskii	MS
Mouminabad	MN
Parkhar	PH
Piandj	PJ
Sovetskii	SU
Vakhm	VH
Vossé	VS
Yavan	YU

Leninabad:

Acht	AT
Aini	AN
Chakhristan	ST
Chaklovsk	CH
Ghantchi	GN
Isfara	IS
Kairakkoum	KR

Kanibadam	KN
Khodjent	NJ
Koudjand	KJ
Matcha	MT
Naou	NU
Pendjikent	PK
Proletarsk	PL
Oura-Tioubé	UT
Tabomar	TB
Zafarabad	ZF

Postal codes

Postal codes consist of a block of 6 digits. This is the same code that was used before the independence of Tajikistan from the Soviet Union. The first two digits indicate the republic and region, the next two the district and the final two the post office. If the fifth digit is '0' then the postal code refers to a rural post office. In all other cases it is an urban post office.

Tanzania

Official name: United Republic of Tanzania, Jamhuri ya Mwungano wa Tanzania
Area: 945 087 sq. km (364 900 sq. miles)
Population: 26 869 000
Capital: Dodoma
Currency: 1 Tanzanian Shilling (TSh) = 100 cents
International telephone access code: 255

Languages

131 languages are spoken in Tanzania. The geographical distribution of these languages is complex. The official languages are English (spoken mainly as a second language by about 1 500 000 people) and Swahili (about 313 200 first-language and 23 000 000 second language speakers). Other widely spoken languages include Bena (568 000 speakers); Chagga (1 000 000 speakers); Gogo (1 300 000 speakers); Ha (800 000 speakers); Haya (1 200 000 speakers); Hehe (750 000 speakers); Kachchi (778 000 speakers); Makonde (900 000 speakers); Nyamwezi (926 000 speakers); Nyaturu (556 000 speakers); Ruguru (520 000 speakers); Shambala (550 000 speakers) and Sukumu (5 000 000 speakers).

Example address format

Miss A. Chome
c/o Mashimoni Enterprises
Private Bag
DODOMA

or

Mr. Abel H.H. Bilia
P.O. Box 10084
DAR ES SALAAM

Addresses consist of a postbox or a private bag and will usually be written in English.

Postal codes

Tanzania has no postal code system.

Thailand
Muang Thai

Official name: Kingdom of Thailand, Muang Thai
Area: 513 115 sq. km (198 062 sq. miles)
Population: 56 800 000
Capital: Krung Thep (Bangkok)
Currency: 1 Baht (B) = 100 satang
International telephone access code: 66

Languages

The official language is Thai, spoken by 20-25 000 000 people. 75 other languages are spoken. The most widespread of these are: Min Nan Chinese (1 081 920 speakers); Northern Khmer (1 000 000 speakers); Pattani Malay (2 384 000 speakers); Northeastern Tai (15-23 000 000 speakers); Northern Tai (6 000 000 speakers) and Southern Tai (5 000 000 speakers).

Address Format

Addresses should be formatted:

Name
{Building/block information}
number[ ]Thoroughfare
{Village and district names}
Settlement
PROVINCE
postal code

For example

Mr Sanya Thongsaphak
95/62 Moo 6 Ban Bua Thong
Talingchan-Suphanburi Road
Amphoe Bang Bua Thong
NONTHABURI
11110

The postal code may also be written immediately following the province name.

Postal codes

Postal codes consist of a block of 5 digits, commencing with a number between 1 and 9. The first two digits of the postal code indicate the province, the last three the post office.

Togo

Official name: Republic of Togo, République Togolaise
Area: 56 790 sq. km (21 941 sq. miles)
Population: 3 810 000
Capital: Lomé
Currency: 1 CFA Franc (CFAFr) = 100 centimes
International telephone access code: 228

Languages

The official language is French (3 000 speakers). 42 other languages are spoken. The most widespread of these is: Aja-Gbe (110 600 speakers); Akposo (94 900 speakers); Éwé (861 900 speakers); Gen-Gbe (200 900 speakers); Gourmanchéma (120 500 speakers); Kabiyé (489 200 speakers); Lama (117 400 speakers); Moba (189 400 speakers); Nawdm (145 600 speakers); Ntcham (100 000 speakers); Tem (204 000 speakers) and Waci-Gbe (365 500 speakers).

Example address format

M. Nicolas Ayi Patatu
BP 526
LOME

Any address written in a non-native language will be written in French. Deliveries are made only to post office boxes (*Boite Postale*, or *BP*).

Postbox

This is written as *Boite Postale*, or *BP*.

Postal codes

Togo has no postal code system.

Trinidad and Tobago

Official name: Republic of Trinidad and Tobago
Area: 5 128 sq. km (1 979 sq. miles)
Population: 1 300 000
Capital: Port of Spain
Currency: 1 Trinidad and Tobago Dollar (TT$) = 100 cents
International telephone access code: 1

Languages

The official language is English. The version spoken in Trinidad and Tobago is a dialect rather than a distinct Creole. There are some 45 000 Hindi-speakers, 36 000 Lesser Antillean Creole English-speakers and a number of Trinidad Creole French-speakers.

Example address format

Mr Michael Naidoo
33 Shende Street
GOPAUL ILANDS
MARABELLA

Addresses will be written in English.

Postal code

Trinidad and Tobago has no postal code system.

Telephone numbers

All telephone numbers in Trinidad and Tobago have the area code 868.

Tunisia
Tunisiyah

Official name: Republic of Tunisia, al Jumhuriyah at-Tunisiyah
Area: 164 150 sq. km (63 362 sq. miles)
Population: 8 413 000
Capital: Tunis
Currency: 1 Tunisian Dinar (TD, D) = 1 000 millèmes
International telephone access code: 216

Languages

The official language is Standard Arabic. Most of the population speak Tunisian Spoken Arabic. There are also 500 speakers of Judeo-Tunisian Arabic; 3 650 of Duwinna (in Chenini town, Douirat Town and Tunis); 11 000 French-speakers; 10 000 speakers of Jerba and 3 000 Tamezret speakers in Tamezret village. Sened is spoken in Sened and Tmagourt villages.

Address Format

Addresses written in Latin script are usually written in French and are similar in format to French addresses. Their format is:

First Name[ ]LAST NAME
number[ ]thoroughfare type[ ]Thoroughfare name
postal code[ ]SETTLEMENT

For example:

Said MOHAMED
10 rue des Jardins
2000 LE BARDO

or

Said MOHAMED
App 100, 1er étage, bloc 9
rue Ksontina
Cité El-Habib
4001 SOUSSE CORNICHE

For the postal regions of Ariana & Ben Arous, Bizerte, Gabès, Sfax, Sousse and Tunis, the post office name is written after the city name. In the above example, *SOUSSE* is the city name and *CORNICHE* the post office name.

Thoroughfare types are written starting with a lower-case letter. For lists of thoroughfare types and other address component information, please refer to the chapter on France.

Postbox

When written in Latin script, this is written as *Boite Postale*, abbreviated to *BP*.

Postal code

Postal codes consists of a block of 4 digits. The first two digits indicate the governorate, the final two the delivery office.

Towns

The following list gives foreign language equivalents of Tunisian town names:

Arabic	*French*	*German*
Bizerte	Binzert	Bizerta
Meuzel Bourguiba		Ferryville
Sousse		Susa
Tabarka		Tabarca

Turkey
Türkiye Cumhuriyeti

At the time of going to press there was continuing unrest and Kurdish rebel action in the south-western areas of the country. Mail deliveries in these areas may consequently be affected.

Official name: Republic of Turkey, Türkiye Cumhuriyeti
Area: 779 452 sq. km (300 868 sq. miles)
Population: 59 200 000
Capital: Ankara
Currency: 1 Turkish Lira (TL) = 100 kurus
International telephone access code: 90

Languages

The official language is Turkish, spoken by some 90% of the population. 35 other languages are spoken. The most widespread of these are: North Mesopotamian Spoken Arabic (400 000 speakers); South Azerbaijani (530 000 speakers in Kars Province) and Kurmanji (Kurdish, 3 950 000 speakers).

There is heavy prejudice against the use of Kurdish and it will therefore rarely be found in addresses.

Company Types

These company types are commonly found in Turkish address databases:

AS (Anonim Sirketi)
TLS (Türk Limited Sirketi)

Address Format

Addresses are written in the following format:

Name
Thoroughfare[ ]number
{more address information such as apartment}
postal code[ ]SETTLEMENT

For example:

Ismet Inönü Bul. 93
Bahçelievler
06700 ANKARA

Postal codes

Postal codes consist of a block of 5 digits.

Towns

The following list provides foreign-language alternatives for Turkish settlement names:

Turkish	*English*	*French*	*German*
Bursa	Prusa		
Edirne			Adrianopel
Gelibolu	Gallipoli		
Izmir	Smyrna	Smyrne	
Sevascedtepe	Giresun		
Tekirdag	Rodosto		

Turkmenistan
Türkmenostan

Official name: Republic of Turkmenistan, Türkmenostan
Area: 488 100 sq. km (188 400 sq. miles)
Population: 3 809 000
Capital: Ashkhabad (Ashgabad)
Currency: Manat
International telephone access code: 993

Languages

The official language, Turkmen, is spoken by some 76% of the population. There are some 349 000 Russian-speakers; 317 000 Northern Uzbek-speakers and 28 000 Western Balochi-speakers. Languages from other parts of the former Soviet Union are also widely spoken.

Example Address Format

744000 ACHGABAT
TURKMENISTAN
Dovletova G.D.
16, pl. Kossaev

The first line contains the postal code and settlement name, the second the country name, the third the contact name and the last the street address.

Postal codes

Postal codes consist of a block of 6 digits. This is the same code that was used before the independence of Turkmenistan from the Soviet Union. The first three digits indicate a main town, the final three the nodal centre of the city or a rural post office.

Tuvalu

Official name: The Tuvalu Islands
Area: 26 sq. km (10 sq. miles)
Population: 9 500
Capital: Funafuti (Fongafale)
Currency: 1 Australian Dollar ($A) = 100 cents
International telephone access code: 688

Languages

The inhabitants of Tuvalu speak Tuvaluan.

Example address format

Mr. Mose Boreham
P.O. Box 33
Vaiaku
FUNAFUTI

Delivery is to postboxes or private bags. The name of the island is mentioned on the last line of the address. The islands making up Tuvalu are:

Funafuti
Nanumanga
Nanumea
Niulakita
Niutao
Nui
Nukufetau
Nukulailai
Vaitupu

Postal codes

Tuvalu has no postal code system.

Uganda

Official name: Republic of Uganda
Area: 241 038 sq. km (150 645 sq. miles)
Population: 17 500 000
Capital: Kampala
Currency: 1 Uganda Shilling = 100 cents
International telephone access code: 256

Languages

46 languages are spoken in Uganda. The geographical distribution of these languages is complex. The official language is English (mainly spoken as a second language by 1 000 000 people). Widely spoken languages include: Acholi (746 796 speakers); Aringa (588 830 speakers); Chiga (1 391 442 speakers); Ganda (3 015 980 speakers); Kenyi (1 200 000 speakers); Lango (977 680 speakers); Masaba (751 253 speakers); Nyankore (1 643 193 speakers); Rwanda (532 692 speakers); Soga (1 370 845 speakers); Swahili and Teso (999 537 speakers).

Example address format

Ms Olive Takubua
P.O. Box 21310
KAMPALA

Addresses will be a postbox number and will be written in English.

Postal codes

Uganda has no postal code system.

Ukraine
Ukraïna

Official name: Republic of Ukraine, Ukraïna
Area: 603 700 sq. km (233 028 sq. miles)
Population: 52 100 000
Capital: Kiev
Currency: 1 Hryvnia (UHR) = 100 kopiyka
International telephone access code: 7

Language

The official language is Ukrainian, spoken by some 58% of the population. There are many speakers of languages from other parts of the former Soviet Union and Eastern Europe, particularly Russian (11 335 000 speakers); Belorussian (440 000 speakers); Polish (1 151 000 speakers) and Romanian (500 000 speakers). Of other indigenous languages, there are some 240 000 Romani-speakers; 100 000 Rusyn-speakers and a small number of Urum-speakers.

The Autonomous Republic of Crimea, now part of Ukraine but previously part of Russia, contains a particularly large number of Russian-speakers, and language-sensitivity in this area especially is required.

Example address format

UKRAINE
252001 KIEV
22, Mazepa pr.
Apt. 22
Alexander Petrenko

Note that the order of address lines in Ukraine is the opposite to that used in Western Europe - the postal code and town comes first, then the street address, then the name of the person or company.

Postal codes

Postal codes consist of a block of 6 digits. The code used is that in use since before independence from the Soviet Union. The first three digits indicate the region, the last three the delivery office.

Towns

There are 166 000 Hungarian-speakers in Ruthenia. In this area, settlement names may be found in Ukrainian, Hungarian or Rusyn:

Ukrainian	*Hungarian*	*Rusyn*
Ardanove		Ardanovo
Ardiv	Beregszász	
Bereznyky		Bereznyk
Berezove		Berezovo
Bilka	Bilke	
Bilovarci		Bilovarec'
Bistra		Bystryj
Borodivka		Barbovo
Borzavs'ke		Velyka Cengava
Brestiv		Brestov
Brid		Brod
Cerveneve		Cerven'ovo
Chabanivka		Bacovo
Chop	Csap	
Chynadieve	Szentmiklós	
Cynadijeve		Cinjad'ovo
Derenkovecj	Beregsom	
Didove	Beregdáda	
Dilove		Bilyj Potok
Dorobratove		Dorohbratovo
Harazdivka	Gút	
Khust	Huszt	
Kosyny	Kaszony	
Mizhhirja	Ökörmezö	
Mukacheve	Munkács	
Nizhni	Vorota	
Rokoshyn	Beregrákos	
Rusjke Pole	Úrmező	
Svaljava	Szolyva	
Tjachiv	Técső	
Uzhhorod	Ungvár	
Velykyy Bereznyy	Berezna	
Vynohradiv	Nagyszőlős	
Vyshkove	Visk	

The following list gives foreign language equivalents of Ukrainian town names:

Ukrainian	*English*	*German*
Kiyev	Kiev	Kiew
Lvov		Lwow
Sevastopol		Sewastopol
Yalta		Jalta

United Arab Emirates
Ittihād al-Imārat al'Arabīyah

Official name: United Arab Emirates, Ittihād al-Imārat al'Arabīyah
Area: 83 600 sq. km (32 300 sq. miles)
Population: 1 990 000
Capital: Abū Zaby (Abu Dhabi)
Currency: 1 United Arab Emirates Dirham (DH) = 100 fils
International telephone access code: 971

Languages

The national language is standard Arabic. There are some 744 000 speakers of Gulf Spoken Arabic; 5 000 speakers of Shihhi Spoken Arabic; 100 000 speakers of Southern Balochi; 80 000 speakers of Western Farsi; 100 000 speakers of Eastern Pashto; several thousand speakers of Western Pashto and 100 000 speakers of Somali.

Address format

Addresses are formatted as follows:

Name of addressee
Name of company
[P.O. Box] number
Name of Emirate

Postbox numbers may be repeated in different emirates, so the name of the emirate is very important. The emirates are:

Abū Zaby (Abu Dhabi)
Ajman
Al Fujayrah
Ash Shāriqah (Sharjah)
Dubayy (Dubai)
Ras al Khaymah
Umm al Qaywayn

Postal codes

There is no postal code system in United Arab Emirates.

UNITED KINGDOM: Postal regions and language areas

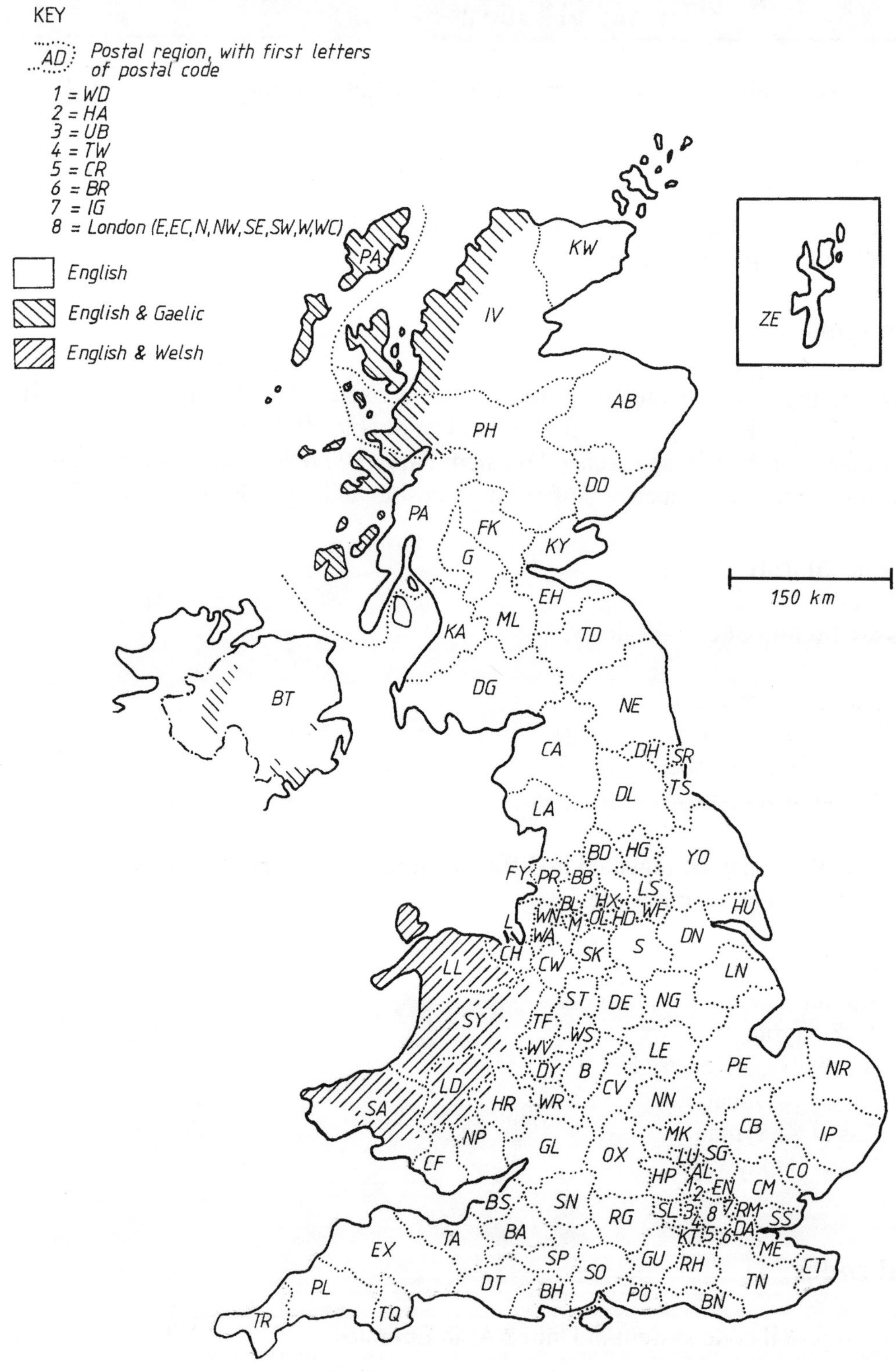

Source some data: Grimes, B., Ethnologue, 1996, Summer Institute of Linguistics

98

United Kingdom

The United Kingdom comprises the nations of England and Scotland, the principality of Wales (Cymru) and the Constituent Region of Northern Ireland. It excludes the Crown Dependencies of the Isle of Man, Jersey and Guernsey. Great Britain is the island which comprises England, Scotland and Wales. Letters from outside the United Kingdom should be addressed correctly. Avoid especially using 'England' for destinations in other parts of the United Kingdom.

Official name: United Kingdom of Great Britain and Northern Ireland
Area: 256 668 sq. km. (160 418 sq. miles)
Population: 57 384 000
Capital: London
Currency: 1 Pound Sterling (£) = 100 pence
International telephone access code: 44

Languages

English, the official language, is spoken by 98% of the population. Welsh is spoken by 575 102 people, of whom 32 700 speak no other language, mainly in northern and central Wales. Scottish Gaelic is spoken by 88 892 people in Ross, the Isle of Skye and the Western Isles of Scotland (of which 477 speak no other language) and Irish Gaelic is spoken in parts of Belfast and in parts of the counties of Armagh and Fermanagh in Northern Ireland.

Angloromani is spoken by 90 000 people. Traveller Scottish is spoken by 1 000 people in Scotland. Welsh Romani is also spoken.

Company names

Words indicating the *nature* of a company, when forming part of the company name, will always follow the *name* of the company, either after a comma or in brackets, thus:

John Smith, Bakers
John Smith (Bakers)

Company types

The company types Limited (abbreviated to Ltd - private limited company) and PLC (Public Limited Company) are those most commonly found in address databases. Other types include

Company Limited by Guarantee
Foreign Registered Company
Friendly Society
Limited Partnership
Partnership

Private Limited Company
Private Unlimited Company
Public Corporation
Sole Proprietorship

Addresses

Addresses in the United Kingdom are the least formatted of any country in Europe. Whilst many countries limit addresses to, at most, three lines, the structure of addresses in the United Kingdom seems very much to have been left to the discretion of the sender, with the result that addresses are often long, contain not strictly necessary information and some almost provide the postman with a route description from the nearest large town to the address concerned. Naming houses or company locations is as common in the United Kingdom as it is rare in other parts of Europe. The postal code is also not as instinctively used as it is in other European countries. The address is written in the following format:

Contact name
{Job Title}
Company Name
number[ ]Thoroughfare name[ ]Thoroughfare type
{District/suburb of town etc. or village name (double dependent locality)}
{District/suburb of town etc. or village name (dependent locality)}
Postal Town
{County}
Postal code

Some addresses contain a house name and no house number. In these cases the house name must be used. However, a house name must not replace a house number where this is available.

The street address may also be written as follows:

Number[,]Thoroughfare name[ ]Thoroughfare type

The address may also contain one or more of the following parameters:

Floor number
Unit number
Industrial Estate name
Building name

The order of these parameters varies. Punctuation (commas at the end of lines) is optional. There must be no punctuation on the same line as the postal code. For example:

Smiths the Bakers
Flour House
Unit 3, Mary Street Industrial Estate
Benson
Oxford
OX9 1AA

Smiths the Bakers
3 Mary Street
Benson
OX9 1AA

Smiths the Bakers
Flour House, 1st floor
Unit 3
Mary Street Industrial Estate
Benson
Nr. Oxford
OX9 1AA

The thoroughfare type is written after and separately from the thoroughfare name, thus:

Saint Helen's Avenue

An exception is the thoroughfare type '-gate', which is of Scandinavian origin and is usually attached to the thoroughfare name, thus:

Friargate

UK addresses will also often use a whole series of other directional indications, such as 'c/o' (care of), 'r/o' (rear of), 'near', 'off' and so on.

There are 11 postal town names in the United Kingdom which are duplicated. These are:

Town	*County*	*Postal codes*
Alford	Aberdeenshire Lincolnshire	AB33 LN13
Ashford	Kent Middlesex	TN23-27 TW15
Bangor	Co. Down Gwynedd	BT19-20 LL57
Bridgend	Isle of Islay Mid Glamorgan	PA44 CF31-35
Gillingham	Dorset Kent	SP8 ME7-8
Newcastle	Co. Down	BT33

	Staffordshire	ST5
Newport	Dyfed Gwent Isle of Wight Staffordshire	SA42 NP1, NP6, NP9 PO30 TF10
Richmond	Surrey North Yorkshire	TW9-10 DL10-11
St Agnes	Cornwall Cornwall (Isles of Scilly)	TR5 TR22
Talybont	Gwynedd Dyfed	LL43 SY24
Whitchurch	Hampshire Shropshire	RG28 SY13

This will cause no problems provided that the postal code is used. Where the postal code is unknown, the county is required.

Thoroughfare types

Below is a list of commonly occurring thoroughfare types, with the abbreviated form(s) which you are most likely to find in address databases:

English

Thoroughfare	*Abbreviation*
Alley	
Avenue	Ave.
Boulevard	Bd.
Centre	Ctr.
Chambers	
Circus	
Close	
Court	Ct.
Crescent	Cr.
Drive	
Drove	
Estate	
Field	
Gardens	
Gate	
Grove	
Hill	
Lane	
Market	Mkt.
Mews	
Parade	
Park	
Place	Pl.

Quay	
Road	Rd.
Route	Rte.
Row	
Square	Sq.
Street	St.
Terrace	
Way	
Yard	

NB: Though the abbreviation for Saint is *St* and that for street is *St.* (with a full stop), they are both commonly incorrectly abbreviated to the same format (with or without the full stop).

Welsh

Thoroughfare	*English version*
Bron	Hill
Cae	Field
Fford	Park, Way
Maes	Field
Marchnad	Market
Sgwar	Square
Sgwar y Marchnad	Market Square

Nouns, adjectives and prepositions commonly found in address databases

Welsh

NB: Welsh has no indefinite article (a, an)

Welsh	*English*
y, yr (before a, e, h, i, o, w, y)	the
tua	till
tan	until
am, i	for
o	of
i	to
at	towards
wrth, gan	by
ar	on
yn	in
tu ol	behind
yn y blaen	in front of
rhwyng	between
dros	over

gyda, efo (Northern Wales)	with
y Dwyrain	East
o'r Ddwyrain	Eastern
y Gorllewin	West
o'r Gorllewin	Western
y De	South
o'r De	Southern
y Gogledd	North
o'r Gogledd	Northern
Bach (Fach for female nouns)	Little
Mawr (Fawr for female nouns)	Great
newydd	New
hen	Old
Hwyr	Long
Sant. Note that the Saint's name comes first in Welsh - for example Dewi Sant=St David's.	Saint

Postbox

This is written as P.O. Box, Post Office Box, PO Box or Postbox.

Note that in the United Kingdom, a postbox is not necessarily a number. It can also be a part (usually the last part) of a postal code. Thus, for example:

> Mr Bun the Bakers
> P.O. Box 1PT
> NE17 1PT

Postal codes

Postal codes must be placed on a separate line at the bottom of the address, after the town name. There must be nothing else written on this line.

Postal code areas do not correspond to administrative districts. Each code represents a single large user or a small number of addresses in a street or neighbourhood.

Each postal code has two parts, separated by a space. No postal code is longer than 8 characters.

The first part of the postal code (outward code) can take the following forms:

A9	e.g. E1
A99	e.g. E11
A9A	e.g. E1A
AA9	e.g. EX1
AA99	e.g. EX11
AA9A	e.g. EC1A (This format is found only in London.)
AAA	For one postal code only - GIR

The second part of the postal code (inward code) is always a digit followed by 2 letters, e.g. lAP.

The first part of the postal code relates to the postal distribution centre, the letters deriving from the town name, and the part of that district. The second part relates to a street and to which side of the street the house is found or whether the house is odd- or even-numbered; or it may be unique to a single large user. The user cannot derive these details from the code itself.

The following list gives all possible initial characters of U.K. postal codes, with their corresponding postal town:

AB	Aberdeen
AL	St.Albans
B	Birmingham
BA	Bath
BB	Blackburn
BD	Bradford
BH	Bournemouth
BL	Bolton
BN	Brighton
BR	Bromley
BS	Bristol
BT	Belfast
CA	Carlisle
CB	Cambridge
CF	Cardiff
CH	Chester
CM	Chelmsford
CO	Colchester
CR	Croydon
CT	Canterbury
CV	Coventry
CW	Crewe
DA	Dartford
DD	Dundee
DE	Derby
DG	Dumfries
DH	Durham
DL	Darlington
DN	Doncaster
DT	Dorchester
DY	Dudley
E	London (East)
EC	London (East Central)
EH	Edinburgh
EN	Enfield

EX	Exeter
FK	Falkirk
FY	Blackpool
G	Glasgow
GL	Gloucester
GU	Guildford
HA	Harrow
HD	Huddersfield
HG	Harrogate
HP	Hemel Hempstead
HR	Hereford
HU	Kingston upon Hull
HX	Halifax
IG	Ilford
IP	Ipswich
IV	Inverness
KA	Kilmarnock
KT	Kingston upon Thames
KW	Kirkwall
KY	Kirkcaldy
L	Liverpool
LA	Lancaster
LD	Llandrindod Wells
LE	Leicester
LL	Llandudno
LN	Lincoln
LS	Leeds
LU	Luton
M	Manchester
ME	Medway
MK	Milton Keynes
ML	Motherwell
N	London (North)
NE	Newcastle upon Tyne
NG	Nottingham
NN	Northampton
NP	Newport
NR	Norwich
NW	London (Northwest)
OL	Oldham
OX	Oxford
PA	Paisley
PE	Peterborough
PH	Perth
PL	Plymouth
PO	Portsmouth
PR	Preston

RG	Reading
RH	Redhill
RM	Romford
S	Sheffield
SA	Swansea
SE	London (Southeast)
SG	Stevenage
SK	Stockport
SL	Slough
SM	Sutton
SN	Swindon
SO	Southampton
SP	Salisbury
SR	Sunderland
SS	Southend-on-Sea
ST	Stoke-on-Trent
SW	London (Southwest)
SY	Shrewsbury
TA	Taunton
TD	Galashiels
TF	Telford
TN	Tunbridge Wells
TQ	Torquay
TR	Truro
TS	Cleveland
TW	Twickenham
UB	Southall
W	London (West)
WA	Warrington
WC	London (West Central)
WD	Watford
WF	Wakefield
WN	Wigan
WR	Worcester
WS	Walsall
WV	Wolverhampton
YO	York
ZE	Lerwick

The letter J is never found as one of the first two letters (except for Jersey, Channel Islands, which is not part of the United Kingdom but is part of the U.K. postal code system). Q, V and X are never found in the first position of the postal code. I and Z are not found in the second position (except for the single postal code GIR 0AA which refers to the Girobank). Only the letters A, E, H, M, N, P, R, T, V, X and Y can appear in the third position. Only the letters A, B, E, H, M, N, P, R, V, W, X and Y can appear in the fourth position.

In the inward (second half) of the code, the letters C, I, K, M, O and V are never found.

As both the International sorting code and UK postal codes begin with letters, confusion can occur (e.g. CH indicating Switzerland can be confused with CH indicating Chester), and for this reason the British Post Office prefers that the International sorting code is not used for international mail posted within the United Kingdom.

Postal codes beginning GY are in the crown dependency of Guernsey, those beginning JE are in Jersey and those beginning IM in the Isle of Man.

Towns

London is known as *Londres* in French and Spanish, *Londra* in Italian and *Londen* in Dutch.

Edinburgh is known as *Edimbourg* in French, *Edimburgo* in Spanish and Italian, and *Edinburg* in Dutch.

Dover is known as *Douvres* in French.

Welsh is widely spoken in Wales, and many settlements in Wales have both Welsh and English names. The British Post Office caters for Welsh place names. These alternative names are listed below. Where more than one settlement of the same name exists in Wales, the county in which it is situated is given in brackets after the English version of the name. Much of this information is derived from Oliver Mason's *Bartholomew Gazetteer of Places in Britain* (1989 edition).

Welsh	*English*
Abaty Cwmhir	Abbeycwmhir
Aberafan	Aberavon
Aberbargod	Aberbargoed
Aberbig	Aberbeeg
Abercastell	Abercastle
Abercynffig	Aberkenfig
Aberdaugleddau	Milford Haven
Aberddawan	Aberthaw
Aberdyfi	Aberdovey
Abergwaun	Fishguard
Aberhonddu	Brecon
Aberllynfi	Three Cocks
Abermiwi	Abermule
Abermo	Barmouth
Aberogwr	Ogmore-by-Sea
Aberpennar	Mountain Ash
Aberriw	Berriew
Abertawe	Swansea
Aberteifi	Cardigan

Abertyleri	Abertillery
Allt Melyd	Meliden
Arberth	Narberth
Arddleen	Ardd-lin
Bangor-is-y-Coed	Bangor-on-Dee
Bargod	Bargoed
Basaleg	Bassaleg
Bedwellte	Bedwellty
Begeli	Begelly
Bers	Bersham
Betws	Bettws
Betws Bledrws	Bettws Bledrws
Biwmares	Beaumaris
Blaenafon	Blaenavon
Blaenau	Blaina
Blaendulais	Seven Sisters
Bochrwyd	Boughrood
Breudeth	Brawdy
Bugeildy	Beguildy
Bwcle	Buckley
Caerdydd	Cardiff
Caerffili	Caerphilly
Caerfyrddin	Carmarthen
Caergybi	Holyhead
Caeriw	Carew
Caernarfon	Caernarvon
Camros	Camrose
Capel Newydd	Newchapel
Capel Uchaf	Upper Chapel
Carwe	Carway
Cas-bach	Castleton
Cas-blaidd	Wolf's Castle
Cas-fuwch	Castlebythe
Cas-gwent	Chepstow
Casilwchwr	Loughor
Cas-mael	Puncheston
Casmorys	Castle Morris
Casnewydd-ar-Wysg	Newport (Gwent)
Casnewydd-bach	Little Newcastle
Castellhaidd	Hayscastle
Castellhenri	Henry's Moat
Castellmartin	Castlemartin
Castell-nedd	Neath
Castell-paen	Painscastle
Cas-wis	Wiston
Cathedin	Cathedine
Ceigidfa	Guilsfield

Ceinewydd	New Quay
Cemais	Kemeys Inferior
Cemais Comawndwr	Kemeys Commander
Cendl	Beaufort
Chwitffordd	Whitford
Cilgeti	Kilgetty
Cilmeri	Cilmery
Cleirwy	Clyro
Clunderwen	Clynderwen
Clydau	Clydey
Coed-duon	Blackwood
Coed-llai	Leeswood
Coed-y-paun	Coed-y-paen
Coedcernyw	Coedkernew
Coety	Coity
Conwil Elvet	Cynwyl Elfed
Corntwn	Corntown
Crai	Cray
Crindai	Crindau
Cronwern	Crunwear
Crucywel	Crickhowell
Crugion	Criggion
Crymlyn	Crumlin
Crynwedd	Crinow
Cwmafan	Cwmavon (West Glamorgan)
Cwmafon	Cwmavon (Gwent)
Cwmbrân	Cwmbran
Cwmcarfan	Cwmcarvan
Cwmcou	Cwmcoy
Cwmlline	Cwm Llinau
Cwmtyleri	Cwmtillery
Cydweli	Kidwelly
Cynffig	Kenfig
Cyncoed	Kingcoed
Derwen-fawr	Broad Oak
Derwen-gam	Oakford
Dinbych	Denbigh
Dinorwic	Dinorwig
Diserth	Dyserth
Drenewydd	Newton (Mid Glamorgan)
Drenewydd Gelli-farch	Shirenewton
Dynbych-y-pysgod	Tenby
Dynfant	Dunvant
Eglwys Fair y Mynydd	St. Mary Hill
Eglwys Wen	Whitechurch
Eglwys Wythwr	Monington
Erbistog	Erbistock

Ewenni	Ewenny
Faerdre	Vardre
Felindre	Velindre (2 in Dyfed, Powys)
Felin-wen	White Mill
Ffontygari	Font-y-gary
Ffwl-y-mwn	Fonmon
Ffynnongroew	Ffynnongroyw
Ffynnon Taf	Taff's Well
Gelli	Gelly
Glan-bad	Uppcr Boat
Glasgoed	Glascoed
Glyn-nedd	Glyn-neath
Gresffordd	Gresford
Gwenfo	Wenvoe
Gwerneshi	Gwernesney
Gwndy	Undy
Helygain	Halkyn
Hendy-gwyn	Whitland
Hwiffordd	Haverfordwest
Lacharn	Laugharne
Landimor	Landimore
Larnog	Lavernock
Lecwydd	Leckwith
Llanandras	Presteigne
Llanarthne	Llanarthney
Llanbadog	Llanbadog
Llanbedr	Llanbeder
Llanbedr Felffre	Lampeter Velfrey
Llanbedr Pont Steffan	Lampeter
Llanbydderi	Llanbethery
Llancaeach	Llancaiach
Llancaeo	Llancillo
Llancatal	Llancadle
Llandaf	Llandaff
Llan-dawg	Llandawke
Llanddewi Felffre	Llanddewi Velfrey
Llanddewi Nant Hodni	Llanthony
Llanddingad	Dingestow
Llanddinol	Itton
Llandeilo Bertholau	Llantilio Pertholey
Llandeilo Gresynni	Llantilio Crossenny
Llanddunwyd	Welsh St. Donats
Llandegfedd	Llandegveth
Llandeilo Ferwallt	Bishopston
Llandenni	Llandenny
Llandudoch	St. Dogmaels
Llandw	Llandow

Llandyfai	Lamphey
Llandyfalle	Llandefalle
Llanedern	Llanedeyrn
Llanedi	Llanedy
Llaneirwg	St. Mellons
Llanelen	Llanellen
Llaneleu	Llanelieu
Llanelltud	Llanelltyd
Llanelwy	St. Asaph
Llanfable	Llanvapley
Llanfaches	Llanvaches
Llanfaes	Llanmaes
Llan-fair	St. Mary Church
Llanfair Isgoed	Llanvair Discoed
Llanfair Llythynwg	Gladestry
Llanfair-ym-Muallt	Builth Wells
Llanfarthin	Llanmartin
Llanfeuthin	Llanvithyn
Llanfihangel-ar-Elai	Michaelston-super-Ely
Llanfihangel Crucornau	Llanvihangel Crucorney
Llanfihangel Troddi	Mitchel Troy
Llanfihangel y Bont-faen	Llanmihangel
Llanfihangel-y-fedw	Michaelston-y-Vedw
Llanfihangel-y-gofion	Llanvihangel Gobion
Llanfihangel-y-pwll	Michaelston-le-Pit
Llanfihangel Ystum Llywern	Llanvihangel Ystern Llewern
Llanfleiddan	Llanblethian
Llanfocha	St. Maughan's
Llangatwg	Llangattock
Llangatwg Dyffryn Wysg	Llangattock nigh Usk
Llangatwg Feibion Afel	Llangattock Vibon Avel
Llangatwg Lingoed	Llangattock Lingoed
Llangeinwyr	Llangeinor
Llangiwa	Llangua
Llangofen	Llangofen
Llangors	Llangorse
Llangrallo	Coychurch
Llangybi	Llangibby
Llangyfiw	Llangeview
Llamgynnwr	Llangunnor
Llangynydd	Llangennith
Llanhari	Llanharry
Llanhiledd	Llanhilleth
Llanilltern	Capel Llanilltern
Llanilltud Faerdref	Llantwit Fardre
Llanilltud Fawr	Llantwit Major
Llanisien	Llanishen

Llanismel	St. Ishmael
Llan-lwy	Llandeloy
Llannarth	Llanarth
Llannewydd	Newchurch (Dyfed)
Llanofer Fawr	Llanover
Llanrheithan	Llanreithan
Llanrhian	Llanrian
Llan Sain Siôr	St. George (Clwyd)
Llan Sain Siôr	St. George's (South Glamorgan)
Llansanffraid-ar-Elai	St. Bride's-super-Ely
Llansanffraid Gwynllwg	St. Bride's Wentlloog
Llansanwyr	Llansannor
Llansawel	Briton Ferry
Llan-soe	Llansoy
Llansteffan	Llanstephan
Llantrisaint (or Llantrissent)	Llantrisant
Llantydewi	St. Dogwells
Llanwarw	Wonastow
Llanwytherin	Llanvetherine
Llanychar	Llanychaer Bridge
Llanymddyfri	Llandovery
Llwyneliddon	St. Lythans
Llysfaen	Lisvane
Llyswyrny	Llysworney
Maenorbyr	Manorbier
Maerdy	Mardy
Maerun	Marshfield
Maesyfed	New Radnor
Magwyr	Magor
Mamheilad	Mamhilad
Marcroes	Marcross
Matham	Mathern
Mathri	Mathry
Meisgyn	Miskin
Melin If an Ddu	Blackmill
Morfil	Morvil
Mynwar	Minwear
Mynwent y Crynwyr	Quaker's Yard
Nant-y-deri	Nant-y-derry
Niwdwl	Newgale
Nyfer	Nevern
Ogwr	Ogmore
Pant-teg	Panteg
Pedair-hewl	Four Roads
Penarlag	Hawarden
Pen-bre	Pembrey
Pencam	Pelcomb

Pencraig	Old Radnor
Pendeulwyn	Pendoylan
Penffordd-Las	Staylittle
Penfro	Pembroke
Pengelli-ddrain	Grovesend
Penhelyg	Penhelig
Penmarc	Penmark
Pentremeurig	Pentre Meyrick
Pomtarfynach	Devil's Bridge
Pontaman	Pontamman
Pont-henri	Pont Henry
Pontneddfechan	Pontneathvaughan
Pontrhydyrynn	Pontrhydyrun
Pontsenni	Sennybridge
Pont-y-pwl	Pontypool
Port Einon	Port Eynon
Porth Sgiwed	Portskewett
Radur	Radyr (South Glamorgan)
Radur	Rhadyr (Gwent)
Rhaeadr Gwy	Rhayader
Rhaglan	Raglan
Rhisga	Risca
Rhiwabon	Ruabon
Rhiwbeina	Rhiwbina
Rhiwderyn	Rhiwderin
Rhoscrowdder	Rhoscrowther
Rhos-goch	Red Roses
Rhos-hyl	Rhos-hill
Rhuthun	Ruthin (Clwyd)
Rhuthun	Ruthin (South Glamorgan)
Rhydri	Rudry
Rhymni	Rhymney
Sain Dunwyd	St. Donats
Sain Ffagan	St. Fagans
Sain Ffred	St. Brides
Sain Nicolas	St. Nicholas (Dyfed and South Glamorgan)
Sain Pedrog	St. Petrox
Sain Silian	St. Julians
Saint Andras	St. Andrews Major
Sain Tathan	St. Athan
Saint-y-brid	St. Bride's Major
Sancler	St. Clears
Sgethrog	Scethrog
Sgiwen	Skewen
Sili	Sully
Silstwn	Gileston

Slebets	Slebech
Solfach	Solva
Sychdyn	Soughton
Talbenni	Talbenny
Talyllychau	Talley
Trap	Trapp
Trawsgoed	Crosswood
Trebefered	Boverton
Tredynog	Tredunnock
Trefaldwyn	Montgomery
Trefalun	Trevalyn
Trefaser	Trefasser
Trefdraeth	Newport (Dyfed)
Trefelen	Bletherston
Trefesgob	Bishton
Trefflemin	Flemingston
Trefforest	Treforest
Treffynnon	Holywell
Trefin	Trevine
Trefonnen	Nash
Trefor	Trevor (Clwyd and Gwynedd)
Treforgan	Morganstown
Trefwrdan	Jordanston
Trefyclo	Knighton
Trefynwy	Monmouth
Tregolwyn	Colwinston
Tre-groes	Whitchurch (Dyfed)
Tre-gŵyr	Gowerton
Trelales	Laleston
Treletert	Letterston
Treopert	Granston
Treorci	Treorchy
Tre'r-gaer	Tregare
Tresimwn	Bonvilston
Treteio	Tretio
Tretomas	Thomastown
Tretwr	Tretower
Trewallter	Walterston
Trewiliam	Williamstown
Trewyddel	Moylgrove
Trostre	Trostrey
Tryleg	Trelleck
Tyddewi	St. David's
Tŷ-dû	Rogerstone
Waltwn Dwyrain	Walton East
Waltwn Gorllewin	Walton West
Wrecsam	Wrexham

Y Barri	Barry
Y Batel	Battle
Y Bont-faen	Cowbridge (South Glamorgan)
Y Bont-faen	Pontfaen (Dyfed)
Y Clas-ar-Wy	Glasbury
Y Crwys	Three Crosses
Y Ddraenen Wen	Hawthorn
Y Ddwyryd	Druid
Y Drenewydd	Newton (South Glamorgan)
Y Drenewudd	Newtown (Powys)
Y Faenor	Vaynor
Y Fan	Van (Powys)
Y Farteg	Varteg
Y Ferwig	Verwick
Y Fflint	Flint
Y Forlan	Vorlan
Y Garn	Roch
Y Gelli	Hay-on-Wye
Y Goetre-hen	Coytrahen
Ynysgynwraidd	Skenfrith
Ynysowen	Merthyr Vale
Y Pil	Pyle
Yr As Fawr	Monknash
Yr Eglwys Lwyd	Ludchurch
Yr Eglwys Newydd	Newchurch (Powys)
Yr Eglwys Newydd ar y Cefn	Newchurch (Gwent)
Yr Hengastell	Oldcastle
Y Rhws	Rhoose
Yr Orsedd	Rossett
Yr Wyddgrug	Mold
Y Sblot	Splottlands
Ystras-fflur	Strata Florida
Y Trallwng	Welshpool
Y Transh	Tranch
Y Tymbl	Tumble
Y Waun	Chirk
Y Wig	Wick

Less widely spoken than Welsh and less likely to be found in address databases, though still commonly used in Ross, the Isle of Skye and the Western Isles, this list provides the Scottish Gaelic equivalents of place names in Scotland:

English	*Scottish Gaelic*
Aberdeen	Obair Dheathain
Airdrie	Àrdruigh
Arbroath	Obair Bhrothaig

Ardrossan	Àrd Trossain
Arran	Arrain
Ayr	Inbhir Àir
Ballingry	Bail' a Gharaidh
Balloch	Bealach
Balquhidder	Both phuidir
Banff	Banbh
Barra	Barraidh
Berwick	Bearuig
Black Isle	An t-Eilean Dubh
Bridge of Allan	Drochaid Ailein
Bridge of Dee	Drochaid Dèagh
Cambuslang	Camus Long
Cambelltown	Ceannloch
Charlestown	Baile Thearlaich
Coatbridge	Drochaid a' Chota
Cowal	Còmhal
Culross	Cùl Rois
Cumbernauld	Comar nan Allt
Dalkeith	Dail Ché
Dingwall	Inbhir Pheofharain
Dumbarton	Dun Breatunn
Dumfries	Dun Fris
Dunblane	Dun Blathan
Dundee	Dun Dèagh
Edinburgh	Dun Eideann
Falkirk	An Eaglais Bhreac
Fort William	An Gearasdan / Gearadan Inbhir Lòchaidh
Fraserburgh	Baile nam Frisealach
Glasgow	Glaschu
Golspie	Goillspidh
Greenock	Grianaig
Harris	Na h-Earradh
Inverness	Inbhir Nis
Iona	Ì Chaluim Chille / Eilean Ì
Islay	Ìle

Jura	Diùra
Kilmarnock	Cill Mheàrnag
Kilsyth	Cillsaidh
Kincardin	Cinn Chardainn
Kirkudbright	Cille Chuithbeirt
Kirkwall	Baile na h-Eaglaise
Lanark	Leanndraic
Largs	Na Leargaidh
Lewis	Leòdhas
Linlithgow	Gleann Iucha
Loch Lomond	Loch Laomuinn
Loch Ness	Loch Nis
Lochgilphead	Ceann Loch Gilp
Milngavie	Muileann Dhaibhidh
Mull	Muile
Mussleburgh	Baile nam Fiasgan
Nairn	Inbhir Narunn
North Uist	Uibhist my Thuath
Oban	An t-Oban
Paisley	Paislig
Perth	Peairt
Peterhead	Ceann Phàdruig
Pitlochry	Baile Chloichridh
Portree	Port Rìgh
Rothesay	Baile Bhóid
Skye	An t-Eilean Sgitheanach
South Uist	Uibhist mu Dheas
Stewarton	Baile nan Stiùbhartach
Stirling	Sruighlea
Stonehaven	Caladh nan Clach
Stonehouse	Taigh nan Clach
Stornoway	Steòrnabhaig
Stranraer	Sròn Reamhair
Tain	Baile Dubhthaich
The Lothians	Lodainn
The Trossachs	Na Tròiseachan
Tillicoultry	Tulaich Caoltraigh

Uist	Uibhist
Ullapool	Ullapul
Wick	Inbhir Ùig

Irish Gaelic is spoken in parts of Belfast and in parts of the counties of Armagh and Fermanagh in Northern Ireland. The use of the Irish Gaelic or English settlement name is closely tied to the political opinions of the user concerning the future of Northern Ireland as part of the United Kingdom (English place names) or as part of Ireland (Irish Gaelic place names). Given the civil unrest in this part of the United Kingdom, you should consider very carefully indeed before using Irish Gaelic place names except where your contact person has used them him/herself. This list provides the Irish Gaelic equivalents of place names in Northern Ireland:

English	*Irish Gaelic*
Armagh	Ard Mhacha
Ballymena	An Baile Meánach
Ballymoney	Baile Monaidh
Bangor	Beannchar
Belfast	Béal Feirste
Carrickfergus	Carraig Fhearghais
Coleraine	Cúil Raithin
Larne	Latharna
Lisburn	Lios na gCearrbhach
Londonderry / Derry	Doire / Doire Cholm Cille
Newtonabbey	Baile na Mainistreach
Newry	An tIúr (Iúr Chinn Trá)
Omagh	An Ómaigh
Portadown	Port an Dúnáin

There are few rules to govern the correct punctuation of town names. A good place to look for correct spellings is Oliver Mason's *Bartholomew Gazetteer of Places in Britain*. The UK has many charmingly and idiosyncratically named settlements, and space limitations do not allow me to list all of them. However, the list below, limited to settlements with more than 5 000 inhabitants (2 000 for settlements in Scotland or Wales) shows the correct way of writing the names of settlements which can be wrongly or alternatively spelt, with their respective postal codes:

Settlement	*Postal code*
Ackworth Moor Top	WF7
Adwick le Street	DN6
Alderley Edge	SK9
Annfield Plain	DH9
Ashby-de-la-Zouch	LE65
Ashton-in-Makerfield	WN4
Ashton-under-Lyne	OL5-7
Barnard Castle	DL12

Barrow-in-Furness	LA13-14
Barton-upon-Humber	DN18
Barton on Sea	SO41
Bayston Hill	SY3
Berwick-upon-Tweed	TD15
Bettws-y-Coed	LL24
Bexhill-on-Sea	TN39-40
Bishop Auckland	DL13-14
Bishop's Cleeve	GL52
Bishop's Stortford	CM22-23
Blackhall Colliery	TS27
Blaenau Ffestiniog	LL41
Blandford Forum	DT11
Blaydon-on-Tyne	NE21
Bo'ness	EH51
Boar's Hill	OX1
Bognor Regis	PO21-22
Bolton-le-Sands	LA5
Boston Spa	LS23
Bourne End	SL8
Bradford-on-Avon	BA15
Bridge of Allan	FK9
Bridge of Weir	PA11
Bromley Cross	BL7
Builth Wells	LD2
Burgess Hill	RH15
Burley in Wharfedale	LS29
Burnham-on-Crouch	CM0
Burnham-on-Sea	TA8
Burry Port	SA16
Burscough Bridge	L40
Burton Latimer	NN15
Burton upon Trent	DE13-15
Bury St Edmunds	IP28-33
Caister-on-Sea	NR30
Canvey Island	SS8
Carlton in Lindrick	S81
Castle Donington	DE74
Catterick Garrison	DL9
Cefn-Mawr	LL14
Chalfont St Giles	HP8
Chalfont St Peter	SL9
Chapel-en-le-Frith	SK12
Charlton Kings	GL52-53
Chester-le-Street	DH2-3
Chipping Norton	OX7
Chipping Ongar	CM

Chipping Sodbury	BS17
Church Village	CF38
Clacton on Sea	CO15-16
Clay Cross	S45
Clayton-le-Moors	BB5
Cleator Moor	CA25
Colwyn Bay	LL28-29
Connah's Quay	CH5
Conon Bridge	IV7
Coupar Angus	PH13
Cove Bay	AB1
Cross Hands	SA14, SA67
Dalgety Bay	KY11
Dalton-in-Furness	LA15
Dinas Powis	CF6
Easton-in-Gordano	BS20
Eaton Socon	PE19
Ebbw Vale	NP3
Ellesmere Port	L65-66
Farnham Royal	SL2
Fort William	PH33
Gilfach Goch	CF39
Glyn-Neath	SA11
Guide Post	NE62
Gwaun-Cae-Gurwen	SA18
Hayling Island	PO11
Haywards Heath	RH16-17
Hazel Grove	SK7
Hedge End	SO3
Hemel Hempstead	HP1-3
Henley-in-Arden	B95
Henley-on-Thames	RG9
Herne Bay	CT6
Hetton-le-Hole	DH5
Higham Ferrers	NN9
Higher Walton	PR + WA
Houghton-le-Spring	DH4-5
Hoyland Nether	S74
Huyton-with-Roby	L36
Ince-in-Makerfield	WN
Isle of Walney (or Walney Island)	LE
Iver Heath	SL0
King's Lynn	PE30-34
Kings Langley	WD4
Kingston upon Hull (more commonly known as Hull)	HU
Kingston upon Thames	KT1-2

Kirby Muxloe	LE
Lee-on-the-Solent	PO13
Leighton Buzzard	LU7
Little Lever	BL3
Llandrindod Wells	LD1
Llandudno Junction	LL31
Llantwit Fardre	CF38
Llantwit Major	CF6
Locks Heath	SO3
Lytham St Anne's	FY8
Mansfield Woodhouse	NG19
Marske-by-the-Sea	TS11
Melton Mowbray	LE13-14
Menai Bridge	LL59
Merthyr Tydfil	CF47-48
Merthyr Vale	CF48
Milford Haven	SA73
Milton Keynes	MK
Milton of Campsie	G65
Mountain Ash	CF45
Newark-on-Trent	NG22-24
Newbiggin-by-the-Sea	NE64
Newcastle-under-Lyme	ST5
Newcastle upon Tyne	NE
Newport on Tay	DD6
Newport Pagnell	MK16
Newton-le-Willows	WA12
Newton Abbot	TQ12-13
Newton Aycliffe	DL5
Newton Mearns	G77
Newton Stewart	DG8
Norton Canes	WS11
Ogmore Vale	CF32
Paddock Wood	TN12
Pembroke Dock	SA72
Penrhyn Bay	LL30
Port Glasgow	PA14
Port Talbot	SA12-13
Potters Bar	EN6
Poulton-le-Fylde	FY6
Princes Risborough	HP27
Radcliffe on Trent	NG12
Richmond upon Thames	TW9-10
Ross-on-Wye	HR9
Royal Tunbridge Wells	TN1-4
Saltburn-by-the-Sea	TS12-13
Seven Sisters	SA10

Shepton Mallet	BA4
Sonning Common	RG4
Southend-on-Sea	SS1-3
Sowerby Bridge	HX6
Stanford le Hope	SS17
Stansted Mountfitchet	CM24
Stockton-on-Tees	TS
Stockton Heath	WA4
Stoke-on-Trent	ST
Stoke Poges	SL2-3
Stourport-on-Severn	DY13
Stratford-upon-Avon	CV37
Sunbury-on-Thames	TW16
Sutton Coldfield	B72-75
Sutton in Ashfield	NG17
Taff's Well	CF4
Telford Dawley	TF4
Ushaw Moor	DH7
Virginia Water	GU25
Waltham Abbey	EN9
Walton-on-Thames	KT12
Wath upon Dearne	S63
Welwyn Garden City	AL7-8
Westbury-on-Trym	BS9
Weston-super-Mare	BS22-24
Westward Ho!	EX39
Whitley Bay	NE25-26
Wide Open	NE13
Wimborne Minster	BH21
Woburn Sands	MK17
Wootton Bassett	SN4

Londonderry, in Northern Ireland, is known to some of the population as Derry. The use of either name is heavily politically coloured, and care needs to be taken. Use the same version that the contact person uses.

Furthermore, there is generally no hyphenation for names beginning with the following words:

Bishop
Castle
East
Far
Great
Greater
High
Higher
Lesser

Little
Low
Lower
Market
Mid
Middle
Near
Nether
New
North
Old
St
South
The
Upper
West
Y
Yr

In some databases, these words may sometimes be found following the rest of the settlement name in this way:

Tew, Great

Saint is always printed as St.

Administrative districts

There have been a number of re-organizations of counties and other administrative districts within the United Kingdom in the past 25 years which has caused confusion especially in the use of these names in addresses. Counties have been merged, un-merged and had name changes. Many people still use county names in addresses, though they may use old (pre-1974) names, new names, or the name that was used in the intervening period. Some still use the names of counties which no longer exist. To add to this confusion, administrative areas which are not counties but have the same administrative rôle as counties, have been brought into being. The British Post Office have not made changes to the official way that counties are used in addresses to conform to the most recent changes.

It is not necessary to use a county in an address provided that the postal code is used. Given the problems in identifying the correct county name, it is probably best not to add them to addresses at all unless you have a good reason to do so.

For a small number of addresses, especially for those near a county boundary, the county added to the address is not necessarily that where the address is geographically situated - it may be that of the postal town.

The following list of counties provides common abbreviations in brackets. Those names followed by an asterisk (*) are newly created districts and are unlikely to be in common usage in addresses. Those followed by the symbol (†) no longer exist as counties but may still be found in address databases. Those followed by the symbol (‡) are counties or districts which were abolished in 1974 but have recently been re-incarnated. Those followed by the symbol (§) are new urban districts which are unlikely to become used as county names - the old county will be used.

England

Avon (†)
Bath and North East Somerset (*)
Bedfordshire (Beds)
(Royal) Berkshire (Berks)
Bournemouth (*)(§)
Brighton & Hove (*)(§)
Buckinghamshire (Bucks)
Cambridgeshire (Cambs)
Cheshire
City of Bristol (*)(§)
City of Kingston upon Hull (*)(§)
City of Stoke-on-Trent (*)(§)
Cleveland (†)
Cornwall
Cumbria
Darlington (*)(§)
Derby City (*)(§)
Derbyshire
Devon
Dorset
(County) Durham
East Riding of Yorkshire (‡)
East Sussex (E Sussex)
East Yorkshire (E Yorks)
Essex
Gloucestershire (Glos)
Greater London
Greater Manchester
Hampshire (Hants)
Hartlepool (*)(§)
Hereford & Worcester
Hertfordshire (Herts)
Isle of Wight
Isles of Scilly (*)
Kent
Lancashire (Lancs)
Leicester City (*)(§)
Leicestershire (Leics)
Lincolnshire (Lincs)
Luton (*)(§)
Merseyside
Middlesbrough (*)(§)

Milton Keynes (*)(§)
Norfolk
North Lincolnshire (*)
North East Lincolnshire (*)
North Somerset (*)
North Yorkshire (N Yorks)
Northamptonshire (Northants)
Northumberland (Northd)
Nottinghamshire (Notts)
Oxfordshire (Oxon)
Poole (*)(§)
Portsmouth City (*)(§)
Redcar and Cleveland (*)
Rutland (‡)
Shropshire (for a short period renamed Salop)
Somerset
South Gloucestershire (*)
South Yorkshire (S Yorks)
Southampton City (*)(§)
Staffordshire (Staffs)
Stockton-on-Tees (*)(§)
Suffolk
Surrey
Swindon (*)(§)
Tyne and Wear
Warwickshire
West Midlands (W Midlands)
West Sussex (W Sussex)
West Yorkshire (W Yorks)
Wiltshire (Wilts)
York (*)(§)

Wales

Blaenau Gwent (*)
Bridgend (*)
Caerphilly (*)
Cardiff (*)
Carmarthenshire (‡)
Clwyd (†)
Conwy (*)
Ceredigion (*)
Denbighshire (‡)
Dyfed (†)
Flintshire (‡)
Gwent (†)
Gwynedd
Isle of Anglesey
Merthyr Tydfil (*)
Mid Glamorgan (M Glam) (†)

Monmouthshire (‡)
Neath Port Talbot (*)
Newport (*)
Pembrokeshire (‡)
Powys
Rhondda Cynon Taff (*)
South Glamorgan (S Glam) (†)
Swansea (*)
Torfaen (*)
Vale of Glamorgan (*)
West Glamorgan (W Glam) (†)
Wrexham (*)

Scotland

Aberdeen City (*)(§)
Aberdeenshire (‡)
Angus (‡)
Argyll & Bute
Central (†)
City of Edinburgh (*)(§)
Dumfries and Galloway
Dundee City (*) (§)
East Ayrshire (*)
East Dunbartonshire (*)
East Lothian (‡)
East Renfrewshire (*)
Falkirk
Fife
Glasgow City (*)(§)
Grampian (†)
Highland
Inverclyde (*)
Lothian (counties of East Lothian, Lothian, West Lothian)
Midlothian (‡)
Moray (‡)
North Ayrshire (*)
North Lanarkshire (*)
Orkney
Perth and Kinross (*)
Renfrewshire (‡)
Scottish Borders
Shetland
South Ayrshire (*)
South Lanarkshire (*)
Stirling (‡)
Strathclyde (†)
Tayside (†)
The Clackmannanshire (‡)

West Dunbartonshire (*)
West Lothian (‡)
Western Isles

Northern Ireland

County Antrim
County Armagh
County (London)Derry
County Down
County Fermanagh
County Tyrone

Crown dependencies

Alderney
Guernsey
Isle of Man
Jersey
Sark

Counties may be written in addresses without the word 'shire', especially where the county is named after a town. Thus, Gloucestershire is often written as Gloucester, Oxfordshire as Oxford, etc. This is especially the case with the old Scottish counties, where the 'shire' is rarely used.

If you want to use counties in addresses, it is necessary to note a number of idiosyncratic differences between the existing administrative regions and the county names that the Royal Mail prefers are used in addresses. These idiosyncrasies are as follows:

1. In Scotland, the administrative regions which replaced the old counties in 1975 are not referred to at all by the Post Office. The old county names are still used. The old Scottish counties are as follows:

Aberdeenshire
Angus
Argyllshire
Ayrshire
Banffshire
Berwickshire
Buteshire
Caithness
Clackmannanshire
Dumfriesshire
Dunbarton
East Lothian
Fife
Inverness-shire
Kincardineshire

Kinross-shire
Kircudbrightshire
Lanarkshire
Midlothian
Morayshire
Nairnshire
Peeblesshire
Perthshire
Renfrewshire
Ross & Cromarty
Roxburghshire
Selkirkshire
Stirlingshire
Sutherland
West Lothian
Wigtownshire

2. For London, the Post Office uses the pre-1965 boundary. So, for example, Harrow is addressed as Middlesex, and Sidcup as Kent. Middlesex no longer exists as a county but is still used in postal addresses.
3. The county name Hereford & Worcester is not used by the Post Office. The separate names Herefordshire and Worcestershire are used.

London boroughs will often be found in addresses. In order to be able to recognise these, a list of the currently existing boroughs follows:

Barking and Dagenham
Barnet
Bexley
Brent
Bromley
Camden
City of London
City of Westminster
Croydon
Ealing
Enfield
Greenwich
Hackney
Hammersmith and Fulham
Haringey
Harrow
Havering
Hillingdon
Hounslow
Islington
Kensington and Chelsea
Kingston upon Thames

Lambeth
Lewisham
Merton
Newham
Redbridge
Richmond upon Thames
Southwark
Sutton
Tower Hamlets
Waltham Forest
Wandsworth

United States of America

Official name: United States of America
Area: 9 160 454 sq. km (3 535 935 sq. miles)
Population: 255 600 000
Capital: Washington
Currency: 1 United States Dollar ($, US$) = 100 cents
International telephone access code: 1

Languages

The official language is English (210 000 000 first-language speakers). There are 175 other indigenous languages (including Indian languages) and large numbers of imported languages. The state of New Mexico is officially bilingual English and Spanish, and there are large Spanish-speaking minorities in certain areas of the United States. There are a total of 22 400 000 Spanish-speakers. Addresses may be found written in Spanish, especially in states along the Mexican border and in Florida. There are an estimated 1 000 000 speakers of Cajun French and Louisiana Creole French in Southern Louisiana. About half the population of the state of Hawaii speak Hawai'i Creole English, about 150 000 of whom do not also speak standard English. There are some 650 000 Vlach Romani-speakers.

Different languages are spoken in the United States Territories which are included in the United States' Postal Service coverage - please see the chapters on each of these for the relevant information.

Address Formats

The USPS (United States' Postal Service) have strict guidelines on address format. Following these guidelines requires upper casing and abbreviation of address elements which will enable you to take advantage of mailing discounts but will result in highly unattractive address layouts.

The address should contain

- standard abbreviations
- no punctuation
- be in upper case
- contain the full 5+4 postal code (ZIP®+4)

The address is formatted as follows:

NAME
NUMBER[ ]THOROUGHFARE{[ ]APARTMENT INDICATOR}
CITY[ ]STATE ABBREVIATION[ ]POSTAL CODE

For example, the address:

Mr S. Holmes
2978 West Main Street # 12
Minneapolis MN 23876

is written as preferred by the USPS:

MR S HOLMES
2978 W MAIN ST # 12
MINNEAPOLIS MN 23976-4542

There should be two spaces between the state abbreviation and the postal code.

The abbreviation "RR" indicates "Rural Route" (*ruta rural* in Spanish) and is formatted in address lines as, for example:

RR 5 BOX 12 A

The hash (#) symbol is used to indicate a floor or apartment number following the street name. The apartment may also be written on its own on a line above the thoroughfare information as follows:

MR S HOLMES
APT 12
2978 W MAIN ST
MINNEAPOLIS MN 23976-4542

When both a street address and a postbox number are used in the same address block, the mail will be delivered to the point to which the postal code refers.

The United States mail system includes a number of Pacific and Caribbean Island dependencies. When mail is addressed to one of these, the island name may be included in the address. The format then becomes:

SETTLEMENT
ISLAND[ ]STATE CODE[ ]POSTAL CODE

for example

SAIPAN
MARIANA ISLANDS MP 96950

The abbreviations APO (Army Post Office) and FPO (Fleet Post Office) are used for armed forces mail. They have the state code AA, AE or AP according to their geographical location. The street address line is replaced by unit numbers, ship names and so on. An example address last line might read:

APO AE 09081

Foreign city of country names in armed forces mail should not be used.

For dependents residing with military personnel, a "c/o" must be used:

MS G SMITH
C/O MSG H SMITH
REST OF ADDRESS

Though not included in official lists from the USPS, addresses may contain Spanish thoroughfare types (see chapter on Spain for a list of these). The USPS regards them as part of the thoroughfare name rather than a thoroughfare type. However, if addressing in mixed case, be sure to write the Spanish thoroughfare types commencing with a lower-case letter.

For Puerto Rico, where addresses are written in Spanish, the most important part of the address is the Urbanization District (*Urb*). These may be known as *extensiones, jardines, mansiones, parques, repartos* or *villas*. If these names are present, the word *Urb* is then obsolete. For example:

SR JUAN CARLOS
URB LOS AMIGOS
23 CALLE JUANITA
SAN JUAN PR 00602-1211

Building Indicators (Unit Designators)

This is the United States Postal Service's official list of building indicators and abbreviations. The USPS prefers that the abbreviation, in upper case, is used in addresses.

Full String	*Required Abbreviation*
APARTMENT	APT
BASEMENT	BSMT
BUILDING	BLDG
DEPARTMENT	DEPT
FLOOR	FL
FRONT	FRNT
HANGAR	HNGR
LOBBY	LBBY
LOT	LOT
LOWER	LOWR
OFFICE	OFC
PENTHOUSE	PH
PIER	PIER
REAR	REAR
ROOM	RM
SIDE	SIDE
SLIP	SLIP
SPACE	SPC
STOP	STOP

SUITE	STE
TRAILER	TRLR
UNIT	UNIT
UPPER	UPPR

Thoroughfare Types

This is the United States Postal Service's official list of thoroughfare types and abbreviations. The USPS prefers that the abbreviation, in upper case, is used in addresses.

Full String	*Required Abbreviation*
ALLEY	ALY
ANNEX	ANX
ARCADE	ARC
AVENUE	AVE
BAYOO	BYU
BEACH	BCH
BEND	BND
BLUFF	BLF
BLUFFS	BLFS
BOTTOM	BTM
BOULEVARD	BLVD
BRANCH	BR
BRIDGE	BRG
BROOK	BRK
BROOKS	BRKS
BURG	BG
BURGS	BGS
BYPASS	BYP
CAMP	CP
CANYON	CYN
CAPE	CPE
CAUSEWAY	CSWY
CENTER	CTR
CENTERS	CTRS
CIRCLE	CIR
CIRCLES	CIRS
CLIFF	CLF
CLIFFS	CLFS
CLUB	CLB
COMMON	CMN
CORNER	COR
CORNERS	CORS
COURSE	CRSE
COURT	CT
COURTS	CTS
COVE	CV

COVES	CVS
CREEK	CRK
CRESCENT	CRES
CREST	CRST
CROSSING	XING
CROSSROAD	XRD
CURVE	CURV
DALE	DL
DAM	DM
DIVIDE	DV
DRIVE	DR
DRIVES	DRS
ESTATE	EST
ESTATES	ESTS
EXPRESSWAY	EXPY
EXTENSION	EXT
EXTENSIONS	EXTS
FALLS	FLS
FERRY	FRY
FIELD	FLD
FIELDS	FLDS
FLATS	FLTS
FORD	FRD
FORDS	FRDS
FOREST	FRST
FORGE	FRG
FORGES	FRGS
FORK	FRK
FORKS	FRKS
FORT	FT
FREEWAY	FWY
GARDEN	GDN
GARDENS	GDNS
GATEWAY	GTWY
GLEN	GLN
GLENS	GLNS
GREEN	GRN
GREENS	GRNS
GROVE	GRV
GROVES	GRVS
HARBOR	HBR
HARBORS	HBRS
HAVEN	HVN
HEIGHTS	HTS
HIGHWAY	HWY
HILL	HL
HILLS	HLS

HOLLOW	HOLW
HOUSE	HSE
INLET	INLT
ISLAND	IS
ISLANDS	ISS
ISLE	ISLE
JUNCTION	JCT
JUNCTIONS	JCTS
KEY	KY
KEYS	KYS
KNOLL	KNL
KNOLLS	KNLS
LAKE	LK
LAKES	LKS
LANDING	LNDG
LANE	LN
LIGHT	LGT
LIGHTS	LGTS
LOAF	LF
LOCK	LCK
LOCKS	LCKS
LODGE	LDG
LOOP	LOOP
MANOR	MNR
MANORS	MNRS
MARKET	MKT
MEADOW	MDW
MEADOWS	MDWS
MILL	ML
MILLS	MLS
MISSION	MSN
MOTORWAY	MTWY
MOUNT	MT
MOUNTAIN	MTN
MOUNTAINS	MTNS
NECK	NCK
ORCHARD	ORCH
OVAL	OVAL
OVERPASS	OPAS
PARK	PARK
PARKS	PARK
PARKWAY	PKWY
PARKWAYS	PKWY
PASS	PASS
PASSAGE	PSGE
PATH	PATH
PIKE	PIKE

PINE	PNE
PINES	PNES
PLACE	PL
PLAIN	PLN
PLAINS	PLNS
PLAZA	PLZ
POINT	PT
POINTS	PTS
PORT	PRT
PORTS	PRTS
PRAIRIE	PR
RADIAL	RADL
RAMP	RAMP
RANCH	RNCH
RAPID	RPD
RAPIDS	RPDS
REST	RST
RIDGE	RDG
RIDGES	RDGS
RIVER	RIV
ROAD	RD
ROADS	RDS
ROUTE	RTE
ROW	ROW
RUE	RUE
RUN	RUN
SHOAL	SHL
SHOALS	SHLS
SHORE	SHR
SHORES	SHRS
SKYWAY	SKWY
SPRING	SPG
SPRINGS	SPGS
SPUR	SPUR
SPURS	SPUR
SQUARE	SQ
SQUARES	SQS
STATION	STA
STRAVENUE	STRA
STREAM	STRM
STREET	ST
STREETS	STS
SUMMIT	SMT
TERRACE	TER
THROUGHWAY	TRWY
TRACE	TRCE
TRACK	TRAK

TRAFFICWAY	TRFY
TRAIL	TRL
TUNNEL	TUNL
TURNPIKE	TPKE
UNDERPASS	UPAS
UNION	UN
UNIONS	UNS
VALLEY	VLY
VALLEYS	VLYS
VIADUCT	VIA
VIEW	VW
VIEWS	VWS
VILLAGE	VLG
VILLAGES	VLGS
VILLE	VL
VISTA	VIS
WALK	WALK
WALKS	WALK
WALL	WALL
WAY	WAY
WAYS	WAYS
WELL	WL
WELLS	WLS

Postbox

This is known as PO Box or *Apartado* in Spanish.

Postal codes

Known as the *ZIP*® code, this can contain a block of 5 digits or, for more accurate delivery, 9 digits in this format:

99999[-]9999

This is known as *ZIP*® + 4.

Towns

New Orleans is known as *La Nouvelle Orléans* in French.

Administrative Areas

The United States consists of 50 states. The state code must be used in addresses between the settlement name and the postal code. State codes for mailing purposes have also been assigned to dependent and other overseas territories and ex-territories. The full list of codes is:

State	*Abbreviation*
Alabama	AL
Alaska	AK
American Samoa	AS (an unincorporated territory - postal code 96799)
Arizona	AZ
Arkansas	AR
California	CA
Colorado	CO
Connecticut	CT
Delaware	DE
District of Columbia	DC
Federated States of Micronesia	FM (became independent of the USA in 1979 - see below)
Florida	FL
Georgia	GA
Guam	GU (an unincorporated territory - postal codes 96910-31)
Hawaii	HI
Idaho	ID
Illinois	IL
Indiana	IN
Iowa	IA
Kansas	KS
Kentucky	KY
Louisiana	LA
Maine	ME
Marshall Islands	MH (became independent of the USA in 1986 - see below)
Maryland Massachusetts	MD MA
Michigan	MI
Minnesota	MN
Mississippi	MS
Missouri	MO
Montana	MT
Nebraska	NE
Nevada	NV
New Hampshire	NH
New Jersey	NJ
New Mexico	NM
New York	NY
North Carolina	NC
North Dakota	ND
Northern Mariana Islands	MP (commonwealth territory postal codes 96950-2)
Ohio	OH
Oklahoma	OK

Oregon	OR
Palau	PW (became independent of the USA in 1994 - see below)
Pennsylvania	PA
Puerto Rico	PR (commonwealth territory - postal codes 00601-799; 00901-999)
Rhode Island	RI
South Carolina	SC
South Dakota	SD
Tennessee	TN
Texas	TX
Trust Territories	TT
Utah	UT
Vermont	VT
Virgin Islands	VI (an unincorporated territory - -postal codes 00801-51)
Virginia	VA
Washington	WA
West Virginia	WV
Wisconsin	WI
Wyoming	WY

Military "State"	*Abbreviation*
Armed Forces Africa	AE
Armed Forces Americas (not Canada)	AA
Armed Forces Canada	AE
Armed Forces Europe	AE
Armed Forces Middle East	AE
Armed Forces Pacific	AP

The Pacific island states of Federated States of Micronesia, the Marshall Islands and Palau are all independent of the USA but are part of its postal system. They can be identified by their postal codes:

Federated States of Micronesia (FM)	96941-4
Marshall Islands (MH)	96960 and 96970
Palau (PW)	96940

Please see the relevant chapters on these countries.

United States Virgin Islands

United States Virgin Islands is an unincorporated territory of the United States. It forms part of the United States' postal system. The three inhabited islands are St Croix, St Thomas and St John.

Official name: United States Virgin Islands
Area: 342 sq. km (132 sq. miles)
Population: 101 809
Capital: Charlotte Amalie
Currency: 1 United States Dollar (US$) = 100 cents
International telephone access code: 1

Languages

The national language is English, with 8 414 mother-language speakers. There are some 52 250 speakers of Lesser Antillean Creole English.

Address Information

United States Virgin Islands forms part of the United States' postal system. Its state code is VI and its postal codes fall in the range 00801-51.

Please refer to the chapter on the United States of America for further information.

Telephone codes

All telephone numbers in the United States Virgin Islands have the area code 340.

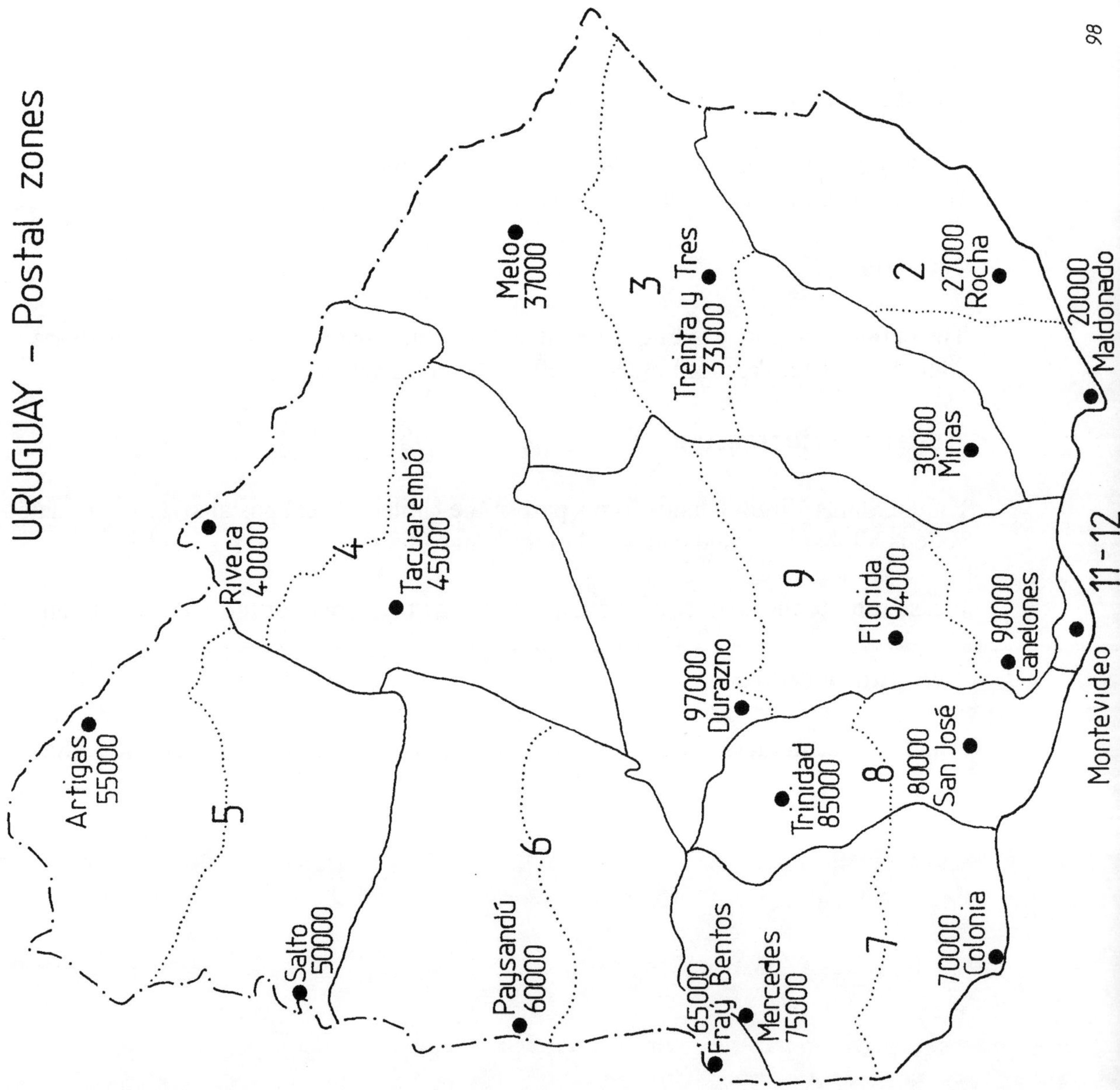
URUGUAY - Postal zones
Artigas 55000
Rivera 40000
Salto 50000
Tacuarembó 45000
Melo 37000
Paysandú 60000
65000 Fray Bentos
Mercedes 75000
97000 Durazno
Trinidad 85000
Treinta y Tres 33000
Florida 94000
80000 San José
70000 Colonia
30000 Minas
27000 Rocha
20000 Maldonado
90000 Canelones
Montevideo
2
3
4
5
6
7
8
9
11-12
98

Uruguay

Official name: Republic of Uruguay, República del Uruguay
Area: 176 215 sq. km (68 018 sq. miles)
Population: 3 130 000
Capital: Montevideo
Currency: 1 New Uruguayan Peso (Nur$m UrugN$) = 100 centésimos
International telephone access code: 598

Languages

The official language, Spanish, is spoken by virtually the whole population.

Address Format

Addresses are formatted:

Name
{thoroughfare type[ ]}Thoroughfare name[ ]number
postal code[ ]City

For example:

Sr. Julio Pérez
Buenos Aires 500
11000 Montevideo

As is usual in Spanish-speaking countries, if the thoroughfare type is *calle* (Street), then this is not written in the address. The thoroughfare type is written commencing with a lower-case letter. For a full list of thoroughfare types, please refer to the chapter on Spain.

Postal codes

Uruguayan postal codes consist of a block of 5 digits, commencing with a number between 1 and 9. The first digit indicates the region or department. The final two digits indicate a block of houses (in towns) or a village.

Uzbekistan
Ozbekiston Republikasy

Official name: Republic of Uzbekistan, Ozbekiston Republikasy
Area: 447 400 sq. km (172 696 sq. miles)
Population: 20 300 000
Capital: Tashkent
Currency: 1 Rouble (R) = 100 kopecks
International telephone access code: 7

Languages

The official language, Northern Uzbek, is spoken by some 71% of the population. There are large numbers of speakers of languages from other parts of the former Soviet Union, particularly Russian (1 661 000 speakers), Tajiki (934 000 speakers), Tatar (468 000 speakers) and Turkmen (228 000 speakers). Also spoken are Uzbeki Spoken Arabic (700 speakers); Bukharic (10 000 speakers); Crimean Turkish (189 000 speakers); Karakalpak and Turkish (197 000 speakers).

Example Address Format

Irgachev Abdulla Yaliévicke
rayon 13
dom 6, kvartira 5
702100 CHIRCHIK
TACHKENT oblast

Addresses are also found with this format inverted - i.e. with the region on the first line, then the postal code and settlement and so on. *Oblast* means region, *rayon* means district, *dom* means building and *kvartira* means apartment.

Postal codes

Postal codes consist of a block of 6 digits. This is the same code that was used before the independence of Uzbekistan from the Soviet Union. The code refers to a delivery post office.

Vatican City
Città del Vaticano

Official name: State of the Vatican City, Stato dell Città del Vaticano
Area: 0.44 sq. km (0.17 sq. miles)
Population: 752 (1988 estimate)
Currency: The Vatican has its own currency, and the monetary system is independent of that of Italy, although Italian Lire are valid within the Vatican. The Vatican coins are the gold lira 1000 (nominal), silver lira 500; 'Acmonital' lira 100 and 50, 'Italma' lira 10, 5 and 1, and 'bronzital' lira 20.
International telephone access code: 39

Languages

Latin is used for Church affairs, whilst the language used on a day-to-day basis is Italian.

Addresses

For details of address formats, please refer to the chapter on Italy.

Postal codes

All addresses within Vatican City share the postal code 00120.

Telephone numbers

The Vatican City forms part of the Italian Telephone system. The area code is 06 (shared with Rome and surrounds).

Venezuela

Official name: Republic of Venezuela, República de Venezuela
Area: 912 050 sq. km (352 051 sq. miles)
Population: 20 185 000
Capital: Caracas
Currency: 1 Bolivar (B) = 100 Céntimos
International telephone access code: 58

Languages

The official language is Spanish, spoken by 97% of the population. There are 39 other spoken languages, many Indian languages spoken in the interior. The most widely spoken of these is Wayuu (170 000 speakers).

Example address format

Sr. Pedro E. López
Apartado 60125
Chacao
CARACAS 1060, D.F.

or

Sr Juan Pérez
Edifico Exa, piso 8, oficina 302
avenida Francisco de Miranda entre Ppal
Country Club c/C Mohedano
CARACAS 1060 R.C. 10

The name of the administrative region may appear after the postal code or on the line above the postal code. This is the case in the example with the abbreviation *D.F. (Distrito Federal)*. *R.C.* in the second example indicates a route carrier number.

The administrative regions are:

Amazonas
Anzoátegui
Apure
Aragua
Barinas
Bolívar
Carabobo
Cojedes
Delta Amacuro
Distrito Federal
Falcón
Guárico

Lara
Mérida
Miranda
Monagas
Nueva Esparta
Portuguesa
Sucre
Táchira
Trujillo
Yaracuy
Zulia

When addresses are written in Spanish, *calle*, the Spanish word for street, is rarely written. The Spanish thoroughfare type, when included, is written before, and separately from, the thoroughfare name. It should be written with the first letter in lower case.

Postbox

The word for postbox is *Apartado* or *Apdo.*

Postal codes

These consist of a block of 4 digits written after the settlement name. The first two digits refer to the region, the final two to the delivery office.

Administrative Regions

One of the 23 region names may be found in addresses. Please see the section on 'Example address format'.

Vietnam
Công Hòa Xã Hôi Chu Nghĩa Viêt Nam

Official name: Socialist Republic of Vietnam, Công Hòa Xã Hôi Chu Nghĩa Viêt Nam
Area: 329 566 sq. km (127 212 sq. miles)
Population: 69 200 000
Capital: Hanoi
Currency: 1 Dông = 10 hao = 100 xu
International telephone access code: 84

Languages

Vietnam has 86 languages. The official language is Vietnamese (65 051 000 speakers). Other widespread languages are: Yue Chinese (500 000 speakers); Hre (100 000 speakers); Iu Mien (300 000 speakers); Central Khmer (700 000 speakers); Muong (767 000 speakers); Nung (700 000 speakers); Phu Thai (150 000 speakers); Rade (120 000 speakers); Tai Daeng (100 000 speakers); Tai Dam (500 000 speakers); Tai Dón (190 000 speakers) and Tày (1 000 000 speakers).

54 ethnic communities are recognized by the Vietnamese authorities, and recognized language use is equally diverse.

Example Address Format

Lam Hoang Vinh
18 Nguyen Du Street
HANOI 10000

Postal codes

Postal codes consist of a block of 5 digits. The first two digits indicate the province or city, the last one the post office.

Towns

Ho Chi Minh City is sometimes still referred to incorrectly as Saigon. It is known as *Ho Chi Minh Ville* in French.

Wallis and Futuna
Wallis et Futuna

Wallis and Futuna is an Overseas Territory of France. It forms part of the French mail system.

Area: 274 sq. km (106 sq. miles)
Population: 16 000
Capital: Matu Utu
Currency: 1 French Franc (Ffr) = 100 centimes
International telephone access code: 681

Languages

The official language is French (120 speakers). There are 3 600 speakers of East Futuna and 7 500 speakers of Wallisian.

Address formats

Please refer to the chapter on France for address information.

Western Samoa
Samoa i Sisifo

Official name: Independent State of Western Samoa, Malotuto'atasi o Samoa i Sisifo
Area: 2 842 sq. km (1 097 sq. miles)
Population: 190 000
Capital: Apia
Currency: 1 Tala (WS$) = 100 sene
International telephone access code: 685

Languages

The official languages are English and Samoan (spoken by 86% of the population).

Example address format

Mr Sapa'u R. Petaia
Director
Posts and Telecommunications Department
APIA

Postal codes

Western Samoa has no postal code system.

Yemen
Al-Yaman

Official name: Republic of Yemen, al-Jumhurïyah al-Yamaniyah
Area: 531 570 sq. km (205 186 sq. miles)
Population: 12 150 000
Capital: Sana'a (Sana)
Currency: 1 Yemeni Riyal (YR, YRI) = 100 fils
International telephone access code: 967

Language

The official language is standard Arabic. There are 300 000 speakers of Hadrami Spoken Arabic; 1 000 speakers of Judeo-Yemeni Arabic; 7 600 000 speakers of Sanaani Spoken Arabic; 6 760 000 speakers of Ta'izzi-Adeni Arabic; 58 000 speakers of Mahri; 290 000 speakers of Somali and 70 000 speakers of Soqotri.

Example address format

Abdullah Mohamed Abdul-Kader
17, Al-Ma'ehad
Habra
SANA'A

Postal codes

Yemen has no postal code system.

Towns

Al 'Adan is known as *Aden* in English.

Yugoslavia
Jugoslavija

Yugoslavia consists of the republics of Serbia and Montenegro.

Official name: Federal Republic of Yugoslavia, Federativna Republika Jugoslavija
Area: 102 173 sq. km (39 438 sq. miles)
Population: 10 400 000
Capital: Beograd (Belgrade)
Currency: 1 Yugoslav Dinar (D, Din) = 100 paras
International telephone access code: 381

Languages

The official language is Serbian (Serbo-Croat). Language is a sensitive issue in this area and rights to use or to be forbidden from using a language are important. There are 1 372 750 Gheg Albanian-speakers, mainly in the province of Kosovo across the border from Albania and 450 500 Hungarian speakers in Vojvodine across the border from Hungary. Also spoken are Romanian (2-300 000 speakers); Romani (150 000 speakers in two different forms) and Slovakian (100 000 speakers).

Address Format

Addresses are formatted in this way:

Name
thoroughfare type[ ]Thoroughfare name [ ]number
postal code[ ]SETTLEMENT

For example:

Markovic Marko
ul. Takovska br. 28
11000 BEOGRAD

Postal codes

The postal codes consist of a block of 5 digits. The code is the same as that used before Slovenia, Croatia, Bosnia Herzegovina and Macedonia left the federation. Serbian codes begin with 1, 2 or 3; Montenegran codes with 81, 84 or 85.

Towns

The city in Montenegro previously known as *Titograd* is now called *Podgorica.*

There is a large Hungarian-speaking minority in Vojvodine. Settlements may be given both a Serbo-Croatian and a Hungarian name:

Serbo-Croatian	*Hungarian*
Banatsko Arandelovo	Oroszlámos
Bečej	Becse
Bela Crkva	Fehértemplom
Čenta	Csenta
Jasenovo	Karasjeszenő
Kikinda	Nagykikinda
Mužlja	Felsőmuzslya
Nakovo	Kákófalva
Novi Sad	Újvidék
Pančevo	Pancsova
Senta	Zenta
Smederovo	Szendrő
Sombor	Zombor
Srpska Crnja	Csernye
Subotica	Szabadka
Uljma	Homoszkil
Vračev Gaj	Varászilget
Vrbas	Verbász
Vršac	Versec
Zemun	Zimony
Zrenjanin	Nagybecskerek

Gheg Albanian-speakers form a 90% majority in Kosovo, but they suffer major discrimination at the hands of the Serbs. Though towns will have both Serbo-Croatian and Albanian names, the Serbian authorities heavily discourage the use of the Albanian names. Albanian-speakers are also found in Montenegro along the border with Albania. In the following table, those settlements located in Kosovo are marked with an asterisk (*):

Serbo-Croatian	*Albanian*
Bar	Tivar
* Decani	Deçan
* Djakovica	Gjakova
* Gnjilane	Gjilan
Gusinje	Gusia
* Kosovska Mitrovica	Mitrovica
* Pec	Peja
Plave	Plava
* Pristina	Prishtina

Ulcinj	Ulqin
* Urosevac	Ferizaj

The Slovakian minority in Vojvodine have alternative names for some settlements:

Serbo-Croatian	*Slovakian*
Djurdjevo	Djurdjov
Kucura	Kocur
Ruski Krstur	Kerestur
Vrbas	Verbas

These settlements have alternative names in other languages:

Serbo-Croatian	*English*	*German*	*Italian*
Beograd	Belgrade	Belgrad	Belgrado
Novi Sad		Neusatz	
Požarevac		Passarowitz	
Zemun		Semlin	
Zrenjanin		Gr.-Betschkerck	

Zambia

Official name: Republic of Zambia
Area: 752 613 sq. km (290 586 sq. miles)
Population: 8 400 000
Capital: Lusaka
Currency: 1 Kwacha (K) = 100 ngwee
International telephone access code: 260

Languages

The official language is English. 38 other languages are spoken. The most widespread are: Bemba (2 000 000 speakers); Kaonde (240 000 speakers); Lala-Bisa (439 000 speakers); Lozi (473 000 speakers); Lunda (220 000 speakers); Luvale (203 000 speakers); Mambwe-Lungu (262 800 speakers); Nsenga (427 000 speakers); Nyanja (989 000 speakers); Nyiha (320 000 speakers); Tonga (990 000 speakers) and Tumbuka (406 000 speakers).

Example address format

Mr Richard Chunda
10 Nyimba Road
50100 NDOLA

Addresses written in a non-native language will be written in English.

Postal codes

The postal code consists of a block of 5 digits. The first two indicate the routing province, the third the routing area, the fourth the delivery area and the final digit indicates the method of delivery.

Zimbabwe

Official name: Republic of Zimbabwe
Area: 390 759 sq. km (150 873 sq. miles)
Population: 10 300 000
Capital: Harere
Currency: 1 Zimbabwe Dollar (Z$) = 100 cents
International telephone access code: 263

Languages

The official language is English (375 490 speakers). 18 other languages are spoken. The most widespread are: Fanagolo (300 000 speakers); Manyika (348 350 speakers); Ndau (391 000 speakers); Ndebele (1 485 000 speakers); Nyanja (251 800 speakers) and Shona (6 225 000 speakers).

Example address format

Mr Joe John
P.O. Box AY 30
Amby
HARARE

or

Ms Sue Susan
34-6th Crescent
Warren Park 1
HARARE

Addresses written in a non-native language will be written in English.

Postal codes

Zimbabwe has no postal code system.

Other Sources

If you haven't been able to find what you need here, try Marian Nelson's *Guide to Worldwide Postal-Code & Address Formats*, which is updated annually. Contact Marian Nelson at:

Nelson Intersearch Company
35 West 90th Street
New York NY 10024
United States of America
Telephone: (+1) 212-362-9855
Fax: (+1) 212-362-9855
e-mail: MarNelson@aol.com

The Internet is another excellent source, but trying to find the right pages can be time-consuming and expensive. Rather than list useful pages, the URL's of which change regularly, I provide a central links page, updated regularly, to allow you to find the postal code, post office and language pages that you are looking for. Point your browser at:

http://www.grcdi.nl/links.htm

Bibliography

Alitalia, *Arrivederci,* III, 34, Rome, December 1992.

Aulestia, Gorka and White, Linda (1992), *Basque-English, English-Basque Dictionary,* Reno, USA: University of Nevada Press.

Bartholomew & Co. Ltd. (1966), *Gazetteer of the British Isles,* Edinburgh.

Beard, Jonathan (1991), 'Computer Code Speaks in Many Tongues', in *New Scientist,* no. 1759, 9 March, p. 28.

Belgisch Staatsblad, 15.10.91.

Boer-Den Hoed, Dr. P.M. (1953), *Van Goor's Zweeds Handwoordenboek Nederlands-Zweeds,* Den Haag: Van Goor.

British Telecom (1990), *The Code Book, National and International Dialling Codes,* February.

Canadian Connexions Canadienne - A Guide to Building Direct Mail Business in Canada, (1991), Ottawa, Canada Post Corporation/Société Canadienne de postes.

Correos u Telégrafos (1992), *Guia Codigo Postal,* 1992, Madrid: Ministerio de Obras Públicas u Transportes.

Crystal, David (ed.) (1994), *The Cambridge Factfinder*, Cambridge: Cambridge University Press.

Delphos, William A. (ed.) (1992), *Direct Marketing Guide to Canada*, Alexandria, United States Postal Service.

Deutsche Bundespost (1977), *Die Postleitzahl.*

Deutsche Bundespost (1993), *Das Postleitzahlenbuch, Alphabetisch geordnet.*

Deutsche Bundespost (1993), *Das Postleitzahlenbuch, Numerisch geordnet.*

Deutsche Telekom (1990), *Vorwahlnummern.*

Diccionario Empresarial Stanford (1990), Area Ed., Madrid: SA Expansion.

Dipartiment Tal-Posta (Malta) (1991), *Direttorju Tal-Kodiċi Postale,* Valletta, Malta: Media & Graphic Services Ltd.

Dominicus, Jo (1981, 1991 edition), *Kanaaleilanden,* Haarlem: J.H. Gottmer.

Everson, Michael (1996), *Repertoires of Characters Used for Writing the Indigenous Languages of Europe - Fourth Draft for CEN/TC304 Project 11*, unpublished.

Gams, Ivan (1996), *Geografske Značilnosti Slovenije*, Ljubljaná Založba Mladinska knjiga.

Gobierno de Navarra/Nafarroako Gobernua (1986), *Ley de la Lengua Vasca / Euskarari Buruzko Foru Legea.*

Great World Atlas (1993), London: George Philip Ltd.

Grimes, Barbara F. (1996), *Ethnologue Languages of the World, 13th Edition*, Dallas, Summer Institute of Linguistics, Inc.

Guardian, 4.8.1993, p. 1.

Guardian, "Chilly Kazakhs hail new capital", 12.11.1997.

Guardian, 'High Hopes of End to Abkhaz Conflict, 16.8.1997, page 5.

Guardian, 'Language', G2, 10.1.1995, page 16.

Guardian, 'Nevis MPs vote to secede', 15.10.1997.

Guardian, 'On the Line' [Estonian international telephone code], 2.2.1993.

Guardian, 'Racist Language Brought to Book', 6.9.1996.

Guardian, 'Three Hundred Years in Search of Acadia', 12.7.1996.

Hammond, Robin (1981), *A German Reference Grammar,* Oxford: Oxford University Press.

Heinemann-Philip Atlases (1995), *Philips Geographical Digest*, Heinemann-Philip Atlases.

Hoffman, Dietrich "Die Entwicklung des Nordfriesischen", *Friesiesch Heute. Beiträge zu einer Tagung über nordfriesische Sprache und Sprachpflege*, eds. Walker, Alistair & Wilts, Ommo. Schriftenreihe der Akademie Sankelmark neue Folge 45/56.

Ihre Post (1996), *Postleitzahlen*, Wien: Ihre Post.

Lautensach, Dr. Phil. Dr. H. C. Hermann (1964), *Atlas zur Erdkunde,* München: Keysersche Verlagsbuchhandlung.

Katzner, Kenneth (1977), *The Languages of the World,* London: Routledge & Kegan Paul.

Kompass Publishers (1987), *Kompass UK Register of British Industry and Commerce,* East Grinstead.

Kossman-Putto, J.A. and Kossman, E.H. (1989), *The Low Countries - History of the Northern Southern Netherlands,* Rekkem, Belgium: Stichting Ons Erfdeel vzw.

L'Evenement, no. 357, 5-11 September 1991.

Mason, O. (1989), *Bartholomew Gazetteer of Places in Britain,* Edinburgh: Bartholomew.

Medhurst, Professor Kenneth (1982), *The Basques and the Catalans,* Minority Rights Group Report no.9, London: Minority Rights Group.

Meijes Tiersman, Pieter (1985), *Frisian Reference Grammar,* Dordrecht: Forsi Publications.

Meio Caminho Andado (1991), *Lista do Código Postal 1991 ediça 2,* Lisboa, Correios e telecomunicaçõ es de Portugal.

Miles, Louella (1991) 'Direct Marketing in the United States', *European Direct Marketing,* Issue 1, Summer, pp. 15-16, 18.

Minority Rights Group (1991), *Minorities and Autonomy in Western Europe,* London: Minority Rights Group.

National Geographic (1997), 'Reincarnating India', Vol. 191, no. 5, May 1997, pp 24-33, Des Moines - National Geographic Society./

National Geographic (1997), 'A Dream Called Nunavut', Vol. 192, no. 3, September 1997, pp 68-91, Des Moines - National Geographic Society.

Nederlandse Taalunie (1993), *Voorzetten 41 - Lijst van Landnamen - Namen van landen, alsmede opgave van de daarbij behorende bijvoeglijke naamwoorden en inwoneruanduidingen en van de namen van de hoofdsteden, Officiële schrijfwijze voor het Nederlandse taalgebied,* 's-Gravenhage: Stichting Bibliographia Neerlandica.

Nelson, Marian (Ed.) (1993), *Guide to Worldwide Postal-Code & Address Formats*, New York.

Nelson, Marian (Ed.) (1996), *1996 Guide to Worldwide Postal-Code & Address Formats*, New York: Nelson Intersearch Company.

Nelson, Marian (Ed.) (1997), *Guide to Worldwide Postal-Code & Address Formats*, New York: Nelson Intersearch Company.

Nordiska DM-Dagar (1990), *Nordic D.M. Guide - Postal Opportunities in Direct Marketing.*

Office Fédéral de la Statistique, 1993, *Mémento Statistique de la Suisse 1993,* Bern.

Pebesma, H. (1982), *Van Goor's Klein Fries Woordenboek,* Ljouwert: Algemiene Fryske Underrjocht Kommisje.

PTT (Switzerland), *Numerisches Verzeichnis der Postleitzahlen / Liste des numéros postaux d'acheminement dans l'ordre numérique / Elenco dei numeri postali d'avviamento in ordine numerico,* Bern.

PTT (Switzerland) (1989), *Verzeichnis der Postleitzahlen / Liste des numéros postaux d'acgeminement / Elenco dei numeri postali d'avviamento,* Bern.

PTT Post (Netherlands) (1978), *Postal codeboek.*

PTT Post (Netherlands) (1991), *Postal code, aunvulling nr. 24.*

PTT Post (Netherlands) (1993), *Postal code Databank.*

PTT Telecom (NL) (1989), *Buitenlandse Netnummers, juli 1989,* Den Haag.

Quick Reference Guide New Number Plan in France, (1996), Paris: France Telecom.

The Reader's Digest (1966), *The Reader's Digest AA Book of the Road,* London.

Royal Mail International (1991), *Royal Mail International Business Travel Guide,* London: Columbus Press.

Royal Mail International (1992), *Royal Mail International Business Travel Guide 1992/93,* London: Columbus Press.

Serryn, Pierre (1980), *Nouvel Atlas Bordas*, Paris: Editions Bordas.

Società Italiana per l'Esercizio delle Telecommunicazioni p.a. (1988), *Prefessi Teleselettivi,* Torino.

South African Post Office (1991), *Postal codes/Poskodes. Alphabetical Postal code List 1991.*

Streetnames: Guidelines / Sráidainmneacha: Treoirlínte (1992), Dublin / Baile Átha Cliath: An Coimisiún Logainmneacha.

Swedish Postoffice (1988), *Postnummerkatalog 1988,* Stockholm.

Unicode Consortium, The (1997), *The Unicode Standard, Version 2.0,* Reading, MA: Addison-Wesley Developers Press.

United States Postal Service (1992), *Direct Marketing Guide to Canada*, Alexandria VA, Braddock Communications Inc.

Universal Postal Union (1997), *Postal Addressing Systems*, Genève, UPU.

Van Goor (1984), *Van Goor's Noors-Nederlands Woordenboek,* Amsterdam: Van Goor Zonen.

Venâncio, Fernando (1983) *Basis Woordenlijst Portugees,* Muiderberg: Dick Coutinho .

Venâncio, Fernando (1989), *Basis Grammatica Portugees,* Schiedam: Blok Uitgeverij.

Venâncio, Fernando (1989), *Boa Sorte - Leer en Oefenboek Portugees 1,* Muiderberg: Dick Coutinho.

Visser-Boezaardt, ir. G. and Schram-Pighi, dr. L. (1980), *Prisma Woordenboek Nederlands Italiaans,* Utrecht/Antwerpen: Het Spectrum.

Vliegher, J. De (1991), *Gids voor Vaticaanstad,* Antwerpen/Baarn: Uitgeverij Hadewijck.

Wilson, Kathryn (ed.) (1991/92), *Marketing Without Frontiers,* London: Royal Mail International.

Wouters, dr. Herman (1976), *Volken en Stammen - Noordelijk Europa,* Amsterdam: Amsterdam Boek.

Wouters, dr. Herman (1977),*Volken en Stammen - Zuid-Europa en de Balken,* Amsterdam: Amsterdam Boek.

Maps used

AA-Macmillan *Cyprus Traveller's Map*, 1:275 000, Basingstoke.

Bartholomew (1992) *Europe 1992 - Political Map of the New Europe,* Edinburgh.

Bartholomew (1997) *1998 Map of Britain* scale 9 miles to 1 inch, Edinburgh.

Ciemen Internationales Zentrum Escarré für Etnische Minderheiten und Nationen *Das Europa der Sprachen (Versuch einer Annäherung an seine Vielfalt),* Barcelona.

De Rouck Cartography (1993) *Administratieve Kaart van België en van Groothertogdom Luxemburg,* scale 1:300 000, Brussels, 5th edition.

Deutsche Bundespost (1993) *Postleitzahlen, Ubersichtskarte der Postleiteinheiten,* scale 1:800 000.

Edizioni Uerre, *Italia Postale,* Umberto Ronca.

Falkplan-Suurland BV, *Gemeentekaart van Nederland,* scale 1:250 000, Eindhoven.

Freytag & Berndt (1995), *Road Map Slovenia*, scale 1:250 000, Wien.

Geodetski Zavod Slovenije (1992), *Slovenija - Karta Slovenskih Narečij,* scale 1:500 000, Ljubljana.

Jakez Derouet (1989) *Celtica,* Pluguvan, Brittany.

John Bartholomew & Son Ltd (1974) *The World Atlas,* Edinburgh.

Johnson & Perrott Ltd (1983) *Map of Ireland,* Ordnance Survey.

Kümmerley & Frey *Road Map of France,* scale 1:1 000 000, Zürich.

Kümmerley & Frey *Österreich-Süd Road Map,* scale 1:200 000, Zürich.

Kümmerley & Frey *Österreich-Ost Road Map,* scale 1:200 000, Zürich.

Recta Foldex *France Administrative, Départements, Régions,* scale 1:100 000.

RV Reise- und Verkehrsverlag *Map of Postal code areas of Germany,* Berlin, scale 1:700 000.

Shell *Touring Map of Italy.*